UNEQUAL DEMOCRACY

DEMOCRACY, DIVERSITY, AND CITIZEN ENGAGEMENT SERIES

Series editors: Alain-G. Gagnon and Yasmeen Abu-Laban

Vibrant movements both new and old, inspired by Indigeneity, national self-determination, anti-racism, migrant precarity, and their intersections with other forms of identity, raise profound questions about social justice. Such movements also provoke backlash. These developments beg the interrogation of institutional mechanisms for inclusion as they relate to democracy, citizenship, public policy, and rights across different state forms, including settler colonial and federal states. Centring the heterogeneity of mobilizations and claims-making by citizens, non-citizens, nations, and groups in the twenty-first century, the Democracy, Diversity, and Citizen Engagement Series invites consideration of how people and interests are represented. In light of how nations and people are often divided by state frontiers, the series, with the support of the Interdisciplinary Research Centre on Diversity and Democracy, also showcases work that identifies how interests and representation might be enhanced at local, national, or global levels.

UNEQUAL DEMOCRACY

The Social Construction of Citizenship in Latin America

EDITED BY

FRANÇOISE MONTAMBEAULT

and TINA HILGERS

McGill-Queen's University Press
Montreal & Kingston

ISBN 978-0-2280-2881-9 (paper)
ISBN 978-0-2280-2986-1 (ePDF)
ISBN 978-0-2280-2956-4 (ePUB)
ISBN 978-0-2280-3010-2 (open-access ePDF)
ISBN 978-0-2280-3011-9 (open-access ePUB)

Legal deposit third quarter 2026
Bibliothèque et Archives nationales du Québec

Printed in Canada on acid-free paper that is 100% ancient-forest-free, containing 100% sustainable, recycled fibre, and processed chlorine-free.

This book has been published with the help of a grant from the Federation for the Humanities and Social Sciences, through the Scholarly Book Awards, using funds provided by the Social Sciences and Humanities Research Council of Canada. This book was published in open access with assistance from the Canadian Association of Research Libraries Fund for Advancing Open Access Book Publishing.

We acknowledge the support of the Canada Council for the Arts.
Nous remercions le Conseil des arts du Canada de son soutien.

McGill-Queen's University Press in Montreal is on land which long served as a site of meeting and exchange amongst Indigenous Peoples, including the Haudenosaunee and Anishinabeg nations. In Kingston it is situated on the territory of the Haudenosaunee and Anishinaabek. We acknowledge and thank the diverse Indigenous Peoples whose footsteps have marked these territories on which peoples of the world now gather.

Library and Archives Canada Cataloguing in Publication

Title: Unequal democracy : the social construction of citizenship in Latin America / edited by Françoise Montambeault and Tina Hilgers.
Other titles: Unequal democracy (2026)
Names: Montambeault, Françoise, editor | Hilgers, Tina, 1971– editor
Series: Democracy, diversity, and citizen engagement series ; 15.
Description: Series statement: Democracy, diversity, and citizen engagement series ; 15 | Includes bibliographical references and index.
Identifiers: Canadiana (print) 20260183393 | Canadiana (ebook) 20260183423 | ISBN 9780228028819 (paper) | ISBN 9780228029564 (ePUB) | ISBN 9780228030119 (open-access ePUB) | ISBN 9780228029861 (ePDF) | ISBN 9780228030102 (open-access ePDF)
Subjects: LCSH: Citizenship—Social aspects—Latin America.
Classification: LCC JL967.A2 U54 2026 | DDC 323.6098—dc23

This book was designed and typeset by Sayre Street Books in 10.5/13 Sabon.
Copyediting by Correy Baldwin.

McGill-Queen's University Press
Suite 1720, 1010 Sherbrooke St West, Montreal, QC, H3A 2R7

Authorized safety representative in the EU: Mare Nostrum Group BV, Doelen 2, 4831 GR Breda, the Netherlands, gpsr@mare-nostrum.co.uk

Contents

Foreword • vii
Terry Lynn Karl
Acknowledgments • xi

Introduction: Civil Society, the State, and the Social Construction of Citizenship Under Neopluralism • 3
Françoise Montambeault and Tina Hilgers

SECTION ONE: LATIN AMERICA

1 Neopluralism, Citizenship, and Clientelism: The Urban Popular Movement in Mexico City • 27
Tina Hilgers

2 Where Did All the Parties Go? Civil Society, Social Protest, and the Crisis of Representation in Chile's Constitutive Stalemate • 52
Kenneth M. Roberts

3 Neopluralist Maternalism and Women's Citizenship in Peru • 77
Stéphanie Rousseau

4 Displacing the Social Construction of Indigenous Citizenship at the International Level: Comparing Guatemala and Paraguay • 96
Garance Robert and Andréanne Brunet-Bélanger

5 The Media's Role in the Social Construction of Citizenship: Neopluralism and the Public Sphere in Latin America • 129
Michelle D. Bonner

6 The Media, Neopluralism, and the Public Sphere in Veracruz, Mexico • 156
Julián Durazo Herrmann

SECTION TWO: COMPARATIVE PERSPECTIVES

7 The Making of Immigrant Inequality in the US: The Privileging of Cubans • 185
Susan Eckstein

8 Civil Society Construction, Hybrid Regimes, and Political Change in the Middle East: Egypt and Syria, Before, During, and After the Arab Spring • 207
Aviad Rubin

9 Neopluralism, Violent Policing, and South Africa's Low-Intensity Democracy • 235
Daniel L. Douek

SECTION THREE: CONCLUDING REFLECTIONS

10 Constructing Citizenship at the Margins: Assessing the Work of Transnational Civil Society Through an Oxhornian Lens • 267
Mónica Treviño González

Conclusion: Bringing Norms Back In: The Neopluralist Legacy and the Need to Rethink Our Assumptions About Democracy • 273
Philip Oxhorn

Contributors • 291
Index • 299

Foreword

Latin America turned Phil Oxhorn into a "bottom up" scholar. Thank you, Latin America.

Phil did not start out as a social movements researcher but rather an undergraduate attracted to dependency theories. Thus, when he came to Harvard as a doctoral student and embraced the study of civil society, he did not need to be influenced by his eventual dissertation advisers (Philippe Schmitter, Sidney Verba, and me, who were firmly against dictatorships and domination), much less his political science training (which often did not share the same stance in the 1960s through the 1980s). He was already there. Indeed, he was so quietly self-directed, persevering, smart, and curious, I am not exactly sure why he needed any of our advice at all!

I first met Phil in 1982 – a first-year graduate student with a hunger to learn about Latin America. He did not speak Spanish, and had never been in any Latin American country, and his greatest research experience to date had been about earthquake preparedness – not surprising for an undergraduate from a California university but quite unlike the other doctoral students studying Latin America who generally had fallen in love with a particular country. Instead, he came well armed with dozens of questions. "I want to go to Chile," he later announced.

Talk about diving in. At the time of his graduate studies, the Harvard Government Department was in an uproar over accusations of sexual harassment, which meant that students like Phil lost some classes and sometimes had little preparation for field work. Not surprisingly to those of us who admired him, Phil took a brave ethical stance at Harvard with the "gang of four" and others, siding with the least powerful. His tenacity, curiosity, and sheer smarts served him well throughout his career. I still remember him when he started out to conduct field research in General Pinochet's Chile – perhaps insufficiently warned about the difficulties of working inside an incipient, fearful, and rightly suspicious opposition. More than anything else, the same set of values, dogged determination, and perseverance that he had shown at Harvard guaranteed his success.

Imagine trying to do participant research in a place where trust is absent, people are afraid to talk, and a *gringo* researcher was most likely to be viewed as part of the same US government effort that helped to put Pinochet in power. Phil arrived in Chile with terrific contacts but quickly discovered that the academics he wanted to speak with were in prison or exile, and almost no one would talk to him. What are now called the Jornadas de Protesta Nacional were in full swing – massive protests against the military dictatorship despite its severe repression. Slowly but surely, Phil would win over an influential German nun, convince well over a hundred women in one community that he was an okay guy, and design research that compared civil society communities throughout Santiago that were protesting despite the potential consequences they faced. And in the process he met his wonderful wife, Rosa, and later became a family man. He also produced his first book from this research: *Organizing Civil Society: The Popular Sectors and the Struggle for Democracy in Chile* (Pennsylvania State University Press, 1995).

"Once you are in Latin America, you are hooked for life," Phil once told me. And hooked he still is! Widely recognized as an expert in civil society, social inclusion, and democratic mobilization, Phil has done it all: engaging Latin Americanists throughout the Americas, developing open access publishing platforms for interdisciplinary research on Latin America, editing the *Latin American Research Review* for almost a decade, organizing annual workshops and a speakers series at McGill, founding the McGill Institute for the Study of International Development, and often partnering with Canada's International Development Research Centre and the Canadian Department of Foreign Affairs.

What I suspect Phil most loves and what hopefully fills him with pride is his work with students, both undergraduates and graduates. Teaching and mentoring, especially in a thoroughly interdisciplinary manner, has permitted him to not only convey his passion for the Americas and the rigour he first brought to his study of Chile but also to reach well beyond his initial work. Both his teaching and his writing extends to Mexico, Brazil, Argentina, Peru, and, most recently, Colombia. His work on civil society has been expanded in a number of published works, most notably *Sustaining Civil Society: Economic Change, Democracy, and the Social Construction of Citizenship in Latin America* (Pennsylvania State University Press, 2011). This book sets out to explain why Latin America remains so profoundly unjust, due to the paradoxical juxtaposition of often profound political rights with very weak social and economic rights. Democratic citizenship is a form of agency – one that needs to be reinforced and nurtured at every turn – and not only throughout the Americas.

A preface for this type of book usually ends by talking about lifetime legacies, but while Phil's contribution to Latin American studies is exceptional already, it is not yet done. His commitment to understanding and undoing lifelong inequities, building civil societies, and helping make all of the Americas a better place, from the far north to the far south, is bound to continue, as is his wonderful sense of humour, legendary perseverance, deep intelligence, and almost inconceivable humility.

Terry Lynn Karl
Stanford University and San Francisco

Acknowledgments

We are very happy to present this book to honour our colleague and friend Philip Oxhorn, not only for his significant contributions to Latin American studies and comparative politics but also for the profound impact he has had on our lives as academics, and as a community of scholars.

Phil has been an essential figure in our intellectual journeys, guiding and supporting us during our formative years and beyond. As Françoise's PhD supervisor and Tina's postdoctoral advisor at McGill University and the McGill Institute for the Study of International Development, he provided invaluable mentorship, encouragement, and insight, shaping our work in lasting ways. All the contributors to this volume have had the privilege of having a long-standing collaboration with Phil – whether as supervisor, supervisee, or academic collaborator – and we all share a deep sense of gratitude for his generosity, intellectual rigour, and unwavering support. This book is a tribute to the scholarship, mentorship, and the meaningful connections he has fostered throughout his career.

The vitality of Latin American studies in Montreal and the strength and cohesiveness of the community of scholars working on these issues – spanning political science, sociology, international development studies, and beyond – are a direct reflection of Phil's legacy as a community builder. His commitment to fostering collaboration and intellectual exchange at McGill and in Montreal has left an indelible mark, enriching the academic environment for generations of scholars.

The idea for this volume first emerged during a conference held in Phil's honour in November 2022 at McGill University, the institution where he pursued most of his brilliant academic career. The conference was co-organized by Françoise Montambeault, Erik Kuhonta, and Manuel Balán, with the generous support of the McGill Institute for the Study of International Development, the Canada Research Chair in Participation and Citizenship, the Fonds de recherche du Québec – Société et culture (FRQSC) Équipe de recherche interuniversitaire sur la gouvernance et l'inclusion en Amérique latine (ÉRIGAL), the McGill Department of Political Science, and the McGill Faculty of Arts.

Along with the contributors to this volume, many more colleagues were involved and presented ideas during the conference, and we would like to thank them for their contributions to the ideas in the book: the Right Honorable Joe Clark, Evelina Dagnino, Rohinton Medhora, Julie Moreau, and Cynthia Sanborn. We wish to express our deepest gratitude to everyone who was involved in the logistical aspects of the conference. Iain Blair, Andréanne Brunet-Bélanger, and Sherryl Ramsahai were crucial to making the event happen, despite a number of challenges along the way, including the COVID-19 pandemic, which pushed the conference – originally planned for 2020 – to 2022.

Finally, we would like to express our heartfelt gratitude to all the contributors to this manuscript. Each of you has played an essential role in bringing this volume to life, and we deeply appreciate the time, effort, and expertise you have shared. Your contributions have enriched this project, reflecting Phil's lasting influence on the field and the intellectual community he helped shape.

We would also like to extend special thanks to our editor at McGill-Queen's, Emily Andrew, who has been exceptional in guiding us through the process of submitting, revising, and publishing the manuscript. Her support has been invaluable. We are also grateful for the excellent and thought-provoking comments made by the three anonymous readers. Their attentive reading made the final manuscript much stronger, and we would like to highlight their important, while sometimes invisible, work. Finally, we are grateful to the research assistants, Roman Perdomo and Millena Navega, who helped us with background research for and final formatting of the manuscript, respectively. Their rigour and attention to detail made a tremendous difference.

Thank you all for your collaboration and dedication, and the thought-provoking work you have brought to this book.

UNEQUAL DEMOCRACY

INTRODUCTION

Civil Society, the State, and the Social Construction of Citizenship Under Neopluralism

Françoise Montambeault and Tina Hilgers

Across the world, populist leaders are rallying citizens increasingly frustrated with politics and markets, while analysts struggle to explain where liberal democracy has failed. This book places lessons from the Latin American experience in comparative perspective in order to pinpoint the development of inequality and polarization, which limit citizenship and undermine democracy.

Latin America remains one of the cornerstones of the literature on contemporary democracy. Indeed, a considerable share of the political science approach to understanding democratic regime transitions, consolidation, quality, variation, and, more recently, stagnation and erosion is based on comparative studies of the Latin American context (see, for example, O'Donnell and Schmitter 1986; Collier and Collier 1991; Przeworski 1991; Rueschemeyer et al. 1992; Linz and Valenzuela 1994; Helmke and Levitsky 2006; Mainwaring and Scully 2009; Balán and Montambeault 2020; Kapiszewski et al. 2021; Mainwaring and Pérez-Liñán 2023). Many observers argue that one of the key problems impeding the deepening of quality democracy in Latin America is unresolved social conflict surrounding inequalities and the extension of citizenship, from electoral and political rights to the civil and social rights that sustain equal political participation (Balán and Montambeault 2020; Hilgers 2012). Contemporary dissatisfaction with democracy across the world, including in the United States and Europe, once again points to the significance of lessons learned from Latin America.

Citizenship and inclusion in unequal Latin American democratic regimes have been studied from institutional (Yashar 2005) and cultural perspectives (Alvarez et al. 1998), but also from a political economy approach focusing on the interaction of the state–society relationship with larger patterns of interest representation and economic change. Among these perspectives, Oxhorn's (2011) theory of the relation between neopluralism, weak civil societies, and the social construction of citizenship is compelling and has influenced a generation of scholars of the region. Economic crises and increasing polarization across the world over the last several decades have reinforced an interest in Latin American cases, characterized by deeply embedded patterns of economic inequality and unequal access to the civil, political, and social rights of citizenship (Oxhorn 1995b).

This introduction synthesizes Oxhorn's work and broadens it, based on the contributions to the volume, to present a unified theory of the nature and consequences of contemporary neopluralism – the relatively unhindered political participation of civil society in a context of neoliberalism, weak state institutions, and extensive inequality. The contributing authors critically engage Oxhorn's theory using evidence from Latin America, the United States, the Middle East, and South Africa. Their empirically based accounts of the links between social movements and political parties, marginalized groups and social policy, immigrants and immigration policy, the media and institutions, and the role of the state, including through its policing of racially and socioeconomically marginalized populations, put Oxhorn's ideas to the test. The chapters' comparative findings regarding state interests and civil society heterogeneity reaffirm the power of Oxhorn's theory, all the while broadening its scope both within Latin America and beyond. We reconfirm that, as a model of interest intermediation defining the interaction between state and society that is embedded in neoliberalism, neopluralism deepens socioeconomic inequalities and political polarization, weakens civil society, and limits the social construction of citizenship. We concur with Oxhorn that neopluralism undermines democracy and its institutions. Furthermore, we contend that the state has political interests that may lead it to provide differential opportunities to civil society sectors. Indeed, we find that civil society is characterized by multiple, sometimes intersecting, identities and capacities beyond the economic and place-based features at work in Oxhorn's theory. In part because of this fragmentation, collective mobilization leading to the overarching political change for which Oxhorn hoped, may be less likely to occur than incremental learning.

CIVIL SOCIETY, THE STATE, AND THE SOCIAL CONSTRUCTION OF CITIZENSHIP

T.H. Marshall (1950), whose work is informed by the British shift from traditional feudal social divisions and inequalities to capitalism, is among the most influential scholars of modern citizenship. His definition of citizenship as a bundle of civil, political, and social (and human) rights and responsibilities posits that it is a *status* universally granted by the state to all members of a political community. He explained that civil rights gradually expanded in the seventeenth and eighteenth centuries, followed in the nineteenth and twentieth centuries by political rights and finally social rights in the welfare states of the twentieth century. While his notion of citizenship as rights and responsibilities remains influential, scholars like Charles Tilly and, in Latin America, Oxhorn have contributed to an important conceptual shift in comparative theories of citizenship: where citizenship was formerly seen as a status or as an expression of formal rights, it is now considered a relational construct, created through the "struggle and bargaining between expanding states and their subjects" (Tilly 1996, 9).

Critics generally disagree with the functionalist and deterministic nature of citizenship in Marshall's theory, in which it is understood to be the "architect of legitimate social inequality" in modern capitalist economies (Turner 1992; Oxhorn 2003). Contrary to what Marshall suggested, they argue that citizenship is neither irreversible, nor acquired through linear progress (Paquet et al. 2018). The Latin American process of rights acquisition, for example, has followed an uneven path since the early twentieth century: capitalist economic development has been associated with growing social inequalities (Oxhorn and Ducatenzeiler 1999), and both the scope of rights and the boundaries of inclusion/exclusion within citizenship regimes have moved over time (Montambeault et al. 2020). For Oxhorn, then, citizenship rights "are not the outcome of the functional requirements of capitalism or a consequence of a new social consensus associated with modernity" (2011, 25). Rather, a causal theory of the emergence, evolution, or stagnation of citizenship rights must consider social struggles: it must go beyond class conflict to take seriously civil society capacity to act and demand inclusion.

Arguing that citizenship rights develop through a relational process, in which autonomous civil society organizations formulate demands in the public sphere and press for state responsiveness,

Oxhorn claims that the granting of the social, political, and civil rights of citizenship is the result of a "social construction" (2011, 21). He defines civil society as "the social fabric formed by a multiplicity of self-constituted territorially – and functionally-based units which peacefully coexist and collectively resist subordination to the state, at the same time that they demand inclusion into national political structures" (Oxhorn 1995b, 9). Strong democratic regimes are sustained by a state–society "synergy" (Oxhorn 2011, 18), driven by two components: citizens with agency who formulate demands to extend the scope and depth of their citizenship rights, and the state as guarantor of those rights (O'Donnell 2010). For Oxhorn, the synergistic relationship that leads to the social construction of inclusive citizenship rights involves an effective civil society built on a variety of autonomous groups capable of determining and representing their interests in competition with others. We call this formulation of a strong civil society *cooperative competition*, to highlight the competitiveness of policy-influencing mobilization, while also drawing attention to the broadly inclusionary pressures it exerts on citizenship regimes. Indeed, Oxhorn (2011) holds that a responsive state creates opportunities for civil society to exert pressure on the state and opens spaces for policy co-production.

However, some economic development models constrain the social construction of citizenship, affecting the scope and depth of citizenship rights development. Economic regimes influence how states shape the political arena and the opportunities for, and capacities of, interest organization (Oxhorn 1998b, 2006). Inclusionary economic regimes enable state–society synergy, while exclusionary ones motivate the state to constrain opportunities for interest organization and, thereby, civil society autonomy. Weak civil societies underwrite the restricted and/or exclusionary citizenship rights characteristic of authoritarian regimes and weak democracies. Civil society thus reflects the distribution of power in society (Oxhorn 1995b).

INDUSTRIALIZATION AND SOCIAL MODERNIZATION: CITIZENSHIP AS AGENCY VERSUS CITIZENSHIP AS COOPTATION

Oxhorn's theory rests on meticulous examinations of Latin American political economic history in comparison especially with Western European developments. In Western Europe, slow industrialization and urbanization processes profoundly affected class structures and the ensuing expansion of citizenship rights. The development of a labour-intensive industrial sector reduced the size of the informal sector, creating a robust industrial proletariat capable of consolidating civil society organizations that were demanding inclusion, first through political rights and then through universal social rights. Gradual industrialization and social modernization sustained the creation of societal corporatist interest intermediation through cooperation between state, labour, and capital (Schmitter 1974), and the development of pluralist democratic regimes associated with relatively inclusive citizenship rights regimes. Progressive social and political change during economic modernization gave rise to citizenship as agency. Groups with diverse interests began to focus on unifying, despite sharing few commonalities, to enable cooperative competition and negotiate with a benevolent state (Oxhorn 2003, 2011).

In Latin America, on the other hand, rapid industrialization and social modernization reproduced socioeconomic inequalities and controlled inclusion (Oxhorn 2003, 2011). Most countries industrialized in the early twentieth century under delayed dependent capitalist development. Their export-based economies suffered during the Great Depression and the Second World War as the core countries turned their attention inward. A weak, divided Latin American bourgeoisie proved incapable of creating the inclusive democratic and economic development that would have supported a modernization of socioeconomic structures. Instead, populist leaders and technocrats imposed state–corporatist interest intermediation, centralizing decision-making over industrial relations, and import substitution industrialization (ISI), favouring protectionist economic policy and state-led investment to replace imports with domestic production. Industrial labour market expansion was limited by developments in modern capital-intensive technology and investors preferring speculative over productive investment, as well as overseas versus domestic investment. Workforce expansion was concentrated in the service sector, but wages remained low due to high population growth, rapid migration to urban centres, and increasing numbers of women workers. People altogether excluded from decent work and unable to find housing came up with their own solutions for work and shelter in the informal sector (see Hilgers and Mayer 2024). Populist elites used ISI and state corporatism to enforce a form of social peace, redistributing the resources from economic growth to a relatively small, state-allied labour sector, while repressing independent lower-class-interest organization. In the absence of full civil and political rights, the state led a controlled inclusion of certain social sectors, restraining the development of strong and autonomous civil society agency, restricting the expansion of social rights, and producing what Oxhorn has called citizenship as cooptation (Oxhorn 1998a, 2003). Revolutionary leftist groups opposing controlled inclusion idealized a social construction of citizenship based on a civil society mobilization that included the poor, but their exclusion of unaligned interests from the public sphere would also have hindered the development of citizenship as agency (Oxhorn 2011). Ultimately, the demise of citizenship as cooptation came with conservative hands.

In the 1960s and 1970s, the consensus surrounding Latin American state corporatism and citizenship as cooptation crumbled. Conservative alliances that feared socialism ousted populist leaders, and the new (often military) authoritarian regimes began to dismantle the social foundations of corporatism and the ISI developmentalist economic model, restricting political rights, repressing popular-sector mobilization, and imposing more orthodox economic policy (Oxhorn 1995b). The most violent of these regimes, in Argentina, Brazil, Chile, and Uruguay, replaced controlled inclusion with "coerced marginalization," constricting the public arena and violating basic rights, especially those of the popular sectors (Oxhorn 2011, 30).

NEOLIBERALISM AND DEMOCRACY: NEOPLURALISM AND CITIZENSHIP AS CONSUMPTION

Following civil society demands, leadership changes, and international pressure, the region's regimes transitioned to democracy in the late 1970s and early 1980s, raising hopes for positive change in citizenship rights. Internal differences had been overcome within civil society: united by the struggle for democracy, diverse groups organized more cooperatively than they had in previous eras (Oxhorn 1995a). Activists and scholars believed that the universal political rights of democracy would further strengthen civil society and that state–society synergy in policymaking would result in measures to end social exclusion and socioeconomic inequality. However, the new economic paradigm impeded progress in citizenship rights (Oxhorn and Ducatenzeiler 1999; Weyland 2004).

With the global oil crises of the 1970s, stagflation, and the 1980s debt crisis, global economic experts and policymakers gradually came to the consensus that market-oriented policies had to replace interventionist ISI and Keynesianism. As core countries focused on the stability of the international system, Latin American elites sought opportunities to better insert their countries into the international arena. Together, they pushed a neoliberal policy consensus that involved state retrenchment, trade liberalization, privatization, fiscal discipline, and attracting foreign investment (Oxhorn 1998b). Labour flexibilization policies aimed at increasing economic competitivity in the context of free markets significantly reduced social protection measures for workers and negatively impacted job security, benefits, and wages. The rising popularity of short-term contracts without benefits blurred the line between formal and informal work. Unemployment rates rose, up to 90 per cent of new jobs were in the informal sector, and inequality intensified. Although economic growth rates improved, reaching 15 per cent in the first half of the 1990s, the structural causes of poverty and inequality remained (Oxhorn 2004).

Neoliberalism deeply affected the model of interest intermediation, especially in Latin America (Oxhorn 1998b). The bourgeoisie were strengthened with ISI policies, gaining independence from the state, but they remained fragmented as they divided into different business associations under neoliberalism. Organized labour, a privileged corporatist sector, withered to little more than an interest group working to maintain its leadership's privileges under a neoliberal economic development model. The popular sectors – urban low-income groups with limited resources – fared no better. Neoliberal poverty reduction programs targeted only the most needy, aiming for short-term help at the individual level, with the reasoning that the poor should become self-sufficient in the long term. Needs-based payments supplanted general welfare in housing, employment, health care, and other policy sectors. The administration of programs became decentralized, often to the local level, with communities expected to participate in planning and budgeting. After having been instrumental to national demands for free and fair elections, the popular sectors demobilized at all but the community level once elections consummated the transition to democracy and political parties took centre stage. Chile's post-Pinochet popular sector organizations illustrate this phenomenon, which Oxhorn encapsulated in the question, "Where did all the protesters go?" (Oxhorn 1994). Paradoxically, popular organizations had been more mobilized and successful under authoritarian regimes than they were within democracy (Oxhorn 1998a, 1998b, 2004, 2011).

Oxhorn conceptualizes the new mode of interest intermediation as neopluralism (1998a, 1998b, 2011). Like the classic US pluralist model, the market-centred approach to lower-class incorporation exhibits many forms of participation that are unstructured and unlimited by the state, with the reasoning that the free competition of civil society ideas will generate a healthy equilibrium of interests and societal progress. The individual freedom to compete is ensured through the protection of private property and the rule of law (though the latter is limited in Latin America). While this system requires executive electoral legitimacy, the new form of pluralism differs from the traditional US model in its weakened state institutions and the addition of authoritarian elements to democratic participation. Military participation in governance, one-party rule, clientelism through the exchange of political support for resources, the remainders of state corporatism, and weak post-electoral executive accountability coexist with democratic elections and organized interest participation. Also different from US pluralism is the much greater level of social interest fragmentation and mass marginalization because of inequality (Oxhorn 1998b, 2011). However, inequality and poverty do not become a threat to democracy because neopluralism "deflects public debate away from the structural causes of poverty and toward a focus on its most notorious consequences" (Oxhorn 2004, 30).

While the success of civil society in negotiating for universal political rights was remarkable, the subsequent fragmentation of civil society and the individualization of welfare responsibilities forestalled progress on civil and social rights. The market logic of neoplural interest intermediation leaves civil society free to organize as it desires and to make itself heard through using economic resources or democratic votes, ostensibly facilitating citizenship as agency. However, state responsiveness to such demands remains limited and groups suffering from economic resource scarcity have difficulty making themselves heard. Neopluralism thus fosters a model of citizenship-as-consumption in which the rights of democratic citizenship accrue to groups that are able to purchase them (Oxhorn 1998a, 1998b, 2004, 2011).

NEOPLURALISM, THE PINK TIDE, AND THE NEW AUTHORITARIAN DYNAMIC

In the long run, neopluralism has allowed high levels of poverty and inequality to coexist with demands for diverse rights and with relatively free and fair elections that have brought to power progressive forces, but also – increasingly – with authoritarian tendencies (Oxhorn, conclusion to this volume). Indeed, popular sector political participation changed across Latin America as the region's governments turned away from state-led economic development programs and toward unpopular neoliberal measures in the 1980s and 1990s.

As state support for corporatist sectors was dismantled, the labour unions and professional associations that traditionally had strong ties to political parties lost power (Morgan 2007). Civil society created new, often intersectional interest- and identity-based organizations and networks that were more flexible than the old corporatist structures and able to protest against, negotiate with (Rich et al. 2019), or even circumvent governments (Robert and Brunet-Bélanger, this volume). Many old parties failed to meaningfully embrace these organizations, as well as the growing sectors of urban poor and informal workers, losing much of their popular support to new parties (Morgan 2007; see also Roberts, this volume). At the same time, a new generation of issue-committed bureaucrats created programs to respond to the newly expressed interests, energizing state–society links. New spaces and resources became available, including the expansion or founding of state agencies in areas such as health, the environment, race, and gender (among others); the development of participatory policymaking venues; and changes in the judiciary, enabling the voicing of individual and group demands for accountability through claims against violations of social or economic rights (Rich et al. 2019).

Increasingly diverse social movements, civil society organizations, and community-based organizations have framed their demands in terms of access to the rights of citizenship (Dagnino 2006). Inequality has become both more complex and a more important issue on the public political agenda. The scope of the debate has expanded beyond poverty and economic inequality to include injustice based on gender, space (physical and social terrain), language, race, ethnicity, education, and access to technology. The impact of these newly recognized forms of inequality can be difficult to measure, as various bases for injustice intersect, affecting opportunities and outcomes in historically and contextually dependent ways (Oxhorn and Jouve-Martín 2017). Despite the diversity of civil society groups, their causes, and their use of social, civil, or political rights to express their goals, they have also found common ground in the overall language of rights (Dagnino 2006). In their mobilizing of economic resources, imagining cultural identities, and negotiating with political power, these groups constructed citizenship from below (see Holston 2008).

Through their struggles, women, landless peasants, Indigenous peoples, the urban poor, organizations fighting for post-authoritarian truth and justice, and others helped to bring progressive political parties to power in the period known as the "pink tide" – with varying outcomes. Left-wing candidates won presidential elections beginning in the late 1990s on broad promises of equality, inclusion, justice, and economic growth, but the resulting reforms varied across countries; within countries across space, social sectors, and policies; and over time. Policy processes and outcomes were uneven, as different levels of government reformed institutions, allied groups and individual people used their identities to influence the political process at all levels, and tensions arose between individual and collective rights claims and between the recognition of equality and difference. A pluralistic approach could be seen in the number of active civil society groups, in their membership's intersectional identities, and in differential understandings of what was meant by inclusion. Varying levels of access to, and relationships with, the state and political power also continued to affect policy outcomes, particularly as left-leaning governments remained committed to the global neoliberal policy paradigm (Montambeault et al. 2020).

While the left in power may not have lived up to ideological and redistributive expectations, it did succeed in creating more policies designed to benefit the poor and in fostering inclusion. In Bolivia, Indigenous peoples mobilized around ideas of identity and decolonization to protest against neoliberal elites and to elect Evo Morales to the presidency in 2005. While subsequent Morales administrations ceded to domestic and global pressures to maintain neoliberal market and liberal political structures, they did bring Indigenous peoples into politics in unprecedented ways. The 2009 Constitution enshrines Indigenous rights, including those of territory, culture, and self-government (Postero 2017). In Mexico City, the Urban Popular Movement has been central to the election of an unbroken series of leftist mayors since 1997. While these mayors and their parties have failed to break with the clientelistic tendencies of the preceding undemocratic regime, they have brought in policies making important goods and services universally accessible, benefitting the poor (Hilgers, this volume). In some cases, officials have also unwittingly strengthened civil society by bringing in skilful citizens to act as intermediaries for popular sectors. In La Paz, officials lacking the resource capacity to enforce regulations for the use of public space by informal workers have helped the workers to organize. These officials provide organization leaders with incentives (licenses, access to the bureaucracy, cash payments) to enforce behaviour in their stead. However, once organized, workers often negotiate for expanded rights and their leaders have become candidates in elections (Hummel 2021).

Regardless of their origin, popular organizations nurture the political participation of marginalized groups by broadening networks that help them overcome barriers of limited education and access to information. Most people gather information about electoral candidates and issues through political discussions in their networks and by seeking the counsel of contacts whom they perceive as knowledgeable (Baker et al. 2020). For example, religious organizations provide people with opportunities to meet and debate the problems of their communities. Religious leaders and congregations discuss politics, motivating members to inform themselves and to vote, which has an especially notable effect on political knowledge among those with low levels of education and living in low-education neighbourhoods. These people otherwise have limited access to civic education, varied media outlets, and sources able to relate electoral platforms to popular realities (Smith 2017; see also Rubin, this volume, for the role of religious organizations in politics). Baker, Ames, and Rennó (2020) contend that such political discussions are effective, linking them with polls showing that 20 to 50 per cent of voters will change their candidate preferences during presidential elections. Importantly, networks help voters to shape their political opinions independent of elite and media influences (Baker et al. 2020).

As a consequence, we observe a quantitative increase in political engagement among the poorest sectors in Latin America over the past twenty years. In fact, the overall figures from the 2006 to 2014 Latin America Public Opinion Project's (LAPOP) AmericasBarometer surveys show that the poor (about 30 per cent of the population) are no longer less politically active than the wealthy. While they still tend to vote at lower rates than the wealthy (73 per cent versus 77 per cent turnout) and protest less than the wealthy (7 per cent versus 9 per cent activity over twelve months), they contact or petition local and federal government officials at higher rates than the wealthy (24 per cent versus 22 per cent, and 44 per cent versus 40 per cent, respectively). Aggregate participation rates show the poor to be more politically active than the wealthy in five of the eighteen surveyed countries and about equally as active in another six countries (Boulding and Holzner 2021, 5–6).

However, as the chapters in this collection highlight, more participation by the poor does not equate to improved impact on the fundamental quality of inclusion if participation remains fragmented across interests. As Oxhorn writes in the conclusion to this volume, the "paradox of neopluralism" is that the combination of poverty and social exclusion with democratic elections has made progressive reform possible, but weak against authoritarian backlash. Reform efforts continue to target the symptoms of inequality over their structural causes. As much as the popular sectors (and different identity groups) desire real democratic accountability, representation, and participation, they are compelled by their marginalized status to make practical choices that meet their immediate resource needs, at the cost of reproducing their own political and economic vulnerability (see also Hilgers, this volume). They support authoritarian elites who offer stability in the face of economic or political crisis, despite their violence and disregard for democracy.

The emerging "new authoritarian dynamic ... may prove to be the most important political innovation of the twenty-first century" (Oxhorn, this volume, 281). Democratic elections have brought authoritarian presidents to power in Brazil, Argentina, Ecuador, El Salvador, Guatemala, and Nicaragua. Neopluralism directly affects the institutions that might otherwise constrain the new authoritarian dynamic. Free, investigative journalism (see both Bonner and Durazo Herrmann, this volume), the rule of law and the seeds of democratic policing (see Douek, this volume), and the courts and other state institutions have all been weakened by the unequal and market-based logic of interest intermediation that is characteristic of neopluralism. As much as civil society groups have mobilized around rights discourses, weak collective mobilization of the poor allows for the new authoritarian dynamic to reinforce their social, political, and economic exclusion (Oxhorn, this volume).

LESSONS FROM LATIN AMERICA AND BEYOND

How do Oxhorn's theoretical insights on Latin America's unequal democracies resonate and travel today, in a world marked by social and political polarization, increased and diverse forms of inequality, and a trend of democratic backsliding? Oxhorn (1998a) conceptualized the popular sectors as a place-based source of collective identity formation that could replace the concept of class to allow for a better understanding of the rise of unequal democracies and the social construction of limited forms of citizenship in Latin America. However, evidence in the chapters of this collective volume leads to the conclusion that differences in identity, interest, and capacity are the building blocks of contemporary societies. This focus on difference may be to the detriment of a particular similarity – resource poverty – that could bind many identities together under the larger notion of disadvantage or subalternity. As many chapters in this collection show, centuries of oppression have evolved into competition both between similar interests and among diverse demands and needs.

The contributions to this volume offer many insights, including two important general lessons for comparative politics in building on and expanding Oxhorn's work on the social construction of citizenship. First, if a strong and autonomous civil society is at the core of the development of citizenship as agency in democracy, the capacities (and interests) of the state also matter, as citizenship is a relational construct. Second, the significance of cooperative competition – heterogeneous civil society and popular sector interests, identities, and resource capacities organizing autonomously, competing peacefully, and demanding inclusion collectively – cannot be overstated. If we are to understand the successes and shortfalls in developing equality, citizenship, and democracy, we must look to both the quantity and the quality of participation and inclusion. In sum, despite an increase in civil society participation, the challenge of cooperation across heterogeneous groups, in addition to gaps in state capacity and interests, keeps civil society weak and hinder the construction of quality citizenship. These lessons are not only important to understanding the limits of democracy in Latin America today, but also to thinking beyond the region and into dynamics of democratic erosion, political polarization, and authoritarian drifts across the world.

1. States and governments are key actors in the creation and reproduction of inequality. While early theories of citizenship were generally considered to be state centric, Oxhorn and others emphasized how agency mattered in defining the width and depth of citizenship regimes (Oxhorn 2011). In fact, a strong civil society is essential in demanding and struggling for inclusion. However, as he emphasized in his argument, citizenship is a relational construct. This means that states remain an important actor, one that creates opportunities for the inclusion or exclusion of disadvantaged groups by crafting institutions, adopting policies, and developing economic models according to their own interests and capacities. States and governments have the capacity to choose which (or whether) civil society groups are deemed worthy of support, or innocuous enough not to repress. This is, of course, as Oxhorn explained, in part because they act with the interests of the resource wealthy, who are able to make themselves heard through social intermediation models like corporatism and, eventually, neopluralism.

However, as the authors of this collection emphasize, states and governments also act because executives, bureaucracies, and legislators have reasons of their own to consider it worth supporting (or tolerating) certain subaltern groups. Studying US–Cuba relations, Eckstein (this volume) shows that US administrations operating in the international context of the Cold War chose to embrace Cuban immigration for strategic reasons. This began a cycle through which a growing Cuban American voter base was able to demand further entitlements and become relatively immune to anti-immigrant pressures in subsequent decades. This dynamic stands in stark contrast to the restricted access and rights of Haitians seeking to be immigrants, who are arguably more in need than Cubans, but whose plight has not served US political interests. Hilgers (this volume) provides a similar account of municipal politics in Mexico. Mexico City mayors and legislators with electoral ambitions, as well as bureaucrats facing resource shortages, have supported the demands of certain subaltern groups for better housing and urban services, in exchange for their votes and to enable the smooth functioning of bureaucratic processes. In both cases, state and government interests contribute to the fragmentation of civil society.

States and governments thus have a variety of interests and capacities regarding the inclusion (or exclusion) of certain civil society or subaltern groups and in creating opportunities for them to organize autonomously, but this capacity is also embedded in the historical paths of state (and regime) formation. This is what Robert and Brunet-Bélanger (this volume) show in their comparative account of Indigenous struggles for inclusion and recognition in Guatemala and Paraguay. The two models of Indigenous citizenship regimes, respectively qualified by the authors as ambivalent and closed, are built into historically constructed and institutionally embedded relationships with the colonial state. Different paths generated distinctive legislation and policy, along with varying (though limited in both cases) opportunities and constraints for collective, national-level Indigenous organization and mobilization to demand inclusion and recognition.

Neoliberal state policies also structure group identities and struggles, as demonstrated by Rousseau (this volume) in her account of the Peruvian state's policy responses to demands by women's movements for citizenship rights. In the context of neopluralism, the Peruvian state's policy priorities and orientations created differentiated inclusion patterns and identities among women's groups. While certain sectors of the women's movement gained political representation and economic and reproductive rights, social policy responses aimed at the popular sectors remained mostly assistentialist (helping only with the immediate symptoms of poverty) and guided by a gendered – and unequal – division of carework. They reproduced exclusion within the women's movement by emphasizing the identities of women from the popular sectors as mothers and caregivers, and not as workers and democratic actors.

For both Rubin and Douek (this volume) it is not only states but more specifically regime types and institutional legacies/structures that play a decisive role in defining the scope and outcome of popular protest and of civil society's capacity to organize autonomously. In his comparative account of popular protest in Middle Eastern republics, Rubin shows that civil society dynamics are embedded in opportunities opened (or not) by preceding undemocratic societies. While the literature distinguishes authoritarian regimes from hybrid ones by degree of state control, Rubin suggests that the distinguishing factor should rather be regime tolerance of civil society activity. Where fully authoritarian regimes seek complete social control, hybrid regimes tolerate some societal challenge as a solution to problems of legitimacy, allowing democratic enclaves to form within an autonomous civil society. These enclaves diffuse ideas and coordinate popular action, defining civil society's capacity to bring about change, even in the event of massive social protests such as those of the Arab Spring. For Douek, low-intensity, neopluralist, unequal democratic regimes like South Africa are also characterized by a legacy of violent and repressive policing. Neoliberal state policies enable the privatization and militarization of police and security forces – key actors in intermediating the state–society relationship and the construction of (unequal) citizenship rights. Repressive structures embedded in these violent, low-intensity democractic institutions and reproduced through (and by) neopluralism, he argues, limit the capacity of civil society groups and popular sectors to organize collectively to demand inclusion, and serve the interests of certain (elite) groups to the detriment of others.

2. *Cooperative competition: Civil society and the popular sectors are heterogeneous* in terms of gender, ethnic, racial, religious, and other forms of identification, as well as in terms of organizational mission – and in terms of capacities. This leads to three important insights for theorizing the social construction of citizenship in neopluralist contexts through a comparative lens.

First, because civil society and the popular sectors are heterogeneous, *opportunity structures may not yield desired or expected outcomes*. One example is the expansion of women's rights in Peru. From 2001 to 2017, the country held democratic elections, had advantageous macroeconomic conditions, and functioned under pluralism. While women's groups took the opportunity to make demands and the state expanded social programs and advanced women's rights, the focus of these demands and responses was narrow. Women's inclusion in social policy was brought about according to instrumentalist visions of motherhood that were focused on improving indicators of maternal mortality, child nutrition, and school enrollment. More progressive policy demands regarding carework and equal labour market opportunities only entered the public agenda with the COVID-19 pandemic (Rousseau, this volume).

Moreover, even when state and government are entirely amenable to acting on civil society demands, civil society may choose not to engage with the state. In Chile, citizens used their democratic power to overturn the status quo of the post-authoritarian regime and its institutions. Following a decade of social protest, they elected a leftist president with roots in the student movement, as well as a constituent assembly, in 2021. But citizens did not transform their street power into support for this new institution or the government, which was constituted of allies. Instead, they rejected the new constitution and distanced themselves from the president and other elected movement leaders. Civil society thus coalesced to defeat the pre-existing order, but the coalition subsequently disintegrated as some members moved to occupy the vacated spaces of power, while others seemed neither willing to support such spaces in the longer term nor able to propose alternatives (Roberts, this volume).

Second, *identity heterogeneity means that civil society groups have different capacities*. To be sure, civil society groups have differing human and financial resources. In addition to this, their identities per se carry different opportunities. Indigenous peoples have suffered exclusion and repression for centuries. Their identity continues to be a basis for their exclusion, while at the same time being a basis for their special status. Latin American countries have largely, and more easily than other regions, conceded special status to their Indigenous populations, according to their traditions. Yet these legal rights tend not to be translated into practice. Indeed, Indigenous people's access to the state and to citizenship rights tends to be more restricted than for other citizens. Nonetheless, many have remained strongly mobilized civil society actors by taking their struggles for the social construction of citizenship to the international level. Indeed, in both Paraguay and Guatemala, Indigenous people's movements made claims through the instruments of international law (Robert and Brunet-Bélanger, this volume).

Heterogeneity in the capacities of civil society is also emphasized in Rubin's contribution (this volume). He argues that, as observed in the Middle East, consensus among popular sector organizations may be thin and the population may not trust them very much, hindering their capacity to mobilize and to push for democratic reforms and inclusion. In certain cases, however, this low level of trust can be mediated by religious groups and organizations, which, as part of civil society, are able to encourage mobilization through their support of the consensus, in otherwise fragmented and neopluralist contexts.

Third, *the media and organized religion are important mediating groups*, with significant resources and internal heterogeneity, that sit uneasily within civil society. They are affected by neopluralism alongside civil society and have to compete amongst themselves; yet they also play a (re)productive role within the public sphere. Bonner,

Durazo Herrmann, and Rubin (each this volume) consider the media as an important intervening group between state and society (while Oxhorn has discounted its importance). For Bonner, the mass media play an important role in the social construction of citizenship. She argues that forced competition within neopluralism weakens investigative journalism, lending power to elite voices while undermining protest. This reinforces neopluralism and further weakens civil society. Durazo Herrmann similarly concludes that neopluralism makes itself felt even in media systems, including affecting diverse voices and platforms that could otherwise contribute to a dynamic public sphere (such as is the case in Veracruz). Unequal resources mean that some media have limited reach and some actors and issues receive less coverage than others, weakening the public's access to information. This, he argues, reinforces neopluralism.

MOVING FORWARD: STILL THE CENTURY OF NEOPLURALISM?

Thinking about authoritarian drifts and democratic erosion in Latin America and across the world, as Oxhorn does in the concluding chapter for this volume, reminds us of the acuteness of his contribution for understanding democracy, but most importantly the current challenges to democracy.

Because they unfold in a context of neoliberal economies and elite-driven minimalist democracies or hybrid regimes, state–civil society relations in Latin America sustain the construction of an exclusionary model of citizenship as consumption. Even if some institutional reforms are implemented, some inclusionary policies are adopted, and some underprivileged groups are struggling for inclusion and recognition, neopluralism remains central to interest intermediation in the public sphere. As the empirical and comparative contributions in this collective volume illustrate, however, the relative strength of civil society as an agent (measured by its capacity for cooperative competition – coexisting peacefully and organizing autonomously to demand inclusion) is driven both by state/government interests and by generally weak, heterogeneous, and often conflict-prone civil societies with diverging interests, identities, and capacities. This means that, in Latin America and in many countries of the Global South, citizenship regimes remain generally limited, exclusionary, and unequal. Even in the older democracies of Europe and the US, such logics can be at play, in particular when it comes to policies regarding the extension (or withholding) of citizenship rights to different categories of migrants.

Divisions and polarization are on the rise, as contemporary liberal democracies face the pressure of democratic erosion, authoritarian drift, or Oxhorn's "new authoritarian dynamic." This context brings to the fore the importance of the concept of neopluralism and the enduring and self-reproducing effect this mode of interest intermediation has had on democracy and inequalities across the world. Democracy has been emptied of its inclusionary essence by neoliberal policies and elitist institutions. Meeting the contemporary challenges posed by the "new authoritarian dynamic" and democratic erosion across the world invites us to redefine democracy, as Oxhorn suggests, not as electoral arrangements meant to serve elite interests, but rather as responsive, accountable (and inclusive) governments brought about through active citizen participation.

REFERENCES

Alvarez, Sonia E., Evelina Dagnino, and Arturo Escobar, eds. 1998. *Culture of Politics/Politics of Cultures: Re-Visioning Latin American Social Movements*. Boulder, CO: Westview Press.

Baker, Andy, Barry Ames, and Lúcio Rennó. 2020. *Persuasive Peers: Social Communication and Voting in Latin America*. Princeton, NJ: Princeton University Press.

Balán, Manuel, and Françoise Montambeault, eds. 2020. *Legacies of the Left Turn in Latin America: The Promise of Inclusive Citizenship*. Notre Dame, IN: University of Notre Dame Press.

Birdsall, Nancy, Nora Lustig, and Christian J. Meyer. 2013. "The Strugglers: New Poor in Latin America?" CGD Working Paper 337, Center for Global Development, Washington, DC.

Boulding, Carew, and Claudio A. Holzner. 2021. *Voice and Inequality: Poverty and Political Participation in Latin American Democracies*. Oxford, UK: Oxford University Press.

Collier, Ruth Berins, and David Collier. 1991. *Shaping the Political Arena: Critical Junctures, the Labor Movement, and Regime Dynamics in Latin America*. Princeton, NJ: Princeton University Press.

Dagnino, Evelina. 2006. "Meanings of Citizenship in Latin America." *Canadian Journal of Latin American and Caribbean Studies/Revue canadienne d'études latinoaméricaines et caribéennes* 31, no. 2: 15–51.

Helmke, Gretchen, and Steven Levitsky, eds. 2006. *Informal Institutions and Democracy: Lessons from Latin America*. Baltimore, MD: Johns Hopkins University Press.
Hilgers, Tina. 2012. *Clientelism in Everyday Latin American Politics*. London: Palgrave Macmillan.
Hilgers, Tina, and Jean François Mayer. 2024. "Le secteur informel urbain en Amérique latine." In *L'Amérique latine en transformation: mobilisation et citoyenneté*, edited by Françoise Montambeault, Dan Furukawa Marques, and Nora Nagels, 155–76. Montreal: Presses de l'Université de Montréal.
Holston, James. 2008. *Insurgent Citizenship: Disjunctions of Democracy and Modernity in Brazil*. Princeton, NJ: Princeton University Press.
Hummel, Calla. 2021. *Why Informal Workers Organize: Contentious Politics, Enforcement, and the State*. Oxford, UK: Oxford University Press.
Kapiszewski, Diana, Steven Levitsky, and Deborah Yashar, eds. 2021. *The Inclusionary Turn in Latin American Democracies*. New York: Cambridge University Press.
Linz, Juan J., and Arturo Valenzuela, eds. 1994. *The Failure of Presidential Democracy*. Baltimore, MD: Johns Hopkins University Press.
Mainwaring, Scott, and Aníbal Pérez-Liñán. 2023. "Why Latin America's Democracies Are Stuck?" *Journal of Democracy* 34, no. 1: 156–70.
Mainwaring, Scott, and Timothy R. Scully, eds. 2009. *Democratic Governance in Latin America*. Redwood City, CA: Stanford University Press.
Marshall, T.H. 195 *Citizenship and Social Class, and Other Essays*. Cambridge, UK: Cambridge University Press.
Montambeault, Françoise, Manuel Balán, and Philip Oxhorn. 2020. "Widening and Deepening Citizenship from the Left? A Relational and Issue-Based Comparative Approach." In *Legacies of the Left Turn in Latin America: The Promise of Inclusive Citizenship*, edited by Manuel Balán and Françoise Montambeault, 17–43. Notre Dame, IN: University of Notre Dame Press.
Morgan, Jana. 2007. "Partisanship During the Collapse of Venezuela's Party System." *Latin American Research Review* 42, no. 1: 78–98.
O'Donnell, Guillermo. 2010. *Democracy, Agency and the State: Theory with Comparative Intent*. Oxford, UK: Oxford University Press.
O'Donnell, Guillermo, and Philippe C. Schmitter. 1986. *Transitions from Authoritarian Rule: Tentative Conclusions About Uncertain Democracies*. Baltimore, MD: Johns Hopkins University Press.

Oxhorn, Philip. 1994. "Where Did All the Protesters Go? Popular Mobilization and the Transition to Democracy in Chile." *Latin American Perspectives* 21, no. 3: 49–68.

Oxhorn, Philip. 1995a. *Organizing Civil Society: The Popular Sectors and the Struggle for Democracy in Latin America.* University Park, PA: Penn State University Press.

Oxhorn, Philip. 1995b. "From Controlled Inclusion to Coerced Marginalization: The Struggle for Civil Society in Latin America." In *Civil Society, Theory and Comparison*, edited by John Hall, 250–77. Cambridge, UK: Polity Press.

Oxhorn, Philip. 1998a. "The Social Foundations of Latin America's Recurrent Populism: Problems of Popular Sectors Class Formation and Collective Action." *Journal of Historical Sociology* 11, no. 2: 212–46.

Oxhorn, Philip. 1998b. "Is the Century of Corporatism Over? Neoliberalism and the Rise of Neopluralism." In *What Kind of Democracy? What Kind of Market?: Latin America in the Age of Neoliberalism*, edited by Philip Oxhorn and Graciela Ducatenzeiler, 195–217. University Park, PA: Penn State University Press.

Oxhorn, Philip. 2003. "Social Inequality, Civil Society and the Limits of Citizenship in Latin America." In *What Justice? Whose Justice?: Fighting for Fairness in Latin America*, edited by Susan A. Eckstein and Timothy P. Wickham-Crowley, 35–63. Berkeley, CA: University of California Press.

Oxhorn, Philip. 2004. "Neopluralism and the Challenges for Citizenship in Latin America." *Soundings: An Interdisciplinary Journal* 87, nos. 1–2: 27–58.

Oxhorn, Philip. 2006. "Conceptualizing Civil Society from the Bottom Up: A Political Economy Perspective." In *Civil Society and Democracy in Latin America*, edited by Richard Feinburg, Carlos S. Waisman, and Leon Zamiosc, 54–82. New York: Palgrave Macmillan.

Oxhorn, Philip. 2011. *Sustaining Civil Society: Economic Change, Democracy and the Social Construction of Citizenship in Latin America.* University Park, PA: Penn State University Press.

Oxhorn, Philip, and Graciela Ducatenzeiler. 1999. "The Problematic Relationship Between Economic and Political Liberalization: Some Theoretical Considerations." In *Markets and Democracy in Latin America: Conflicts or Convergence?*, edited by Philip Oxhorn and Pamela K. Starr, 13–41. Boulder, CO: Lynne Rienner.

Oxhorn, Philip, and José R. Jouve-Martin. 2017. "Inequality and Inclusion in Latin America." *Latin American Research Review* 52, no. 2: 203–7.

Paquet, Mireille, Nora Nagels and Aude-Claire Fourot, eds. 2018. *Citizenship as a Regime: Canadian and International Perspectives.* Montreal: McGill-Queen's University Press.

Postero, Nancy. 2017. *The Indigenous State: Race, Politics, and Performance in Plurinational Bolivia.* Berkeley, CA: University of California Press.

Przeworski, Adam. 1991. *Democracy and the Market: Political and Economic Reforms in Eastern Europe and Latin America.* New York: Cambridge University Press.

Rich, Jessica A.J., Lindsay Mayka, and Alfred P. Montero. 2019. "Introduction: The Politics of Participation in Latin America – New Actors and Institutions." *Latin American Politics and Society* 61, no. 2: 1–20.

Rueschemeyer, Dietrich, Evelyne Huber Stephens, and John D. Stephens. 1992. *Capitalist Development and Democracy.* Chicago: University of Chicago Press.

Schmitter, Philippe C. 1974. "Still the Century of Corporatism?" *Review of Politics* 36, no. 1: 85–131.

Smith, Amy Erica. 2017. "Democratic Talk in Church: Religion and Political Socialization in the Context of Urban Inequality." *World Development* 99: 441–51.

Tilly, Charles. 1996. "Citizenship, Identity and Social History." In *Citizenship, Identity and Social History*, edited by Charles Tilly. Supplement 3, *International Review of Social History*, 1–17. Cambridge University Press.

Turner, Bryan. 1992. "Outline of a Theory of Citizenship." In *Dimensions of Radical Democracy: Pluralism, Citizenship, Community*, edited by Chantal Mouffe, 33–63. London: Verso.

Weyland, Kurt. 2004. "Neoliberalism and Democracy in Latin America." *Latin American Politics and Society* 46, no. 1: 135–57.

Yashar, Deborah J. 2005. *Contesting Citizenship in Latin America: The Rise of Indigenous Movements and the Postliberal Challenge.* New York: Cambridge.

SECTION ONE

Latin America

I

Neopluralism, Citizenship, and Clientelism: The Urban Popular Movement in Mexico City

Tina Hilgers

Philip Oxhorn's seminal contribution to the study of democracy has centred on the importance of a mobilized and autonomous civil society, highlighting the impact of economic structures on its capacity to construct inclusive citizenship. One of his key arguments has been that the weakness of democracy across Latin America is grounded in the lack of resolution of economic conflicts surrounding citizenship rights (2011). Indeed, the scope of his analysis that populism could gain from perceptions that democratic elites and institutions are disconnected from the reality of most citizens widened beyond Latin America (1998a, 2007, 2011) in the era following the 2008 financial crisis to encompass "the West" (Oxhorn and Jouve-Martín 2017).

In this chapter, I use Oxhorn's insights on civil society, economic paradigms, and populism, and clientelism (the exchange of political support for resources) to analyze the case of Mexico City. Oxhorn's work has highlighted the inclusionary weaknesses of the economic and political structures shaping the context in which actors negotiate policy content and implementation, as well as political participation. I meet his macro arguments with a view from below, elaborating on why citizens are swept up in clientelistic relationships that personalize politics, seemingly running counter to democratic practices. To do so, I focus on the politics and practices linking the Movimiento Urbano Popular (Urban Popular Movement, or MUP) to the left-wing Partido de la Revolución Democrática (Democratic Revolutionary Party, or PRD) and the Movimiento Regeneración Nacional (National Regeneration Movement, or MORENA).

The first section of this chapter outlines Oxhorn's economic analysis of civil society in Latin America, focusing on the concepts of neopluralism and the social construction of citizenship. The second section uses these insights to construct three categories of incentives – economic, institutional, and community – that motivate citizens to turn to clientelism as an informal mechanism of inclusion. The third section provides historical context for the Mexican case, looking at the methods of controlled inclusion used by the authoritarian regime of the Partido Revolucionario Institucional (Institutional Revolutionary Party, or PRI) to demobilize civil society and the MUP. The fourth section covers the fraught relationship between the MUP and both the PRD and MORENA in Mexico City. I argue that, under the democratically elected governments formed by the PRD and MORENA, the MUP has enjoyed greater freedom of action, but has fragmented. Elements of the parties and administrations have sought simultaneously to include the MUP and to demobilize it through clientelism, as is characteristic of citizenship under neopluralism. However, MUP leaders and members have also sought these clientelistic relationships as mechanisms to meet the institutional, economic, and community demands on which their elected governments are weak.

OXHORN'S NEOPLURALISM AND CITIZENSHIP

Oxhorn (2011) argues that the problem underlying democratic weakness across Latin America is the lack of resolution of conflicts surrounding citizenship rights (2011). His explanation develops a collectivist perspective on the struggle to construct consensus about the structure of society, drawing attention to the differentiated economic resources and organizational capacities (power and power resources) of groups, their relationships with each other, and their relationships with the state.

In a robust democracy, civil society – autonomous territorial and functional groups with varying interests – and the state together construct citizenship through confrontation and synergy. Civil society holds the state accountable for providing equal inclusion in politics, the state provides opportunities for participation, and both work together to create policy change (Oxhorn 2011).

However, democratic states, governments, and civil societies function *mutatis mutandis*. Democratic participation, representation, and public administration; interest intermediation; and political–economic paradigms are interconnected (Dagnino 2005; Hilgers and Mayer 2022). The weakness of Latin American democracy and civil society and the fragmentation of citizenship are related to the political economies in imbrication with which they developed (see also Robert and Brunet-Bélanger, this volume). Marginalized from meaningful political participation by ruling elites and crushed by economic crises, low-income sectors (the majority of the population) have not developed the organizational capacities necessary to press for change (Oxhorn and Ducatenzeiler 1998). Rather than acting as an autonomous agent in the construction of citizenship, civil society has largely been controlled and (de)mobilized from above. In the state-centred industrialization/urbanization era (1930s to 1980s), citizenship developed through cooptation, as states used corporatist sectors to control inclusion by trading resources for political allegiance. In the market-oriented democratic/neoliberal era (1980s to 1990s), citizenship evolved into a matter of individual consumption, as citizens gained universal political rights but were obliged to use votes and economic resources as currency to privately access what should be universal social and civil rights. In both eras, state accountability remained weak (Oxhorn 1998b, 2007, 2011). Oxhorn (1998b) conceptualizes the new method of interest intermediation that is replacing corporatism as neopluralism. As was the case in the classic US model of pluralism, neopluralism involves widely varying interests competing to bring public and policy attention to their demands. But under the market-centred approach to lower-class inclusion, inequality fragments civil society, repression interweaves with democratic participation, and clientelism and neocorporatism persist. Paradoxically, popular organizations were more successful under authoritarianism than they are in democracy (Oxhorn 1998a, 1998b, 2011).

The persisting problems of inclusion have resulted in a crisis of democratic representation. Citizens are frustrated by their incapacity to hold accountable political elites whom they perceive as disconnected from the average person's reality. The free vote seems meaningless when other rights of citizenship are disrespected, while democratic institutions and elites appear to be obstacles, not solutions, to problem solving (Oxhorn 2007; Oxhorn and Jouve Martín 2017).

Populist leaders exploit this dissatisfaction. They use the context of economic and political exclusion to rally the fragmented interests of the popular sectors, capitalizing on mass support to convince the popular sectors to negotiate their own admittance to elite circles in a reaffirmation of class hierarchy that stalls more profound social change. Nonetheless, populism, clientelism, and other forms of controlled inclusion may be better than their alternative. Where inequality is rampant in the absence of any attempt at inclusion, extreme polarization may lead to civil war, such as in Haiti, Paraguay, Cuba, El Salvador, and Nicaragua (Oxhorn 1998a).

INCENTIVES FOR CLIENTELISM UNDER NEOPLURALISM

We can use Oxhorn's macro arguments and concepts at the micro level to shed further light on how citizens respond in such contexts. I argue that citizens evaluate regime quality according to three interrelated rubrics – institutional, economic, and community – and use personalistic opportunities for inclusion where official channels fall short.

Many voters hold broad conceptions of what democratic citizenship should accomplish. These include concerns about political and civil rights, such as free and fair elections and guarantees of civil liberties, but also social rights of equality, economic opportunities, and improved access to education, health care, and other social welfare programs (Baviskar and Malone 2004; Segovia et al. 2021; Lustig 2020).[1] In the processes of democratization beginning in the mid-1970s, voters were encouraged to believe in the power of democracy to increase economic well-being and social welfare. For instance, in his campaign for the presidential election that would end the Argentine military dictatorship in 1983, Raúl Alfonsín used the slogan, "with democracy one eats, one is cured, one is educated" (cited in Tedesco 1999, xiii).

Yet, in the years following the initial presidential transitions, it became increasingly clear that citizenship rights would remain limited. Candidates for public office continued to break promises, corruption and mismanagement remained widespread, the rule of law was uneven at best, and living standards failed to improve (O'Donnell 1998; Oxhorn 2003). In classifying the results of a 2001 survey on democratic government performance in Argentina, Brazil, Chile, and Guatemala, researchers had to include the category "there is no democracy" because as many as 15 per cent of respondents voiced this opinion (Baviskar and Malone 2004).

This context changed briefly with what I identify as the "pink boom," the decade spanning 2004 to 2014, during which Latin American social democracy overlapped with a global commodity supercycle. Civil society mobilized to bring a series of social democratic presidents to power in the first surge of the "pink tide," from the late 1990s to 2015. The popular sectors felt the benefits of these administrations investing the returns of the 2004 to 2014 global commodities boom in order to decrease poverty and inequality. General satisfaction with democracy rose by as much as 30 per cent across the region (Foa et al. 2020, 29) and the 2006 to 2014 Latin America Public Opinion Project (LAPOP) AmericasBarometer surveys show an increase in political engagement among the poorest sectors for this period (Boulding and Holzner 2021). Had the rallying of civil society during the pink boom consolidated into a sustained mobilization combining broad inclusionary pressures and autonomous policy-influencing organization, we might have seen the sort of cooperative competition that makes for a strong and effective civil society (see Montambeault and Hilgers, introduction to this volume). But civil society dynamism, inclusionary politics, and state–society synergy in constructing citizenship were short-lived. Economic hardship and political discontent returned as the political-economic fallout of the Great Recession hit, the pink boom ended, and the COVID-19 recession began. By 2020, "more than three in every four citizens across the region register[ed] discontent with the performance of democracy – the highest level since the start of public opinion surveys" (Foa et al. 2020, 28), and only 48 per cent supported democracy (Latinobarómetro 2023).

I argue that citizens evaluate regimes according to their capacity to meet everyday institutional, economic, and community needs and that negative evaluations have consequences beyond manifesting as discontent. Where democratic representatives and institutions are found to be inadequate, citizens often turn to informal channels to look for solutions to their problems. Their evaluation of institutional, economic, and community needs does not follow a ranked order. The relative importance of the elements that constitute a democracy differ from one country to another (Camp 2003) and from one voter to another (Miller et al. 1997; Crow 2009).

Citizens assess government commitments to upholding *institutionalized political and civil rights*: free and fair elections, the rule of law, and the protection of basic rights and freedoms (Miller et al. 1997;

Foa et al. 2020). Among the rubrics according to which these factors are assessed are accountability and access to the state. Elections are a method for holding leaders accountable for their actions, and it is through the organs of the state that voters can make demands or seek recourse regarding their rights. Where sanctions through voting do not appear to influence the policy orientation of a government (such as with democracies that are plebiscitarian; see Oxhorn 2007) and access to the state through official channels is difficult, voters will seek alternatives for ensuring accountability and making demands (Gay 1999; Krishna 2007; Anciano 2018).

Having a formal political voice and equality are not in themselves satisfactory unless they are perceived as directly affecting access to *economic benefits*. Voters have pressing, immediate needs that include housing, health care, education, urban services, employment, and nutrition. It is difficult to separate the popularity of a particular government or regime from citizens' economic considerations. As much as poor voters are interested in political change, the democratic forms of organization must be able to meet their material needs or voters will seek other options (Oxhorn 2011; Shefner 2012; Anciano 2018; Hilgers and Mayer 2022).

Voters respond to the attraction of *community*. Under neopluralism and citizenship as consumption, participation, rights, and equality are individualized, while notions of community have lost relevance (Oxhorn and Ducatenzeiler 1998; Oxhorn 2011). But protections guaranteeing individual rights and freedoms are restricted to the political sphere (Oxhorn 2011),[2] while most citizens are helpless vis-à-vis fluctuations in market and household economies (Güneş-Ayata 1994; Birdsall 2015; Hilgers et al. 2022). The contradictions inherent in individualizing politics and separating it from the market generate outcomes that encourage voters to seek alternative means of representation and of meeting their resource needs. At the same time, impersonal and individualized political arrangements are alienating. Voters not only want leaders to be present at the local level, so that they may interact with them and challenge the results of their work (Tejera Gaona 2003), they also want to have personal relationships with leaders and other voters that will generate a shared identity and a support network (Güneş-Ayata 1994; Auyero 1999a; Auyero 1999b; Hagene and González-Fuente 2016; see also Koster and Eiró 2022).

The alternative to formal democratic channels for representation, participation, and resource mobilization is often a personalistic exchange such as clientelism, in which people and groups with a lower income trade political support for resources with higher status patrons (Hilgers and Mayer 2022; Hilgers 2018). Clientelism is often regarded as anti-democratic because patrons are not elected, clients do not have formal rights, public resources are privatized, and benefits are not universal. In addition, individualized competition for finite goods and services divides the popular classes, undermining solidarity organization (Montambeault 2015). But in a move to decolonialize political analysis (in the sense of decoupling it from the "Western" ideals held by foreign and local elites), some propose that clientelism is a form of democratic participation (Hilgers 2012; Anciano 2018).[3] Evidence from the local level in Mexico demonstrates that clientelism can sometimes respond successfully to the three interconnected areas of performance – institutional, economic, and community – in ways that formal, but weak, democratic citizenship cannot.

MUP: ORIGINS AND CLIENTELISM UNDER AUTHORITARIANISM

Oxhorn has analyzed the Mexican case, studying the PRI's authoritarian regime (1929–2000) through the lenses of citizenship as cooptation in the corporatist years until the early 1980s, and citizenship as consumption in the subsequent technocratic neoliberal years (Oxhorn 2011). Much of the PRI's national-level controlled inclusion was reproduced at the local level in Mexico City, where the MUP's autonomy was restricted by having to work with PRI regents to meet members' immediate needs for shelter, work, health care, and other services.

Popular mobilization in Mexico related to urban housing needs in the post-revolutionary authoritarian era can be divided into four periods: 1920s to 1940s, 1940s to 1968, 1968 to 1985, and 1985 to the late 1990s (1997, in the case of Mexico City). All were marked by a mix of repression and cooptation through corporatism and clientelism, characterizing the links between MUP organizations and the government. As Mexico's major urban centre, Mexico City has been central to many developments of the MUP, but these also occurred in other cities, including Veracruz, Guadalajara, and Puebla.

In the PRI's early years, mobilization was limited and easily controlled, but industrial expansion and its related demographic shift eventually increased the intensity and scope of housing, service, and employment problems and related demands. From the 1920s to the 1940s, tenants associated with revolutionary unions primarily demanded rent controls, but their mobilization did not develop broadly because the state both met their demands and repressed their activities. The PRI constructed itself as a corporatist party in the 1930s, with hierarchically organized sectors engineered to turn the processes of mobilizing and making demands into a family affair. The labour, peasant, and popular sectors channelled their demands directly to the party, rather than taking to the streets in protest, and their loyalty was rewarded with consideration of their needs as well as resource provision.[4] The popular sector – the Confederación Nacional de Organizaciones Populares (National Confederation of Popular Organizations, or CNOP) – included all those who did not fall into the categories of industrial workers, peasants, or large capital. This was the organization through which claims related to the problems of urbanization might have been made. However, it also included the middle classes, professionals, and bureaucrats, who wanted a beautiful city unmarred by informal markets and shelters – demands at odds with the needs of the poor for space and resources. While the CNOP's membership was vast, its diversity made it an unfit advocate for the poor (Davis 1991). The inclusion it did offer was through *caudillo* (strongman) leaders who negotiated with the government, which responded with both targeted fulfillment of specific demands and cooptation. Attempts to organize outside the corporatist system were met with violent repression and eviction (Ramírez Sáiz 1986, 1999).

After the Second World War, the PRI's desire to enter the ranks of industrialized countries led to the development of import substitution industrialization (ISI) and urban renewal. ISI involved spending on infrastructure development, easing access to credit, purchasing foreign-made industrial machinery, and regulating foreign access to Mexican markets. The industrialization of agriculture and the expansion of urban production and markets created a demographic shift, as increasing numbers of people migrated from rural to urban areas. In 1940, Mexico City counted 1.8 million inhabitants, and in 1947 about 2.3 per cent of the population lived in precarious housing. By 1960, the population had more than doubled to 4.9 million, including 1.8 million rural migrants to the centre of the city. The poverty rate exceeded 30 per cent, and over 50 per cent of all housing was inadequate because of structural problems and/or a lack of services such as fresh water. By the end of the decade, there was a shortage of 1.3 million homes within the city (Jordan 2013). Seeking to make the city more cosmopolitan, the regent Ernesto P. Uruchurtu (1952–66) invested in public green spaces, drainage, sewerage, lighting, housing, and markets, while criminalizing street vending and using the police to repress the lower classes (Cross 1998; Jordan 2013).

The year 1968 marked a turning point in urban politics and mobilization. Thousands of students – supported by workers, teachers, and members of the public – took to the streets in a call for social, political, and education reform. The regime's response of military and police repression, in which an estimated three hundred protesters were killed and another one thousand arrested, incited popular disgust. The PRI successfully calmed the population by accommodating some demands and coopting student leaders, but the seeds of opposition were sown (Haber 2006). President Luis Echeverría (1970–76) brought opponents back into the fold of the PRI with political and economic reforms, including changes to electoral laws and significant increases in social spending. By the early 1970s, at least 50 per cent of the population lived in precarious, self-constructed housing on the northern and eastern outskirts of the city. Echeverría moved to formalize tenure and extend the urban infrastructure of sewerage, running water, electricity, and paved roads. Nonetheless, delivery of the programs remained politically motivated, with access largely going to neighbourhoods affiliated with the corporatist sectors (Maffitt 2014). Independent neighbourhood organizations trying to challenge the CNOP's power were either co-opted or repressed.

The earthquake that ravaged Mexico City in September 1985 galvanized the urban popular movement. Measuring 8.0 on the Richter scale, the quake killed over 10,000 people and left another 250,000 without adequate shelter, especially within low-income zones in the city centre. President Miguel de la Madrid's (1982–88) administration responded slowly, initially refusing to fully deploy the military and to accept international aid. Citizens organized independently to rescue survivors and supply victims with necessities. In the weeks and months following the quake, existing popular organizations and new groups composed of victims mobilized to demand that the government supply them with proper shelter. These groups coalesced into the Coordinadora Única de Damnificados (Single Coordinating

Committee of Earthquake Victims, or CUD) and then the Asamblea de Barrios (Neighbourhood Assembly, or AB), as well as smaller, more radical groups, such as the Frente Popular Francisco Villa (Francisco Villa Popular Front, or FPFV), which began to make broader demands for social, economic, and political change.

The postwar era of growth had ended definitively by the late 1970s, and the 1980s saw the beginnings of economic restructuring: the state-centred development model of investment in domestic industry (ISI) was abandoned in favour of a neoliberal economic paradigm that called for restricted state spending and free trade. In the so-called "lost decades" of the 1980s and 1990s, economic opportunities disappeared, the middle classes shrank, and poverty and inequality rose. Popular organizations that were already mobilized around issues of shelter now linked their demands to socialist and social democratic ideals of equality and justice. Debates about the advantages of joining established political parties in working toward regime change divided the movement, with some groups remaining autonomous and others establishing political links.

The relationship between the MUP and city government were fraught. There were periods of openness from the government and others of repression, depending, among other things, on the personal convictions of the city's regent regarding the best manner of responding to the conflicting demands of the poor and the middle classes (Cross 1998). There were also periods of increased mobilization by the MUP, often in response to what were seen as particular excesses in state disinterest in the plight of the poor, combined with openings in the political opportunity structure – that is, opportunities to access the political system (Haber 2006). Despite its desire to oust the PRI, the MUP had to work with the party in power. Its membership's primary needs were immediate – shelter, work, health care, and other services – and these could only be met by the PRI and the state apparatus. Thus, groups such as the AB and the FPFV in Mexico City, and others around the country, felt compelled to negotiate with the PRI.

MUP: FRAGMENTATION AND CLIENTELISM UNDER DEMOCRACY

The slow transition to democracy began with electoral reforms after the 1968 student movement and culminated in the 2000 election of the conservative opposition Partido Acción Nacional (National

Action Party, or PAN) to the presidency. In 1989, former members of the PRI, left-wing opposition parties, and social organizations, including parts of the MUP, formed the centre-left PRD as an electoral vehicle to bring about democracy. While PRD presidential candidates would not be victorious, the party became successful at all other electoral levels and especially in Mexico City, which it governed from 1997 to 2018. It was a key force in the democratic opposition movement, was considered the champion of the poor masses, and drew support from across social, economic, and age groups (see Klesner 2007 for an analysis of PRD supporters). The PRD splinter group, MORENA, registered as a competing political party in 2014, winning both the Mexico City governorship and the presidency in 2018 and 2024. Both the PRD and MORENA have been riven by internal power disputes, with party posts, bureaucratic jobs, electoral candidacies, and public resources being distributed according to patronage and for clientelistic reasons, in order to benefit one faction or another.

The Mexican electorate's level of satisfaction with their democracy has been uneven. Voters have varied expectations of a democratic system, including free and fair elections, the rule of law, civil rights and freedoms, equality, welfare, and community, but for a plurality, socioeconomic factors appear to be more important than others (Camp 2003; Crow 2009; see Tejera Gaona 2003 for expectations regarding the community presence of representatives). Providing an overview of Mexicans' feelings about democracy, the 2009 Latinobarómetro survey results (Latinobarómetro 2009) showed that only 44 per cent of Mexicans considered democratic governments as better prepared than others to confront economic crises and only 20 per cent believed that democracy guaranteed a fair distribution of wealth. If they had to choose between democracy and economic development without democracy, only 30 per cent would have chosen the former. Fourteen years later, the Latinobarómetro (2023) survey suggests that the Latin American region is undergoing democratic decline as economic crises increase poverty and inequality, and with governments incapable of meeting policy demands and of guaranteeing civil and social rights, while political elites are perceived by the people as ever more corrupt. In evaluating the capacity of their regime to meet their needs, 35 per cent of surveyed Mexicans support democracy, 28 per cent believe there is no difference between a democratic and a non-democratic regime, 33 per cent believe that an authoritarian regime might be preferable, and 56 per cent would not care if a non-democratic government were in power if it solved their problems. Mexico City has the third-highest rate of dissatisfaction with democracy (71 per cent) among Mexican states, and 67 per cent of its residents think that their state functions under little to no democracy (Moreno 2019).

The mediocre will and capacity of the PRD and MORENA to meet citizens' everyday institutional, economic, and community needs have had consequences beyond fostering discontent. Clientelism and other personal exchanges amount to a meeting of supply and demand (Shefter 1994; Hilgers and Mayer 2022). They exist not only because leaders offer privileges to their supporters, but also because voters seek alternatives to official channels that do not meet their needs when it comes to representation and resources.

Democratic Institutions

The PRD's and MORENA's track records on promoting democratic institutions in Mexico City have been moderate, at best. Internal and popular elections have been marked by fraud and other illegalities, including ballot box theft or stuffing, and illegal mobilizations, and little will to change the status quo (Corona Armenta 2004; García Soto 2009; Cárdenas Solórzano 2009; Bruhn 2021; Esteinou Madrid 2024). During popular elections, leaders of both parties buy votes and use the traditional method of *acarreo* (transporting citizens to vote or to demonstrate, with strict instructions on how to behave), and between elections they create clientelistic relationships with social organizations and local brokers that then become reliable sources of votes (Sánchez 1999, 2001; Tejera Gaona 2021; Reveles Vázquez and Moreno Delgado 2022; Langston and Castro Cornejo 2023; field observations 2004, 2012). PRD administrations were also at the centre of several financial scandals, resulting from officials accepting significant sums of cash from private donors.

Important sectors of the MUP have seen the practices of the PRD and MORENA in power as problematic and have dissociated themselves from the parties. Many organizations supported the PRD's bid for power in 1997 because the party's discourse was one of remaining close to the masses and using intervention to ease their economic plight, and because it offered a democratic alternative to the PRI (Bruhn 1997). But several soon withdrew from their alliance with the party, feeling that it inhibited their political autonomy and angered by the party's non-democratic actions. MUP leaders criticized PRD administrations for centralizing power, engaging in fraudulent activities, individualizing services and presenting them as party goodwill, redistributing just enough resources to create voter allegiance rather than generating programs with lasting economic effects, demobilizing civil society, and encouraging social organization leaders to use their membership as a base from which to compete for power in the party and in public elections.[5] Under the MORENA administration, MUP mobilization has sometimes been in line with official policy positions, but there is also friction as groups chafe against the centralization of power (Bruhn 2021).

For the individual voter, the situation remains complex and the choice is not one of being for or against the PRD or MORENA, but of how best to deal with the status quo. Voters have had low opinions of national and Mexico City institutions (Mitofsky 2009; Covarrubias 2005; Moreno 2019), but the PRD and MORENA perform well enough on other rubrics to maintain support, and voters must engage with each of their various administrations in order to have their demands met.[6] If improving institutional safeguards through electoral sanctions is not considered a viable option, then voters feel they must ensure accountability and access in other ways.

On 27 June 2012, hundreds of thousands of people filled Mexico City's Zócalo, the main square, for the closing ceremony of Andrés Manuel López Obrador's presidential election campaign (at the time, for the PRD). In the sea of PRD-yellow T-shirts, flags, and banners were spots of orange, red, and white, identifying allied parties and social organizations. People milled about, talking, eating, drinking, and cheering with nominal enthusiasm at the appropriate moments. Following the final speech, the masses squeezed out of the plaza and into the contiguous streets to find their way home via subway or on the multitude of buses chartered to *acarrear* participants. The FPFV had a delegation in the plaza and was also busily *acarreando* people from outside the city in preparation for the 1 July election, lodging them in its social housing complexes (field observations 2012). Aware that politics based on such activities is a sham, *acarreados* participate because they enjoy the immediate benefits of the events (food, drink, campaign swag, entertainment) and because they need the long-term benefits of their relationship with their patrons (preferential access to government subsidies and programs) (field observations 2004, 2012). Regardless, many of them would have voted for López Obrador at the national level (at 32 per cent, he came second to the PRI, at 39 per cent) and the PRD at the local level (which won with 60 per cent), regarding the PRD's ideological position and policy platform as more advantageous than those of the rivaling parties. But they knew that there were never enough resources to turn proposed universal programs into concrete universal goods and services.

Although clientelistic exchanges can have a series of pernicious effects, in competitive political contexts, clients can use them effectively to meet their needs. Patrons cannot be formally held accountable through elections or the courts, but where there is viable political competition, clients can – and do – use "voice and exit" to express their disapproval of patron actions. Members and former members of several PRD client groups talked of shopping for patrons to find the one who most suited their needs, of challenging patrons, and of leaving organizations for which the costs of participation outweighed the benefits.[7] The link of accountability is also clear and direct. In a clientelistic relationship, the patron is available at the borough or neighbourhood level; clients know their face, have a relationship with them, and know whether the relationship is providing tangible benefits. Although the patron is not formally required to justify their actions, competitive politics encourages effectiveness. When clients have a problem, they are not faced with incomprehensible bureaucratic institutions and requisites, and having to contact distant officials, but have a familiar figure to whom to turn for help.

Economic Benefits

Weaknesses in the functioning and protection of democratic institutions are often matched by relatively poor economic performance. Many Mexicans consider economic growth to be an integral element of democracy, and their dissatisfaction with their country's post-transition economic performance has translated to disillusionment with democracy (Crow 2009). Under the PAN and PRI presidencies since 2000, voters' economic dissatisfaction was often aimed at the conservative federal governments, whose policies failed to generate growth or opportunities that extended much beyond the wealthier classes. In Mexico City, the PRD and MORENA have tried to ease the burden of the poor by offering financial aid to the elderly, accessible health care, education subsidies, housing subsidies, and so on (Luccisano and Macdonald 2017; Reveles Vázquez 2022). Popular movement leaders and intellectuals have criticized the PRD for giving out dependency-creating handouts instead of creating programs to change society (author interview with Elena, see note 5, Mexico City, 18 October 2004), but the masses tend to support such policies. They saw first the PRD and then MORENA as the only party whose programs demonstrate concern for public welfare and have tangible effects. Nonetheless, the repercussions of stagnation play out at the local level, in voters' daily lives and through their choices.

In the people's eyes, the primary success of the PRD in government was the provision of a monthly pension payment to all senior citizens, which was so popular that it was taken over by the federal government and became a constitutional right in 2020. But despite these efforts – and those of MORENA – to confront poverty and inequality from the standpoint that citizens have universal rights, not just particular needs (Luccisano and Macdonald 2017; Reveles Vázquez 2022), city administrations have not had enough resources to sustain these programs. Over half (52.5 per cent) of the city's population continues to live in poverty and 19.6 per cent lives in extreme poverty, while about half of the economically active population does some informal work and 29 per cent works entirely in the informal sector (Reveles Vázquez 2022). The housing deficit remains a pressing problem, with about 65 per cent of housing self-built or informal (Tellman et al. 2021). Those who need to survive and protect their families cannot afford to wait as their opportunity for decent shelter becomes stalled in apparently interminable official processes. Instead, they are forced to seek special relationships with friends in the administration.

In the 1980s and 1990s, independent urban popular organizations such as the AB grew from consisting of successful representatives of Mexico City squatters, the homeless, and the urban poor to participatory movements demanding political change at the national level. Many movement leaders, in the struggle for democracy, became candidates for the PRD, effectively decapitating their own organizations. The new politicians were no longer present in the streets, furthering the material demands of their movements, but they also did not have access to enough state resources to alleviate the housing shortage in the short term. The MUP lost momentum, broke apart, and the remaining splinter groups survived on patronage links with their former leaders in public office (interviews with Elena, Rafael, Alberto, Francisco Saucedo, and Marco Rascón, see note 5; field observations 2004, 2012; see also Grajeda 2005). A good number of these former MUP leaders and remaining social organizations then shifted their allegiance to MORENA (Tejera Gaona 2020). Although special relationships like these undermine the establishment of programs with universally applicable regulations and benefits, from the perspective of the citizen in need, they are better than the alternative of waiting patiently for uncertain results.

Depending on their position and connections, patrons can give clients improved access to health care, education, and subsidized housing; provide them with jobs; and organize urban service delivery on their behalf. Clientelism creates inequalities but can also be a mechanism of social inclusion (Hilgers 2012). This was the case in Gay's (1999) famous example of "The Broker and the Thief," featuring a Rio de Janeiro neighbourhood leader brokering deals to exchange community access to urban services for votes. The key to the success of his efforts lay in requiring political candidates to deliver payment prior to election day. The broker's activities may not have been strictly democratic, but he ensured that the community's votes were not wasted on candidates who were making promises that they would forget after the elections. When the community experimented with having leadership that left electoral choices to individual people, residents found that they no longer received any state support at all. Where democratic institutions and organizations are not capable of providing material benefits and services, clientelism remains a viable choice that solves the immediate resource problems of at least some citizens.

Community

The discourse of the PRD and MORENA – at the national as well as at the state level – has been populist, revolving around participation and closeness to the masses, but the core of these parties has remained self-contained elites. In its electoral struggles, first against the hegemonic PRI and then against the PAN, the PRD positioned itself as the people's party, as the force that would not only generate economic policy geared toward fulfilling the needs of the masses, but would also give these masses a direct voice by including them in government. This populist discourse of inclusiveness was arguably at the core of the PRD's success. At the same time, in their decision-making styles, party leaders have been anything but close to the people. Cuauhtémoc Cárdenas, the PRD's moral leader and first mayor of Mexico City, tended to make decisions with a small circle of trusted advisors (Prud'homme 1996). López Obrador, the other great leader of the PRD and, later, linchpin of MORENA, knows how to rouse the masses in public squares, but only engages in carefully scripted interactions. Despite their rhetoric, neither these nor other PRD or MORENA figures have introduced functioning mechanisms of democratic participation beyond elections.[8]

The gap left at the local level by distant elites, a lack of participatory mechanisms, and people's inability to meet all of their material needs has been filled by local intermediaries. Political operators with experience in popular organizing for employment, housing, and representation have long established themselves in Mexico City's popular neighbourhoods. They use their local presence and image as skilled political entrepreneurs to gather supporters. Based on the strength of their following, the operators then negotiate with the PRD, MORENA, and the city administration for resources for their supporters, as well as for positions of power within the parties and for candidacies for public election for themselves. In many of the city's poor boroughs, such operators, aided by their families and friends, have taken over public offices in the name of the PRD and then MORENA, and turned them into personal fiefdoms.[9]

To be sure, such patrons engage in all manner of un-democratic and anti-democratic activity, subverting resources, buying votes, engaging in fraudulent electoral processes, and so on, yet their voting clients often evaluate their performance based on other factors. Long-term clientelistic relationships can provide a desirable feeling of community and identity. Clients tolerate the asymmetrical nature of the relationship because the patron is generous and shows concern for them. Clients identify with the patron because they come from the same region or neighbourhood, hold similar jobs, or belong to the same ethnic or religious group (Güneş-Ayata 1994; Hagene and González-Fuente 2016).

Members of client groups in Mexico City expressed happiness about having found people with similar experiences, with whom they interacted and worked toward a common goal, and on whom they could rely for support – benefits that seemed to outweigh their non-democratic leadership actions.[10] Auyero (1999a, 1999b) observed a similar phenomenon in his work on clientelism in Buenos Aires, where patron–client relationships were the basis for feelings of solidarity and family-belonging in a poor community. Patrons knew their clients personally, understood their problems, and solved their pressing resource needs, and their clients responded with respect and affection. While the relationship was one of dominance, it made shantytown life bearable.

FINAL DISCUSSION

The Mexican case is emblematic of Oxhorn's analysis of corporatist citizenship as cooptation and of neopluralist citizenship as consumption. Whereas in the first period the PRI manipulated access to power by creating group hierarchies that divided civil society, in the second period the market plays an important role in controlling access. All groups and individual people are nominally free to organize and make demands, but only the wealthy and powerful have the resources to do so in practice. The popular sectors are left to wield their votes as bargaining chips. The PRD's and MORENA's Mexico City governments have created programs making important goods and services universally accessible, but there are not enough resources to meet demands, and personalistic exchanges providing selective benefits continue.

The macro insights developed by Oxhorn on the construction of citizenship under varying political and economic constraints are helpful at the micro level to explain why citizens engage with personalistic mechanisms of inclusion. Writing about the crisis of representation, Oxhorn (2007) argues that citizens believe in the good of democracy but are dissatisfied with how it is practised. As electoral promises of economic and social inclusion fail to materialize, trust in democratic institutions weakens and political apathy grows. This chapter has argued that gaps in institutional procedures, economic benefits, and community-creating processes are filled by alternative methods, so that democracy and hierarchical, personalistic methods of problem solving intertwine.

NOTES

1 For a hard-hitting indictment of US democracy, arguing that negative pressure on economic and social rights by elected representatives will eventually result in a revolt against democracy, see Klarman 2020. For a similar analysis on the Latin American region, analyzing the decline of democracy and resulting citizen frustration, see Latinobarómetro 2023.

2 And even here they may be losing ground (see Klarman 2020 on the United States).

3 See also Montambeault and Dias Félix (2021) on building participatory institutions on clientelistic networks.

4 The military was initially included as a corporatist sector, but this was subsequently disbanded. For a general discussion of corporatism, see Schmitter 1974. For the Mexican case, see Middlebrook 1995.

5 Interviews in Mexico City with several movement leaders: Elena (one of the original leaders of the city's MUP), 18 October 2004; Rafael (a leader of the Unión Popular Revolucionaria Emiliano Zapata [Popular Revolutionary Union Emiliano Zapata, or UPREZ] within the MUP), 8 November 2004; Alberto (leader of a housing organization with roots in the MUP), 30 September 2004; Francisco Saucedo (one of the early leaders of the AB, and then federal congressman for the PRD), 29 October and 3 November 2004; and Marco Rascón (one of the early leaders of the AB and one of the originators of "Superbarrio Gómez" – the superhero figure representing the AB's struggle), 19 October 2004. The names of interview participants have been changed, except in the case of public figures.

6 For an in-depth discussion regarding the complex motivations of social organizations and their members, see Haber (2006), who argues that urban popular movements engage both in sociopolitically transformative projects and in activities intended to meet the basic needs of their members.

7 Interviews in Mexico City with Beatriz (a former member of a FPFV housing organization), 24 November 2004; Ana (a resident in an FPFV shantytown), 8 December 2004; Lupe and Carmelita (initially members and then leaders of a housing organization created by a PRD politician), 28 October 2004.

8 See Harbers (2007) for a detailed discussion of the PRD's participatory mechanisms. See Montambeault and Dias Félix (2021) for an example of participatory security being embedded in clientelistic networks in Mexico City's greater metropolitan area.

9 The PRI and PAN hardly function differently at the municipal level.
10 Interviews in Mexico City with Luisa (who has lived in various shantytowns for over twenty years and was living in an FPFV shantytown at the time of the interview), 8 December 2004; Lupe (see note 7); and Catalina (member of a senior citizens' group), 27 November 2004; as well as a general discussion at a senior citizens' group meeting, 4 November 2004.

REFERENCES

Anciano, Fiona. 2018. "Clientelism as Civil Society? Unpacking the Relationship Between Clientelism and Democracy at the Local Level in South Africa." *Journal of Asian and African Studies* 53, no. 4: 593–611.

Auyero, Javier. 1999a. "Performing Evita: A Tale of Two Peronist Women." *Journal of Contemporary Ethnography* 27, no. 4: 461–93.

Auyero, Javier. 1999b. "'From the Client's Point(s) of View': How Poor People Perceive and Evaluate Political Clientelism." *Theory and Society* 28: 297–334.

Baviskar, Siddhartha, and Mary Fran T. Malone. 2004. "What Democracy Means to Citizens – and Why It Matters." *European Review of Latin American and Caribbean Studies* 76: 3–23.

Birdsall, Nancy. 2015. "Does the Rise of the Middle Class Lock in Good Government in the Developing World?" *European Journal of Development Research* 27, no. 2: 217–29.

Bruhn, Kathleen. 1997. *Taking on Goliath: The Emergence of a New Left Party and the Struggle for Democracy in Mexico*. University Park, PA: Pennsylvania State University Press.

Bruhn, Kathleen. 2021. "AMLO y su partido." *Política y gobierno* 28, no. 2: 19–27.

Camp, Roderic Ai. 2003. "Democracy through Latin American Lenses: An Appraisal." In *Citizen Views of Democracy in Latin America*, edited by Roderic Ai Camp, 3–23. Pittsburgh, PA: University of Pittsburgh Press.

Cárdenas Solórzano, Cuauhtémoc. 17 July 2009. "Un último llamamiento a los militantes del PRD." *La Jornada* (Mexico).

Corona Armenta, Gabriel. 2004. "La renovación de las dirigencias nacionales en el Partido de la Revolución Democrática (1989–2002)." In *Partido de la Revolución Democrática: Los problemas de la institucionalización*, edited by Francisco Reveles Vázquez, 73–133. Mexico City: Universidad Nacional Autónoma de México and Gernika.

Covarrubias, Ana Cristina. 2005. *Las Instituciones ante el Espejo de la Opinión Pública*. Mexico City: Pulso Mercadológico y Covarrubias y Asociados. www.amai.org/datos_files/las_inst_ante_el_espejo.pdf.

Cross, John C. 1998. *Informal Politics: Street Vendors and the State in Mexico City*. Stanford, CA: Stanford University Press.

Crow, David Bradley. 2009. "Citizen Disenchantment in New Democracies: The Case of Mexico." PhD diss., University of Texas at Austin.

Dagnino, Evelina. 2005. "Meanings of Citizenship in Latin America." IDS Working Paper 258, Brighton, UK, University of Sussex, Institute of Development Studies.

Davis, Diane E. 1991. "Urban Social Movements, Intrastate Conflicts over Urban Policy, and Political Change in Contemporary Mexico." In *Breaking Chains: Social Movements and Collective Action*, edited by Michael P. Smith, 133. New Brunswick, NJ: Transaction.

Esteinou Madrid, Francisco Javier. 2024. "Elecciones 2024: La Mañanera Electoral." *Siempre!* No. 3709, 14 July.

Foa, Roberto Stefan, Andrew Klassen, Micheal Slade, Alex Rand, and Rosie Collins. 2020. *The Global Satisfaction with Democracy Report 2020*. Cambridge, UK: University of Cambridge, Bennett Institute for Public Policy.

García Soto, Salvador. 2009. "René y el plato frío de la venganza." *El Universal*, 13 June.

Gay, Robert. 1999. "The Broker and the Thief: A Parable (Reflections on Popular Politics in Brazil)." *Luso-Brazilian Review* 36, no. 1: 49–70.

Grajeda, Ella. 16 January 2005. "Benefician perredistas con créditos de Vivienda." *El Universal*, Ciudad, 2.

Güneş-Ayata, Ayşe. 1994. "Clientelism: Premodern, Modern, Postmodern." In *Democracy, Clientelism, and Civil Society*, edited by Luis Roniger and Ayşe Güneş-Ayata, 19–28. Boulder, CO: Lynne Rienner.

Haber, Paul L. 2006. *Power from Experience: Urban Popular Movements in Late Twentieth Century Mexico*. University Park, PA: Pennsylvania State University.

Hagene, Turid, and Íñigo González-Fuente. 2016. "Deep Politics: Community Adaptations to Political Clientelism in Twenty-First-Century Mexico." *Latin American Research Review* 51, no. 2: 3–23.

Harbers, Imke. 2007. "Democratic Deepening in Third-Wave Democracies: Experiments with Participation in Mexico City." *Political Studies*, 55, no. 1: 38–58.

Hilgers, Tina. 2008. "Causes and Consequences of Political Clientelism: Mexico's PRD in Comparative Perspective." *Latin American Politics and Society* 50, no. 4: 123–53.

Hilgers, Tina. 2012. "Democratic Processes, Clientelistic Relationships, and the Material Goods Problem." In *Clientelism in Everyday Latin American Politics*, edited by Tina Hilgers, 3–22. New York: Palgrave Macmillan.

Hilgers, Tina. 2018. "*Gestión* (Mexico)." In *The Global Encyclopedia of Informality*, vol. 2, edited by Alena Ledeneva, 216. London: UCL Press.

Hilgers, Tina, Anna Calderón, and Max Honigmann. 2022. "Tensions Between the Middle Classes and the 'New Middle Class' in Brazil: An Accidental Biographical Ethnography." *Latin American Research Review* 57, no. 3: 536–53.

Hilgers, Tina, and Jean François Mayer. 2022. "Negociar inclusão pelo clientelismo: democracias neoliberais, pobreza e desigualdade." *Revista Extraprensa* 16, no. 1: 52–81.

Jordan, Robert M. 2013. "Flowers and Iron Fists: Ernesto P. Uruchurtu and the Contested Modernization of Mexico City, 1952–1966." PhD diss., University of Nebraska–Lincoln.

Klarman, Michael J. 2020. "Foreword: The Degradation of American Democracy – and the Court." *Harvard Law Review* 134, no. 1: 1–264.

Klesner, Joseph L. 2007. "The 2006 Elections: Manifestation of a Divided Society?" *PS: Political Science and Politics* 40, no. 1: 27–32.

Koster, Martijn, and Flávio Eiró. 2022. "Clientelism in Northeast Brazil: Brokerage Within and Outside Electoral Times." *Contemporary Social Science* 17, no. 3: 222–34.

Krishna, Anirudh. 2007. "Politics in the Middle: Mediating Relationships Between Citizens and the State in Rural North India." In *Patrons, Clients, and Policies: Patterns of Democratic Accountability and Political Competition*, edited by Herbert Kitschelt and Steven I. Wilkinson, 141–58. New York: Cambridge University Press.

Langston, Joy, and Rodrigo Castro Cornejo. 2023. "Why Do Clientelist Brokers Go Rogue? Parties, Politicians, and Intermediaries in Mexico." *Perspectives on Politics* 21, no. 1: 43–58.

Latinobarómetro. 2009. *Informe Latinobarómetro 2009*. Santiago: Corporación Latinobarómetro.

Latinobarómetro. 2023. *Informe Latinobarómetro 2023*. Santiago: Corporación Latinobarómetro.

Luccisano, Lucy, and Laura Macdonald. 2017. "Guns and Butter: Social Policy, Semiclientelism, and Efforts to Reduce Violence in Mexico

City." In *Violence in Latin America and the Caribbean: Subnational Structures, Institutions, and Clientelistic Networks*, edited by Tina Hilgers and Laura Macdonald, 132–49. New York: Cambridge University Press.

Lustig, Nora. 2020. "Desigualdad y descontento social en América Latina." *Nueva Sociedad* 286 (March–April): 53–61.

Maffitt, Kenneth M. 2014. "Nueva política social, viejor contrato social: Políticas de vivienda y protesta urbana en la periferia de la Ciudad de México, 1960s–1980s." *Historia* 47, no. 1: 113–32.

Middlebrook, Kevin J. 1995. *The Paradox of Revolution: Labor, the State, and Authoritarianism in Mexico*. Baltimore, MD: Johns Hopkins University Press.

Miller, Arthur H., Vicki L. Hesli, and William M. Reisinger. 1997. "Conceptions of Democracy Among Mass and Elite in Post-Soviet Societies." *British Journal of Political Science* 27, no. 2: 157–90.

Mitofsky. 2009. *Monitor Mitofsky: Economía, gobierno y política.* Mexico City: Consulta Mitofsky.

Montambeault, Françoise. 2015. *The Politics of Local Participatory Democracy in Latin America: Institutions, Actors, and Interactions.* Stanford, CA: Stanford University Press.

Montambeault, Françoise, and Annabelle Dias Félix. 2021. "When Informality Matters: Participatory Security Reform and Mechanisms of Social Embeddedness in Nezahualcóyotl, Mexico." *Journal of Latin American Studies* 53, no. 3: 465–92.

Moreno, Alejandro. 25 September 2019. "Yucatán y Querétaro, los estados más satisfechos con la democracia." *Nación 321*. https://www.nacion321.com/encuestas/yucatan-y-queretaro-los-estados-mas-satisfechos-con-la-democracia.

O'Donnell, Guillermo. 1998. "Polyarchies and the (Un)Rule of Law in Latin America." In *The Rule of Law and the Underprivileged in Latin America*, edited by Juan Méndez, Guillermo O'Donnell, and Paulo Sérgio Pinheiro, 303–38. Notre Dame, IN: Notre Dame University Press.

Oxhorn, Philip. 1998a. "The Social Foundations of Latin America's Recurrent Populism: Problems of Popular Sector Class Formation and Collective Action." *Journal of Historical Sociology* 11, no. 2: 212–46.

Oxhorn, Philip. 1998b. "Is the Century of Corporatism Over?" In *What Kind of Democracy? What Kind of Market?: Latin America in the Age of Neoliberalism*, edited by Philip Oxhorn and Graciela Ducatenzeiler, 195–217. University Park, PA: Pennsylvania State University Press.

Oxhorn, Philip. 2003. "Social Inequality, Civil Society, and the Limits of Citizenship in Latin America." In *What Justice? Whose Justice?: Fighting for Fairness in Latin America*, edited by Susan E. Eckstein and Timothy P. Wickham-Crowley, 35–63. Berkeley, CA: University of California Press.

Oxhorn, Philip. 2007. "Citizenship as Consumption or Citizenship as Agency? The Challenge for Civil Society in Latin America." In *Civil society, Religion and Global Governance: Paradigms of Power and Persuasion*, edited by Helen James, 126–55. Abingdon, UK: Routledge.

Oxhorn, Philip. 2011. *Sustaining Civil Society: Economic Change, Democracy, and the Social Construction of Citizenship in Latin America.* University Park, PA: Pennsylvania State University Press.

Oxhorn, Philip, and Graciela Ducatenzeiler. 1998. "Economic Reform and Democratization in Latin America." In *What Kind of Democracy? What Kind of Market?: Latin America in the Age of Neoliberalism*, edited by Philip Oxhorn and Graciela Ducatenzeiler, 3–20. University Park, PA: Pennsylvania State University Press.

Oxhorn, Philip, and José R. Jouve-Martín. 2017. "Inequality and Inclusion in Latin America." *Latin American Research Review* 52, no. 2: 203–7.

Prud'homme, Jean François. 1996. "Party Strategies and Negotiations over the Rules for Electoral Competition: Mexico (1988–1994)." PhD diss., York University.

Ramírez Sáiz, Juan Manuel. 1986. "Organizaciones populares y lucha política." *Cuadernos Políticos* 45: 38–55.

Ramírez Sáiz, Juan Manuel. 1999. *El movimiento urbano popular en México.* 2nd ed. Mexico: Siglo veintiuno editores.

Reveles Vázquez, Francisco. 2022. "El primer gobierno de MORENA en la CDMX: ¿En busca de la igualdad social?" In *La 4T y el régimen político*, edited by Godofredo Vidal de la Rosa, 349–81. Mexico City: Universidad Autónoma Metropolitana.

Reveles Vázquez, Francisco, and Daniel Patricio Moreno Delgado. 2022. "La ilusión democrática en México: La revocación del mandato presidencial de 2022." *El Cotidiano* 38, no. 234: 7–16.

Sánchez, Marco Aurelio. 1999. *La Élite en Crisis: Problemas Organizativos, Indeterminación Ideológica y Deficiencias Programáticas.* Mexico City: Plaza y Valdés.

Sánchez, Marco Aurelio. 2001. *PRD: El Rostro y la Máscara – Reporte de la Crisis Terminal de una Élite Política.* Mexico City: Centro de

Estudios de Política Comparada and Centro de Estudios para la Transición Democrática.
Schmitter, Philippe C. 1974. "Still the Century of Corporatism?" *Review of Politics* 36, no. 1: 85–131.
Segovia, Joselin, Nicola Pontarollo, and Merci Orellana. 2021. "Discontent with Democracy in Latin America." *Cambridge Journal of Regions, Economy and Society* 14, no. 3: 417–38.
Shefner, Jon. 2012. "What Is Politics for? Inequality, Representation, and Needs Satisfaction Under Clientelism and Democracy." In *Clientelism in Everyday Latin American Politics*, edited by Tina Hilgers, 41–59. New York: Palgrave Macmillan.
Shefter, Martin. 1994. *Political Parties and the State: The American Historical Experience*. Princeton, NJ: Princeton University Press.
Tedesco, Laura. 1999. *Democracy in Argentina: Hope and Disillusion*. London: Frank Cass Publishers.
Tejera Gaona, Héctor. 2003. "'No se olvide de nosotros cuando esté allá arriba': Cultura, ciudadanos y campañas políticas en la ciudad de México." Mexico City: Universidad Autónoma Metropolitana, Universidad Iberoamericana, Miguel Ángel Porrúa.
Tejera Gaona, Héctor. 2020. "Estructura política y elecciones en la Ciudad de México." In *México 2018: Elecciones, partidos y nuevos clivajes sociales*, edited by Esperanza Palma and Sergio Tamayo, 129–54. Mexico City: Universidad Autónoma Metropolitana.
Tejera Gaona, Héctor. 2021. "La formación y funcionamiento de las relaciones político-clientelares asociadas al mantenimiento y reproducción de la estructura política de la Ciudad de México." Mexico City: Universidad Nacional Autónoma de México, Centro de Investigaciones Interdisciplinarias en Ciencias y Humanidades.
Tellman, Beth, Hallie Eakin, Marco A. Janssen, Felipe de Alba, and B. L. Turner. 2021. "The Role of Institutional Entrepreneurs and Informal Land Transactions in Mexico City's Urban Expansion." *World Development* 140: 105374.
Ward, Peter M., and Elizabeth Durden. 2002. "Government and Democracy in Mexico's Federal District, 1997–2001: Cárdenas, the PRD and the Curate's Egg." *Bulletin of Latin American Research* 21, no. 1: 1–39.

2

Where Did All the Parties Go? Civil Society, Social Protest, and the Crisis of Representation in Chile's Constitutive Stalemate

Kenneth M. Roberts

In a provocative and deeply insightful article on Chile's democratic transition published shortly after General Augusto Pinochet abandoned the presidential palace, Philip Oxhorn (1994) posed the trenchant question, "Where Did All the Protesters Go?" As a leading chronicler of Chile's massive mid-1980s protest movement against Pinochet's military dictatorship, Oxhorn tackled the paradox of popular demobilization in the midst of democratic transitions – a paradox presaged in the pathbreaking work of transitology by Guillermo O'Donnell and Philippe Schmitter (1986, 48–56). Simply put, the paradox emerges when grassroots activists politically mobilize against a brutal dictatorship, despite the closure of formal political arenas and the risk of violent repression, only to demobilize when political repression is relaxed and institutional channels of participation are reopened.

Oxhorn tackled this paradox by examining how regime change was associated with basic shifts in the locus of political agency and contestation. Authoritarian rule, he argued, produced "a shift in the locus of political activity to nonparty arenas where it is more difficult to repress." The urban poor and grassroots civil society actors were often at the forefront of this basic shift, as new "political experiences and new forms of organization and participation emerge as a result of repression that targets political parties, political elites, and the leadership of most collective actors, particularly organized labour" (Oxhorn 1994, 49). Nevertheless, the popular upsurge associated with "the resurrection of civil society" was destined to be "ephemeral," as O'Donnell and Schmitter had suggested (1986, 55–6). Oxhorn noted that as a democratic transition unfolds and elections are scheduled, political contestation is redirected from the streets to more formal institutional arenas. In the process, "political parties once again come to the fore," and a "demobilization of mass actors" occurs. Wary of a backlash from authoritarian hardliners, "political parties become agents for moderation and social control to ensure that the transition runs its course." Chile's 1988 to 1990 democratic transition, therefore, was "dominated by elite actors who actively sought to limit social mobilization and channel political activity into exclusively electoral forms" (Oxhorn 1994, 50–1).

Revisiting Oxhorn's account a generation later is instructive, and more than a little puzzling, as Chile appears to have travelled full circle in its articulation of party–society relations. For the better part of three decades, Chile was widely regarded to have one of Latin America's most stable and institutionalized democratic regimes (Rhodes-Purdy 2017), anchored by an electorally dominant multiparty system (Valenzuela et al. 2018) and a transpartisan elite and technocratic consensus around the country's vaunted neoliberal economic model – one of the Pinochet regime's most durable and restrictive political legacies. The social demobilization that Oxhorn (1994, 1995) analyzed continued well beyond Chile's elite-negotiated and controlled regime transition, seemingly taking on the appearance of a systemic trait in the country's technocratic, internationally acclaimed *democracia de los acuerdos* (democracy of agreements) (Roberts 1998; Rhodes-Purdy 2017).

Over time, however, evidence mounted that Chile's once deeply rooted and highly institutionalized party system had become hollowed out and detached from its social bases. As parties became increasingly professionalized and technocratic, their capacity to articulate, aggregate, and represent a plurality of social demands – that is, to institutionally channel and control social mobilization, as Oxhorn described – severely decayed (Luna and Altman 2011; Roberts 2016). Student-led protests in 2006 and 2011 set the stage for a mass social uprising in October 2019 that paralyzed the democratic regime and forced it to accept what was previously unimaginable: the election of a constituent assembly in May 2021 aimed at refounding the political order bequeathed by Chile's military junta and its civilian brain trust. Both the constituent assembly election and subsequent national presidential and legislative elections confirmed that Chile's traditional parties had been eclipsed by new civil society and movement-based political fronts.

Chile's 2019 mass uprising, or *estallido* in Spanish, was a paradigmatic expression of what Jason Frank (2010, 8) calls a "constituent moment," when "underauthorized" actors "enact a political power that transcends the state's legal organization," basing their claims "wholly on the democratic authority of the people themselves." As Negri (2009, 11) argues, constituent power can be an insurgent force "that bursts apart, breaks, interrupts, unhinges any preexisting equilibrium and any possible continuity." The Chilean *estallido* surely had such disruptive effects, as it shattered the carefully constructed institutional equilibrium imposed during the regime transition and reproduced across three decades of democratic contestation. Arguably, the constraints placed on popular political claims under this institutional equilibrium suppressed the more quotidian "micropolitical enactments" (Frank 2010, 33) of constituent power and channelled it toward explosive and insurgent eruptions of mass political agency.

As Negri (2009, 1) emphasized, however, "constituent power resists being constitutionalized." Despite unprecedented levels of social mobilization, which placed an estimated 1.2 million people on the streets of Santiago on 25 October 2019, the constituent power of Chile's insurgent popular movements proved averse to institutional crystallization or representation. The political effervescence of the streets and barricades was very partially transmitted to partisan, electoral, and governing institutions, and formal institutions arguably had the effects anticipated by Negri – those of segmenting, denaturalizing, and disempowering constituent power itself (see Negri 2009, 11).

This chapter explores the challenges and pitfalls of transmitting this constituent power to formal democratic arenas in Chile. Chile's popular democratic movements succeeded in electing a constituent assembly dominated by representatives of civil society organizations and new political fronts, rather than traditional political parties, and they proceeded to draft a progressive constitution recognizing a broad swath of new social citizenship rights. They also helped to elect a leftist president in 2021, Gabriel Boric, with roots in the student protest movement. The popular bloc splintered, however, as it tried to mobilize mass support for the new constitution, and the constitution itself was decisively rejected in a September 2022 popular referendum – yet another exercise of constituent power, perhaps, but a radically different one from that which precipitated the crisis in 2019, and a rarity for a constitution drafted by an elected assembly.

Similarly, Boric and other movement leaders who entered into electoral politics had little in the way of a party organization to support them, and they quickly became detached from the movement bases that spawned their political careers. As such, Chile's new leftist administration was placed on the political defensive from the moment it assumed executive office, beset by conflicts over crime, immigration, and Indigenous rights that fanned the flames of conservative opposition. By May 2023, elections for a new Constitutional Council to draft yet another version of the constitution produced a conservative supermajority that empowered a relatively new far-right party led by an avowed proponent of Pinochet's legacy, José Antonio Kast, who had been defeated by Boric in the 2021 presidential election. The centrist Partido Demócrata Cristiano (Christian Democratic Party, or PDC), the dominant political party during the period of democratic transition, was unable to elect a single representative to the new Constitutional Council. The mainstream Partido Socialista de Chile (Chilean Socialist Party, or PSCh), which allied with the PDC during the transition and governed with its support across three presidential administrations, was relegated to secondary status in a new, but thoroughly defeated, leftist electoral front led by Boric's supporters. A second, more staunchly conservative new constitution drafted by this Constitutional Council was subsequently rejected in yet another popular referendum in December 2023. Chile was thus left to operate by default under a Pinochet-era constitutional framework that had been rejected by an overwhelming majority of voters, but sustained by the political gridlock vetoing the adoption of any proposed alternative.

Consequently, with mainstream parties on the left, centre, and right in precipitous decline, and no major new progressive party emerging from iterative cycles of mass social protest – although, notably, a major new far-right party emerging as a counter-reaction to them – Chile's constituent moment has seemingly deepened rather than resolved the country's crisis of democratic representation.

Rather than reconstitute the political order, it deconstituted the old one (Luna 2020) and produced a constitutive stalemate, leaving Chilean democracy in political limbo. Majoritarian popular constituencies have repeatedly demonstrated their ability to mobilize as an opposition force and paralyze state institutions (Meléndez 2022) – a "negative" expression of constituent power, perhaps – but they have yet to demonstrate their foundational or originary capacity to anchor the construction of an alternative democratic order with majoritarian support and constitutive authority.

Ultimately, the Chilean case demonstrates that the demobilization studied by Oxhorn was not necessarily a permanent condition. But it also demonstrates the supreme difficulty of overcoming the social and political fragmentation of Latin America's popular sectors and constructing a cohesive popular political *subject* on a neoliberal structural landscape of social atomization and heterogeneity – a central concern woven throughout Oxhorn's corpus of scholarship (see the introduction to this volume by Montambault and Hilgers). Oxhorn (1998, 2011) persuasively attributed Latin America's heterogeneous, "neopluralist" landscape to historical processes of class formation that were heavily conditioned by delayed industrialization, crisis-induced market liberalization, and extreme inequalities in the region's dependent capitalist economies. He also recognized the historical proclivity to rely on populist leadership to overcome the collective-action problems intrinsic to fragmented social landscapes, and thus construct popular subjects from the top down, at considerable cost to the political autonomy and democratic agency of the popular sectors themselves (Oxhorn 1998). Chile's popular sectors have, to date, resisted the populist temptation, but they have failed to construct a more autonomous, movement-based alternative capable of translating transversal forms of social protest into cohesive institutional and constitutive power. They have demonstrated their ability to mobilize as an oppositional force on a massive scale – but this mobilization has been cyclical or episodic rather than sustained, and it is too organizationally diffuse to cohere around a positive and hegemonic transformative project that is amenable to articulation within governing institutions. Absent the latter, it has yet to secure the expanded citizenship rights that are at the core of protesters' demands.

FROM DEMOBILIZATION TO MASS PROTEST: CONTESTING SOCIAL CITIZENSHIP RIGHTS

Chile's iterative cycles of mass protest against neoliberalism in 2006, 2011, and 2019 were not without precedent in Latin America, but they were qualitatively different from the modal patterns of anti-neoliberal protest in the region. Elsewhere, mass protests have typically erupted in response to financial crises in liberalized market economies (i.e., the uprisings that toppled Jamil Mahuad in Ecuador in 2000 and Fernando de la Rúa in Argentina in 2001), or the adoption of unpopular liberalization and structural adjustment measures that posed threats of serious economic hardships or dislocations (i.e., Bolivia's water privatization reform in 2000, or the austerity and structural adjustment measures that triggered Venezuela's mass urban uprising, the *Caracazo*, in 1989) (see Silva 2009; Simmons 2016). What made Chile different was the absence of a severe financial crisis or wrenching new austerity and adjustment measures at the onset of any of these protest cycles – unless one counts the four-cent hike in metro fares that led high school students to leap over metro turnstiles, setting off the 2019 *estallido*, as a wrenching adjustment measure. Chile's protest cycles were neither crisis nor adjustment induced, which is perhaps why they took so many people by surprise; they seemingly came "out of the blue." They were protests against a stable, mature, and thoroughly liberalized market economy – indeed, the region's neoliberal showcase, with one of its most dynamic and internationally competitive economies. But this neoliberal showcase suffered from a chronic deficit of social rights, and as the steady drumbeat of demands for expanded social citizenship bumped up against the constraints of extant representative institutions, periodic – if unpredictably timed – uprisings occurred. For all Chile's international acclaim, LAPOP/AmericasBarometer 2021 public opinion survey of Chilean citizens ranked the country *last* among all Latin American countries in their belief that basic rights were well-protected, with only 20 per cent of Chilean respondents claiming that they were (Perry 2023, 2).

To understand Chile's protest cycles, it is thus essential to juxtapose the twin deficits of the post-1990 democratic order: the weakness of social citizenship rights, and the progressive hollowing out of party-mediated political representation in a highly technocratic political order, which enervated state responsiveness to mobilized social citizenship claims. The first deficit was deeply embedded in Chile's neoliberal model – Latin America's, and the world's, first, most doctrinaire, and most comprehensive program of post-Keynesian neoliberal restructuring. All Latin American countries, with the exception of socialist Cuba, eventually followed Chile's lead in imposing neoliberal austerity and structural adjustment measures – including free trade, the privatization of state-owned industries, and financial deregulation (Edwards 1995) – in response to the 1980s debt crisis and subsequent hyperinflationary spirals. Chile under Pinochet, however, went well beyond these macroeconomic structural reforms to create the social pillars of a neoliberal order, or what Polanyi (1944) referred to as "market society."

Foremost among these social pillars were the privatization and commodification of social goods like education, health care, and social security, along with the liberalization or "flexibilization" of labour markets. Steeped in the market orthodoxy of Friedrich Hayek and Milton Friedman, Pinochet's Chicago school technocrats were handed the reins of state economic policymaking in early 1975, and proceeded to restructure Chilean society according to the principles of market individualism (see Silva 1996). Unencumbered by popular democratic pressures or civil society mobilization, thanks to the iron fist of the dictatorship and the complete closure of democratic spaces, the "Chicago Boys" constructed an order in which social goods were selectively allocated by the marketplace – and, therefore, heavily stratified by class position – rather than by claims to social citizenship rights. The Christian Democratic– and Socialist-led governments of the centre-left Concertación alliance that succeeded Pinochet following the 1990 regime transition largely reproduced these neoliberal social pillars, even while introducing technocratic reforms to broaden their coverage (see Pribble 2013).

Like many new democratic regimes (Albertus and Menaldo 2018), Chile inherited a constitutional order that originated in dictatorship. The institutional compromises embedded within the country's pacted democratic transition imposed severe constraints on the Concertación's ability to modify the neoliberal model, given the presence of unelected right-wing senators appointed by the dictatorship, a highly disproportional electoral system that overrepresented conservative parties in Congress, and a constitutional and juridical order that fiercely defended property rights and eschewed rights of social citizenship. Policy continuity, however, was not simply a function of institutional constraints, which were gradually lifted under Chile's Socialist presidents. Although Christian Democratic and Socialist leaders had been highly critical of the neoliberal model under Pinochet, they softened their opposition and pledged to keep the core of the model intact in order to alleviate military and business elite fears of a restoration of democracy. Memories of the trauma associated with the political polarization unleashed by Salvador Allende's experiment in democratic socialism in the early 1970s, which culminated in the 1973 military coup and ferocious military repression, reinforced this cautious and pragmatic approach (Rosenblatt 2021). Indeed, with the economy growing rapidly and generating employment, and the labour movement severely weakened by military repression and economic restructuring, the democratic ruling parties were loath to rock the boat by encouraging new social mobilization around claims for redistribution or expanded social citizenship rights. The top-down, technocratic management of Chile's neoliberal model quickly became a hallmark of the new democratic regime; the Socialist presidents Ricardo Lagos (2000–06) and Michelle Bachelet (2006–10 and 2014–18) introduced reforms to expand education credits, introduce universal basic health care, and broaden social security coverage, but access to and the quality of these and other social goods remained highly stratified by social class, and largely divorced from civil society input and citizen participation (see Pribble 2013; Rhodes-Purdy 2017).

This technocratic detachment from popular constituencies lay at the heart of the second democratic deficit – the hollowing out of Chile's once deeply rooted and institutionalized party system. By the start of Chile's third democratic decade, evidence was mounting that Chile's party system had become uprooted, even if it remained electorally stable – for the time being (Luna and Altman 2011; Roberts 2016; Heiss 2021, 34). Voter registration and turnout had steadily declined, especially among youth who had come of age under the democratic regime. Indeed, public opinion surveys showed that Chileans ranked at or near the bottom of Latin American countries for party identification, interest in politics, and participation in election campaigns and local-level politics (Luna et al. 2010, 135, 143, and 170; UNDP 2015, 34). If, as Oxhorn argued, Chile's parties had succeeded in controlling and demobilizing the shantytown youth protest movements that challenged Pinochet in the mid-1980s, they were woefully incapable of channelling the nascent mobilization of the post-Pinochet generation after 2006.

The student movements that began with the so-called *Pingüino* (penguin) rebellion of high school students in 2006 – named for the black-and-white colour scheme of the students' school uniforms – and continued with the massive university student uprising in 2011, thoroughly politicized the twin deficits of social citizenship and democratic representation. Indeed, the student uprisings were a classic expression of Polanyi's (1944) "double movement" of societal resistance to a market society that leaves citizens vulnerable to market insecurities without means for collective political redress. Student protests took direct aim at Chile's highly privatized and commodified education system, which both reflected and reproduced class inequalities in educational opportunities. Whereas students from well-to-do families had access to expensive and high-quality private schools and universities, those from low-income families were relegated to substandard public schools. Many students could only pursue higher education by assuming substantial debts at for-profit educational institutions. The centrepiece of student demands, therefore, was free universal public education at all levels of instruction – a claim to social citizenship that was well to the left of the platforms proposed by any of Chile's mainstream parties (see Donoso 2017).

This outflanking to the left of mainstream parties would be repeated throughout the decade to follow as other social groups pressed claims for social citizenship rights that clashed with Chile's neoliberal model and the trans-partisan technocratic consensus that upheld it. The student mobilization was amplified by protests against a largely privatized pension system that left many elderly citizens without an adequate income. Temporary contract workers protested against employment insecurity, and other groups mobilized around women's rights, the rights of Indigenous peoples, and the environmental consequences of a neoliberal growth model dependent on natural resource extraction (Donoso and von Bülow 2017). These diverse claims coalesced in the massive October 2019 uprising, which quickly assumed the character of a generalized assault on the party system establishment at the heart of the post-1990 democratic order. Protesters staged mass rallies and called for the resignation of conservative President Sebastián Piñera, placing over a million people on the streets of Santiago in a single day. Many of the protesters blocked streets, while their more radical flanks attacked metro stations and looted shops. By the end of the year, attacks had taken place on over eighty metro stations, along with buses, banks, gas stations, supermarkets, and Santiago's landmark telecommunications tower. With Piñera declaring, "We are at war," the government responded with heavy-handed police and military repression, declaring a state of emergency and deploying military troops in a futile effort to restore order. By the time the *estallido* had run its course, thirty-one people were dead, some seven thousand had been arrested, and over thirteen thousand people had been injured, including more than 350 who suffered eye damage from police shotgun pellets (Amnesty International 2020, 32).

Unable to restore order, the Piñera government acceded to a 15 November accord among party leaders in Congress to hold a national referendum on the convocation of a constitutional assembly. Although the referendum would be delayed by the early 2020 COVID-19 epidemic – which finally brought a halt to the protest movement – Chile's "constituent moment" had placed the country on the precipice of a break with Pinochet's institutional legacy, and a refounding of the democratic regime itself.

SOCIAL PROTEST AND CHILE'S CRISIS OF REPRESENTATION

Despite the scale and intensity of the 2019 uprising and its thorough rejection of the political establishment, social mobilization in the streets had only translated very partially and unevenly into constituent power in more institutionalized arenas. Indeed, it revealed the inherent tensions between civic and institutional expressions of constituent power, as Negri (2009) forewarned, and the formidable obstacles that can impede their bridging. In so doing, it posed in stark terms the institutional dilemma that has plagued radical political projects since the nineteenth century. This dilemma was instrumental to the division of the left historically into its anarchist, Leninist, and social democratic branches, and it heavily conditioned both the sociological study of political organization (Michels 1915) and the ideational study of revolutionary imaginaries (Renaud 2021).

This institutional dilemma lies precisely in the challenge of scaling up grassroots civic and political activism – or *poder popular*, as it is known in Latin America – and projecting it into formal institutional arenas. In local settings, grassroots activism exercised in a union hall or workplace, a school or neighbourhood assembly, or in the streets or public squares can encourage direct – that is, unmediated – forms of democratic deliberation, participation, accountability, and decision-making. The notion of an assembled *demos* acting as a non-hierarchical, self-governing civil society, shorn of the need for rulers, managers, or organized political intermediaries, is intrinsic to anarchist conceptions of revolutionary power constructed from below and within horizontal and decentralized social spaces, rather than captured from above in vertical and centralized governing institutions (Shaffer 2023). It is also prevalent in revolutionary imaginaries that insist on the "prefiguration" of emancipatory social relations in the organizational forms of radical political projects (see Renaud 2021). A long history of partisan capture, cooptation, and instrumentalization of civil society actors in Latin America has not only elicited a staunch defence of the political autonomy of *lo social*, but also, in some sectors of the grassroots, a visceral rejection of parties and formal governing institutions altogether, as alien forces incompatible with the construction of popular democratic alternatives.

The challenge of scaling up, however, is rooted in the fact that overarching legal, regulatory, and public policy frameworks that shape citizens' daily lives, as well as the distribution and exercise of power in society, are determined at higher and more centralized institutional settings that cannot be accessed directly by a *demos* assembled in local sites, or even assembled en masse through protests in the streets.[1] Access to these larger institutional sites inevitably requires some organization of representative agents – that is, political intermediaries – that lie in between the assembled *demos* and any state accountable to it.

Historically, political parties have been the primary collective actors performing such bridging or intermediary roles by organizing social cleavages, aggregating interests, and representing popular constituencies in formal state institutions (Lipset and Rokkan 1967; de Leon et al. 2015). The Latin American experience provides several prominent examples of movement-based party organizations emerging from cycles of mass social protest, such as the Movimiento al Socialismo (Movement Toward Socialism, or MAS) in Bolivia at the turn of the century and the Partido dos Trabalhadores (Workers' Party, or PT) in Brazil in the late 1970s (Anria 2019). This type of institutionalization, however, is fraught with its own tensions and limitations, and it is far from being an inevitable political extension of constituent power expressed in the form of social movements. As Tarrow (2022, 193–210) reminds us, social movements naturally experience cyclical ebbs and flows – that is, cycles of mobilization and demobilization – as they cannot sustain peak periods of extra-institutional mobilization indefinitely. And there is nothing automatic about their transformation into party-movement blocs that expand political representation and realign partisan competition in formal institutional arenas. The political dynamics whereby parties coopt, divide, and/or demobilize social movements "from above" that Oxhorn (1994) identified during Chile's democratic transition have been replicated in other Latin American countries more recently, such as Argentina's *piqueteros* movement and Ecuador's Indigenous movement at the turn of the century (Wolff 2007; Rossi 2017). The regional political landscape is littered with the residue of other protest movements that temporarily gave voice to societal grievances and rocked their national political establishments without leaving durable institutional traces – even where their grassroots social networks survive on the margins and bide their time, waiting for a favourable political opportunity to wage future battles.

Arguably, the advent of new social media has accentuated the institutional dilemma. Platforms like Facebook, Instagram, Twitter, and WhatsApp have made it easier to resolve the horizontal network communication and social coordination impediments to collective action, thereby lowering the barriers to entry for citizens to engage in episodic – even instantaneous – social protest. Paradoxically, however, this networked collective action can be extensive in scope but extraordinarily hollow in its organizational density, and thus difficult to sustain temporally and scale up vertically in order to occupy larger institutional sites (see Tufekci 2017). Indeed, social media provide forums for individual and small-group political self-expression that, however valuable they might be in their own right, stand at odds with any broader logic of party-mediated interest aggregation and representation.[2] As such, they reinforce more long-term trends toward the development of – or, at least, the quest for – functional alternatives to traditional forms of partisan representation (Schmitter 2001; Tormey 2015).

These varied manifestations of the institutional dilemma are readily apparent in contemporary Chilean politics, dating back to the original cycle of student-led mass social protest in the *Pingüino* rebellion of 2006. Starting with local protests triggered by the collapse of a school roof during a rainstorm in the depressed former coal mining community of Lota, the rebellion quickly swelled and took aim at admissions test fees, bus transportation costs, and the entire structure of the decentralized and heavily privatized education system. High school students met in highly participatory assemblies, went on strike, organized mass rallies and marches – the largest mobilizing nearly a million students and sympathizers – and shut down some four hundred schools across the country (Donoso 2013). The Socialist-led Bachelet administration was able to quiet the rebellion by appointing an expert advisory commission to meet with student and teacher representatives and develop a proposal for educational reforms. The proposal that came out of the dialogue, however, was heavily watered down by conservative opposition in Congress, and the package that was finally approved by Congress in 2009 did little to reform the basic structure of the privatized education system (Pribble 2013, 104–5). The student movement was left feeling bitter and betrayed by this party-brokered technocratic compromise on education reform (Bidegain Ponte 2015, 252–5), which ultimately set the stage for the even larger social uprisings looming on the horizon.

The sequel would not take long to emerge. After four consecutive governments led by the centre-left Concertación alliance, the Chilean right took control of the government by democratic means for the first time in half a century, electing wealthy businessman Sebastián Piñera to the presidency in 2010. A younger brother of one of Pinochet's leading Chicago school technocrats, José Piñera – an architect of Chile's neoliberal reforms in social security, health care, and labour markets – Piñera represented a return to neoliberal orthodoxy following the modest social reforms of his Socialist predecessors Lagos and Bachelet. University students ensured that his honeymoon would be short-lived, as they spearheaded a massive wave of protests in 2011 to 2012 whose central target was the heavily privatized education system. High school students joined college students in protesting against the poor quality of public schools, the debts incurred by students in private universities, and the education system's reliance on for-profit schools. Student protests received support from teachers' unions, university professors, and the national labour confederation, forcing the closure of hundreds of universities and secondary schools. With civil society networks for labour rights, women's rights, Mapuche Indigenous rights, and environmental conservation joining in, the protest cycle peaked in August 2011 with over nine hundred demonstrations across the country on a national day of protest against the neoliberal order and the party system establishment that upheld it (Guzman-Concha 2012, 410; Donoso and von Bülow 2017).

This protest cycle articulated myriad demands for structural reforms – including free universal public education and an end to for-profit schools – well to the left of the positions adopted by Chile's mainstream parties, including the PSCh on the left flank of the Concertación. This outflanking was readily apparent in civil society as well, as leadership of the activist networks spearheading the student and labour movements had moved steadily leftward since the 1990s, beyond the parties of the Concertación. Leadership of the university federations in the powerful Confederación de Estudiantes de Chile (Confederation of Chilean Students, or CONFECH), a central player in the 2011 to 2012 protest cycle, was largely in the hands of Christian Democratic and Socialist student activists in the 1990s, but over time these leaders were displaced by activists belonging to the Communist Party and, eventually, independent left "social collectives" (*colectivos sociales*) as waves of student protest transformed the organizational landscape (Bidegain Ponte 2015, 235). Similarly, in 2012, Socialist leadership of the central labour confederation, the Central Unitaria de Trabajadores de Chile (United Workers Central, or CUT), also passed to a Communist slate headed by a leader of the teachers' union with close ties to the student protest movement. Social activism in civil society, therefore, was channelled outside and against the mainstream party establishment, and it increasingly assumed the characteristics of a generational divide in the Chilean body politic.

Widespread social mobilization was not yet capable of dislodging Chile's party system establishment, but in the aftermath of the 2011 to 2012 protests, it began to crack it open. In contrast to Bolivia at the turn of the century – where the MAS effectively channelled diverse social movements into a party-building project that transformed it from a regional movement of coca growers into a hegemonic national party organization (Anria 2019) – Chile's student movement did not generate a major, unifying party organization. To the extent that the movement gave expression to a generational cleavage in Chilean society – one that divided Chileans who lived through the polarized conflicts and trauma of the Allende and Pinochet eras from those who grew up in an era of democratic convergence around neoliberal technocracy – it was not a cleavage that crystallized in the form of an organized party, as did class cleavages historically (Lipset and Rokkan 1967). Indeed, some of the students' grassroots networks and *colectivos* opposed any effort to found a party organization or engage in institutional political arenas. Nevertheless, several new movement-based parties emerged from the protest cycle, and four student leaders were elected to Congress in 2013. Two of them were leaders of the Communist Youth organization – Camila Vallejo, the former president of the University of Chile's student federation (Federación de Estudiantes de Chile, or FECh) and the spokesperson for CONFECH during the 2011 protests, and Karol Cariola, a former president of the University of Concepción's student federation. A third, Giorgio Jackson, had been president of the Catholic University student federation during the protest cycle and a founder of a new movement party, Democratic Revolution. The fourth, Gabriel Boric, was elected as an independent, having been active in the Autonomous Left *colectivo* and the successor to Vallejo as the president of FECh.

The 2013 elections returned Bachelet to the presidency at the head of a new, broader centre-left coalition known as *Nueva Mayoría* (New Majority). Although the PDC remained in the new coalition, it also incorporated the Communist Party (Partido Comunista de Chile, or PCCh), which had previously been excluded from the Concertación. The inclusion of the PCCh was a clear signal that Bachelet and the Socialists needed a partner with stronger ties to social activist networks, and were committed to a reform agenda that addressed at least some of the demands of the protest movement. The new government thus adopted reforms to provide free university education to students from low-income families, and introduce a proportional representation electoral system to replace the highly skewed binomial system left behind by Pinochet.[3]

Nevertheless, Chile's crisis of representation only deepened in the years that followed (Castiglioni and Kaltwasser 2016; Luna 2016; Piñeiro Rodríguez and Rosenblatt 2020). Mainstream parties from across the ideological spectrum were seriously tainted by a series of corruption scandals that reinforced long-term trends toward declining partisan identification and voter turnout, especially among Chilean youth. Cycles of protest against the privatized pension system, gender inequalities, and sexual violence erupted between 2016 and 2018. Meanwhile, trends toward party system fragmentation were reinforced by the new system of proportional representation in the run-up to national elections in 2017. Although Boric joined with Jackson's Democratic Revolution and several other small leftist parties to found a new political front, the *Frente Amplio* (Broad Front), much of the leadership of Boric's Autonomous Left movement opted out of this party-building venture and rejected its emphasis on seeking public office through institutional channels, including municipal governments (von Baer 2021). The *Frente Amplio* supported an independent journalist, Beatriz Sánchez, for president in 2017; Sánchez finished third in the race with 20.3 per cent of the vote, and narrowly missed making it into the second-round runoff. In steep decline, the centrist PDC broke its three-decade alliance with the PSCh to leave *Nueva Mayoría* and run its own candidate, who finished in fifth place with less than six per cent of the vote, behind the independent far-right candidate, José Antonio Kast. The mainstream conservative party coalition then defeated *Nueva Mayoría* in the runoff, returning Piñera to presidential office for what would prove to be the last stand of Chile's post-1990 party system establishment.

Although the *Frente Amplio* made a respectable showing in the presidential race and elected twenty deputies to Congress (out of 155 seats), it remained a limited institutional expression of Chile's vibrant student and civil society networks. Indeed, the deepening detachment of those networks from *all* political parties, including those with roots in prior protest cycles, was soon made abundantly clear when the *estallido* erupted in October 2019, midway into Piñera's second year in office. This unprecedented manifestation of constituent power would force Chile's party establishment to open the door to a refounding of the constitutional order – but, as explained below, it would ultimately fail to achieve it.

CONSTITUENT POWER, CONSERVATIVE BACKLASH, AND CHILE'S CONSTITUTIONAL STALEMATE

As a former student activist and a prominent leftist member of the Chamber of Deputies, Boric played a major role in brokering the 15 November 2019 multiparty agreement to hold a popular referendum on the drafting of a new constitution. The accord was controversial, however, as neither Boric nor any other parties to the agreement had been delegated to speak on behalf of the movement, or movements, that converged in the *estallido*. Any such delegation would have clashed with the uprising's political logic, as it was remarkably diffuse organizationally – a confluence of myriad activist, grassroots, and social media networks with no apparent organizational core, minimal coalitional structure, an absence of centralized leadership, and certainly no unifying partisan instrument to speak on the movements' behalf. Not surprisingly, then, Boric's role was opposed by much of the leadership of his own political front (von Baer 2021), not to mention many of the protesters – still on the streets – who rejected any party-mediated strategy to tame the uprising, leave Piñera in office, and redirect Chile's constituent moment into formal institutional settings. The protest slogan "*el pueblo unido avanza sin partidos*" (the people united advance without parties) captured the mood of many on the streets. Nevertheless, the institutional wheels continued to turn as the protest cycle retreated in the face of pandemic-induced social distancing. As Chileans prepared to vote in a constitutional referendum that was first delayed and then scheduled for 25 October 2020, civil society networks gradually shifted toward an institutional sphere that offered – so it seemed – an unprecedented opportunity to make a decisive break with the political order bequeathed by Pinochet.

The effort to translate the political crisis into an institutional refounding or "reconstitution" of Chilean democracy got off to an auspicious start. Although right-wing parties protective of Pinochet's legacy campaigned against a new constitution, an overwhelming majority of Chilean voters – 78 per cent – supported the proposal to draft a new constitution in the October referendum. Reflecting widespread anti-party and anti-establishment sentiments, 79 per cent also voted for a directly elected constitutional convention, rejecting any role for sitting members of Congress. Elections were thus held for a 155-member constitutional convention in May 2021 under rules explicitly designed to allow for the expression of constituent power and give voice to traditionally underrepresented sectors of society. The election rules mandated gender parity, allowed independent candidates and non-party lists, and reserved seventeen seats for representatives of Indigenous communities. As stated by Piscopo and Siavelis (2023, 144), "more than 67 per cent of the delegates elected had no party affiliation," while the "vast majority of winning candidates (87 per cent) had never held elected office, and 78 per cent had never stood for office before." A coalition of right-wing parties managed to elect thirty-seven delegates, less than the third they needed to veto constitutional measures, while a centre-left alliance of parties – a successor to the Concertación – elected twenty-five delegates. The *Frente Amplio* formed a list with the Communist Party and other small leftist groups to elect twenty-eight delegates, while an independent list of civil society actors known as *La Lista del Pueblo* (the list of the people) elected twenty-six delegates. Another twenty-two delegates were elected as independents or representatives of other independent lists, along with seventeen Indigenous representatives. The new Convention began its work in July 2021, with a mandate to produce a final draft of a constitution by 21 July 2022.

The eclipse of Chile's traditional parties was subsequently ratified in the November 2021 national elections and the December second-round presidential runoff. In the first-round presidential election, the mainstream right-wing and centre-left coalitions finished in fourth and fifth place, respectively, with only 12.8 and 11.6 per cent of the vote. The two leading candidates from the first round were the far-right candidate Kast of the Republican Party, with 27.9 per cent, and Boric, with 25.8 per cent, at the head of a reconfigured movement-left coalition that included the Communist Party and other small leftist groups. Boric proceeded to win the runoff election, with 55.9 per cent of the vote, assuming presidential office in March of 2022 as the Constitutional Convention was vigorously debating the content of a new charter.

The Convention began its work with a broad base of support and substantial democratic legitimacy. It elected a Mapuche Indigenous rights activist, Elisa Loncón, its first president, and it condemned police brutality during the 2019 uprising. Citizens could gather signatures to make proposals to the Convention, and they could follow the Convention's deliberations as they livestreamed on YouTube. The Convention ultimately wrote a constitutional draft that was widely recognized to be among the most progressive in the world. The proposed constitution would have preserved a market economy in Chile, but supplemented it with a far stronger set of social citizenship rights. It recognized rights to social goods and services – including education, social security, housing, health care, water, and digital connectivity – that were heavily commodified under the neoliberal model and that were focal points of chronic social protest. Declaring Chile to be a plurinationalist sate, the constitution proclaimed new rights for Indigenous peoples and other minority groups, along with women, LGBTQI+ persons, those with disabilities, and the environment (see Green Rioja et al. 2022; Piscopo and Siavelis 2023).

By the time the draft was complete, however, it had already been placed on the political defensive, along with the Convention itself and the newly inaugurated Boric government. Chileans may have voted for a constitutional process dominated by civil society activists rather than party elites and professional politicians, but many were not prepared for the unconventional and performative elements of an assembly comprised of activists. Right-wing and social media opponents of the Convention tried to discredit the entire process, playing up breaches of tradition and professionalism, along with a high-profile scandal of a delegate elected after making fraudulent claims about his personal medical history. Politicizing the constitution's plurinationalist character and social rights, opponents made incendiary and misleading claims about threats the new constitution would pose to national unity, economic stability, and individual rights (Bauer 2022; Piscopo and Siavelis 2023, 148–50). Meanwhile, the incoming Boric administration – the leadership ranks of which included other prominent figures from the 2011 to 2012 student uprising, such as Jackson and Vallejo – was immediately confronted with political conflicts over crime, narcotrafficking, immigration, inflation, and unrest in Mapuche Indigenous communities. These issues – centrepieces of Kast's far-right candidacy for the presidency in 2021 – fanned the flames of conservative opposition, and forced Boric to redirect attention from his social reform agenda to national security concerns as his public support frayed (Winter 2023).

The shift in the political winds was readily apparent when a stunning 62 per cent of Chileans voted against the proposed constitution in the popular referendum on 4 September 2022. Chile's constituent moment had effectively come to an end, well short of its refoundational goals, bottled up and ultimately vetoed as it struggled in vain for institutional expression. Since there was no plan B, the resounding defeat of constituent power left Chilean democracy in a constitutive stalemate that would be addressed in the time-honoured fashion – through negotiations among rival political elites ensconced in formal institutions. Party leaders in Congress passed a law to formalize the process for drafting yet another new constitution – a process with a starkly different political logic than that of the now-defunct Constitutional Convention. The new formula magnified the role of

Congress, parties, and technical expertise, rather than civil society representation. It called for Congress to appoint a Commission of Experts dominated by lawyers to draft a new charter based on constitutional principles established by Congress itself. The draft would then be debated and approved or modified by a Constitutional Council elected from party lists, and the final draft would undergo review by a technical committee of jurists to ensure its conformance with the base principles outlined by Congress. Finally, Chilean citizens would vote to approve or reject the new constitution in yet another popular referendum in December 2023.

The Constitutional Council elected on 7 May 2023 reflected Chile's shifting political winds, along with the displacement of social issues like education, pensions, and health care by those centred on crime and security. The far-right Republican Party of Kast won over a third of the vote and the largest number of seats, twenty-three of the fifty elected seats in the Council – enough to exercise unilateral veto power over constitutional measures. When combined with the eleven seats won by the traditional conservative parties, right-wing forces controlled a majority of the new Council. A left-wing coalition aligning Boric's supporters with the PSCh won 28.6 per cent of the vote and sixteen seats on the Council. In a graphic indication of how thoroughly things had changed, the centrist PDC – the largest party during Chile's 1989 to 1990 democratic transition – failed to elect any members of the Council (Jacob and Erdmannsdörffer 2023). Under mandatory voting rules, which expanded the electorate to include a large number of citizens who had previously abstained, 20 per cent of Chileans voted blank or annulled their ballot. Paradoxically, the lead role in the drafting of Chile's new constitution was assumed by a pro-Pinochet party – that of Kast – which had opposed any effort to draft a new constitution from the very outset of the process. The second, far more conservative constitution, however, met the same fate as the progressive one written by civil society activists; it was decisively rejected by over 55 per cent of voters in the popular referendum of December 2023. Chile, once again, had seemingly gone full circle.

CONCLUSION

In a poignant retrospective on the failures of Chile's Constitutional Convention, feminist leader and convention delegate Alondra Carrillo Vidal stated that "as popular organizations we always imagined a deepening of the revolt's spirit of tearing down the old, and we were not necessarily so clear about the leading role we would have to play in the Convention and its role in building the new" (Green Rioja et al. 2022, 384). Chile's constituent moment did, in fact, tear down much of the old, demonstrating the impermanence of the partisan capture and demobilization of societal actors that Oxhorn (1994) so insightfully analyzed during the country's democratic transition. But as Negri (2009, 1) anticipated, the newfound expression of constituent power proved extraordinarily difficult to constitutionalize. Its mobilizational capacity, so impressive in late 2019, was ultimately shown to be episodic and unsustainable. Part of the social networks that comprised it resisted any transfer from the streets to institutional arenas, and those who embraced this transfer were ultimately unable to break out of Chile's historical leftist "third" to win over centrist voters to a progressive constitutional project, or at least prevent them from aligning en masse with right-wing opponents. Chile's constitutive stalemate rests precisely in the ease of mobilizing "negative" popular majorities in opposition to constituted power, and the difficulty of mobilizing a "positive" democratic majority in support of any alternative within formal representative institutions. Chilean civil society is hardly alone in facing this challenge in Latin America, but its recent history provides a unique vantage point on the potentialities of, and the constraints on, constituent power.

NOTES

1 Even in the exceedingly rare circumstances in which mass social protest results in an insurrectionary removal of governing officials or overthrow of state institutions, the challenge of scaling up invariably arises in the reconstitution of new authority structures.

2 I am indebted to Manuel Antonio Garretón for his insight on this dimension of contemporary representational crises.

3 Under the binomial system, each district elected two representatives to congress, which operated in practice to overrepresent the conservative coalition and exclude leftist parties outside the centre-left Concertación alliance.

REFERENCES

Albertus, Michael, and Victor Menaldo. 2018. *Authoritarianism and the Elite Origins of Democracy*. New York: Cambridge University Press.

Amnesty International. 2020. *Human Rights in the Americas: Review of 2019*. London: Amnesty International.

Anria, Santiago. 2019. *When Movements Become Parties: The Bolivian MAS in Comparative Perspective*. New York: Cambridge University Press.

Bauer, Kelly. 2022. "Untangling Elite Opposition to Indigenous Rights." NACLA *Report on the Americas* 54, no. 4: 430–7.

Bidegain Ponte, Germán. 2015. "Autonomización de los movimientos sociales e intensificación de la protesta: Estudiantes y mapuche en chile (1990–2013)." PhD diss., Pontificia Universidad Católica de Chile.

Castiglioni, Rossana, and Cristóbal Rovira Kaltwasser. 2016. "Challenges to Political Representation in Contemporary Chile." *Journal of Politics in Latin America* 8, no 3: 3–24.

de Leon, Cedric, Manali Desai, and Cihan Tuğal, eds. 2015. *Building Blocs: How Parties Organize Society*. Stanford, CA: Stanford University Press.

Donoso, Sofía. 2013. "Dynamics of Change in Chile: Explaining the Emergence of the 2006 Pingüino Movement." *Journal of Latin American Studies* 45, no. 1: 1–29.

Donoso, Sofía. 2017. "Outsider and Insider Strategies: Chile's Student Movement, 1990–2014." In *Social Movements in Chile: Organization, Trajectories, and Political Consequences*, edited by Sofia Donoso and Marisa von Bülow, 65–97. New York: Palgrave Macmillan.

Donoso, Sofia, and Marisa von Bülow, eds. 2017. *Social Movements in Chile: Organization, Trajectories, and Political Consequences*. New York: Palgrave Macmillan.

Edwards, Sebastian. 1995. *Crisis and Reform in Latin America: From Despair to Hope*. Oxford, UK: Oxford University Press.

Green Rioja, Romina, Elisa Roncón, and Alondra Carillo Vidal. 2022. "Transforming Chile from the Ground Up." NACLA *Report on the Americas* 54, no. 4: 382–8.

Guzman-Concha, Cesar. 2012. "The Students' Rebellion in Chile: Occupy Protest or Classic Social Movement?" *Social Movement Studies* 11, nos. 3–4: 408–15.

Heiss, Claudia. 2021. "Latin America Erupts: Re-Founding Chile." *Journal of Democracy* 32, no. 3: 33–47.

Frank, Jason. 2010. *Constituent Moments: Enacting the People in Postrevolutionary America*. Durham, NC: Duke University Press.

Jacob, Olaf, and Caroline Erdmannsdörffer. 5 May 2023. "La derrota del gobierno de Gabriel Boric." *Diálogo Político*.

Lipset, Seymour Martin, and Stein Rokkan, eds. 1967. *Party Systems and Voter Alignments: Cross-National Perspectives*. New York: Free Press.
Luna, Juan Pablo. 2016. "Delegative Democracy Revisited: Chile's Crisis of Representation." *Journal of Democracy* 27, no. 3: 129–38.
Luna, Juan Pablo. 26 October 2020. "El problema de las tres comunas: Cómo evitar que las elites dominen la constituyente." CIPER.
Luna, Juan Pablo, and David Altman. 2011. "Uprooted but Stable: Chilean Parties and the Concept of Party System Institutionalization." *Latin American Politics and Society* 53, no. 2: 1–27.
Luna, Juan Pablo, Elizabeth J. Zechmeister, and Mitchell A. Seligson. 2010. *Cultura política de la democracia en Chile, 2010: Consolidación democrática en las Americas en tiempos difíciles*. Nashville, TN: Latin American Public Opinion Project, Vanderbilt University.
Meléndez, Carlos. 2022. *The Post-Partisans: Anti-Partisans, Anti-Establishment Identifiers, and Apartisans in Latin America*. New York: Cambridge University Press.
Michels, Robert. 2015. *Political Parties: A Sociological Study of the Oligarchical Tendencies of Modern Democracy*. New York: Hearst's International Library.
Negri, Antonio. 2009. *Insurgencies: Constituent Power and the Modern State*. Minneapolis, MN: University of Minnesota Press.
O'Donnell, Guillermo, and Philippe C. Schmitter. 1986. *Transitions from Authoritarian Rule: Tentative Conclusions about Uncertain Democracies*. Baltimore, MD: Johns Hopkins University Press.
Oxhorn, Philip. 1994. "Where Did All the Protesters Go? Popular Mobilization and the Transition to Democracy in Chile." *Latin American Perspectives* 21, no. 3: 49–68.
Oxhorn, Philip. 1995. *Organizing Civil Society: The Popular Sectors and the Struggle for Democracy in Chile*. University Park, PA: Pennsylvania State University Press.
Oxhorn, Philip. 1998. "The Social Foundations of Latin America's Recurrent Populism: Problems of Popular Sector Class Formation and Collective Action." *Journal of Historical Sociology* 11, no. 2: 212–46.
Oxhorn, Philip. 2011. *Sustaining Civil Society: Economic Change, Democracy, and the Social Construction of Citizenship in Latin America*. University Park, PA: Pennsylvania State University Press.
Perry, Lauren. 2023. *Who Perceives Well-Protected Basic Rights in the Americas?* Insights Series #159. Nashville, TN: LAPOP/Americas Barometer.

Piñeiro Rodríguez, Rafael, and Fernando Rosenblatt. 2020. "Stability and Incorporation: Toward a New Concept of Party System Institutionalization." *Party Politics* 26, no. 2: 249–60.

Piscopo, Jennifer M., and Peter Siavelis. 2023. "Chile's Constitutional Chaos." *Journal of Democracy* 34, no. 1: 141–55.

Polanyi, Karl. 1944. *The Great Transformation*. New York: Farrar and Rinehart.

Pribble, Jennifer. 2013. *Welfare and Party Politics in Latin America*. New York: Cambridge University Press.

Renaud, Terrence. 2021. *New Lefts: The Making of a Radical Tradition*. Princeton, NJ: Princeton University Press.

Rhodes-Purdy, Matthew. 2017. *Regime Support Beyond the Balance Sheet: Participation and Policy Performance in Latin America*. New York: Cambridge University Press.

Roberts, Kenneth M. 1998. *Deepening Democracy? The Modern Left and Social Movements in Chile and Peru*. Stanford, CA: Stanford University Press.

Roberts, Kenneth M. 2016. "(Re)Politicizing Inequalities: Movements, Parties, and Social Citizenship in Chile." *Journal of Politics in Latin America* 8, no. 3: 125–54.

Rosenblatt, Fernando. 2021. *Party Vibrancy and Democracy in Latin America*. Oxford, UK: Oxford University Press.

Rossi, Federico M. 2017. *The Poor's Struggle for Political Incorporation: The Piquetero Movement in Argentina*. New York: Cambridge University Press.

Schmitter, Philippe C. 2001. "Parties Are Not What They Once Were." In *Political Parties and Democracy*, edited by Larry Diamond and Richard Gunther. Baltimore, MD: Johns Hopkins University Press.

Shaffer, Kirwin. 2023. "Anarchists vs. the State." NACLA *Report on the Americas* 55, no. 1: 74–81.

Silva, Eduardo. 1996. *The State and Capital in Chile: Business Elites, Technocrats, and Market Economics*. Boulder, CO: Westview Press.

Silva, Eduardo, ed. 2009. *Challenging Neoliberalism in Latin America*. New York: Cambridge University Press.

Silva, Eduardo, and Federico M. Rossi, eds. 2018. *Reshaping the Political Arena in Latin America: From Resisting Neoliberalism to the Second Incorporation*. Pittsburgh, PA: University of Pittsburgh Press.

Simmons, Erica S. 2016. *Meaningful Resistance: Market Reforms and the Roots of Social Protest in Latin America*. New York: Cambridge University Press.

Tarrow, Sidney. 2022. *Power in Movement: Social Movements and Contentious Politics*, 4th ed. New York: Cambridge University Press.

Tormey, Simon. 2015. *The End of Representative Politics*. Cambridge, UK: Polity Press.

Tufekci, Zeynep. 2017. *Twitter and Tear Gas: The Power and Fragility of Networked Social Protest*. New Haven, CT: Yale University Press.

UNDP (United Nations Development Programme). 2015. *Auditoría a la democracia: Más y mejor democracia para un Chile inclusivo*. Santiago: UNDP.

Valenzuela, J. Samuel, Nicolás Somma, and Timothy R. Scully. 2018. "Resilience and Change: The Party System in Redemocratized Chile." In *Party Systems in Latin America: Institutionalization, Decay, and Collapse*, edited by Scott Mainwaring, 135–63. New York: Cambridge University Press.

von Baer, Alex. 20 July 2021. "Jorge Sharp: La historia de cómo pasó de estrecho aliado a detractor de Boric." *Ex-Ante*.

Winter, Brian. 5 May 2023. "In Chile and Elsewhere, Crime Is the New Corruption." *Americas Quarterly*.

Wolff, Jonas. 2007. "(De-)Mobilising the Marginalised: A Comparison of the Argentine Piqueteros and Ecuador's Indigenous Movement." *Journal of Latin American Studies* 39, no. 1: 1–29.

3

Neopluralist Maternalism and Women's Citizenship in Peru

Stéphanie Rousseau

Among the many contributions that Philip Oxhorn made to the study of Latin American politics, his views on the neopluralist features of contemporary democracies promoted critical perspectives on citizenship studies. Through this lens, the predominant form of political incorporation in post-1980s Latin America is market based, generating what Oxhorn (2006) called "citizenship as consumption." Political power is concentrated rather than distributed, and at the same time the state has few incentives to adopt redistributive schemes. Social inequality, economic exclusion, and fragmented civil societies lead the agency component of citizenship to be seriously truncated for the majority of the population. Weak party systems add to the obstacles that most of the population face to organize collective interest representation and influence policymaking.

In what follows, I want to address what can be considered one of the most understudied aspects of neopluralist democracy: in many Latin American countries, state–society relations have defined the parameters of women's citizenship in the last decades largely without considering the structural causes and effects of the unequal – and gendered – division of care work. And yet women's movements have been key actors in Latin American politics since the 1970s or 1980s, leading to important gains in women's access to political representation. While recognizing that Latin America is a huge region with great diversity, I present some insights into this paradox based on my research on the case of Peru. I argue that even though Peru has benefited from roughly two decades of stable democracy and constant economic growth from the early 2000s until the COVID-19 pandemic, neither the market, the state, nor even the community offer solutions to women's need to reconcile caring and income-generation activities. The social costs of care continue to be born by women through their personal time and resources, which overshadows their economic opportunities. The explanation I put forward relies on the analysis of two different but interrelated dynamics: on one hand, the agendas of social actors who sought to represent women's interests during these years have contributed – even if unwillingly – to maintaining the exclusion of most women from citizenship – both as consumers and as agents. On the other hand, social policy paradigms and the characteristics of social programs put forward by the Peruvian state as a response to persistent poverty were based on social assistance rather than citizenship rights and left traditional gender roles intact.

Thus, this chapter builds on two central concepts of Oxhorn's work that I have incorporated into my own since the time I was a graduate student working under his supervision. First, citizenship is socially constructed through the interactions between organized civil society and the state. To study the construction of women's citizenship means paying attention to the shape, agendas, and opportunities of women's organizations and how they build claims on the state. Second, the broad political context within which I analyze women's citizenship construction in Latin America is neopluralism. I propose here the expression "neopluralist maternalism," for a double purpose: first, to describe the weakness of the public sphere when it comes to the articulation of collective interests – in this case those of women and more particularly those of the poorest sectors; and second, to characterize the dominant discourse through which the state addresses women's interests, as well as that through which women's mobilization frequently legitimizes its claims. Maternalism is a concept that was developed in the social sciences to reflect the paradox of women's emergence as social and political actors claiming recognition as citizens, but on the basis of their traditional gender roles. As such, maternalistic ideologies vindicate women's contribution to society as mothers and, by extension, as caretakers. They have notably been behind the development of new social protection schemes in the early twentieth century (Koven and Michel 1993). Franceschet, Piscopo, and Thomas define maternalism as "cultural ideologies that ascribe to women the morally superior qualities of selflessness, nurturing, and caring, which govern how they rear their own children as well as how they serve communities and nations" (2017, 65).

Various authors have used the concept of maternalism to analyze different aspects of women's movements and state policy in Latin America in the past and currently (see, among others, Dore and Molyneux 2000; Ramm and Gideon 2020). In an interesting discussion of the literature on maternalism in Latin American politics, Franceschet, Piscopo, and Thomas (2017) argue that, even though some recent reforms are oriented towards greater gender equality, maternalistic ideas continue to shape debates on maternity leave, reproductive rights, and childcare, which are fundamental policy issues for women's autonomy. Applying the lens of neopluralism to maternalist politics allows us to analyze the way market-based "inclusion" and liberal rights, combined with conventional gender roles reinforced by state policy, leave the question of social care invisible and unresolved. Neopluralist maternalism reflects what Nancy Fraser (2013) and other authors have discussed when pointing to the limits of feminist-inspired reforms as they were designed and implemented jointly with the turn to neoliberalism in the 1980s and 1990s. A selective integration of gender-equality reforms allowed for a massive entry of women in the labour market and in the state, without ensuring that carework would be adequately redistributed between women and men, and among families, the market, and the state.

I begin this chapter by exploring several socioeconomic indicators to show the enduring gender gaps after two decades of sustained growth in Peru up until the COVID-19 pandemic. Then, I analyze the two key factors of my argument: a) the divorce between the agendas of feminist and grassroots women's organizations, associated with the absence of social mobilization around social and economic rights from a gendered perspective; and b) social policy based on technocratic criteria and techniques of the "social investment state" (Jenson 2020), devoid of gender analysis.

SUSTAINED GROWTH, GENDER GAPS, AND ECONOMIC INEQUALITY

Peru has had a relatively high level of political and economic stability from 2001 until at least 2016, when its political regime started to experiment with institutional fragility (Dargent and Rousseau

2021, 2022). Economic stability remained high up until the COVID-19 pandemic, and after this tremendous shock for the whole region, Peru has managed to recuperate basic macroeconomic health, but in the context of a severe increase in poverty levels.

The 1990s in Peru were marked by the adoption of neoliberal reforms that installed a set of new rules dismantling prior channels of state–society relations such as unions (Carrión 2006; Rousseau 2009). Moreover, Alberto Fujimori's self-coup in 1992 facilitated the authoritarian adoption and implementation of these reforms. After two decades of turmoil due to internal conflict between terrorist organizations and security forces, the end of Fujimori's government in 2000 allowed for the re-establishment of democracy and the adoption of some important political reforms such as decentralization. Peru is also one of the Latin American countries that, in macroeconomic terms, has been a "good student" of fiscal prudence and economic stability recipes since the widespread adoption of neoliberal policies. Annual growth rates from 2002 to 2008 fluctuated between 4 per cent and 9 per cent. They remained between 2 per cent and 9 per cent from 2010 to 2019. Its worst year prior to the pandemic was 2009, with 1.1 per cent.[1] At the same time, Peru managed to reduce poverty consistently from 2005 (with 61.5 per cent of the population living on less than $6.85 a day, in 2017 purchasing parity dollars) to 2019 (28.9 per cent). However, the proportion of the population that was vulnerable to falling below the poverty line increased from 25 per cent in 2005 to 35 per cent in 2011. It remained at around 35 per cent to 37 per cent between 2011 and 2019 (World Bank 2023, 29).

Since the 1990s, the predominant form of inclusion has therefore been through market-based processes, with the erosion and fragmentation of civil society, and most of the economically active population depending on the informal sector (Arroyo 2020; Ilizarbe 2022). In this context, economic growth and poverty reduction have not benefited women and men equally. In fact, most socioeconomic gender gaps have only moderately or barely diminished. Among the key indicators supporting this claim is the percentage of the population without an income of their own, which is key in accounting for women's economic dependency. In 2007, 34.4 per cent of Peruvian women were without an income of their own, while 12.2 per cent of Peruvian men were in the same situation – a gender gap of 22.2 per cent. In 2013, 32.2 per cent of women and 12.2 per cent of men were without an income of their own, while in 2019, it was 29.4 per cent and 11.9 per cent, respectively (a gender gap of 17.5 per cent). Most of the gender gap reduction is attributable to improvements for women in the older age groups (fifty years and above). For younger age groups, in which care responsibilities for children and older parents are more demanding, there has been very little change in the last twenty years: around 30 per cent of women lack an income of their own.[2]

Another way to appreciate the enduring gender gaps is by looking at social protection. Within the economically active population, 18.6 per cent of women and 32.3 per cent of men had access to a pension system in 2008. Ten years later, in 2018, 28.3 per cent of women and 41.2 per cent of men had access to such a system, showing an important improvement overall, but with the same gender gap.[3] In addition, the absolute number and the proportion of single-parent households have increased significantly in the last decades, with women forming the vast majority of heads of households in this category. In 2007, single-parent households represented 6.8 per cent of total households, while in 2017 they represented 9.3 per cent. Women-headed single-parent households formed 82.4 per cent of total single-parent households in 2007 (375,240 households), while in 2017 they increased to 84.3 per cent (645,032 households).[4]

Finally, women work in the informal sector more than men. In 2008, the gender gap in informal work amounted to 7.3 per cent, with 83.6 per cent of women and 75.7 per cent of men having an informal occupation. In 2019 it had reduced to 5.5 per cent, with 75.8 per cent and 70.3 per cent, respectively. But in 2022, the gender gap increased again to 6.3 per cent, with 74 per cent of women and 67.7 per cent of men working in the informal sector.[5] Needless to say, this amounts to three-quarters of economically active women who are completely excluded from social security and formal labour market benefits such as maternity leave, unemployment insurance, or sick leave. Also, the income of economically active women is on average much lower than that of men. In 2009, the gender gap was 34.8 per cent, while ten years later, in 2019, it was 26.9 per cent. Although the gap diminished, women still earned over a quarter less than men, mostly because they often work without wages in family businesses, or because they dedicate fewer hours than men to income-generating activities.[6]

It is important to mention that the fertility rate dropped from 2.8 in 2000 to 2.2 in 2019. This is due in part to a sustained effort at reducing the educational attainment gap between men and women, as well as providing access to family planning, both of which have been key public policy priorities since the 1990s. Nevertheless, these gains were not sufficient to significantly undermine the structural obstacles to gender equality.

A GENDERED DEMOCRACY? FEMINIST AGENDAS AND THE CONTINUING EXCLUSION OF POOR WOMEN'S AGENCY

The gender gaps presented above show that women have faced a systemic persistence of structural inequalities during Peru's economic bonanza in the first two decades of this century. In this section, I look at some key elements of neopluralist maternalism as manifested through the politics of gender interest representation in the last decades. I will go over some of what state policy has focused on directly to address some of the structural bases of gender inequality. These advances were made in response to regional trends in policymaking that were linked with sustained demands and pressure from civil society – mostly feminist – organizations. In line with the broadening of participation by a variety of sectors, as described by Rich et al. (2019) when analyzing the last two decades in Latin America, these policy reforms represent significant gains in broadening the range of issues to which the state pays attention, even if most of the time it is only done formally.

In Peru, it has been difficult for these demands to enter into the agenda of any particular political party, due to the weakness of the party system and the absence of a consolidated centre-left party. Moreover, by the early 1990s onwards, the most important Peruvian feminist organizations had largely lost touch with grassroots popular sector movements (Rousseau 2009). These movements have been extremely fragmented and demobilized throughout most of the 1990s and up until today. As a result, the reforms that were adopted by the Peruvian political system to empower women in the last decades were the product of combined efforts by bureaucratic entrepreneurs and/or nongovernmental organization (NGO) campaigns, in a context marked by a relatively high consensus about the legitimacy of the neoliberal model. The reforms mostly focused on dimensions of women's citizenship that did not have a direct bearing on their social or economic rights. Both state and civil society strategies combined to leave the question of social care largely outside of public debates.

Feminist agendas since the 1990s have revolved mostly around women's civil and political rights as core components of citizenship (Rousseau 2009). Important gains were made on the latter with the adoption as of 1997 of a series of reforms allowing for electoral gender quotas for subnational and national electoral lists. These measures led to some improvements in women's access to party lists and in the proportion of women elected, yet as of 2020, female representatives accounted for only 25.4 per cent of Congress (Melgar et al. 2021, 13). Very recently, in line with a similar pattern in different countries of the region, the Peruvian government adopted Law 31030 to enforce gender parity in national and subnational electoral lists, leading to a record of 38 per cent of seats won by women in 2021 congressional elections (Llanos and Nina Tapia 2021). However, this law lasted only a few years, and in 2024, a Congress dominated by cross-party conservative representatives eliminated gender parity in local, regional, and national elections.

In relation to civil rights, legal reforms were made in the 1980s and 1990s to eliminate explicit discrimination against women; as of the 2000s, discrimination against LGBTQI+ minorities started to be politicized more forcefully by social movements, with bills on civil union and same-sex marriage being debated in Congress, for example. Yet these demands were generally not successful, and Peru became one of the laggards of Latin America on the recognition of sexual minority rights (Corrales 2022).

Women's civil rights are also critically related to two major dimensions: reproductive rights and gender-based violence. Feminist organizations in Peru have always given priority to these issues, at least since the 1980s. Several gains can be noted, although many problems remain crucially unaddressed. To start with the more highly resisted issue, abortion, feminist efforts have led to the adoption of a long-overdue protocol for the implementation of therapeutic abortion. Medically necessary abortion has been legal in the country since early in the twentieth century, and article 119 of the Penal Code protects this right, but only as of June 2014 was the protocol adopted through a resolution by the Ministry of Health, which was necessary for medical health providers to implement it. The resolution was challenged in the courts by conservative groups, and in March 2023, the Supreme Court declared the resolution constitutional, providing more solid grounds for the implementation of therapeutic abortion. Yet numerous obstacles remain for effective access, such as the oppposition of some doctors, bureaucratic delays, and geographical distance from hospitals or clinics that can practice abortions, all of these being much more pronounced for adolescents and women in the poorest sectors of society, which are marked by ethnic and racial disparities.

Efforts at broadening the range of non-punishable abortion to cases of pregnancies resulting from rape remain unsuccessful until today, due to the capacity of conservative sectors to oppose the different bills that have been presented in Congress. The continuing prohibition of abortion amounts to a severe violation of women's right to life and right to health. Unsafe abortions are one of the major causes of the 262,028 cases of women who were treated in public hospitals or health centres for abortion-related complications between 2016 and 2021 (Cuba et al. 2022, 30). It is also one of the three main causes of maternal mortality in Peru (Gianella et al. 2021).

Reproductive rights also include the right to choose a contraceptive method according to one's preferences, which requires having access to a diversity of methods as well as information about the pros and cons of each. Women-focused NGOs have worked for decades to broaden the range of methods included in public health family planning services, while at the same time defending women's reproductive autonomy. In this domain, just like for abortion, social and economic inequalities have a direct impact on access. In many regions of the country, especially in rural areas, only some contraceptive methods are available with some degree of reliability.

Moreover, one of the most controversial reproductive rights issues since the early 2000s has been the inclusion of the "morning-after pill" in public health services. In 2009, Peru's Constitutional Tribunal prohibited the distribution of this pill by public health care providers, which left buying it in a private pharmacy as the only option available. This situation lasted until 2016, when a precautionary measure was dictated by Lima's first Constitutional Court to allow for public distribution under some circumstances. Finally, in April 2023, Peru's Constitutional Tribunal ordered the state to guarantee public distribution of the morning-after pill in all national territory.[7]

Gender-based violence is another key area around which feminist organizations have mobilized in the last decades. Legal advances and the construction of specialized state institutions to address this severe problem have been very slow. In the early 1990s, the first law on family violence was adopted, yet it included no gender perspective. The early 2000s saw some developments with the creation of a national program on violence against women, housed within the Ministry of Women and Social Development. This allowed for more resources to be invested in the creation of first-response centres for victims of violence (Rousseau et al. 2019). Yet the pace of legal and institutional improvements accelerated only after mass mobilizations were organized under the Ni Una Menos (not one more) campaign in 2016. In this effort, leadership did not come from feminist NGOs, but rather from a group of young activists who were inspired by a similar campaign first held in Argentina (Rousseau et al. 2025).

After 2016, the Peruvian state invested many more resources in creating first-response centres and specialized justice institutions in charge of investigating and sanctioning cases of violence against women and family members, as well as to protect victims. Mass mobilization and several high-profile cases of feminicides were the main motivators for state action. Yet on this issue, what is still lacking is state efforts at preventing gender-based violence, notably through education. Such efforts are difficult to enact in light of a new wave of conservative activism in recent years targeting the Ministry of Education, in an attempt to veto some components of the school curriculum dealing with gender equality and sex education (Rousseau 2020).

While political and civil rights, with reproductive rights and gender-based violence in particular, have been the core issues politicized by feminist movements in Peru since the 1990s and even earlier, other dimensions of women's citizenship have remained marginalized within these movements. Issues pertaining to care work, for example, have not become a priority over the years. As well, domestic workers' rights, or daycare services, both of which have clear bearings on gender relations, have not generally been politicized by women's movements.

As a result, for the Peruvian state, care work is almost non-existant on the public policy agenda. While there have been some legal improvements in terms of regulating the labour standards of domestic workers, with a new law adopted in 2020, there is no encompassing discussion about childcare, elderly care, and other dimensions of the social care agenda (Pérez and Gandolfi 2024). A bill to create a national care system was proposed by the Ministry of Women and Vulnerable Populations in 2021, but so far it remains stalled in Congress. Moreover, it is highly declaratory in its content, which threatens its progress in terms of concrete policymaking and service provision.

This relative absence of debate on care work and on women's social and economic rights in general is due to several factors. First, as mentioned above, the agendas of feminist NGOs have been focused on other dimensions of women's citizenship. In addition, grassroots women's organizations lost the political protagonism that they had briefly acquired in the 1980s and early 1990s (Rousseau 2009). This disintegration was part of the general process of the neopluralist weakening of civil society that has affected Peru since that period, leading to sectoral and regional fragmentation, as well as an extremely low level of union affiliation (Manky 2021). When combined with the ultra-volatile political party system, this has left the majority of Peruvian women with very few channels by which to develop and represent their interests as women, mothers, or workers, or other relevant social identities.

SOCIAL POLICY AND TECHNOCRATIC MANAGEMENT OF POVERTY

The second dynamic constitutive of the phenomenon of neopluralist maternalism is connected to the design of the social policy implemented by the Peruvian state in the last decades. Social policy has been elaborated without the consideration of a gender perspective. Needless to say, a gender perspective has also been also completely foreign to the issues that have constituted the country's social care policy agenda. Peru's poverty reduction strategy has been heavily influenced by the social investment perspective, with the majority of social programs targeting children living in poverty (Jenson 2020). The assumption guiding this paradigm is that state intervention to eradicate poverty can be most cost-effective when the playing field is levelled at the beginning of life, during early childhood, and throughout childhood. Results-based social programs targeting children from the poorest families and designed to diminish maternal mortality, infant mortality, child malnutrition, and school dropout rates have been seen as the core social tasks of the state, in Latin America and beyond, as of the early 2000s. While the importance of these tasks is indisputable, there are a number of consequences arising from an overwhelming concentration of social programs in these areas, especially when considering other unattended needs, as well as the missed opportunities to pursue similar goals but through different schemes. Here I will focus on these consequences from the point of view of women in particular.

Peru's social programs targeting poor children carry strong maternalist premises (Nagels 2016). The architecture of many social programs relies on the volunteer work of poor women, mostly to ensure that policy objectives in relation to child welfare be fulfilled while minimizing public spending. In this way, the state contributes directly – although probably inadvertently – to the reproduction of gender inequality. Mothers are involved in the implementation of program objectives, without these programs taking into account the fact that care responsibilities are not remunerated or are very poorly remunerated, and without them promoting changes in the distribution of such responsibilities between women and men, and/or between the state and families (Blofield and Martínez 2014).

The main social programs that were developed in Peru over the last decades and through which poor mothers are indirect beneficiaries are the Programa de Apoyo Directo a los Más Pobres-Juntos, a conditional cash transfer program seeking to improve maternal and infant health, as well as educational attainment; the Programa Nacional de Alimentación Escolar-Qali Warma, a national food program implemented in public schools for children and adolescents; and Cuna Más, a program to improve early childhood development in poor rural and urban districts. Other major social programs that do not rely on the active collaboration of poor mothers are Pensión 65, a cash transfer program for seniors living in poverty, and Fondo de Cooperación para el Desarrollo Social (FONCODES), which promotes economic inclusion and rural development. Neither of these programs integrate a gender perspective into their design and goals, nor has this been considered.

The maternalist social programs share a number of objectives. Relevant to this chapter is that all three of them rely on the principles of new public management as it applies to the governance models of social policy delivery. As several authors have shown, since the 1990s, social programs have often relied on the participation of individuals and/or communities for their delivery, under the close scrutiny of the state (Molyneux 2006; Staab 2012). What is defined as a model of state–community co-management emulates the public–private partnerships of new public management doctrine, whereby the community is in charge of service delivery. The rationale behind this model is that it should allow for greater transparency, as well as community and individual ownership of the responsibility for the use of state resources for the pursuit of program goals. While theoretically this sounds very good, in practice it amounts to the state relying on the volunteer work of women – mostly mothers – to carry out a great proportion of the activities necessary for the functioning of the programs (Cookson 2018). Women's volunteer work is sometimes but not always compensated with monetary incentives. Yet these incentives are not commensurate with the market value of time and energy invested by women in these programs.

With Qali Warma, volunteers are involved in the program in two of the three central processes: in the selection of food providers, and in the reception, preparation, and distribution of food rations for children. Volunteers can be men or women, but they are mostly women. With Juntos, the mothers who enroll as beneficiaries receive a monetary transfer of 200 soles (approximately US$55) every two months. In exchange, they need to comply with regular medical checkups during their pregnancy and for their children, as well as ensure that their children go to school without interruptions. They also need to attend training sessions when called for by the program. With Cuna Más, there are several volunteer roles: community-management committee member, caregiver, and cook. Caregivers and cooks receive a monetary incentive that is less than two-thirds of the value of the minimum wage. Considering that they work from 8 a.m. to 4 p.m., five days a week, one could expect the state to provide monetary incentives that are at least equal to the minimum wage. The majority of volunteers are women, and many are mothers of the children who benefit from the program. To become a volunteer, women are recruited locally by the community-management committee and trained regularly by Cuna Más staff. They do not require any previous experience or post-secondary education.

There are several explanations for why many women agree to participate in these programs and/or enroll their children as beneficiaries. First, some women may need the monetary stipend. Even if they are minimal, they represent a relatively reliable source of monthly income in an environment of scarce economic opportunities. This is especially true if they are mothers of preschool children, because they do not usually have access to affordable childcare and therefore are hard-pressed to find income-generating activities. For this reason, Cuna Más volunteers, for example, are often mothers of children who are themselves beneficiaries of the daycare services that the program offers in urban areas. This allows them to earn some money while remaining close to their child.

Second, Peru has a long history of poor women volunteering to organize and run survival-based initiatives, mostly around food provision. From collective kitchens to breakfasts for school children, these initiatives often have started as "spontaneous" actions coming from civil society organizations, and many have been co-opted or sponsored by churches or the state, or through international cooperation (Blondet and Montero 1995; Rousseau 2009). In the last decades, the Peruvian state has taken over and "technocratized" most of these initiatives, introducing results-based financing and state–community co-management, as the main mechanisms to ensure more efficient processes. In order to justify more public investment in social programs, the government of Ollanta Humala developed tools to establish poverty-reduction targeting criteria, measurable indicators of program goals, and monitoring processes linked to public accountability (Trivelli and Vargas 2014). In this transformation, women's volunteer work in different programs was brought under greater public scrutiny and control by the state. This left very little space for local autonomy amid the number of detailed norms and regulations, leading to the bureaucratization of women's traditional caring roles. In fact, many grassroots women's organizations that had been key actors in the poorest sectors in the 1980s and 1990s simply disappeared or were displaced by new state-created participatory mechanisms. Through the attempt to reduce the scope of political clientelism, corruption, and inefficiency that had historically marked the relation between social assistance, the state, and organized women, this transformation led to a demobilization of women and a new technocratic control over their volunteer work.

In particular, the creation of the Ministry for Development and Social Inclusion (MIDIS) in 2011 at the start of President Humala's government marked the alignment of all social programs in this logic of a targeted, results-based, and state–community co-management model. In an interview, former MIDIS Minister Carolina Trivelli, who was the first head of the ministry and therefore central in its engineering, admitted that the care perspective, associated with recognizing, valuing, and transforming women's roles in social care, was absent from the discussions or policy models that were considered at that time (Trivelli, personal interview, July 2023). The goals were instead to achieve measurable results on the basis of a set of policy instruments that international organizations were promoting as best practice, already in place in countries such as Brazil or Mexico, and which had already produced widely discussed evidence of their capacity to improve key human development indicators.

This agenda had the merit of raising the efficiency and, often, the quality of social programs. Nevertheless, through this process, important dimensions of state intervention were forgotten. One clear example is the Wawa Wasi program, which consisted of daycare services offered by women in their homes, or in daycare centres. One of the main goals of the program was to provide an alternative form of daycare for working mothers of babies and toddlers. Among the criteria used to measure the effectiveness of the program was whether it increased the likelihood of parents – mostly mothers – finding employment, or allowed them to dedicate time to income-generating activities or study ("2003 Evaluation Report on the National Wawa Wasi Program," cited in MIMDES 2011, 13). In the early 2000s, program officials were considering rural demands for such daycare services. While a similar rural program never materialized, it is striking that when Wawa Wasi was transformed into Cuna Más in 2012, the only goals pursued through the new program involved promoting early childhood development. The existing daycare services in urban areas – which were very few and insufficient – were maintained, but in rural areas the daycare option was not adopted. Another strategy – a family-visitation program – was reinforced for the families of rural children.

CONCLUSION

In this piece, I have argued that for the majority of women in Peru, many of whom are poor and vulnerable, traditional care responsibilities act as a fundamental barrier to their ability to access the labour market. Most women are economically active, but their income-generating activities are constrained by the necessity of responding to the direct needs of their children and other household members. The two decades of democratic stability and growth that was initiated in the early 2000s have not led to significant changes in this respect. Up until the COVID-19 pandemic, neither the state nor civil society organizations positioned care work as a public policy issue that was central to addressing gender inequality. Since then, the issue has emerged, but only as a marginal, expert-based debate. The political and economic crisis that followed the pandemic has complicated even further the possibility for significant policy proposals that could transform inequalities that are based on care responsibilities.

While there have been important policy advances on key issues such as gender-based violence and women's political participation, the social and economic dimensions of citizenship remain tilted against women's inclusion in the political realm. Neither democracy nor economic growth has been used to shift the terms of women's inclusion. I have argued that this situation can be described as a form of neopluralist maternalism. Women remain defined by parties and technocrats, and in the media as vehicles acting for the well-being of their families. Maternalist assumptions guide the design of the country's main social programs, through women's volunteer work in preparing food rations, ensuring that their children go to school and get medical checkups, and providing daycare, among other social reproductive tasks required by the state. Social policy designed to reduce poverty is divorced from gender equality goals, and the role assigned to women in social programs is in line with their traditional role as caretakers. Gender equality as pursued by feminist organizations and state institutions focus on the very important dimensions of reproductive autonomy, political participation, and protection from violence. Yet this focus falls short of connecting these issues to social care and its concomittant gender and class inequalities.

What are the prospects of democracy in this context? As Oxhorn wrote in the early 2000s, "It is this contradiction – the apparent inability of citizens to use their political right to vote to find democratic solutions for their most pressing needs – that is perhaps the greatest threat to democracy in the region" (Oxhorn 2006, 121). Twenty years later, this contradiction remains. Even in countries such as Bolivia or Brazil that have mostly been ruled by left-wing governments in the last decades, the legacy of reform is very similar to that in Peru in that it has left social care work on the margins of politics. And the contradiction has acquired even greater saliency in the wake of the COVID-19 pandemic and other recent global turbulences, with rising poverty, inflation, and food insecurity, and the ever more entrenched consequences of regional illegal economies.

Currently, what we see (re)surfacing in Peru and elsewhere in the region are authoritarian and intolerant political discourses. Be it under the guise of religious fundamentalism, or a "quick fix" response to rising crime and drug trafficking, these projects do not augur well for the capacity of poor women to find solutions to the care work conundrum. The absence of public services that would alleviate the burden on women in this regard goes hand-in-hand with widespread distrust and rampant corruption. In this context, the *ollas comúnes*, or collective kitchens – grassroots women's organizations – are undergoing some revival in Lima and other cities of the country, due to the post-pandemic crisis. Can they aspire to become more than a survival strategy? Can they resist the authoritarian appeals?

NOTES

1 "Peru GDP Annual Growth Rate: 3.0%." 2024. London: World Economics. https://www.worldeconomics.com/GrossDomesticProduct/GDP-Annual-Growth-Rate/Peru.aspx.

2 "Perú: Encuesta Demográfica y de Salud Familia." Lima: INEI (Peru's official statistics agency).

3 Encuesta Nacional de Hogares. 2025. Lima: Instituto Nacional de Estadística e Informática (INEI).

4 National Census. 2007, 2017. Lima: Instituto Nacional de Estadística e Informática (INEI). https://www.gob.pe/en/36495-check-information-on-the-censuses-conducted-by-the-inei-national-censuses-of-population-and-housing.

5 Encuesta Nacional de Hogares. 2025. Lima: Instituto Nacional de Estadística e Informática (INEI).

6 Encuesta Nacional de Hogares. 2025. Lima: Instituto Nacional de Estadística e Informática (INEI).

7 "Perú garantiza acceso gratuito a la Anticoncepción Oral de Emergencia." 25 April 2023. Lima: Center for Reproductive Rights. https://reproductiverights.org/peru-garantiza-acceso-gratuito-a-la-anticoncepcion (accessed 2 October 2023).

REFERENCES

Arroyo, Juan. 2020. "Débil competitividad e institucionalidad: El crecimiento no sostenible del modelo informal." *Latin American Research Review* 55, no. 2: 266–77. https://doi.org/10.25222/larr.376.

Blofield, Merike, and Juliana F. Martínez. 2014. "Work, Family and Public Policy Changes in Latin America: Equity, Maternalism and Co-responsibility." *CEPALReview* 114 (December): 101–17.

Blondet, Cecilia, and Carmen Montero. 1995. *Hoy: Menú popular – Los comedores en Lima.* Lima: Instituto de Estudios Peruanos.

Carrión, Julio F., ed. 2006. *The Fujimori Legacy: The Rise of Electoral Authoritarianism in Peru.* University Park, PA: Penn State University Press. https://doi.org/10.1515/9780271030326.

Cookson, Tara Patricia. 2018. *Unjust Conditions: Women's Work and the Hidden Cost of Cash Transfer Programs.* Berkeley, CA: University of California Press. https://doi.org/10.1525/luminos.49.

Corrales, Javier. 2022. *The Politics of LGBTQ Rights Expansion in Latin America and the Caribbean.* New York: Cambridge University Press.

Cuba, Lucero, Mariana Gallo Alarcón, Ella Goñez Fernandez, Eurídice Vargas Velarde, Nicolás Vargas Ugalde, and Francesca Encalada Yong. 2022. *Nacer con útero: Efectos de la criminalización del aborto en el Perú.* Lima: Justicia Verde. https://justiciaverdeperu.org/nacer-con-utero.

Dargent, Eduardo, and Stéphanie Rousseau. 2021. "Peru 2020: The Interruption of Political Continuity?" *Revista de ciencia política* 41, no. 2: 377–400. https://dx.doi.org/10.4067/S0718-090X2021005000112.

Dargent, Eduardo, and Stéphanie Rousseau. 2022. "Choque de poderes y degradación institucional: Cambio de sistema sin cambio de reglas en el Perú (2016–2022)." *Política y gobierno* 24, no. 2: 1–28.

Dore, Elizabeth, and Maxine Molyneux, eds. 2000. *Hidden Histories of Gender and the State in Latin America.* Durham, NC: Duke University Press.

Franceschet, Susan, Jennifer M. Piscopo, and Gwynn Thomas. 2017. "Motherhood and Politics in Latin America." In *Mothers and Others: The Role of Parenthood in Politics*, edited by Melanee Thomas and Amanda Bittner, 64–86. Vancouver: UBC Press.

Fraser, Nancy. 2013. *Fortunes of Feminism: From State-Managed Capitalism to Neoliberal Crisis.* London: Verso.

Gianella, Camila, Jorge Ruiz-Cabrejos, Pamela Villacorta, Andrea Castro, Gabriel Carrasco-Escobar. 2021. "Revertir cinco años de progreso: El impacto de la covid-19 en la mortalidad materna en Perú." CMI Brief no. 2021:2. https://www.cmi.no/publications/7454-revertir-cinco-aos-de-progreso-el-impacto-de-la-covid-19-en-la-mortalidad-materna-en-pero.

Ilizarbe, Carmen. 2022. "Peru: Democratic Erosion Under Neoliberalism." In *Challenges to Democracy in the Andes: Strongmen, Broken Constitutions, and Regimes in Crisis*, edited by Maxwell Cameron and Grace Jaramillo, 121–42. Boulder, CO: Lynne Rienner.

Jenson, Jane. 2020. "Social Investment: Polysemy in Perspective." In *Handbook on Society and Social Policy*, edited by Nicholas Ellison and Tina Haux, 59–74. Cheltenham, UK: Edward Elgar.

Koven, Seth, and Sonya Michel, eds. 1993. *Mothers of a New World: Maternalist Politics and the Origins of Welfare States*. New York: Routledge.

Llanos, Beatriz, and Juana Nina Tapia. 2021. "La paridad aplicada: Rendimiento electoral de las mujeres y condiciones de la competencia electoral bicentenaria." *Revista Elecciones* 20, no. 22: 169–96. https://doi.org/10.53557/Elecciones.2021.v20n22.05.

Manky, Omar, ed. 2021. *Rostros del trabajo: Desigualdad, poder e identidad en el Perú contemporáneo*. Lima: Universidad del Pacífico.

Melgar, Sandy, Narda Carranza Pinedo, Mariuxy Bustos Ocampos, and Fiorella Zamora Cabinillas. 2021. "Paridad y alternancia: Elecciones generales 2021 – Avances hacia una democracia paritaria." Lima: Oficina Nacional de Procesos Electorales.

MIMDES (Ministerio de la Mujer y Desarrollo Social [Ministry of Women and Social Development]). 2011. "Aportes del programa nacional Wawa Wasi a la estrategia nacional Cuna Más, 2011–2016." Lima: Programa Nacional Wawa Wasi, MIMDES. https://www.scribd.com/document/149754003/wawa-wasi.

Molyneux, Maxine. 2006. "Mothers at the Service of the New Poverty Agenda: Progresa/Oportunidades, Mexico's Conditional Transfer Programme." *Social Policy and Administration* 40: 425–49. https://doi.org/10.1111/j.1467-9515.2006.00497.x.

Nagels, Nora. 2016. "The Social Investment Perspective, Conditional Cash Transfer Programmes and the Welfare Mix: Peru and Bolivia." *Social Policy and Society* 15, no. 3: 479–93. https://doi.org/10.1017/S1474746416000105.

Oxhorn, Philip. 2006. "Neopluralism and Citizenship in Latin America." In *Citizenship in Latin America*, edited by Joseph S. Tulchin and Meg Ruthenburg. Boulder, CO: Lynne Rienner.

Pérez, Leda M., and Andrea Gandolfi. 2024. "From Dead Letter to Functional Policy? Domestic Workers' Rights and 'Disformality' in Peru." *International Labour Review* 163: 455–76. https://doi.org/10.1111/ilr.12436.

Ramm, Alejandra, and Jasmine Gideon, eds. 2020. *Motherhood, Social Policies and Women's Activism in Latin America*. Basingstoke, UK: Palgrave Macmillan.

Rich, Jessica A.J., Lindsay Mayka, and Alfred P. Montero. 2019. "Introduction: The Politics of Participation in Latin America – New Actors and Institutions." *Latin American Politics and Society* 61, no. 2: 1–20. https://doi.org/10.1017/lap.2018.74.

Rousseau, Stéphanie. 2009. *Women's Citizenship in Peru: The Paradoxes of Neopopulism in Latin America*. New York: Palgrave Macmillan.

Rousseau, Stéphanie. 2020. "Antigender Activism in Peru and Its Impact on State Policy." *Politics and Gender* 16, no. 1: E5. https://doi.org/10.1017/S1743923X20000070.

Rousseau, Stéphanie, Eduardo Dargent, and Aurora Escudero. 2019. "Rutas de atención estatal a las víctimas de violencia de género: Entre legados e innovaciones." Lima: Consorcio de Investigación Económica y Social. https://cies.org.pe/investigacion/rutas-de-atencion-estatal-las-victimas-de-violencia-de-genero-entre-legados-e.

Rousseau, Stéphanie, Debora Lopreite, and Eduardo Dargent. 2025. "From Aspirational Laws to the Implementation of Legislation Against Gender-Based Violence: Bottom-Up Pressure in Peru and Argentina." *European Journal of Politics and Gender*. https://doi.org/10.1332/25151088Y2025D000000080.

Staab, Silke. 2012. "Maternalism, Male-Breadwinner Bias, and Market Reform: Historical Legacies and Current Reforms in Chilean Social Policy." *Social Politics: International Studies in Gender, State and Society* 19, no. 3: 299–332. https://doi.org/10.1093/sp/jxs010.

Trivelli, Carolina, and Silvana Vargas. 2014. "Entre el discurso y la acción: Desafíos, discusiones y dilemas en el marco de la creación del Ministerio de Inclusión Social." Lima: Instituto de Estudios Peruanos.

World Bank. 2023. *Rising Strong: Peru Poverty and Equity Assessment*. Washington, DC: World Bank.

4

Displacing the Social Construction of Indigenous Citizenship at the International Level: Comparing Guatemala and Paraguay

Garance Robert and Andréanne Brunet-Bélanger

In Latin America, the recognition of Indigenous peoples' citizenship rights reflects a paradoxical situation. On the one hand, unlike in other territories of the world, most countries in the region have, theoretically, acknowledged the existence of their Indigenous populations and have seemingly – albeit slowly – accepted that they should be able to exercise a certain degree of "internal self-determination" within the existing boundaries of the nation-state (Sieder 2014, 414). This is exemplified, for instance, by the widespread ratification of the 1989 International Labour Organization (ILO) Convention 169 on Indigenous and Tribal Peoples,[1] as well as by the constitutional recognition of Indigenous rights in several countries.

On the other hand, most Latin American countries are in practice characterized by particularly exclusionary "citizenship regimes" in which Indigenous people are still treated as *immigrés de l'intérieur* (Jenson and Rousseau, 2006, 10). Here, "citizenship regime" refers to "the institutional arrangements, rules and understandings that guide and shape concurrent policy decisions and expenditures of states, problem definitions by states and citizens, and claims-making by citizens" (Jenson 2007, 5). The concept of citizenship used here therefore goes further than a purely formal notion of rights based on nationality. It centres, instead, on the ways that "citizenship practices identify who has rights, what thoses rights are, and *who is responsible for ensuring they are truly accessible*" (Jenson and Rousseau 2006, 10; our emphasis). In the region, there persists a significant gap between Indigenous peoples' aspirations and demands, and the legal and institutional recognition of these rights. Where these rights and international norms exist, their implementation remains highly limited, creating a substantial gap between rules and their enforcement (Wright and Tomaselli 2020). Moreover, apart from Bolivia and Ecuador, neither of which are exempt from tension in this regard (Aguilar et al. 2010), the representation of Indigenous peoples within democratic institutions remains very limited, especially at the national level. Finally, in terms of citizenship territory, both in the strict sense (of nationality and of holding a passport) and in the more complex sense of national identity and its geographical space, Indigenous peoples are generally discriminated against. Indigenous identities are often either denied, as in the case of Argentina, Chile, and Costa Rica (Kradolfer 2008, David 2023, Loncón 2023), or integrated into a myth of national identity as a synthesis of a harmonious and respectful hybridization between Indigenous and European cultures, as in Mexico and Brazil (Rights and Resources Initiative 2015).

From the 1960s onwards, and even more so since the 1980s and 1990s (Yashar 2005), Indigenous movements have made their voices heard and reclaimed their rights for recognition in Latin America. The opening up of political opportunities, facilitated by democratic transitions, has enabled these groups to interact freely with each other and with the state to articulate new demands (Yashar 2005; Rice 2015), while being strongly conditioned – and thus limited – by their human and financial capacities, due to the emerging neoliberal context. Such mobilization reflects a form of "neopluralism" (Oxhorn 2011), a mode of interest intermediation that highlights the interplay between exclusionary citizenship regimes and Indigenous agency. Neopluralism thus impacts the social construction of Indigenous citizenship rights. Consequently, it affects modes of political, social, and economic inclusion for these groups – although inclusion is far from being the sole focus of these claims, which also include autonomy and auto-determination, and which vary widely cross countries, contexts, and movements. These observations align with what several authors have described as "neoliberal multiculturalism," as highlighted by Postero (2007) regarding Bolivia prior to the presidency of Evo Morales, or as "cosmetic multiculturalism" (Bastos and Camus 2004), concerning Guatemala in the 2000s. These countries adopted multicultural reforms – in the 1990s for Bolivia and the

2000s for Guatemala – recognizing Indigenous rights and cultural diversity. While these measures expanded Indigenous participation in governance, they also served as mechanisms to depoliticize and manage Indigenous populations within the framework of neoliberal development. Despite these limitations, Indigenous movements have not necessarily lost their dynamism. On the contrary, they seem to have gained unprecedented visibility and become impressively vigorous across the region, thus constituting an influential transnational social movement in global politics (Brysk 2000; Van Cott 2005; Jackson and Warren 2005; Yashar 2005; Rice 2015).

This chapter examines the paradox between limited citizenship rights and the resilience of Indigenous movements, building on the concept of *citizenship as agency* (Montambeault et al. 2020). We argue that this de facto exclusion from citizenship regimes does not mean that Indigenous actors are in a position of weakness within the social fabric of civil society (Oxhorn 2011). To explain the persistence of Indigenous actors' mobilization and their vitality in contexts marked by exclusion and state repression, it seems essential to explore the (sometimes punctual, sometimes longer-term) shift in Indigenous struggles towards the supranational arena, which contributed to the shaping of the social construction of Indigenous citizenship in Latin America.

Our discussion builds upon a comparison of Guatemala and Paraguay, two countries with vastly different social, cultural, economic, and institutional contexts, but where Indigenous movements have demonstrated a great capacity for mobilization, despite unfavourable conditions.[2] The comparison shows that Indigenous actors can maintain robust mobilization by leveraging the instruments that are available to them, especially at the international level. In both cases, the demands of Indigenous movements are articulated through instruments of international law, mainly due to the inefficiency or impossibility of formulating claims at the national level. However, as the comparison reveals, it is the degree of closure within the citizenship regime that conditions the extent to which Indigenous movements tend to shift their struggles to the international arena. That said, despite the importance of the international arena in the social construction of citizenship, the state remains the ultimate target of these movements, as it holds the effective means to guarantee these rights.

NEOPLURALISM, CITIZENSHIP AS AGENCY, AND INTERNATIONAL INTERACTIONS

Guatemala and Paraguay are two countries with vastly different institutional, economic, social, and political contexts. While both regimes exhibit authoritarian traits, Paraguayans have never had a taste of true democracy (Sondrol 2007), unlike Guatemala (Torres-Rivas 2011). There is also a significant difference in the proportion of their Indigenous populations, estimated at around 45 per cent in Guatemala (INE 2018), compared to 2.3 per cent in Paraguay (IWGIA 2023). In terms of Indigenous rights recognition, Guatemala has seen notable advancements, including a range of legal provisions protecting and recognizing Indigenous peoples' cultural and territorial rights – although these remain largely ineffective. From a strict legal standpoint, Indigenous rights are more limited in Paraguay, despite some recent initiatives. Nevertheless, in both cases (albeit at different moments), Indigenous movements have articulated significant demands for the recognition of their collective rights, particularly their rights to land and self-determination (Correia 2023; Bastos 2009).

Despite these differences, the concept of neopluralism, as developed by Oxhorn (2005) and discussed in the introduction of this volume, is relevant to both cases. Given the central role that the market plays in the concept of neopluralism, this model of interest intermediation poses three types of threats to democratic stability in Latin America: growing economic insecurity, which threatens the social fabric; increasing crime rates and the predominant responses by the state to this issue, which tend to focus on security policies that reinforce inequalities; and, finally, the fragmentation and atomization of civil society (Oxhorn 2005). These conditions, along with identity-based colonialism, contribute to the continued exclusion of Indigenous peoples from citizenship regimes in Latin America. However, the exclusion of Indigenous peoples does not reflect their level of dynamism, which is why it is important to focus on the concept of citizenship as agency (Oxhorn 2011; Montambeault et al. 2020, 23). Indeed, while Oxhorn warns of the risk of neopluralism, which produces citizenship as consumption and reproduces inequalities, neopluralism does not always preclude agency. However, struggles for the social construction of citizenship rights can take place at multiple and interdependent spatial scales, meaning that the practice of citizenship is experienced, expressed, and understood differently in various contexts (public/private, local/national) by citizens, who have complex and often intersectional identities (Isin 2008; Lister 2007; Moreau 2015, cited in Montambeault et al. 2020, 25). Substantive citizenship rights first emerge in practice and become effective through social processes conditioned by the participation or non-participation of individual people (Oxhorn 2007). To attain these rights, conflicts and struggles between social actors and the state are necessary, leading to compromises and an extension of citizenship rights when hesitant elites realize they have few alternatives (Oxhorn 2007).

In this chapter, we intend to enrich Oxhorn's theoretical conception of citizenship as socially constructed through the interactions of civil society with the state, but also with other entities. We argue that the social construction of Indigenous citizenship allows us to see how the international sphere should be considered a distinct entity in which part of the agency of Indigenous movements is constructed in the context of their struggles for recognition and inclusion by the state. The cases of Guatemala and Paraguay demonstrate that the international arena offers Indigenous movements both substantial and symbolic resources that they can leverage in their national and supranational struggles for inclusion. These resources include legal instruments and international norms that substantiate their claims. Symbolic resources enhance the legitimacy of these claims by providing tools to articulate discourses and justify actions based on international standards, guiding present and future actions (Moura Masiero 2019). We thus align with Postero's definition of Indigenous citizenship as a negotiated process, a notion that highlights its dynamic and contested nature, in which Indigenous actors use both local and global discourses to demand rights and challenge exclusion (Postero 2007, 2017).

Investing in the international sphere as a symbolic resource yields tangible results for Indigenous struggles. First, it enables movements to make their voices heard through undertaking a series of collective actions that underscore their national struggles for recognition. These actions include documenting the violations they have suffered, exposing these violations to a wider audience, fostering solidarity with other groups, obtaining financial resources linked to international cooperation, and ultimately gaining legitimacy in the eyes of national and international societies. Second, international activism can facilitate other types of collective action, such as negotiations with national authorities, awareness campaigns among local populations, and sustainable development projects. Overall, the substantial and symbolic resources provided in the international arena strengthen the capacity of Indigenous groups, which are part of the "social fabric formed by a multiplicity of territorially and functionally self-constituted units," to become agents interacting with the state, "collectively resisting subordination to the state while demanding inclusion in national political structures" (Oxhorn 1995, 251–2).

The comparative examination of Guatemala and Paraguay shows that while legal instruments and resources for action built into the international arena are not a "magic bullet," they serve as a crucial space in which Indigenous peoples in Latin America can practice citizenship as agency, albeit in varying ways across movements and countries. For Guatemalan actors, international actions include legal actions, especially at the inter-American level. More broadly, their actions are also aimed at obtaining material resources through transnational funding. They therefore have tangible effects on Indigenous agency, supporting the funding of struggles and the sharing of experiences. Conversely, in Paraguay, collective action in the international arena is mostly focused on mobilizing supranational courts, such as the Inter-American Court of Human Rights, to address the lack of Indigenous rights recognition at the national level. Thus, as the comparison reveals, the non-linear process of the social construction of citizenship is inseparable from interactions with the international sphere in both cases, but it is the degree of openness of the "citizenship regime" that conditions the modalities of resorting to international law: the more closed it is, the more that actions taken in the international sphere will not only be recurrent but also significant for the Indigenous movement(s) concerned.

GUATEMALA: AN AMBIVALENT CITIZENSHIP REGIME

Guatemala is home to one of the most ethnically diverse populations in Latin America, with a significant proportion being Indigenous.[3] Guatemalan Indigenous peoples have managed to preserve and reinvent much of their specific traditions and cultures since the conquest, maintaining a de facto legal pluralism (Blanco 2014). However, it was not until the late 1970s that Indigenous advocacy movements underwent a significant resurgence, one that emphasized Indigenous identity. This period marked a national reckoning with Indigenous issues, previously largely ignored despite the important proportion of Indigenous people in the population (Bastos 2009).

From 1978 to 1984, successive military governments suppressed Indigenous movements in an attempt to eradicate dissent, leading to atrocities that have been labelled "genocidal" by those involved in Guatemalan transitional justice, including scorched-earth policies, population displacements, and large-scale massacres (CEH 1999; Vela Castañeda 2014). But political instability, economic crisis, and the desire to improve their image both domestically – notably among economic elites – and internationally finally led the Guatemalan military authorities to initiate a "pacted" transition process from the mid-1980s onwards (Brett 2006). Despite somewhat weak support within the army for democracy (Schirmer 1999), this relative openness allowed numerous actors, including Indigenous groups, to seize the opportunity to advocate for the recognition of their rights. In 1985, a new constitution was adopted and Vinicio Cerezo – a Christian Democrat and the first civilian president in two decades – was elected.

Several organizations that had gone underground during years of intense repression resurfaced, such as the Peasant Unity Committee (Comité de Unidad Campesina, or CUC) in 1986. Against the backdrop of intensified transnational activist networks and international human rights promotion (Finnemore and Sikkink 1998; Risse et al. 1999), many predominantly Indigenous organizations emerged to denounce violence and human rights violations, such as the Mutual Support Group (Grupo de Apoyo Mutuo, or GAM) in 1984 or the National Coordination of Widows of Guatemala (Coordinadora Nacional de Viudas de Guatemala, or CONAVIGUA) in 1988, without demanding specific Indigenous rights, however. Simultaneously, other openly "Mayanist" organizations emerged, leading to the creation of federations like the Council of Mayan Organizations of Guatemala (COMG) and Instance of Mayan Unity and Consensus (Instancia de Unidad y Consenso Maya, or IUCM) in the 1990s. For these organizations, the focus and goal was autonomy, along with the promotion of Mayan culture, notably through the state-funded Academy of Mayan Languages (Academia de Lenguas Mayas de Guatemala) and the Council of Mayan Organizations of Guatemala (Bastos 2009). The 1990s marked a period of significant penetration by international organizations and international cooperation, the unprecedented visibility of these issues (such as the Nobel Peace Prize being awarded to Rigoberta Menchú in 1992), and the recognition of Indigenous organizations within civil society and Indigenous people within Guatemalan society.

LEGAL PROVISIONS, STRUCTURAL INEQUALITIES, AND THE VIGOUR OF INDIGENOUS MOVEMENTS

Since 1985, various legal instruments for the recognition of Indigenous rights have been created at both the constitutional and local levels in Guatemala, alongside the formal recognition of numerous international norms by the state. Although Spanish is the official language of Guatemala, the 1985 Constitution acknowledges the nation's multicultural, multiethnic, and multilingual character and recognizes twenty-three vernacular languages. The Constitution also allows collective land ownership and the right of individual people and communities to their cultural identity, but at the same time restricts legal pluralism by establishing the exercise of justice as the exclusive prerogative of the state (Article 203). The judicial functions that some Indigenous leaders traditionally exercised in their communities until 1985 were, in fact, revoked by the Constitution (Blanco 2014).

The Peace Accords signed in 1995 and 1996, which included the Agreement on the Identity and Rights of Indigenous Peoples and the Agreement on Socio-Economic Aspects and Agrarian Situation, bolstered existing constitutional guarantees. For the first time, historical discrimination against Indigenous peoples was officially recognized, and legal, educational, and legislative reparative measures were proposed. A gender perspective was also incorporated, highlighting the role played by Indigenous women and the double discrimination they faced. The agreements also emphasized the need to translate ILO Convention 169 into provisions to guarantee to Indigenous peoples the right to free, previous, and informed consultation (FPIC) and included cultural protection measures. Furthermore, they acknowledged Indigenous authorities and customary law, originally with the intention of integrating them into national legislation. While these provisions were not implemented in the Constitution, due to their rejection in the 1999 constitutional referendum, the Peace Accords remain a crucial reference point for the advocacy efforts of civil society movements, especially for Indigenous movements (Ladisch 2012; Sanabria Arias 2019; Robert 2022).

In 2002, a decentralization reform was initiated in Guatemala through Decrees 12-2002 and 14-2002, establishing a municipal code and a decentralization law. Decree 12-2002, Article 8, recognizes traditional authorities as essential elements of the municipality, with Article 55 officially acknowledging the existence of "Indigenous mayoralties" (*alcaldías indígenas*) and obligating municipal and governmental authorities to acknowledge, respect, and promote the ancestral authority system. Additionally, Decree 11-2002, Article 26, establishes the right to FPIC on development measures for Maya, Xinca, and Garifuna peoples, managed through their representatives within Community Councils of Urban and Rural Development (Consejos Comunitarios de Desarrollo Urbano y Rural, or COCODE), a promise that has often remained unfulfilled in practice. Several jurisprudential texts from Constitutional Court rulings (from 2009, 2011, 2015, and 2017) have supplemented these decentralization initiatives. These rulings assert the fundamental and indisputable right to consultation, grounded in human rights laws ratified by the Guatemalan state, and which interpret consultation as a collective fundamental right that has been integrated into constitutional law. They emphasize that the state cannot argue that an absence of adequate legal and institutional frameworks is an insurmountable obstacle to fulfilling its duty of consultation (Romero and Orantes 2018; Corte de Constitucionalidad de Guatemala 2009).

In sum, the legislative framework at both the national and local levels in Guatemala acknowledges the issues affecting Indigenous peoples, yet its effectiveness remains limited. In practice, these laws are difficult to implement, such as the difficulty of implementing bilingual education due to severe resource shortages within the education system. Similarly, there are obstacles to implementing FPIC due to close ties between economic elites, political elites, and organized crime, all of whom leverage coercive forces to protect extractive projects rather than serve the population (Ilmer 2018). Numerous examples of projects, including the Fenix nickel mine in El Estor, Izabal (Bastos 2021; Masek 2023), the San Rafael mine in Santa Rosa (Weisbart 2018), the Marlin Mine in San Marcos (Vanthuyne and Dugal 2023; Sibrián and van der Borgh 2014), and the hydroelectric project in Santa Cruz Barillas in Huehuetenango (Torres 2019), in which FPIC was not granted have received significant media coverage and academic research attention. Actions against these projects often face state repression, leading to the criminalization of social protest and further human rights violations. Moreover, Indigenous populations continue to face significant discrimination and economic marginalization (IWGIA 2020).

With the limited implementation of Indigenous rights in the country, Indigenous movements suffered a relative loss of momentum in the late 1990s. Bastos and Camus (2004) describe the situation as "cosmetic multiculturalism" within a context of "post-conflict normalization," in which the Guatemalan state masks existing inequalities through demonstrations that it is, ostensibly, fulfilling its duties towards the Indigenous population and international donors. Most actions explicitly addressing ethnic difference are based on the use of politically correct multicultural discourse, accompanied by primarily symbolic gestures reflecting this new mindset (Bastos 2009). Mayans have been able to attain relatively high government positions, and specific spaces have been created to manage policies for the Maya, overseen by Mayans. According to Cojtí (2007), one of the main drawbacks of these units is their lack of political support, often leaving them dependent on external cooperation and fending for themselves. These factors hinder them from bringing about profound changes.

In addition to lacking effectiveness in terms of combating inequalities and advancing Indigenous rights, this institutionalization of Maya struggles has led to their relative demobilization. Although Maya organizations are able to influence public policies, their cooptation by the state has also entailed a loss of radicalism, both in terms of repertoire of action and the formulation of collective demands, as often described in the literature (i.e., Tarrow et al. 2001). At this juncture of the "Maya movement," their interactions with the international sphere have not entirely disappeared, however, especially because groups and institutions advocating for Indigenous rights rely to a large extent on financial resources obtained through international cooperation. However, the significance of these interactions has remained limited and relatively insignificant: it is not a displacement per se, as the movements do not need to resort to other avenues, since the state appears – at least superficially – open to dialogue and cooperation with Indigenous movements. This "moment" of Indigenous struggles in Guatemala thus illustrates that the more open a state is to (in this case, Indigenous) the demands of a movement, the less important becomes that movement's engagement in the international sphere, with its efforts focused at the national level.

LOCAL–GLOBAL INTERACTIONS, THE INTERNATIONAL SPHERE, AND THE SOCIAL CONSTRUCTION OF CITIZENSHIP IN GUATEMALA

Since the 2000s, there has been a revitalization of Indigenous movements in Guatemala, in particular in mobilizing against extractive development projects (hydroelectric, mining, etc.) that affect territories inhabited by Indigenous communities. This revitalization initially stemmed from local dynamics, which were also influenced by the decentralization law of 2002 and the reconstruction of Indigenous municipalities. However, these dynamics also intersect with the actions of Indigenous groups in the international arena, where there has also been a significant revitalization of Indigenous action (relative to other countries, both in terms of the number of actions and their significance), in a context in which the Guatemalan state has shown less openness to Indigenous demands and, generally, has become more repressive towards social (and Indigenous) protest (Doran 2015).

First, local Indigenous mobilizations have focused almost exclusively on the right to FPIC and on natural resources and territorial rights (Brett and Bastos 2010), pushing for the normative framework provided by the ILO Convention 169 on Indigenous rights, ratified by Guatemala in July 1996. Not only are these international legal instruments used by Indigenous groups to legitimize their struggles in the face of a noncompliant state, these Indigenous movements also play a significant role in formulating the international legal instruments, in a co-construction process (Bellier 2012, 2018; Bellier and González 2015), along with other Latin American groups and organizations (especially from the Andean region), and from other regions around the world.

Since their emergence, Guatemalan Indigenous movements, particularly the Maya movement, have always maintained close ties with international organizations and transnational movements. These interactions have played a fundamental role in the evolution of their struggles, both in terms of their language and demands, and the legitimacy of their demands. Therefore, these interactions have also played a role in the social construction of citizenship. When questioned today, Indigenous actors (including lawyers and grassroots activists, and members of ancestral community authorities, from all generations) generally see international actions – whether it be support or intervention from the international community, for the purpose of obtaining resources for their organizations, or the mobilization of international law through international law institutions (particularly the Inter-American Commission on Human Rights and the Inter-American Court of Human Rights) – as an integral part of their strategies for collective mobilization and for making demands.

However, there are differences in perception among different Indigenous actors, both regarding the importance of these actions and the effectiveness of international legal instruments. Although several activist groups have appealed to the inter-American system, only a small number of legal cases have been presented by Indigenous communities themselves. Some cases submitted to the inter-American system involve massacres that occurred during the internal armed conflict, which therefore involved fundamental human rights violations against Indigenous communities that were never addressed in a satisfactory way within the national system. In these cases, the plaintiffs are mentioned by their name or place of residence and are not identified as Indigenous peoples. There are only two cases with resolution in which the name of the community is mentioned and in which explicit reference is made to the rights of Indigenous peoples. The first is *Maya Q'eqchi' Indigenous Community of Agua Caliente v. Guatemala*, in which the community challenges the lack of national legislation guaranteeing their right to collective property and attempts to combat both the establishment of a mining project and the lack of resources to protect their rights. The second is the *Maya Kaqchikel Peoples of Sumpango et al. v. Guatemala*, resolved on 6 October 2021 in favour of the plaintiffs. They accused the state of violating the freedom of expression of four Indigenous communities due to the lack of recognition of community radio stations, legal obstacles to obtaining permits, and persecution of their members. These cases are important, but they demonstrate the limitations of using the inter-American system compared to legal mobilization and collective action undertaken at the national level.

Discussions with Indigenous leaders, lawyers, and advocates for rights and territory, from all generations, reveal a fundamental aspect: most actors do not position themselves in opposition to international legal instruments and norms. Sometimes they consider these to be incomplete, but they always acknowledge their positive aspects. However, they are disillusioned regarding their effectiveness: these instruments and norms are not binding, which limits their scope. Furthermore, the timelines are extremely long, thus delaying their effectiveness. A member of the *alcaldía indigena* [Indigenous mayoralty] of the Ixil of Nebaj expresses it this way:

> The statements are very good, such as those from the United Nations, for example, or declarations on Indigenous peoples in the Americas ... but they have no binding force.[4]

For this Indigenous women's rights activist and co-founder of the organization Mama Maquín, a lot of international norms are well formulated, but their implementation depend on the will of states. Thus, they are only minimally effective:

> It [the state] has an obligation, and we, we hold rights. So, treaties are very good ... but unfortunately [these institutions] almost exclusively provide recommendations. I believe that is where we are weakened. ... There is no instance in which a state that does not fulfill its obligations, its responsibilities, can be punished.[5]

Another interviewee, an activist and lawyer, emphasizes the very long delays that exist in these spaces, therefore limiting the scope of any actions undertaken:

> One of the most significant limitations for us is obviously related to time. ... Sometimes, just to file a request, we have calculated that eligibility is declared almost ten years later, and even then, that's the minimum time. It's always like that. ... Yes, it can be effective, but very slow.[6]

Another interviewee – another activist for Indigenous women's rights – mentioned the lack of accessibility when it comes to the mechanisms available for people whose rights have been violated:

> I think that [these legal instruments] are important, necessary. But often we don't know about them and don't know how to access them. And the people who manage to use them are few.

> For example, participation is so limited ... women, or groups, or collectives ... who don't even have access to this information.[7]

However, another interviewee, a lawyer and co-founder of the Indigenous People Rights law office, emphasizes that it remains essential to work with this system, especially if there are no other solutions at the national level:

> This is our last resort. ... We must go and explain [before these international bodies] why it is necessary to act, and make them understand that there is, from the Indigenous peoples, an invisibility in Guatemala. And that because of this invisibility, we must go there.[8]

Another important aspect – which here echoes the statements of Paraguayan leaders – is the significant foundation provided by international laws in terms of legitimacy, and in symbolic terms, even if they are not binding. One Indigenous leader and ancestral authority of the plurinational government of Akateka, Chuj, Q'anjob'al, and Popti' peoples expresses the strategic importance of these elements:

> The "paper" [international laws and declarations] serves to argue that the struggle is justified. And this is another tool to make demands from those who refuse to understand that there are other groups of people who also have rights.[9]

Finally, the international arena is also crucial in Guatemala from the perspective of material resources: almost all national-level Indigenous organizations and a large portion of local organizations rely, directly or indirectly, on financial support from international cooperation, as confirmed by all the interviews. Consequently, discourse is conditioned based on what these donors require, and these organizations themselves shape the discourse at the international level, in a back-and-forth movement.

However, there are a small number of organizations, with significant reach and presence at the national level, that reject this dependency, which they consider a factor of deradicalization. This is the case with the Peasant Development Committee (Comité de Desarrollo Campesino, or CODECA),[10] as their coordinator states:

> There are many international cooperation organizations that say "we fund human rights, gender, entrepreneurial initiatives, but not politics." ... They talk a lot about human rights, women's rights, but they never know how to drive this agenda, this struggle, this horizon. And that's one of the great limitations that from our perspective has affected and greatly reduced the living conditions in Guatemala. ... That's why, if we receive a small portion of cooperation, it's very little, and it doesn't define what CODECA should do.[11]

In conclusion, the case of Guatemala and the evolution of Indigenous struggles clearly demonstrates how interactions with the international sphere, and sometimes engagement within it (relative to other spaces), have influenced the social construction of Indigenous citizenship: international texts support and legitimize their struggle, providing them with a significant platform from which to denounce the violations committed by the state. Despite its lack of effectiveness, the international sphere cannot be ignored. The rejection of the logic of these spaces by certain organizations also underscores their importance: they convey a certain vision, which remains fundamental for obtaining resources, but which carries the risk of depoliticizing struggles.

The case of Guatemala also demonstrates that the periods when the state was most open (at least superficially) to dialogue, such as in the aftermath of the Peace Accords, were also the times when the international sphere was not the main arena of action for Indigenous movements. Conversely, more recently and in a context of relative closure, the international sphere has gained greater importance, as a source of both substantial and symbolic resources for mobilization and agency. For Indigenous activists, however, the international sphere and its instruments are means and not ends in themselves, an approach that suggest that while the instruments of the international sphere can displace struggles for the social construction of Indigenous citizenship in the international arena to a certain extent, the state remains the primary interlocutor as the entity that grants and guarantees their citizenship rights – both Indigenous and human.

PARAGUAY: A CASE OF LIMITED INDIGENOUS CITIZENSHIP

In Paraguay, the emergence of Indigenous movements can be partially attributed to the interaction between the democratization process initiated in 1989 and the ratification of international legal instruments on human rights. Additionally, financial and advisory support from nongovernmental organizations (NGOs) aimed at strengthening Indigenous claims has played a significant role. Unlike in Guatemala, the rise of Indigenous movements in Paraguay is relatively recent, notably with the formation of the Coordinadora de Líderes Indígenas del Bajo Chaco (CLIBCH) and the Articulación de Mujeres Indígenas de Paraguay (MIPY) in the early 2000s. These movements are primarily composed of members from the same Indigenous community or ethnicity, but this has not precluded support from other communities for the actions taken by one of them.

Indigenous movements, primarily focused on demands for the restitution of ancestral territories, emerged in the 1980s, parallel to the adoption of Law 904/81 on the status of Indigenous communities. At that time, most Indigenous communities in the Chaco region were linked to the Anglican Church through the main Makthlawaiya mission, while in the eastern region, Indigenous peoples were associated with the Catholic Church. In response to both mistreatment that they saw in their missions and restrictions to land access, Anglican and Catholic priests, with the assistance of anthropologists, initiated aid projects for Indigenous peoples, with the Marandú Project, which aimed to educate Indigenous leaders about their legal rights, being the most prominent.

Currently, Indigenous movements are primarily focused on demands for access to territory and autonomy, as well as guaranteeing other fundamental rights such as economic, social, cultural, and environmental rights. This orientation towards territorial rights can be explained by the closed nature of the regime towards Indigenous communities, reflected in the shortcomings of the rule of law, particularly when it comes to issues related to territorial rights. Indeed, there are many cases of human rights violations in Paraguay, mainly arising from land conflicts between Indigenous populations and large landowners. Often, these issues are resolved in favour of the landowning elites, as state land policy is influenced by the close ties between political and landowning elites.

THE CLOSED INSTITUTIONAL CONTEXT: EFFECT ON CITIZENSHIP FOR INDIGENOUS PEOPLES

In Paraguay, despite formal recognition, Indigenous rights are weakly institutionalized, particularly in terms of access to territory. This weak institutionalization also has concrete effects, opening the doors to forced displacements and violations of various human rights.

To date, the only law governing the procedure for the restitution of Indigenous territories was established during the dictatorship. Indeed, in 1981, Law 904/81, "Estatuto de las Comunidades Indígenas," was enacted to delineate the specific rights of Indigenous communities. This legislation led to the creation of a ministry dedicated to Indigenous affairs and the establishment of a legal mechanism allowing for the recognition of Indigenous communities and, eventually, the restitution of their ancestral lands. However, while Law 904/81 aims to preserve the culture and society of Indigenous communities, defend their heritage and traditions, improve their economic conditions, enable their effective participation in the national development process, and guarantee them equal rights to those of other citizens in terms of land ownership and other productive resources, it does not recognize their pre-state existence on the territory, thus creating a legal void for Indigenous populations living on unrecognized territories. This issue of recognizing Indigenous territories stems from a long history of land usurpation: between 1881 and 1914, 64 per cent of what would come to be perceived as the national territory was transferred to private owners (Galeano 2001). The illegal sale of Indigenous territories continued in the 1960s and 1970s under the dictatorial regime for various megaprojects, including the construction of highways and the creation of the Paraguayan–Brazilian Itaipu hydroelectric dam (Villalba Portillo 2022, 85).

After the end of Alfredo Stroessner's dictatorship (1954–89), constitutional reforms during the democratic opening of 1992 strengthened the land rights of Indigenous peoples, as did the country's ratification in 1993 of ILO Convention 169 on the rights of Indigenous and tribal peoples. Other constitutional provisions recognize the right to communal land ownership and Indigenous participation by establishing special measures to protect these rights. For example, Article 64 of the Constitution acknowledges the right of Indigenous communities to the collective ownership of their lands, which are indivisible and inalienable. This article also stipulates that Indigenous people cannot be relocated without their consent. With the democratic transition, Paraguay became a member of the Inter-American Court of Human Rights, while adopting various United Nations instruments relating to human rights. The state adopted the United Nations Declaration on the Rights of Indigenous Peoples (UNDRIP) in 2007. According to both Article 137 (par. 1) and Article 141 of the Constitution (1992), international treaties have the force of law upon ratification and take precedence over national legislation.

However, several factors contribute to conceptual gaps in the national legal framework, leading to the state refusing to recognize ancestral territories, among other rights violations, despite the creation of favourable national legal instruments for such recognition. This formal acknowledgment is often constrained in practice, attributable to the fragility of the rule of law, along with challenges associated with institutional fragmentation and the separation of powers (Bailliet 2013; Hetherington 2011; Pous et al. 2018). In Paraguay, as we will explain, the scope of rights at the national level is weak, significantly diminishing the political power and advocacy of groups defending these rights before national courts. This closure at the national level partly explains the importance of the international arena for the advocacy of Indigenous movements.

One of the reasons for this closure at the national level stems from the definition of land according to the Constitution. Chapter 9 establishes that the economic and developmental dimension of land takes precedence over ancestral Indigenous territory, as defined in Article 64 of the Constitution (Brunet-Bélanger 2022). This orientation is reflected in national laws, notably Law 1863 on agrarian status (2002), which allows for the expropriation of lands claimed by Indigenous communities if those lands are not being used "rationally," meaning "productive," in economic terms. This reform encourages the colonization of lands that are considered to be "underutilized" (Ezquerro-Cañete 2016).

Characterized by close ties between political and landowning elites, the state's land policy favours an economic model oriented toward private enterprises, to the detriment of the interests of Indigenous communities (Correia 2018, 2023). This conception of land exacerbates discriminatory practices against Indigenous communities, as it prioritizes the rational use of land over its traditional use and the cultural and spiritual values associated with it – as emphasized by the United Nations Special Rapporteur on the Rights of Indigenous Peoples during her visit to Paraguay in 2015 (Tauli-Corpuz 2015). This leads to territorial evictions of Indigenous communities, as their lands are not considered to be used rationally, thereby permitting their expulsion under national law. A coordinator of an NGO working with Indigenous communities in the Chaco region illustrates this situation:

> I would unfortunately tell you that there isn't much change in this regard at the moment. Here in Paraguay, we are experiencing a fierce attack on the right to land, with expulsions and invasions of Indigenous properties. Suddenly, there are many of these lands with multiple titles or other emerging problems used as resources for legal battles, etc. But since last year, the expulsions of Indigenous communities from the lands they occupy have been enormous, even expulsions of communities with legal titles, with legal manoeuvers, and legal resources that are not precisely very saintly, true, from local prosecutors and the judicial system, which is probably the most corrupt there is.[12]

In summary, although there is a legal framework for the participation of Indigenous peoples, in practice, it does not allow for truly significant participation. The challenges faced by Indigenous communities stem from structural factors inherited from colonization, such as social, economic, and political inequalities; socioeconomic exclusion; poverty; and lack of access to basic services, which significantly limit opportunities for participation (Duarte-Recalde 2012). Furthermore, the lack of symbolic resources, such as education and access to information, also hinders the ability of Indigenous peoples to exercise their citizenship (Duarte-Recalde 2012, 252). Laws are also not enforced, as explained here by a director of an NGO working on a legal defense for Indigenous communities:

> Well, I think that in our country, in terms of the relationship, let's say on the side of the national constitution that ordains all rights at the national level, it must be said that in the constitution, in the fifth chapter, there are measures to truly protect Indigenous rights. However, as we say here, these are papers with dead letters because there are no policies, and no budgets to make this materialize in the communities.[13]

Thus, Indigenous communities seeking to assert their rights at the national level face complete closure at both the executive and the legislative level. When they attempt to assert their rights before national courts, they encounter not only unfavourable judgments but also laws designed to hinder their claims. An example illustrating this situation is that of the Xákmok Kásek community, which initiated a legal recognition process of its ancestral territory in 1990. Despite a decade of petitions and mobilization before the courts, the bill aimed at returning the community's claimed lands was rejected by the Senate in 2000. This decision was meant to put an end to the community's repeated legal demands and to quash its claims.

Furthermore, the persecution of Indigenous peoples and their allies has intensified since 2021, notably through the amendment of Article 142 of the Penal Code. This amendment, which came into effect in July 2021, seeks to protect large landowners by criminalizing those who demand the recovery of territories or who live on lands without proper title deeds. During the dictatorship, over eight million hectares of land were illegally granted to regime allies, and these lands have never been returned to Indigenous communities. Approximately one million hectares of public lands were irregularly appropriated by soy producers, ranchers, and large landowners, without any government measures to prevent or rectify this situation. This inaction has allowed landowners to retain control of the lands and obstructed Indigenous claims to their ancestral territories. Similarly, the government amended Article 98 of the Agrarian Statute in 2021 to exclude from state social programs and subsidies anyone who is accused of illegally occupying lands.

Given the impossibility of asserting rights at the national level, or the inefficiency of legal tools, Indigenous claims have come to rely on international law, which serves both as a battleground and as source of tools and avenues for engaging with the state – as emphasized by a lawyer specializing in Indigenous rights:

> And as Paraguay has also ratified numerous international agreements such as C169 [Convention 169] ... all of these are, let's say, the instruments that we use to continue defending or engaging in litigation for Indigenous peoples.[14]

RESORTING TO INTERNATIONAL SPACES AS SITES FOR CONSTRUCTING INDIGENOUS CITIZENSHIP

In a context in which the state ignores the claims of Indigenous communities, three such communities in Paraguay appealed to the Inter-American Court of Human Rights (IACtHR)[15] between 2005 and 2010 to claim recognition of their rights – namely, the Yakye Axa, Sawhoyamaxa, and Xákmok Kásek communities. The three requests concern the failure of the state to guarantee the rights of Indigenous communities to their ancestral territory in the Chaco region, despite national legislation allowing such claims, and despite international responsibility to do so. The communities therefore chose to turn to an international forum, with the support of international instruments for the protection of human rights, which the Paraguayan state has also adopted and should, in theory, implement in its national laws. Consequently, we will focus on the use of international law by these three communities, as they illustrate the strength of international law, both symbolically and practically, in Paraguay.

All three cases ruled in favour of the applicant communities. In each case, the IACtHR concluded a violation of property rights due to the inefficiency of Paraguay's legal procedures regarding land claims. Moreover, the IACtHR stipulated in all three cases that the state had not ensured the right to effective participation of community members, by their customs and traditions. The aim was to make the state recognize that it had failed in its duties by prioritizing "productive" landowners over the rights of Indigenous peoples. This is explained by a lawyer specializing in Indigenous law:

> The objective was for the state to change its policy and provide comprehensive and reparative attention to Indigenous peoples who have been and continue to be victims of various violations and denials of their rights. It is not just about territorial rights; they have been denied the right to legal identity. For the state, many Indigenous children and elderly individuals have passed away without having identity documents recognizing them, depriving them of access to health services.[16]

There is no doubt that these various judgments, and, more broadly, international standards, are exceedingly important for the work of the various NGOs working with Indigenous peoples. During our interviews with a dozen NGOs, all unequivocally emphasized the importance of building rights for advocacy through the development of international law, particularly through the IACtHR. According to one NGO coordinator, in explaining the importance of international standards in daily work:

> Issues related to the IACtHR, for example, are important to us. We recently presented cases concerning Indigenous peoples who were here, in Ka'a Poty Square, for seven months. They were evicted three times and have now returned, but we fear for people's safety because there are armed civilians, among other concerns. We have also taken this case to the IACtHR. Paraguay has already faced numerous international sanctions regarding Indigenous rights, notably due to the persistence of slavery in the Chaco. We have many complaints, but we believe that international standards are also extremely important.[17]

Likewise, according to an NGO director we spoke with:

> Yes, indeed, we have extensively used them [international standards], and Paraguay, with the cases it has brought before the Inter-American Court, has contributed to the development of jurisprudence, that is, precedents, in the American Convention on Human Rights, which is the main human rights treaty in the Americas. ... These are arguments that we use internally here and that have been very useful, not only in Paraguay but practically throughout Latin America.[18]

The question has been whether this approach positively and concretely supports the demands of Indigenous communities and opens up questions of citizenship. This question was raised by a retired lawyer who was involved in the restitution of Indigenous territories in the Chaco in the 1990s:

> Jurisprudence is used by lawyers as a very important precedent. If the Paraguayan state says it doesn't have to buy land, the Inter-American Court has already ordered it to buy land, so they must buy land. There needs to be more resources and people so that Indigenous peoples can reclaim all their land, but that's not

> enough. They have their land and remain poor, miserable, and discriminated against.[19]

Despite the shift to the international arena, the decisions of the IACtHR have not had a formal effect on the position of the state, which continues to disregard Indigenous communities' demands for territorial recognition as well as their other rights. Even when communities have prevailed before the IACtHR, the Paraguayan state has not implemented reparations, and no internal legislative changes have been observed.

However, both Indigenous communities and their allies maintain a positive outlook on legal mobilizations, even though few developments are being observed at the national level. This holds for communities who have brought cases before the IACtHR as well as those who have not. This perception is largely explained by the fact that the international space that allowed for the presentation of their cases before the IACtHR has conferred legitimacy to their claims. Thus, our research demonstrates that while international law decisions may not have had a direct influence on the formal and institutional recognition of Indigenous people's territorial rights and their right to participate in decisions concerning them in a legal or political framework, an observable participative opening still exists, through actions and demands created by and for the communities themselves. International norms are also integrated into discourses.

By using the international arena to demand the restitution of their ancestral territories, Indigenous communities and the movements in which they participate can also address social issues, such as violations of social, economic, and environmental rights, which are then reflected in the discourse, framing, and legitimacy gained in the legal process. In closed regimes, movements face enormous obstacles, including high personal risks, unfair trials, and repressive legislation. However, studies on the international space as a space of contestation demonstrate that social movements persist in using supranational courts, which are perceived as safer spaces in which to contest national policy and actions (McCann 2006; Vanhala 2012; van der Vet 2018; Chua 2014, 2019).

Participation in the international arena has allowed communities to push for the opening of the national space. Indeed, for the Yakye Axa, Sawhoyamaxa, and Xákmok Kásek communities, the mobilization process that led to the submission of cases to the IACtHR ultimately conferred new legitimacy to the discourses used by Indigenous communities, shaped by the discourse of the Court, and thus helped these communities establish themselves as political subjects and rights holders within the national sphere.

For example, for the Xákmok Kásek community, the international judgment created pressure at the national level, as explained by one of the community leaders:

> After obtaining the judgment from the Inter-American Court of Human Rights, our strength increased even more, because this instrument exerted pressure on the government in place. Our main demand has always been the restitution of our ancestral land. Furthermore, space was created to examine the implementation of the Court's resolutions, which allowed progress on certain aspects. The judgment of the Inter-American Court is therefore truly fundamental because, through this instrument, we used it against the government. Without this tool, the restitution of our ancestral land would have been very difficult. We consider the judgment of the Court to be of paramount importance.[20]

As a result, according to the interviews conducted, the support of the Court consolidated the sense of security within the community, granting it the necessary legitimacy to persevere in its claims, despite a complete closure on the part of the state. The sense of legitimacy materialized in various ways within the community, including through greater daily political involvement and collective initiatives directed toward the state. These different actions are closely intertwined. The recognition of their rights by the IACtHR and the acknowledgment that the state had violated these rights, opened up a dialogue in which to challenge the actions of the state.

In the case of the Xákmok Kásek community, appearing before the IACtHR has been particularly revelatory. They have learned to politicize their identity in order to continue advocating for their claims at the national level. The recognition obtained from the IACtHR has legitimized their struggles, enabling them to claim external recognition vis-à-vis the state. This has also brought legitimacy to their demands, bestowing to them symbolic significance, and reinforcing their own self-esteem and confidence in their actions (Brunet-Bélanger 2023). The process of appearing before the IACtHR has given the community a sense of having accessed their rights and has amplified their voice by mobilizing the rights outlined in the judgments, without necessarily requiring further judicial recourse (Correia 2023).

In sum, in Paraguay, international standards have, to a certain extent, enabled communities and movements to compel the state to listen and act, at the national level. International law, although not free from power relations, provides communities with tools to challenge structures and assert themselves as political and rights-bearing subjects, advocating for their rights and advancing their recognition by the state. By using the tools developed by international law, communities can hold the state accountable and seek to introduce and establish national legal safeguards. However, in the case of Paraguay, unlike with the Guatemalan case, the use of law has not led to an increase in international cooperation, particularly where resources are concerned. The international sphere remains a limited resource, and its use, from a strictly legal point of view, is hampered by the refusal of the state to interact with international legal processes.

CONCLUSION

The concept of the social construction of citizenship, enriched by meaningful interactions with the international sphere, helps us understand the apparent paradox of Indigenous movements in Latin America having significant vitality despite struggling against generally closed citizenship regimes. These interactions encompass actions taken with intergovernmental organizations (particularly the United Nations and the Organization of American States) as well as other actors in this sphere (especially international NGOs and development agencies from Western countries), as well as the use (both direct and symbolic) of legal norms developed at the international level and ratified by the relevant states. As we have demonstrated, Indigenous citizenship, seemingly limited and exclusive – despite significant formal advances, especially over the past fifteen years – is also legitimized and made concrete in practice through mobilizations, an important part of which take place in the international sphere. These interactions are essential to understand the dynamism of these mobilizations and the construction of a more inclusive citizenship.

We have also demonstrated that the response of states greatly influences this shift to the international sphere. It continues to be central and remains the primary target of the actions of Indigenous movements. The citizenship regime, therefore, remains largely conditioned by the state. When dialogue with the state becomes exhausted, this is where the shift is most pronounced. Thus, our study does not question the importance of the state; rather, it encourages a consideration of the international sphere as an additional fundamental parameter in which to understand this construction – one that has its own proper dynamics and effects. The effective recognition and protection of the rights of Indigenous peoples, particularly in terms of autonomy, are still far from guaranteed. Yet, the way in which this "citizenship in action" is socially constructed and the modalities by which these groups formulate their claims in practice, signal a fundamental change in their perception of themselves and their role within national societies. This shows that demands in terms of rights and, more generally, the "rights paradigm" continue to gain ground in Latin America and around the world, despite the contradictions of this paradigm and immense challenges ahead.

NOTES

1 In total, twenty-four countries in Latin America have signed the Convention, and fifteen have ratified it and translated it into domestic legislation.

2 This contribution is based on data collected in Paraguay (in 2022) and Guatemala (in 2022 and 2023) through semi-structured interviews with around thirty actors involved in the defence of Indigenous rights, human rights, and land rights in each country, supplemented by the analysis of documentation from various Indigenous rights organizations in these two countries.

3 Approximately 44 per cent in 2018, according to the last National Statistics Institute of Guatemala census (INE 2018). The country is home to three ethnic groups and twenty-four subgroups, including twenty-two Mayan language groups, one Xinca group, and the Garifuna. While our focus here is primarily on the Maya movements, it is worth noting the emerging strength of the Xinca movement, which has close alliances with Maya organizations, and the distinct Garifuna claims, albeit somewhat detached from broader Indigenous demands in Guatemala (Virgill Artiaga 2020)

4 Interview in Santa María Nebaj, Guatemala, February 2023. All the names of the interviewees have been withheld. All translations are from Spanish and were done by the author (Robert).

5 Interview in Guatemala City, February 2023.
6 Interview in Guatemala City, March 2023.
7 Interview in Guatemala City, March 2023.
8 Interview in Guatemala City, March 2023.
9 Interview in Guatemala City, June 2022.
10 This name does not reflect the organization's orientation, since it is indeed an Indigenous organization and claims to be so. But the name dates to the 1970s, at a time when peasant and Indigenous struggles were more closely intertwined.
11 Online interview (Zoom), July 2023.
12 Interview in Asunción, Paraguay, June 2022. All the names of the interviewees have been withheld. All translations are from Spanish and were done by the author (Brunet-Bélanger).
13 Interview in Asunción, Paraguay, June 2022.
14 Interview in Asunción, Paraguay, July 2022.
15 In Spanish, the Comisión Interamericana de los Derechos Humanos (CIDH).
16 Interview in Asunción, Paraguay, July 2022.
17 Interview in Asunción, Paraguay, June 2022.
18 Interview in Asunción, Paraguay, July 2022.
19 Interview in Asunción, Paraguay, June 2022.
20 Interview in Asunción, Paraguay, July 2022.

REFERENCES

Aguilar, Gonzalo, Sandra Lafosse, Hugo Rojas, and Rébecca Steward. 2010. "South/North Exchange of 2009: The Constitutional Recognition of Indigenous Peoples in Latin America." *Pace International Law Review Online Companion* 22, no. 2: 44–96.

Bailliet, Cecilia M. 2013. "Measuring Compliance with the Inter-American Court of Human Rights: The Ongoing Challenge of Judicial Independence in Latin America." *Nordic Journal of Human Rights* 31, no. 4: 477–95.

Bastos, Santiago. 2009. "La (ausencia de la) demanda autonómica en Guatemala." *Confluencia/Cuadernos de observación activa*. Guatemala: CANEK: Observatorio Cultural.

Bastos, Santiago. 2021. "Despojo, criminalización, y periodismo comunitario en Guatemala: Entrevista a Carlos Ernesto Choc." *Latin American and Caribbean Ethnic Studies* 16, no. 2: 212–23.

Bastos, Santiago, and Manuela Camus. 2004. "Multiculturalismo y Pueblos Indígenas: reflexiones a partir del caso de Guatemala." *Revista Centroamericana de Ciencias Sociales* 1, no. 1: 87–112.

Bellier, Irène. 2012. "Les peuples autochtones aux Nations unies: Un nouvel acteur dans la fabrique des normes internationales." *Critique internationale* 54: 61–80.

Bellier, Irène. 2018. "Les droits des peuples autochtones: Entre reconnaissance internationale, visibilité nouvelle et violations ordinaires." *L'homme et la société* 206: 137–74.

Bellier, Irène, and Veronica González-González. 2015. "Peuples autochtones: La fabrique onusienne d'une identité symbolique." *Mots: Les langages du politique* 108, no. 2: 131–50.

Blanco Santiago, Valme. 2014. "Les Mayas du Guatemala et la reconnaissance de leurs droits: un difficile parcours." Doctoral thesis in law, Université d'Auvergne, Clermont-Ferrand, France.

Brett, Roddy. 2006. *Movimiento social, etnicidad y democratización en Guatemala, 1985–1996*. Guatemala: F&G editores.

Brett, Roddy, and Santiago Bastos. 2010. *El Movimiento Maya en la Decade despues de la Paz*. Guatemala: F&G editores.

Brunet-Bélanger, Andréanne. 2022. "Inégalités et pandémie dans les communautés autochtones au Paraguay." *Cahiers des Amériques latines* 99, no. 1: 201–17.

Brunet-Bélanger, Andréanne. 2023. "La jurisprudence de la Cour interaméricaine des droits de l'homme et les luttes autochtones: Le cas des communautés du Chaco paraguayen." *Les Cahiers de Droit* 64, no. 3: 493–526.

Brysk, Alison. 2000. *From Tribal Village to Global Village: Indian Rights and International Relations in Latin America*. Redwood City, CA: Stanford University Press.

CEH (Comisión para el Esclarecimiento Histórico). 1999. *Guatemala, memoria del silencio*. Oficina de Servicios para Proyectos de las Naciones Unidas (UNOPS). Guatemala.

Chua, Lynette J. 2014. *Mobilizing Gay Singapore: Rights and Resistance in an Authoritarian State*. Philadelphia, PA: Temple University Press.

Chua, Lynette J. 2019. "Legal Mobilization and Authoritarianism." *Annual Review of Law and Social Science* 15: 355–76.

Cojtí, Demetrio Waqi' Q'anil. 2007. *Nuevas perspectivas para la construcción del estado multinacional*. Guatemala City: Waqib' Kej and Fundación Cholsamaj.

Correia, Joel E. 2018. "Adjudication and Its Aftereffects in Three Inter-American Court Cases Brought against Paraguay: Indigenous Land Right." *Erasmus Law Review* 11, no. 1: 43–56.

Correia, Joel E. 2023. *Disrupting the Patrón: Indigenous Land Rights and the Fight for Environmental Justice in Paraguay's Chaco*. Berkeley, CA: University of California Press.

Corte de Constitucionalidad de Guatemala (Constitutional Court of Guatemala). 2009. Expediente núm. 3878–2007, sentencia del 21 de diciembre.

Dagnino, Evelina, and Luciana Tatagiba. 2010. "Social Movements and Institutional Participation: Range of Collective Actions and Cultural Dynamics in the Difficult Construction of Democracy in Brazil." *Revue internationale de politique comparée* 17, no. 2: 167–85.

David, Carine. 2023. "Le droit des peuples autochtones au Costa Rica: L'envers de la carte postale." *Droit et politiques comparés, Recherche sur la Cohésion sociale.*

Doran, Marie-Christine. 2015. "La criminalisation de l'action collective dans la crise actuelle des droits humains en Amérique latine." *Revue québécoise de droit international.* Special edition (March): 221–46.

Duarte-Recalde, Liliana Rocío. 2012. "Variaciones en el comportamiento electoral en Paraguay." *América Latina Hoy* 60: 117–38.

Ezquerro-Cañete, Arturo. 2016. "Poisoned, Dispossessed and Excluded: A Critique of the Neoliberal Soy Regime in Paraguay." *Journal of Agrarian Change* 16, no. 4: 702–10.

Finnemore, Martha, and Kathryn Sikkink. 1998. "International Norm Dynamics and Political Change." *International Organization* 52, no. 4: 887–917.

Galeano, Eduardo. 2001. *Les veines ouvertes de l'Amérique latine*. Paris: Pocket.

Hetherington, Kregg. 2011. *Guerrilla Auditors: The Politics of Transparency in Neoliberal Paraguay*. Durham, NC: Duke University Press.

Ilmer, Patrick. 2018. "La violencia y las élites en Guatemala: Pactos en la interfaz de lo legal y lo ilegal." *ECA: Estudios Centroamericanos* 73, no. 752: 65–86.

INE (Instituto Nacional de Estadística) Guatemala. 2018. *XII Censo nacional de población y VII de vivienda*. Guatemala City: INE.

Isin, Engin F. 2008. "Theorizing Acts of Citizenship." In *Acts of Citizenship*, edited by Engin F. Isin and Greg Marc Nielsen. London: Zed Books.

IWGIA (International Work Group for Indigenous Affairs). 2020. *El Mundo Indígena 2020*, 34th edition.

IWGIA (International Work Group for Indigenous Affairs). 2023. "Indigenous Peoples in Paraguay." Accessed 20 March 2024. https://iwgia.org/en/paraguay.html.

Jackson, Jean E., and Kay B. Warren. 2005. "Indigenous Movements in Latin America, 1992–2004: Controversies, Ironies, New Directions." *Annual Review of Anthropology* 34: 549–73.

Jenson, Jane. 2007. "The European Union's Citizenship Regime: Creating Norms and Building Practices." *Comparative European Politics* 5: 53–69.

Jenson, Jane, and Stéphanie Rousseau. 2006. "Contesting the Boundaries of Citizenship: Politics and Policies in Contemporary Latin America." *Canadian Journal of Latin America and Caribbean Studies* 31, no. 62: 9–14.

Kradolfer, Sabine. 2008. "Les autochtones invisibles ou comment l'Argentine s'est 'blanchie.'" *Amérique Latine Histoire et Mémoire: Les Cahiers ALHIM* 16.

Ladisch, Virginie. 2012. "The Challenges of Implementation: Guatemala." In *Conflict Management in Divided Societies: Theories and Practice*, edited by Stefan Wolff and C. Yakinthou, 201–16. London: Routledge.

Le Bot, Yvon. 1992. *La guerre en terre maya: Communauté, violence et modernité au Guatemala*. Paris: Éditions Karthala.

Lister, Ruth. 2007. "Inclusive Citizenship: Realizing the Potential." *Citizenship Studies* 11, no. 1: 49–61.

Loncón, Elisa. 2023. "The Mapuche Struggle for the Recognition of Its Nation From a Feminine and Decolonizing Point of View." *ReVista (Harvard Review of Latin America)*.

Masek, Vaclav. 2023. "Memoria colectiva y movimientos indígenas durante la consulta comunitaria en El Estor, Guatemala." In *Estrategias, pedagogías y abordajes clínicos en Derechos Humanos*, edited by Cecilia Gebruers, 15–43. Santa Rosa, Argentina: Editorial de la Universidad Nacional de La Pampa.

McCann, Michael. 2006. "Law and Social Movements: Contemporary Perspectives." *Annual Review of Law and Social Science* 2: 17–38.

Montambeault, Françoise, Manuel Balán, and Philip Oxhorn. 2020. "Widening and Deepening Citizenship from the Left? A Relational and Issue-Based Comparative Approach." In *Legacies of the Left in Latin America: The Promise of Inclusive Citizenship*, edited by Manuel Balán and Françoise Montambeault, 17–43. Notre Dame, IN: Notre Dame University Press.

Moreau, Julie. 2015. "Intersectional Citizenship, Violence and Lesbian Resistance in South Africa." *New Political Science* 37, no. 4: 494–508.

Moura Masiero, Clara. 2019. "Legal Mobilization, Rights and Social Change in Brazil: Reasons for Optimism." In *Justice Alternatives*, edited by Pat Carlen and Leandro Ayres França, 123–35. London: Routledge.

Oxhorn, Philip. 1995. *Organizing Civil Society: The Popular Sectors and the Struggle for Democracy in Chile*. Philadelphia, PA: Penn State University Press.

Oxhorn, Philip. 2005. "Neopluralism and the Challenges for Citizenship in Latin America." Paper prepared for After Neo-Liberalism? Consequences for Citizenship, workshop no. 2 in the series Claiming Citizenship in the Americas, organized by the Canada Research Chair in Citizenship and Governance, Université de Montréal, Canada. Accessed 4–5 November 2005. www.cccg.umontreal.ca.

Oxhorn, Philip. 2007. "Civil Society Without a State? Transnational Civil Society and the Challenge of Democracy in a Globalizing World." *World Futures* 63, nos. 5 and 6: 324–39.

Oxhorn, Philip. 2011. *Sustaining Civil Society: Economic Change, Democracy, and the Social Construction of Citizenship in Latin America*. Philadelphia, PA: Penn State University Press.

Postero, Nancy. 2007. *Now We Are Citizens: Indigenous Politics in Postmulticultural Bolivia*. Stanford, CA: Stanford University Press.

Postero, Nancy. 2017. *The Indigenous State: Race, Politics, and Performance in Plurinational Bolivia*. Berkeley, CA: University of California Press.

Pous, Federico, Alejandro Quin, and Marcelino Viera. 2018. *Authoritarianism, Cultural History, and Political Resistance in Latin America: Exposing Paraguay*. London: Palgrave Macmillan.

Rice, Roberta. 2015. "Indigenous Mobilization in Latin America." In *Latin American Democracy: Emerging Reality or Endangered Species?*, edited by Richard L. Millett, Jennifer S. Holmes, and Orlando J. Pérez, 201–12. London: Routledge.

Rights and Resources Initiative. 2015. "Who Owns the Land in Latin America? The Status of Indigenous and Community Land Rights in Latin America." Washington, DC: Rights and Resources Initiative. https://rightsandresources.org/publication/who-owns-the-land-in-latin-america.

Risse, Thomas, Stephen C. Ropp, and Kathryn Sikkink. 1999. *The Power of Human Rights: International Norms and Domestic Change*. New York: Cambridge University Press.

Robert, Garance. 2022. "Vingt-cinq ans des accords de paix au Guatemala: Des textes ambitieux, une mise en œuvre semée d'embûches." In *Amérique latine: L'année politique 2021/Les Etudes du CERI*, no. 259–260, edited by Olivier Dabène.

Romero, Wilson, and Ana Patricia Orantes. 2018. *Estudio sobre racismo, discriminación y brechas de desigualdad en Guatemala*. Publicación de las Naciones Unidas, CEPALMexico. Mexico.

Sanabria Arias, José Carlos. 2019. "The Roads to Reinvigorate the Peace Agreements: Between Electoral and Justice Reforms in Guatemala." In *International Perspectives on Democratization and Peace*, edited by Narayanan Ganesan, 113–33. Bingley, UK: Emerald Publishing.

Schirmer, Jennifer. 1999. *Intimidades del proyecto politico de los militares en Guatemala*. Guatemala City: Sophos Editorial.

Sibrián, Anabella, and Chris van der Borgh. 2014. "La Criminalidad de los Derechos: La Resistencia a la Mina Marlin." *Oñati Socio-Legal Series* 4, no. 1: 63–84.

Sieder, Rachel. 2014. "Indigenous Peoples' Rights and the Law in Latin America." In *Law and Society in Latin America*, edited by Cesar Garavíto, 143–56. London: Routledge.

Sondrol, Paul. 2007. "Paraguay: A Semi-Authoritarian Regime?" *Armed Forces and Society* 34, no. 1: 46–66.

Tarrow, Sydney, Charles Tilly, and Doug McAdam. 2001. *The Dynamics of Contention*. New York: Cambridge University Press.

Tauli-Corpuz, Victoria. 2015. "Report of the Special Rapporteur on the Rights of Indigenous People: Paraguay." Doc N.U. A/HRC/30/41/Add.1. Accessed 1 November 2023. digitallibrary.un.org/record/803354?ln=en.

Torres, Selvin. 2019. "Conflictividad y represión en Guatemala: Criminalización de la defensa del territorio en Santa Cruz Barillas, Huehuetenango." *Revista de la Carrera de Sociología Entramados y Perspectivas* 9, no. 9: 68–95.

Torres-Rivas, Edelberto. 2011. *Revoluciones sin cambios revolucionários*. Guatemala: F&G editores.

Van Cott, Donna Lee. 2005. "Building Inclusive Democracies: Indigenous Peoples and Ethnic Minorities in Latin America." *Democratization* 12, no. 5: 820–37.

Van der Vet, Frank. 2018. "When They Come for You: Legal Mobilization in New Authoritarian Russia." *Law and Society Review* 52: 301–36.

Vanhala, Lisa. 2012. "The Paradox of Legal Mobilization by the UK Environmental Movement." *Law and Society Review* 46: 523–56.

Vanthuyne, Karine, and Marie Christine Dugal. 2023. "Regenerating Maya-Mam Ways of Governing: Indigenous Emancipatory Politics in the Age of the Extractive Imperative." *Journal of Latin American and Caribbean Anthropology* 28: 251–60.

Vela Castañeda, Manolo Estuardo. 2014. *Los pelotones de la muerte: La construcción de los perpetradores del genocidio Guatemalteco*. Mexico: El Colegio de México.

Villalba Portillo, Sara Mabel. 2022. "Subrepresentación política de pueblos indígenas en Paraguay: A tres décadas del reconocimiento constitucional del derecho a la participación." *Reflexión Política* 24, no. 49: 78–91.

Virgill Artiaga, Scherly. 2020. "Garífuna Voices of Guatemala's Armed Conflict." *NACLA Report on the Americas* 52, no. 4: 422–9.

Weisbart, Caren. 2018. "Diplomacy at a Canadian Mine Site in Guatemala." *Critical Criminology* 26, no. 4: 473–89.

Wright, Claire, and Alexandra Tomaselli. 2020. *The Prior Consultation of Indigenous Peoples in Latin America: Inside the Implementation Gap*. London: Routledge.

Yashar, Deborah J. 2005. *Contesting Citizenship in Latin America: The Rise of Indigenous Movements and the Postliberal Challenge*. Cambridge, UK: Cambridge University Press.

5

The Media's Role in the Social Construction of Citizenship: Neopluralism and the Public Sphere in Latin America

Michelle D. Bonner

The mass media play an important role in the social construction of citizenship. As Philip Oxhorn (2011) argues, citizenship rights do not naturally flow from the elite as they embrace democracy or capitalism. Nor does their extension follow any defined order. They are the result of contestation and compromise between civil society and the state that occurs in the public sphere. Media is a part of these interactions. Civil society organizations rely on the mass media to communicate their ideas, knowledge, and demands to political leaders and the public. In turn, state actors concerned about their re-election care how the media cover their actions, inactions, and policy choices. Indeed, they often make policy decisions based on how different decisions are likely to be covered in the media or what they interpret from the media to be public opinion.

Of course, neither civil society nor state actors need to listen to the mass media. They can use alternative ways to communicate with each other or the public, such as social media, and decision making on both sides sometimes does ignore the mass media. Perhaps as a result, Oxhorn centres his analysis on the interactions between civil society and the state, with little mention of the media. In his model of the social construction of citizenship, the media is an intervening variable with an "ambiguous" impact on the public sphere (2011, 20). It engages in the public sphere but its "commercial nature" neutralizes its impact on policy (2011, 20). This brief mention assumes that the media is not directly affected by economic structures, the state, civil society, or political parties. It is comprised of independent (albeit not unbiased) businesses that contribute to shaping the public sphere in particular ways but does not determine the structure of the public sphere. As Oxhorn notes, political leaders can win elections even when the media are against them (2011, 20). Yet he also recognizes that the media can stoke fear of crime, which can narrow the public sphere "as public opinion shifts in support of authoritarian nondemocratic remedies" (2011, 20). However, as media scholars have long argued, these apparent contradictions are not random. They are the result of the nuanced ways media affect public opinion, as well as the different economic and regulatory models that states choose to use in order to structure a "free" or democratic media.

This chapter aims to bring media into Oxhorn's theoretical framework in a manner that more fully incorporates the scholarship from media studies. In particular, I argue that the mass news media both reflect and reinforce the state and economic structures that shape civil society's participation in the public sphere. The mass news media ("media," for simplification) refers to print, TV, radio, social media, and other digital communication technologies used to communicate politically relevant information to large audiences.

As Oxhorn argues, the public sphere is shaped by power relations, particularly economic ones, that affect how civil society participates in the public contestation of citizenship and who in civil society is able to participate. More specifically, he explains that "[t]o the extent that a given set of economic development policies contributes to a greater dispersal of power resources and increases the capacity of subaltern groups to organize themselves, it should facilitate greater levels of social inclusion and democratization" (2011, 2). Oxhorn argues that, historically, civil society in Latin America has been limited in its ability to engage in the public sphere, owing to either coerced marginalization (state repression) or controlled inclusion (state cooptation of civil society through clientelism and state corporatism). Yet, beginning in the 1970s, a new market-centred development model was embraced, which has contributed to a different state–civil society relationship that he describes as neopluralism.

Neopluralism is pluralist in the sense that it is based in the normative belief that interests are best balanced through a free, market-based "competition among individuals in the rational pursuit of their self-interest" (Oxhorn 2011, 56). In this model, political rights are of central importance, as "ultimate political authority is essentially decided by a free market of votes" (Oxhorn 2011, 56). Unlike with Robert Dahl's (1971) understanding of pluralism, neopluralism in Latin America, Oxhorn argues, has an authoritarian bent, as elections, not democratic checks and balances, are the central meaning of political rights. Beyond elections "[i]ndividuals' personal economic resources largely determine the extent and nature of their political and social inclusion," including the extension of education, health care, and legal protection (Oxhorn 2011, 57). Citizenship thus becomes defined through consumerism, rather than agency. Civil society is then weakened, not by a reduction in the quantity of organizations, but by greater inequality in the dispersal of the power resources needed for organizations to participate fully in the construction of citizenship. Civil society is fragmented, as organizations compete with each other for scarce resources, and democratic rights are won by those able to purchase them. In Latin America, Oxhorn argues, this has resulted in strong political rights with weak civil rights and deteriorating social rights.

I argue that the same state-led market-based economic reforms that have restructured the relationship between the state and society in Latin America, also restructured the media in ways that reflect and reinforce neopluralism and contribute to the weakening of civil society. Like with civil society, mass media participation in the public sphere has been historically shaped by controlled inclusion and coerced marginalization. In this current phase of neopluralism, the state-led economic restructuring of the media, through deregulation and privatization, has altered media actors' (e.g., journalists, editors, producers) practices in ways that reinforce plebiscitary democracy, the voices of the economically powerful (through public relations), and the criminalization of protests. I draw on cases studies of Argentina and Chile to illustrate these processes. The case studies are based in twenty years of research on media and state–society relations in both countries (see, for example, Bonner 2014; Bonner 2019).

MEDIA AND THE SOCIAL CONSTRUCTION OF CITIZENSHIP

In the social construction of citizenship, it matters who is included or excluded in the public sphere. As Oxhorn argues, democracy is strengthened when the state and its chosen economic development model support an autonomous and diverse civil society that is able to both demand inclusion in the state and resist subordination, while using self-restraint in their pursuit of those goals (2011, 9). Like with Oxhorn's ideal civil society, Habermas (2006) argues that an ideal media is also autonomous, diverse, and self-regulating. It is, however, necessarily selective in its interactions with civil society, and the relationship is asymmetrical, in favour of the media. Yet in its ideal form it would support the amplification of those civil society voices that are the most persuasive and beneficial in their diversity for democracy.

In practice, the media play an important role in determining which civil society voices are heard (if any), how their message is presented, and the relative importance they are accorded. A wide range of state and civil society actors compete to have their voices included in the media, and state-chosen economic structures that shape how the media function (the media system) affect how media actors respond to their efforts. Together these practices contribute to the relative inclusivity of the public sphere and the social construction of citizenship.

By changing the placement of the media in Oxhorn's framework, media power and its relationship to economic power are highlighted as central variables in the inclusivity of the public sphere and thus the social construction of citizenship. This is not a new claim, but rather it reflects the rich literature in media studies on media power and media systems.

Media power is important to the social construction of citizenship. Habermas defines media power as the unavoidable result of the work of politically relevant media actors (such as journalists, editors, and producers) who "cannot but exert power, because they select and process politically relevant content and thus intervene in both the formation of public opinions and the distribution of influential interests" (2006, 419). This includes whether civil society voices are heard in mediated public debates, which civil society voices are heard, how their ideas are presented, and the relative importance they are accorded.

Media do not determine public opinion. Nor do state or civil society actors need to accept media portrayals of public opinion as public opinion. However, countless studies have shown that the media do *affect* public opinion, making some policy outcomes more likely than others. Media studies draw our attention to three key ways in which they do this.

The first two are agenda setting and priming (see, e.g., Scheufele and Tewksbury 2007; McCombs and Shaw 1972). Agenda setting is when the mass media place significance on some news items over others through their placement (headlines or top of the web page, first segment in radio or TV broadcasts), space given (word counts or time), or enhanced circulation on social media through, for example, favourable algorithms, as well as other indicators that draw attention to the news item. These news pieces then set the agenda for what people are talking about (including on social media) and audiences are more likely to identify these topics as important policy issues. If a news item, such as crime, is repeatedly featured over days, months, or years, then audiences are likely to be "primed" to view these as top policy issues facing the country, and, when elections occur, are more likely to use these policy topics to evaluate the performance of political leaders (Scheufele and Tewksbury 2007).

The third way media affect public opinion is through framing (see, for example, Valenzuela et al. 2017; Scheufele and Tewksbury 2007; Gamson and Wolfsfeld 1993). Journalists, editors, and producers make decisions as to how to frame news stories. Frames simplify and condense complex issues so that a story resonates quickly with audiences as familiar, relevant, or important. In print and digital media, the title or headline usually summarizes the article frame. On TV, radio, and podcast news segments, frames constitute the main take-away message. When framed well, and especially when audience members know little about the topic, news frames can shape how audiences interpret events, ideas, actions, or inactions. Whereas agenda setting and priming can affect public support for a policy issue (e.g., crime), framing can influence public opinion on the appropriate policy response (e.g., "tough on crime" rather than preventive policies).

These processes are relevant to the social construction of citizenship, as these choices can shape whose ideas and interests, expressed in the public sphere, gain more public attention and are attributed more importance than others. They signal to political leaders what public opinion might be and thus what policy choices may help (or impede) their re-election. Ideally these mediated processes would favour the best ideas from the public sphere, drawing from a plurality of ideas from autonomous and diverse civil society organizations, state actors, and political parties. However, as Oxhorn (2011) details, the public sphere contains power relations that are shaped by state power and the favoured economic model. These power relations affect whose voices and ideas are more likely to be circulated in the mass media, and whose are more likely to be dismissed or ignored. Studies of democracy and democratization often focus on how state power limits what the media report, equating state power with censorship and control (see, for example, Levitsky and Way 2010). Yet, as Oxhorn emphasizes, economic power also matters to the diversity of voices heard in the public sphere and particularly to the strength of civil society. Similarly, different economic models can result in different ways of organizing media in a democracy. Some democratic media systems encourage, more than others, the inclusion of a diversity of civil society voices. I will briefly review two media systems as examples.

Hallin and Macini (2004) describe the democratic media system of Northern Continental Europe as a democratic corporatist media model. In this system, the media are understood as being important for democracy. While some media are businesses, others are publicly run (at arm's length from the government), and all media are regulated to protect and encourage their contribution to democracy. That is, state regulations do not aim to censor, but rather to ensure that a diversity of political perspectives are heard and that journalists have legal protections to pursue news stories as they see best fit (regardless of editorial lines). Some media outlets receive state subsidies because they represent groups within society that are important for democracy but which may not be commercially viable. To some extent this media system is tied to Northern European corporatism, in that protections and subsidies were originally put in place to ensure the existence of media that will enable effective communication between the leaders of corporative groups and their members. While not perfect, in this system, a state uses subsidies and regulations to encourage news coverage of a diverse range of civil society organizations, so that their ideas and interests are included in public debate.

In what Hallin and Mancini (2004) call the liberal model, the media are primarily businesses. There are relatively few state regulations or subsidies, and little public media. The examples they give for the liberal media model are the US and, to a lesser extent, the UK, Canada, and Ireland. In this model the primary role of media outlets is to produce profit. This system assumes that the (near) absence of state involvement makes the media "free" and thus democratic (Levitsky and Way 2010, 57). The ideas and interests of civil society organizations are included when they are consistent with the media outlet's goal of profit. This favours organizations with aims that encourage consumerism, do not offend advertisers, or are politically neutral (see, for example, Gamson and Wolfsfeld 1993; Schradie 2019). Indeed, recent studies have challenged the early optimism that the Internet would liberate civil society. They argue that an unregulated, market-based Internet favours some, particularly economically powerful, actors over others (Schradie 2019; Lupien 2020; Lupien et al. 2021; Deibert 2020).

These two brief examples illustrate how different economic development models affect both which civil society voices are amplified in the media and how they are amplified. Not all "free" or democratic media treat civil society organizations equally.

In sum, the media do not determine political outcomes, but media power is more than an intervening variable in the social construction of citizenship. It both reflects and reinforces existing power relations (especially economic power) within the public sphere. In the next section I review how media has been organized in Latin America in ways that reinforce the historical changes in the state–civil society relations that Oxhorn identifies: controlled inclusion, coerced marginalization, and neopluralism.

MEDIA AND THE PUBLIC SPHERE IN LATIN AMERICA: CONTROLLED INCLUSION, COERCED MARGINALIZATION, AND NEOPLURALISM

The history of mass media in Latin America reflects the history of the region's public sphere. Throughout Latin America in the nineteenth century, the mass media, then limited mainly to newspapers, were run by political parties or the Catholic Church. Their purpose was to communicate with their (mainly elite) constituents. As suffrage, literacy, and export-led growth expanded, the mass media gradually became independent businesses. In the early twentieth century, the mass media began to use some of the new techniques emerging in the United States to draw in audiences and increase profits, such tabloid journalism and "professional" or "non-political" styles of journalism (Waisbord 2000, 14; Caimari 2017). News stories began to centre on drama, entertainment, and immediacy. Voices not conducive to profit (even if important for democracy) struggled to gain coverage. For example, in Argentina, the large labour movement protests occurring in the early twentieth century received very little mass media coverage (Cane 2011, 18–19).

After the Second World War, what Oxhorn calls "controlled inclusion" both shaped and reinforced a new relationship between the state and civil society. Oxhorn defines controlled inclusion as "top-down processes of political and social inclusion in which citizenship rights were segmented, partial, and, ultimately, precarious" (2011, 34). It is, as he puts it, citizenship as cooptation. What this looked like and the role played by the media varied between countries in the region. In Argentina, controlled inclusion was led through the populist government of President Juan Domingo Perón (1946–55; 1973–74) and implemented through state corporatism and clientelism. Consistent with the populist logic, the mass media were divided into those deemed to support "the people" (i.e., Perón) and those who supported "the elite" (i.e., opposition to Perón). Perón centralized and nationalized most mass media (print and radio at the time). Those mass media outlets that remained private businesses (primarily newspapers) either supported Perón or faced state-imposed economic sanctions or harassment. When television emerged, it was state owned and the content was entirely Perónist. For example, the first broadcast was of Eva Perón, the First Lady, on 17 October 1951 (Loyalty to Perón Day) (Waisbord 1998, 44).

As Oxhorn (2011) explains, controlled inclusion in Chile looked different. It occurred through political parties, which spanned the political spectrum but were hierarchical, and which placed partisan, ideological positions above citizens' autonomous interests. The mass media reflected and reinforced this restructuring of the public sphere. While radio, during the early part of this period, focused mainly on entertainment, newspapers spanned the political spectrum. However, they were, like the rest of the public sphere, partisan, often with strong ties to particular political parties. When television emerged, a compromise was struck in which one channel each was assigned to Chile's most prestigious universities on the condition of pluralistic news coverage. In 1969, President Eduardo Frei established Chile's first national TV channel to be run at arm's length from the government by a politically plural governing board (Fox and Waisbord 2002; Davies 1999).

Beginning in the 1950s, media polarization increased as media, like political parties, threw their support behind either the Socialist Party of Chile (eventually led by Salvador Allende) or the opposition political parties. For example, *El Mercurio*, Chile's most important national newspaper, opposed Allende and in July 1973 openly called for a military coup. In contrast, *Clarín*, then Chile's second most circulated national newspaper, supported Allende (Léon-Dermota 2003; Carter and Sepúlveda 1964). More than simply reflecting Chile's version of controlled inclusion, the media reinforced and amplified it to such an extent that the country's truth commission would later hold the media in part to blame for the coup that followed (Human Rights Watch 1998, 27).

In both Argentina and Chile, the military regimes used repression (coerced marginalization) to silence not only civil society but also the media. Indeed, media were among the first targets of the new military regimes. In Chile, opposition radio stations were bombed the day of the coup. Journalists in both countries were disappeared and killed. Opposition media outlets were closed, expropriated, nationalized, or sold to military regime supporters. Media that remained private businesses, primarily newspapers, were subject to censorship and were provided economic opportunities if loyal. The role of the mass media was to communicate to the public what the military regime had to say, not offer a forum for public debate, and certainly not a forum for public debate that included civil society.

However, in the 1980s, what O'Donnell and Schmitter (1986) call "the resurrection of civil society" was accompanied with a flourishing of alternative media that was, like civil society itself, diverse and relatively autonomous. Alternative media provided civil society a venue to have their voices heard by a wider audience, reflecting and reinforcing this civil society activity. In Chile, the power of the media to bring about political change in interaction with civil society was showcased during the 1988 plebiscite and the No campaign that ended the Pinochet regime (Crofts Wiley 2006). However, this democratizing potential of the media and civil society met new challenges with the rise of what Oxhorn (2011) calls neopluralism.

As in most of Latin America, the return to electoral democracy in Argentina and Chile came with market-oriented economic reforms. In Chile, these market-oriented reforms were mostly implemented by the military regime, and in Argentina they were most fully implemented by President Carlos Menem, beginning in 1989. The reforms not only affected employment security, health, education, pensions, and economic inequality, which Oxhorn (2011) outlines, they also restructured the mass media and thus how the media shape the public sphere and represent civil society. The mass media reflect and reinforce neopluralism and citizenship as consumption.

In Chile, Pinochet waited to fully apply market-based economic reforms to the media sector until just prior to leaving office in 1990. During the military regime, newspapers continued to be private companies, but those that remained were supporters of Pinochet. They were able to expand their companies by buying up opposition newspapers, creating a duopoly in which most newspapers were owned by either El Mercurio Group or Copesa, even today. As the government privatized television and reduced trade regulations, these two media groups were in a good economic position to take advantage of the opening market. The first cable provider in the country, Intercom, was owned by El Mercurio Group. The first non-cable private TV channel was bought by Pinochet supporter Ricardo Claro, and aired in 1990.

The flourishing alternative media from the late 1980s had benefited from international solidarity funds that aimed to help end the military regime. With the resumption of electoral democracy, this funding ended and alternative media were left to compete in a market that was far from equal. Not only were the Pinochet-supporting media economically secure, they also owned the only printing presses in the country with a capacity for national distribution, and received large amounts of guaranteed state advertising, and businesses were reticent to advertise in alternative media (Bresnahan 2003; Léon-Dermota 2003). By the end of the 1990s, almost all the alternative media had closed.

In Argentina, there were six years between the return of electoral democracy in 1983 and the state implementation of market-based economic reforms to the media sector. During these six years, *Página/12*, a national left-of-centre newspaper with the goal of promoting democracy and human rights, and pursuing watchdog journalism, was established. This encouraged the other two national newspapers to compete, and a subsequent flourishing of watchdog journalism exposed audiences to a wide variety of issues and perspectives from civil society (Waisbord 2000).

However, beginning in 1989 and slowly expanding until approximately 2001, the government implemented market-oriented economic reforms, which privatized all media outlets that were not already private, deregulated ownership limits across territory and mediums, and opened up foreign investment. Like in Chile, these reforms favoured those companies that had economically benefited from the military regime and thus could easily afford to buy the newly privatized radio and TV stations. This contributed to media ownership concentration and made Grupo Clarín the largest media group in the country, owning the newspaper with the largest circulation, 35 per cent of the print market, 60 per cent of the cable market, and the two leading broadcast companies in Buenos Aires (Becerra 2015; Blanco and Germano 2005; Mastrini et al. 2014). In response, the 2009 broadcasting law (the Audiovisual Communication Services Law) sought to break up this media ownership concentration and included a provision that required 33 per cent of frequencies to be distributed to nonprofits. However, in practice, little changed as a result of the law (Becerra 2015, 105).

Digital media that began with websites in the 1990s and social media in the 2000s emerged in this private and deregulated environment. Thus, while a significant amount of scholarly attention has been given to the Internet's mobilizing potential, recent scholarship has begun to more critically examine how private and deregulated social media reflect and reinforce many of the same features of media found with neopluralism. For example, algorithms are set up to support advertising (Van Dijck and Poell 2013; Guardino 2019). Pressures to produce twenty-four-hour online news content require journalists to produce more stories with less time, resulting in the use of fewer sources and less investigative research by journalists (Guardino 2019; Bonner 2019). Moreover, studies show that these unregulated technologies often reflect and reinforce, in the online world, "real world" class and racial inequalities and their associated economic, technological, power, and knowledge resources (Schradie 2018; Lupien 2020). In this media environment, everyone is free to use or access the media. However, their voices compete with each other and become fragmented, and economic resources elevate some voices over others. In what follows I examine three key ways that the media has reflected and reinforced neopluralism and citizenship as consumption: reinforcing plebiscitary democracy, elevating economically powerful voices through public relations, and criminalizing protests.

MEDIA AND PLEBISCITARY DEMOCRACY

Oxhorn shows that neopluralism in Latin America provides strong political rights, but limits them primarily to elections and voting. This, he argues, increases the gap between citizens and the political elite. The "plebiscitary nature of neopluralism" expects citizens to consume public discourse and react but not participate (Oxhorn 2011, 78). Governing through polling epitomizes this relationship. As Oxhorn explains, "The decision to participate [in a poll] is deliberately random and initially made by others, the participant has no choice but to remain anonymous, there can be no debate among participants, and the decision regarding the focus of the poll is not made by the participant" (2011, 79). The importance of polls to neopluralism is reflected and reinforced in the mass media.

Ideally, journalists spend time investigating a story, interviewing many sources, including a variety of civil society sources. Through these sources, news stories reflect the heterogenous nature of public opinion, encourage debate between different viewpoints, and highlight areas of agreement. However, deregulated private media have profit as their primary goal. Aside from advertising, media companies can make money by hiring fewer journalists to produce more stories more often. With less time allotted to journalists, polls, of varying quality, are quick ways for the media to present public opinion and act as proxies for democratic participation. While the media in many Latin American countries increasingly publish public opinion polls, their history in Chile is particularly emblematic of neopluralism.

In Chile, prior to 1987, public opinion polls were rarely conducted and mainly limited to uses in the social sciences. Indeed, one study found that only seventy-one public opinion polls had been conducted in the country from 1957 to 1986 (Cordero 2009, 81). When the 1988 plebiscite on Pinochet's leadership was announced, the number of public opinion polls exploded. The same study identified eighty-two such polls from 1987 to 1988. With the return of electoral democracy in 1990, public opinion polls have become a regular feature of news reporting. Certainly, since 1999, the media has increasingly published their own public opinion polls (Cordero 2009, 79). However, they continue to rely primarily on other entities, often civil society organizations, to conduct these polls.

Of course, polling is expensive, especially if done well. Thus, not all civil society organizations have the ability to produce them. Those that do are often conservative foundations, research centres, and companies, and their polls are among the most cited in the mass media. For example, two civil society organizations whose polls are regularly disseminated in the media are Citizen Peace (Paz Ciudadana) and the Centre for Public Studies (Centro de Estudios Públicos, or CEP). Citizen Peace was founded in 1992 by El Mercurio Group owner and Pinochet supporter Agustín Edwards. CEP was founded in 1980 by Pinochet-supporting political and business leaders.[1] One of its founders was then director of *El Mercurio* (1978–82), Arturo Fontaine Aldunate. One study of the history of CEP explains that the organization was established to support Pinochet's market-based economic reforms (Jara Barrera 2019). The participation of El Mercurio Group, Chile's most important media group, in the foundation of both of these think tanks highlights the significant links between media and civil society that reflect and reinforce the dominant economic model.

Beyond polling, civil society organizations are rarely mentioned in the mass news media. One study found that the inclusion of civil society voices in Chile dropped by nearly 50 per cent from 1990 to 2011. Their presence as sources in news stories fell from 11 to 6.1 per cent and their mention as actors in the news dropped from 18.1 to 9.2 per cent (Hughes and Mellado 2016, 58). Even during the dramatic 2019 social uprising, a study of news coverage of the police violence found that only 15 to 16 per cent of quotes or paraphrasing on police actions came from human rights organizations or international organizations, combined (Bonner and Dammert 2021, 6). While social media offers civil society organizations the possibility of skipping traditional mass media and speaking directly to the public or political leaders, many civil society organizations, especially the most marginalized, struggle to reach large audiences (Lupien 2020). Occasionally civil society organizations are included in polls. For example, during the massive student protests in 2011, CEP began to include students in their polls on public confidence in various political actors (CEP 2015). However, CEP, not the students, controlled the questions being asked.

The Chilean case exemplifies the plebiscitary approach to democracy as found in neopluralism, while drawing our attention to its impact on media–civil society interactions. Media-published polls, while primarily reducing citizens to consumers of ideas, do not entirely exclude civil society from political participation. Those civil society organizations with access to economic and media power are able to better produce and use polls to support their ideas and interests. They shape the topics on which the public are asked to comment, and when they are asked, and can use the mass media to assert the results as public opinion.

THE RISE OF PUBLIC RELATIONS

When the public sphere supports a strong civil society comprised of a diversity of autonomous organizations that demand inclusion in the state but resist subordination, then a wide range of ideas and interests can help shape government policies and the political, socio-economic, and civil rights of citizenship. As Oxhorn (2011) details, these policies and rights emerge through interactions between state actors and citizens through the meaningful participation of civil society. However, the plebiscitary quality of neopluralism fragments civil society, elevating the impression that the media, like the polls they publish, represent the voice of the people. Thus, while policy change and the expansion of rights can be obtained without the support of the media or even despite the opposition of the media, media support makes both much easier. For many civil society and state organizations, public relations then offers an appealing path to participation in these debates.

The same market-based media reforms that make public opinion polls attractive to journalists also favour journalists' increased use of public relations material. Public relations, especially prepared articles, photos, video, and audio clips, help journalists to produce more stories quickly. The public relations industry first emerged in the United States in the late ninetieth century and gradually expanded, particularly in the US and the UK. Its importance increased exponentially in those countries starting in the 1980s (MacNamara 2014, 73–4; Moloney 2006, 32). It first appeared in Latin America in the late 1950s but began to grow rapidly with the return of electoral democracy and governments' implementation of market-based economic reforms in the 1990s (Ferrari and França 2011, 49–50). In both regions, the public relations industry continues to grow. While its origins are in the private sector, its use by state and civil society organizations has expanded significantly over the last few decades. Of course, effective public relations requires economic and human resources. These resources are not distributed evenly between the state and civil society, nor *within* the state and civil society. This distorts the public sphere, as economic resources largely determine the extent and nature of participation and thus impacts the social construction of citizenship.

Generally, state actors dominate debate in the mediatized public sphere. Yet, within the state, not all state actors have equal access to professional public relations, creating inequalities within the state. What Oxhorn refers to as the "marketization of the rule of law" includes the ability of different state actors within the criminal justice system to publicize themselves as worthy of state resources and to have their voices, over other state actors, amplified in mass media discussions on crime and security.

In Chile, the Carabineros, Chile's national uniformed police, have a large and very well-funded professional communications department. After a scandal in 1985, during the Pinochet regime, the Carabineros invested heavily in reforming and professionalizing their communications department. Among other things, they provide media training to their personnel, provide prepared material for journalists in all formats, and run sophisticated advertising campaigns (Bonner 2013). In 2015, there were approximately sixty people working in their communications department. By contrast, that same year the Investigations Police (Chile's non-uniformed police) had seven people in their communications department and the prison guards service (Gendarmería) had fourteen (Bonner 2019, 109).[2] Prison guards, in particular, spoke of the consequences of their inability to communicate to the public: being unable to explain the important role that prisons play in the rehabilitation of prisoners leads to prisons being underfunded and unable to provide this rehabilitation. Interviewees from the Ministry of the Interior and the Public Prosecutors' Office all spoke of the difficulties they faced in challenging the discursive frames used by the Carabineros, contributing to policies that benefitted the Carabineros rather than the criminal justice system as a whole (Bonner 2019, 116).[3]

In Argentina, communications, at least during the Kirchner governments (2003–15), was centralized in the executive. Consistent with the plebiscitary state–society relations of neopluralism, the populist government sought to control its direct communication with "the people" on pressing questions of security and criminal justice. Certainly, this increased their ability to frame crime as something that is best resolved with preventive socioeconomic polices. However, the importance they placed on the media, as a measure of public support, led not only to the government asserting control over public relations and the mass media (in ways consistent with controlled inclusion) but to the mediatization of policymaking (governments choosing policy based on whether they think the media will present those policies positively or not).

For example, after an important incident of police wrongdoing in 2010, President Cristina Fernández de Kirchner appointed Nilda Garré as Minister of Security, with the task of reforming the Argentine Federal Police. However, when "tough on crime" political leader Sergio Berni was appointed as Secretary of Security in 2012, he gained far more positive media attention than Garré, especially from conservative media. This elevated Berni's political importance, skuttled plans for police reform, and eventually contributed to Garré's resignation in 2013 (Bonner 2016; Bonner 2019, 114).

Civil society organizations are at a disadvantage in the mediatized public sphere, as journalists prefer the authoritative and official sources that state actors provide. Yet civil society organizations are not disadvantaged equally. In both countries, the voices of civil society organizations who can afford professional communications departments are heard more often than those who cannot. Professional communication departments allow civil society organizations to have a dedicated person or staff who can follow the news cycle, know when and how to intervene, and have the knowledge, skills, and funds to produce quality prepared materials. In both countries, these inequalities favour civil society organizations with strong funding and positions that align with dominant state and media actors. Social media has not levelled the playing field, as, among other issues, professional communications staff know how to use social media more effectively and consistently (Bonner 2019; Schradie 2018). Moreover, some civil society organizations, especially the most marginalized, have been targets of online harassment and state surveillance, a situation that can lead such organizations to self-censor or avoid using social media altogether (Lupien et al. 2021).

Using the example of the rule of law again, there are important inequalities in how civil society organizations in Chile and Argentina participate in this public debate. In Chile, the most prominent civil society organization in media discussions on crime and security is Citizen Peace. It is funded by some of Chile's wealthiest donors, such as Banco de Chile, Falabella, and El Mercurio Group. It has a professional communications department, an alignment with the dominant media frame regarding insecurity, and was founded and is directed by the Edwards family (the owners of El Mercurio) (Bonner 2019, chap. 6). The organization reinforces the dominant frame that crime is the most pressing issue facing the country and that increased policing is the solution. Human rights organizations that seek to draw attention to police violence generally do not have professional communications assistance. Indeed, some, like the Ethical Commission Against Torture, do not even have an office. Even those organizations that do have professional communications assistance, such as Amnesty International Chile, are unable to use it as effectively as Citizen Peace.[4]

In Argentina, of eighteen civil society organizations interviewed that work on issues of crime, security, or police violence, only two had professional public relations assistance. These are the Centre for Legal and Social Studies and the Provincial Commission for Memory. Both organizations are well funded and are able to provide journalists with prepared material such as statistics and timely information on trials, and the latter runs an alternative press agency (andaragencia.org). These organizations' contribution to human rights–oriented public debate on crime and security is important. However, their reform-oriented approach is not shared by many less-well-funded civil society organizations (Bonner 2019, 140–2).

Of course, there are moments when civil society organizations can gain significant and positive mass media coverage without a professional public relations assistant. For example, if an organization frames their goals, ideas, or interests in a manner that is consistent with that used by a media outlet or the government, then the organization is more likely to be heard. In Argentina, the Coordinadora contra la Represión Policial e Institucional (CORREPI), a left-wing anti-police-violence organization with little funding, has received coverage in conservative media whenever their political positions intersect (e.g., both opposed the Kirchner government). However, such opportunities are often inconsistent and infrequent compared to organizations with strong public relations capabilities.

As Habermas argues, public relations aims to "engineer consent," and in so doing the publicist subverts the public sphere (1962/1991, 194). The "general interest" no longer emerges from "a rational agreement between publicly competing opinions" because "the publicist self-presentations of privileged private interests have adopted it for themselves" (195). Neopluralism thus fragments civil society into a market-based competition to define public opinion that, owing to the costs of public relations, favours those with economic and political resources. Certainly, protests can be a cheap form of public relations. However, as the next section reveals, economic structures shape how the media cover these events.

MEDIA AND THE CRIMINALIZATION OF PROTESTS

Oxhorn argues that protests, like elections, are plebiscitary in nature. They are able to paralyze governments and act as a veto over specific policies (Oxhorn 2011, 3). Massive demonstrations, he argues, "are a double-edged sword that invite manipulation of the crowd by opportunistic leaders at the same time that they establish the undemocratic precedent of extraconstitutional popular vetoes" (2011, 14). In contrast, he argues, a strong civil society is one that is autonomous, in the sense that civil society organizations "define and defend their interests in interaction with other actors, including the state" (2011, 12). It is about conflict and compromise, with a "thin" level of consensus that necessitates that civil society organizations self-limit their "demands and expectations (even reluctantly) with other civil society actors" (2011, 13). Thus, rather than civil society organizations being antagonistic toward the state and other civil society organizations, a strong civil society is comprised of organizations that interact in the public sphere with other actors in a manner that, ideally, brings about change and entails compromise (2011, 17). This requires that civil society organizations be organized and empowered enough to negotiate with the state once protests and media have drawn attention to their issue, and that the state is willing to make the profound political and economic changes needed to address citizens' most pressing concerns around issues such as education, health, employment, and pensions. Neopluralism weakens civil society by creating conditions that make it more likely that the media and political leaders will criminalize protests. The frame of criminality dismisses civil society organizations as illegitimate public sphere actors. Once criminalized, they lose their negotiating power with the state, since public opinion is likely to turn against them.

Chile, as Oxhorn identifies, is an ideal model of neopluralism. The conservative media in Chile have a long history of criminalizing strikes and protests (Salazar 1990, 1994; Bonner 2014). Pinochet's market-oriented media reforms created a conservative mass media duopoly. Not only do these media continue with news coverage that criminalizes protests, but there are now added commercial benefits to doing so. First, crime news is cheap, entertaining, quick to produce, plentiful, and draws large audiences. This has elevated the voice of the police as the quickest source for producing crime news. Many journalists on the crime beat start their day at the

Carabineros communications department (Bonner 2019, 92). When protests occur, media outlets have strong existing relationships with the police and are motivated not to harm these relationships, as it could reduce their access to the regular crime news that they rely on. Thus, often, mass media outlets send their police journalists to cover protests (Bonner 2014, 171). Police, aiming to justify their repression of protests, are motivated to frame protesters as criminals, and these protesters are then often described in media reports as *lumpen*, delinquents, vandals, hooded (*encapuchados*), or violent people (*violentistas*), or even as linked to soccer hooliganism (*barra bravas*) and drug trafficking (Bonner 2014; Bonner and Dammert 2021).

In reaction to this coverage, political leaders on both the left and the right have passed legislation that further criminalizes protests. For example, in response to student protests in 2006, *El Mercurio* reported that President Bachelet's government had:

> prepared a new law that will be applied more rigorously against all those who are caught [during protests] provoking disturbances in the street. According to high-level sources in the Interior Ministry, the initiative is due to the preoccupation of the executive with the almost zero per cent of formal changes laid by the Public Ministry in relation to the number of people arrested.[5]

That is, the issue is not the arbitrary arrests, but rather the insufficiency of the laws available to charge protesters. Similarly, during the 2019 Chilean social uprising, *El Mercurio* quoted President Piñera as stating that his government would use the Internal Security Law against protesters who "have incited, promoted, fostered or participated in the commission of serious crimes."[6] A week later, Piñera clarified that "the modern concept of national security is related to those who impede the normal functioning of the state and the normal functioning of society."[7] In short, protesters are criminals who pose a serious threat to the state and will be confronted with the most powerful laws available.

Of course, civil society can bring about political change despite the influence of the media (Hughes and Mellado 2016). For example, some modest changes to education policy came as a result of the 2006 student protests in Chile. However, as Oxhorn notes, the failure of civil society to bring about fundamental change to the education system was, in part, the result of the eventual loss of public support. The public had come to equate political participation with "protests, destruction and lawlessness" (Patricio Navia, quoted in Oxhorn 2011, 129). The media played a role in the public's interpretation of the protests in this manner. This can be seen most clearly when police repression of protests becomes excessive. In these instances, state actors aim to limit the policy consequences of police actions by reducing these actions to the excesses of individual officers or suggesting that they are justified given the threat that police face from protesters (Bonner 2014, chap. 10).

Indeed, despite national and international condemnation of police repression of protests during the 2019 social uprising, Chilean mass media continued to rely predominantly on the police, and their state supporters, as their primary sources for news coverage (Bonner and Dammert 2021). These sources justified the repression, which included sexual abuse and thousands of ocular wounds, as necessary and proportionate, given the criminal threat the protesters posed (Bonner and Dammert 2021). To be sure, despite this coverage, the 2019 protests did eventually result in a change in government, talk of police reform, and attempts at constitutional reform. Yet, as noted earlier, the Carabineros have a well-funded communications department that is skilled in public relations, and benefits from a media system that profits from journalists' reliance on the police as an authoritative source. Consequently, the police successfully managed this image crisis, and police reform was taken off the public agenda by the end of 2021.

Neopluralism provides little space in the public sphere for protests, as protests challenge people's freedom of movement and the belief that the best balance of interests emerges from "some form (however limited) of free competition among individuals in their rational pursuit of their self-interest," not collective action (Oxhorn 2011, 56). As shown, in Chile, neopluralism combines with coerced marginalization, albeit the latter is more restrained (for most but not all citizens) than repression under the authoritarian regime. In democracy, the rule of law can be used to justify police repression of protests.

Similar to Oxhorn's case study of Mexico, in Argentina, neopluralist democracy "represents an uneasy mix of citizenship as co-optation and as consumption" (2011, 186–7). The media underwent profound privatization and deregulation from 1989 to 2001, which, like in Chile, favoured media groups that had benefited from the military regime (1976–83). By the late 1990s, media coverage of crime had substantially increased, as such news is cheap, plentiful, and profitable (Bonner 2019; Fernández Roich 2017). However, for historical reasons, journalists in Argentina are more reticent than Chilean journalists to use the police as an authoritative source (Bonner 2019). Instead, clientelism plays a more important role in how and when media actors use the protest-as-crime frame.

Most media in Argentina rely on state advertising for a significant portion of their revenue. Governments distribute this advertising strategically to their clients in exchange for uncritical support (Becerra 2015). This practice increased significantly with the Kirchner governments (2003–15; and as vice president, 2020–23) (O'Donnell 2007). Indeed, even the 2009 broadcast law reform maintained the government's power to distribute state advertising. Consequently, media coverage of protests reflects both market and clientelist pressures, creating unique opportunities and limitations to the inclusion of civil society voices in the public sphere.

When protesters' demands correspond with the views of a media outlet's clientelist network, those protesters are more likely to receive positive media coverage by that outlet and their demands are more likely to be heard by large audiences. For example, on 11 June 2021, approximately 15,000 *piquetero* (unemployed workers), along with the organizations 29 de mayo and Organización Clasista Revolucionaria (civil society organizations from the popular classes), protested the Fernández–Kirchner government's policies addressing unemployment and the pandemic. The protest received substantial positive news coverage on the conservative news outlet La Nación's television channel, LN+.[8] In contrast, the conservative media are more likely to cover protests that favour the Kirchner government in a manner that either criminalizes their behaviour or emphasizes the chaos or financial costs of protests. For example, a 2016 *piquetero* protest against the Macri government was framed as "violent," justifying the use of rubber bullets against them by police.[9]

In turn, protests that favoured the Kirchner government received substantial positive coverage in government-supporting media. Beginning in 2004, the Kirchner governments had an official protest management policy of dialogue, not repression (Perelman 2008; Bonner 2014). Such dialogue generally gained positive media coverage (especially in Kirchner-supporting media) but often came with predetermined outcomes and acted as an opportunity for cooptation.

This was the case during an anti-mining protest in Catamarca in 2012 in which conflict, including police repression, led the Kirchner government to call for "dialogue" (Taylor and Bonner 2017). The dialogue proposed was between national and provincial governments and excluded civil society organizations. Its aim, as then governor of Catamarca, Lucía Corpacci (a supporter of the Kirchner government), put it, was to build "the necessary social consensus [in order to grow] Catamarca mining."[10] Reducing or ending mining, which the environmentalists who were protesting were calling for, was not part of the discussion. The Kirchner-supporting media's positive coverage of the remedy of "dialogue" reduced the space available for civil society organizations to challenge the government's position or persuade the public of the strength of their position.

Protests are thus managed as public relations events that either showcase public support for the government or ignore, reject, or criminalize the protests. In this manner, the media reinforce the plebiscitary nature of protests, in which protests are the passing of judgment on elite positions. This media frame limits the potential role of protests as a first step toward initiating or establishing meaningful avenues for exchange and compromise between the autonomous ideas and interests of state and civil society actors.

CONCLUSION

Oxhorn offers us an important vocabulary for understanding the social construction of citizenship. His concepts of controlled inclusion, coerced marginalization, and neopluralism reveal significant challenges to the development of a strong civil society in Latin America and draw our attention to practices that could contribute to the erosion of democratic citizenship in the region and elsewhere. His theoretical framework centres on state–civil society relations. However, as this chapter has argued, his concepts are equally relevant to understanding the place of mass media in the social construction of citizenship. Thus, with only small adjustments, his framework can highlight how the state's chosen economic development model structures the mass media and its ability to reflect and reinforce a strong or weak civil society.

Oxhorn's theory of the social construction of citizenship opens many new questions for further research, the most pressing of which is how citizenship as consumption can be challenged in ways that strengthen civil society, rather than weaken it in new (or old) ways. His framework suggests that the state's economic development model will be part of the answer, and, as I have argued, so will the associated media reforms.

NOTES

1 The founders of CEP are Sergio de Castro Spíkula (Chicago school economist and Minister of Livestock [Hacienda] under Pinochet [1976–82]), Jorge Cauas Lama (Minister of Livestock [Hacienda] under Pinochet [1974–76]), Pablo Baraona Urzúa (a leader of the Chicago Boys and Minister of the Economy under Pinochet [1976–78]), Julio Philippi Izquierdo (conservative lawyer and Minister of State under President Alessandri [1958–64]), Roberto Kelly Vásquez (former member of the Chilean army), Arturo Fontaine Aldunate (director of *El Mercurio* from 1978–82), and Carlos Urenda Zegers (business owner, lawyer, and adviser to the large economic groups) (Jara Barrera 2019, 229–30). From 1987 to 2015, the chairman was billionaire Eliodoro Matte (whose family wealth comes from forestry and paper products).

2 Author interviews with Ariella Olivares (head of communications for the Gendarmería) in Santiago (3 July 2015), and an anonymous member of public affairs (asuntos públicos) for the Investigations Police (Policía de Investigaciones, or PDI), in Santiago (7 July 2015).

3 Author interviews with anonymous employees from the communications department of the National Prosecutors of the Public Ministry, in Santiago (15 July 2009); three anonymous employees from the communications department, Ministry of the Interior, in Santiago (18 June 2009, 3 July 2015, 15 July 2015); and three anonymous employees from the Ministry of the Interior, in Santiago (17 June 2009, 2 July 2015).

4 Author interviews with anonymous members of Comité Ética contra la Tortura (30 June 2015), and Amnestía Internacional Chile (Amnesty International Chile), in Santiago (1 July 2015).

5 Rodrigo Vergara and Francisco Águila, "Gobierno prepara dura ley contra violentistas," *El Mercurio*, 7 June 2006, C5. My translation.

6 "Presidente llama a acuerdos por la paz, la justicia y la Constitución tras jornada de graves desmanes," *El Mercurio*, 13 November 2019. My translation.

7 Donoso, M, "Las tensiones que reveló el acta del Cosena," *La Tercera*, 20 November 2019. My translation.

8 Author notes from viewing LN+ via YouTube, 11 June 2021. In another example, see La Nación, "Miles de piqueteros se concentraron en Plaza de Mayo con reclamos de planes y trabajo," 12 May 2022.

9 For example, La Nacion, "La Gendarmería desalojó con balas de goma una violenta protesta de piqueteros en una autopista," 25 August 2016.

10 "Corpacci: 'La minería se desarrolla orgullosamente en Catamarca,'" *Página/12*, 14 February 2012. My translation.

REFERENCES

Becerra, Martín. 2015. "Transgresión, propaganda, convergencia y concentración: El sistema de medios en el kirchnerismo." In *¿Década Ganada? Evaluando el legado del kirchnerismo*, edited by Carlos Gervasoni and Enriquie Peruzzotti, 89–111. Buenos Aires: Random House Mondadori.

Blanco, Daniela, and Carlos Germano. 2005. *20 años de medios y democracia en la Argentina*. Buenos Aires: La Crujía.

Bonner, Michelle D. 2013. "The Politics of Police Image in Chile." *Journal of Latin American Studies* 45, no. 4: 669–94.

Bonner, Michelle D. 2014. *Policing Protest in Argentina and Chile*. Boulder, CO: Lynne Rienner (First Forum).

Bonner, Michelle D. 2016. "Rethinking Debates on Media and Police Reform in Argentina." *Policing and Society* 26, no. 8: 925–43.

Bonner, Michelle D. 2019. *Tough on Crime: The Rise of Punitive Populism in Latin America*. Pittsburgh, PA: Pittsburgh University Press.

Bonner, Michelle D., and Lucía Dammert. 2021. "Constructing Police Legitimacy During Protests: Frames and Consequences for Human Rights." *Policing and Society*. https://doi.org/10.1080/10439463.2021.1957887.

Bresnahan, Rosalind. 2003. "The Media and the Neoliberal Transition in Chile: Democratic Promise Unfulfilled." *Latin American Perspectives* 30, no. 6: 39–68.

Caimari, Lila. 2017. *While the City Sleeps: A History of Pistoleros, Policemen, and the Crime Beat in Buenos Aires Before Perón*. Oakland, CA: University of California Press.

Cane, James. 2011. *The Fourth Enemy: Journalism and Power in the Making of Peronist Argentina, 1930–1955*. University Park, PA: Pennsylvania State University Press.

Carter, Roy E., and Orlando Sepúlveda. 1964. "Some Patterns of Mass Media Use in Santiago de Chile." *Journalism Quarterly* 41: 216–24.

CEP (Centro de Estudios Públicos). 2015. "Encuesta CEP y confianza en Carabineros." PowerPoint prepared for author by Ricardo González T., Coordinator, Public Opinion Area.

Cordero, Rodrigo. 2009. "Dígalo con números: La industria de la opinión público en Chile." In *La Sociedad de la Opinión: Reflexiones sobre encuestas y cambio político en democracia*, edited by Rodrigo Cordero, 69–92. Santiago: Ediciones Universidad Diego Portales.

Crofts Wiley, Stephen B. 2006. "Assembled Agency: Media and Hegemony in the Chilean Transition to Civilian Rule." *Media, Culture and Society* 28, no. 5: 671–93.

Dahl, Robert A. 1971. *Polyarchy: Participation and Opposition*. New Haven, CT: Yale University Press.

Davies, Matt. 1999. *International Political Economy and Mass Communication in Chile*. New York: St. Martin's Press.

Deibert, Ronald J. 2020. *Reset: Reclaiming the Internet for Civil Society*. Toronto: House of Anansi.

Fernández Roich, Cynthia. 2017. *Media and Crime in Argentina: Punitive Discourse During the 1990s*. New York: Palgrave Macmillan.

Ferrari, Aparecida María, and Fabio França. 2011. *Relaciones públicas: Naturaleza, función y gestión en las organizaciones contemporáneas*. Buenos Aires: La Crujía.

Fox, Elizabeth, and Silvio Waisbord. 2002. "Latin Politics, Global Media." In *Latin Politics, Global Media*, edited by Elizabeth Fox and Silvio Waisbord, 1–21. Austin, TX: University of Texas Press.

Gamson, William A., and Gadi Wolfsfeld. 1993. "Movements and Media as Interacting Systems." *Annals of the American Academy of Political and Social Sciences* 528: 114–25.

Guardino, Matt. 2019. *Framing Inequality: News Media, Public Opinion, and the Neoliberal Turn in US Public Policy*. New York: Oxford University Press.

Habermas, Jürgen. 1991. Originally published 1962. *The Structural Transformation of the Public Sphere: An Inquiry into a Category of Bourgeois Society*. Cambridge, MA: MIT Press.

Habermas, Jürgen. 2006. "Political Communication in Media Society: Does Democracy Still Enjoy an Epistemic Dimension? The Impact of Normative Theory on Empirical Research." *Communication Theory* 16, no. 4: 411–26.

Hallin, Daniel C., and Paolo Mancini. 2004. *Comparing Media Systems: Three Models of Media and Politics*. New York: Cambridge University Press.

Hughes, Sallie, and Claudia Mellado. 2016. "Protest and Accountability Without the Press: The Press, Politicians, and Civil Society in Chile." *International Journal of Press/Politics* 21, no. 1: 48–67.

Human Rights Watch. 1998. *The Limits of Tolerance: Freedom of Expression and the Public Debate in Chile*. New York: Human Rights Watch.

Jara Barrera, Maximiliano. 2019. "El Origen de Centro de Estudios Públicos: Importando el liberalismo para una transición ideológica, 1980–1982." *Historia 396* 9, no. 1: 225–53.

Léon-Dermota, Ken. 2003. *And Well Tied Down: Chile's Press Under Democracy*. Westport, CT: Praeger.

Levitsky, Steven, and Lucan A. Way. 2010. *Competitive Authoritarianism: Hybrid Regimes after the Cold War*. Cambridge, UK: Cambridge University Press.

Lupien, Pascal. 2020. "Indigenous Movements, Collective Action, and Social Media: New Opportunities for New Barriers?" *Social Media and Society* 6, no. 2: 1–11. doi.org/10.1177/2056305120926487.

Lupien, Pascal, Gabriel Chiriboga, and Soledad Machaca. 2021. "Indigenous Movements, ICTs and the State in Latin America." *Journal of Information Technology and Politics* 18, no. 4: 387–400.

MacNamara, Jim. 2014. *Journalism and PR: Unpacking "Spin," Stereotypes, and Media Myths*. New York: Peter Lang.

Mastrini, Guillermo, Martín Becerra, and Santiago Marino. 2014. "State Intervention and Market Structures: The New Overview of the Argentinian Audio-visual Sector." In *Media Systems and Communication Policies in Latin America*, edited by Mireya Márquez-Ramírez and Manuel Alejandro Guerrero, 194–207. New York: Palgrave MacMillan.

McCombs, Maxwell E., and Donald L. Shaw. 1972. "The Agenda-Setting Function of Mass Media." *Public Opinion Quarterly* 36, no. 2: 176–87.

Moloney, Kevin. 2006. *Rethinking Public Relations: PR, Propaganda and Democracy*. London: Routledge.

O'Donnell, Guillermo, and Philippe C. Schmitter. 1986. *Transitions from Authoritarian Rule: Tentative Conclusions about Uncertain Democracies*. Baltimore, MD: Johns Hopkins University Press.

O'Donnell, María. 2007. *Propaganda K: Una maquinaria de promoción con el dinero del estado*. Buenos Aires: Planeta.

Oxhorn, Philip. 2011. *Sustaining Civil Society: Economic Change, Democracy, and the Social Construction of Citizenship in Latin America*. University Park, PA: Penn State University Press.
Perelman, Marcela. 2008. "La regulación de los operativos de seguridad en el marco de las manifestaciones públicas: Arances y cuestiones pendientes." *Cuadernos de Seguridad* 6 (April): 51–66.
Salazar, Gabriel. 1990. *Violencia Política Popular en las "Grandes Alamedas": Santiago de Chile, 1947–1987*. Santiago: Ediciones Sur.
Salazar, Gabriel. 1994. "Construcción de Estado en Chile: La historia reversa de la legitimidad." *Proposiciones* 24: 92–110.
Scheufele, Dietram A., and David Tewksbury. 2007. "Framing, Agenda Setting, and Priming: The Evolution of Three Media Effects Models." *Journal of Communication* 57, no. 1: 9–20.
Schradie, Jen. 2018. "The Digital Activism Gap: How Class and Costs Shape Online Collective Action." *Social Problems* 65: 51–74.
Schradie, Jen. 2019. *The Revolution that Wasn't: How Digital Activism Favors Conservatives*. Cambridge, MA: Harvard University Press.
Taylor, Ariel, and Michelle D. Bonner. 2017. "Policing Economic Growth: Mining, Protest, and State Discourse in Peru and Argentina." *Latin American Research Review* 52, no. 1: 112–26.
Valenzuela, Sebastián, Martina Piña, and Josefina Ramírez. 2017. "Behavioral Effects of Framing on Social Media Users: How Conflict, Economic, Human Interest, and Morality Frames Drive News Sharing." *Journal of Communication* 67, no. 5: 803–26.
Van Dijck, José, and Thomas Poell. 2013. "Understanding Social Media Logic." *Media and Communication* 1, no. 1: 2–14.
Waisbord, Silvio. 1998. "The Unfinished Project of Media Democratization in Argentina." In *Communicating Democracy: The Media and Political Transitions*, edited by Patrick H. O'Neil, 41–62. Boulder, CO: Lynne Rienner.
Waisbord, Silvio. 2000. *Watchdog Journalism in South America: News, Accountability, and Democracy*. New York: Columbia University Press.

6

The Media, Neopluralism, and the Public Sphere in Veracruz, Mexico

Julián Durazo Herrmann

How has the media contributed to the democratization of the public sphere in the state of Veracruz – a subnational state within the Mexican federation – since 2016? After eighty-seven years of hegemonic party rule (the Institutional Revolutionary Party, or PRI [Partido Revolucionario Institucional]), Veracruz belatedly transitioned to a plural party system,[1] in which both a coalition of the right-wing National Action Party (Partido Acción Nacional, or PAN) and the centre-left Party of the Democratic Revolution (Partido de la Revolución Democrática, or PRD), and the left-wing National Regeneration Movement (Movimiento de Regeneración Nacional, or MORENA) have occupied the seat of the subnational government since 2016.

In this chapter, I argue that Veracruz's longstanding tradition of political coverage and regional media diversity, and the existence of multiple technological platforms currently guarantees the existence of a diverse media system that includes numerous actors and issues. However, limitations in the dissemination of certain media and the difficulties certain actors face in obtaining real and direct coverage of their demands create a neoplural political system, in which democratic procedures are formally in force but reproduce important marginalization dynamics (Oxhorn 1998). Certain groups with high social capital have created alternative media that contribute to the formation of counter-publics (Fraser 2001). This allows for the dissemination and discussion of certain issues in thematically or sectorally restricted spaces.

It is undeniable that democratization has expanded and reinforced political and media pluralism in Veracruz. Cities, with good access to the Internet, with a more consolidated rule of law, and with organized movements better endowed with social and human capital, have benefited from this process. However, the rural areas of the state lag behind, deepening already very marked social inequalities. Furthermore, the digital divide has created sharply differentiated access to the public sphere.

However, maintaining a media vehicle and effectively navigating local political deliberation rules in order to shape public opinion and define the common good require significant access to human and financial capital, which is often beyond the reach of lower classes. It also requires spaces of deliberation that are relatively free of violence, which is not the case everywhere in Veracruz. Even in more democratized areas, in the absence of explicitly inclusive public policies, existing media structures promote the reproduction of authority structures inherited from the previous regime (Marques-Pereira and Garibay 2011; Bonner, this volume). This reinforces social inequalities despite the formal opening of the public sphere, fragments the arenas for debate, excludes key issues from public debate, and isolates individual efforts to overcome this overwhelming trend. Briefly stated, it promotes neopluralism.

THE THEORETICAL FRAMEWORK

In this chapter I use the liberal definition of democracy, which, in addition to the division of powers, free and competitive elections, alternation between parties in government, and freedom of association, prescribes social pluralism, freedom of expression, and access to varied and independent sources of information (Dahl 1971). In turn, democratization is the transition from a regime that could be classified as authoritarian to a liberal democracy, a process marked by elite agreements (O'Donnell and Schmitter 1986). As self-governing polities, Latin America's subnational units, such as Veracruz, are also subject to democratization and its pitfalls.

A characteristic feature of Latin American democratization processes – marked by the double transition to democracy and neoliberalism – is neopluralism (Oxhorn 1998, 2014). This phenomenon is marked by the formal and actual recognition of democratic pluralism, combined with persistent structural socioeconomic inequality and fragile institutional systems of checks and balances, and accountability mechanisms (Isunza 2013). Hybrid political systems thus emerge in which formal democratic processes coexist with informal authoritarian practices, with the former legitimizing the latter and allowing for their reproduction and renewal. Because of their marginal role in federal politics and their propensity to nurture particular political cultures, subnational polities are prime breeding grounds for hybrid regimes (Durazo Herrmann 2010).

Neopluralism fragments society by forcing social groups to compete for the attention of a relatively weak and absent state and by closing public spaces for negotiating conflicting organizational logics (for example, between urban and Indigenous organizations, or between demands for access to land and protection of natural resources). These dynamics prevent the creation of common fronts that would facilitate the insertion in the public sphere of subordinated social groups and their demands. For this reason, in addition to reproducing historical inequalities, neopluralism makes social movements with fewer social, economic, and political resources invisible to the public sphere (Oxhorn 2014; see also Hilgers, this volume, and Robert and Brunet-Bélanger, this volume).

I resort to the notion of the public sphere – distinct from "public space" – to denote a virtual, non-physical space in which different social actors present and debate topics of their interest through rational deliberation, a process that creates a consensual understanding of the common good. In a democratic public sphere, political procedures are those of liberal democracy, and, in principle, there are no restrictions on access to the public sphere in terms of either actors or specific issues (Habermas 1962/1992).

The media play a fundamental role in the construction of the democratic public sphere, since they are the mechanism that allows mass societies to deliberate, giving publicity to all political activity and presenting to the public the actors involved in political debate, the issues discussed, and the arguments put forward. The media also help fulfill the values of pluralism and freedom of expression that define democracy (Matos 2012). Private media, dominant in contemporary societies, face the paradox of simultaneously having a public social communication mandate and a private profit imperative (Weber 1910/1999, Habermas 1962/1992). From a liberal perspective, it is the existence of competition and of varied and independent sources of information that allow for the construction of a truly democratic public sphere (Dahl 1971).

Within federal countries, subnational states often become the home of subnational media systems, in which local media vehicles coexist with and complement national networks, creating a properly subnational public sphere. With its many radios, papers, and news sites, Veracruz certainly has an autonomous media system and hence its own public sphere (see the overview of Veracruz below).

Despite is democratic promises, the actually existing public sphere (Fraser 2001) is limited in its democratic character by processes that enforce and reproduce various social hierarchies (class, gender, ethnicity, regional, etc.). The resulting heterogeneity translates into differentiated access to democratic processes for certain social actors and an unequal capacity to concretely influence political decision making. Not all actors are equally admissible in the public sphere, nor do all issues have the same weight in their deliberations (Mazzuca 2010; Levy and Martínez 2019).

The expansion of freedom of expression derived from democratization does not by itself eliminate the important biases present in the media and inherited from previous periods. In Latin America, state attrition and the privatization of public broadcasters reinforced media concentration and consolidated private conglomerates, controlled by an oligarchy that imposed its economically liberal and socially conservative agenda (Oxhorn 2003). Despite the legal recognition of community broadcasting, social movements were reduced to marginal spaces and vehicles, consolidating neopluralism in the media system. This is as much the case at the national level as at the subnational level (Prudêncio et al. 2022; Bonner, this volume).

In some cases, depending on their human and financial capacity to create effective media, some groups may form counter-publics, that is, small spheres isolated from the general public sphere in which these groups and their allies can deliberate on the issues of their concern, and formulate consensus regarding these – though restricted to the particular counter-public – thus contributing to a haphazard and heterogeneous democratization process (Fraser 2001). As we will see in the case of Veracruz, these counter-publics can be defined both territorially – for example, referring to an urban neighbourhood or a rural community – and sectorally – within unions or other social movements.

Both the marginalization that results from neopluralism and its effects on the media system sustain heterogeneous political systems in which different democratic processes work at different speeds, selectively and often marginalizing different social groups in order to maintain and legitimize a formally democratic regime, while also reproducing existing social hierarchies and tolerating limited-scope dissidence and resistance at the margins. Marginalization is an important constraint on the ongoing democratization processes in Latin America (González Casanova 1965/2013; Oxhorn 2003). The concrete workings of marginalization are local, and the actors involved – in enforcing them as much as in enduring them – are subnational in nature.

Therefore, focusing on Veracruz allows us to apply the subnational comparative method to my analysis (Snyder 2001). Studying a geographically constrained polity with almost all the trappings of a state (including population, territory, and government, as well as a partial claim to legitimate coercion, but not internationally recognized sovereignty) makes field research both easier and more profound. We can thus identify how local dynamics – often obscured by national bias and its focus on large-scale trends based in the capital – give concrete meaning to neopluralism, affecting citizenship, the public sphere, and, ultimately, the quality of democracy.

While I do not study other empirical cases in this chapter, uncovering how the media embodies neopluralism in the Veracruz public sphere contributes to enlarging the theoretical depth and the applicability of the concept of neopluralism, as well as its relationship to the social construction of citizenship – this book's main aim (see Montambeault and Hilgers, this volume). We thus gain a finer understanding of democratization and its challenges in Mexico and beyond.

METHODOLOGY

Veracruz is an ideal case to study the links between media, neopluralism, and the public sphere, as it embodies many of the elements of a neoplural polity: an extremely diverse society, numerous but fragmented and disconnected social organizations, late alternation, and incomplete democratization. Moreover, it has one of Mexico's richest and most prestigious media ecosystems, but also faces precariousness, charges of corruption, and intense violence against journalism.

To answer the research question – how has the media contributed to the democratization of the public sphere in the Mexican state of Veracruz since 2016? – I study how the Veracruz media system contributes to the make-up of a subnational public sphere. I also identify the actors participating in this system and the issues that they address there. Finally, I seek to determine how the Veracruz public sphere has changed (Azevedo 2004; Muñiz 2015).

My analysis runs from October 2016 to March 2023. This time frame begins with the abrupt end of the last PRI government of Veracruz and includes the two alternation governments: Miguel Ángel Yunes Linares, from the PAN–PRD coalition (2016–18), and Cuitláhuac García Jiménez, elected by MORENA for the period 2018 to 2024. This period encompasses, in public discourse at least, the alternation and consolidation of democracy in Veracruz.

In this chapter, I study the Veracruz media system as a whole, including commercial and community radio, news websites, and print newspapers and magazines. I also analyze the role of the subnational public broadcaster (Radio y Televisión de Veracruz, or RTV). I do not address commercial television, dominated by Mexico City conglomerates with little subnational production (Mariscal 2011) – although they capture a substantial part of the audience.

I draw on data from a survey of the available scientific literature and a selection of media items collected in the field. It should be noted that, given the research question, I focus on the "general," political, and (given the prevalence of insecurity and violence) crime sections of the various news media. I do not address topics such as business, sports, or celebrities.

I also conducted a series of semi-directed interviews in August 2019 and between June and December 2022. During these two periods, I spoke with journalists (reporters, editors, and media owners), politicians, and subnational officials, as well as with social organizers in various cities in the state of Veracruz. In 2022 I also did an ethnography on the relationship between journalists and politicians, and the issues they addressed in the two weekly press conferences held in Xalapa, the state capital: the leader of the opposition, the PAN (on Monday mornings), and the Labour Party (Partido del Trabajo, or PT, a small left-wing party in coalition with MORENA, on Tuesday mornings). For security reasons, in this chapter I cite all published texts, both scientific and journalistic, but have anonymized all the interviews.

BRIEF OVERVIEW OF VERACRUZ

Located along Mexico's Gulf Coast, the state of Veracruz is the country's fourth state by population, with over eight million inhabitants (INEGI 2024). Embraced by both the ocean and Mexico's highest mountains, Veracruz is divided into ten distinct geographical regions.

Mexico's traditional hegemonic party, the PRI, remained in power in Veracruz from 1929 to 2016 – sixteen years after alternation at the federal level. Amid growing accusations of corruption and authoritarianism, Javier Duarte, the last PRI governor, fled the country after he was issued an arrest warrant a few weeks before the end of his term (Olvera 2018). In 2016, Miguel Ángel Yunes, supported by a PAN–PRD coalition, was elected governor for a two-year transition mandate. In 2018, Cuitláhuac García Jiménez, of MORENA, was elected governor on the coattails of President Andrés Manuel López Obrador's overwhelming federal victory. MORENA also won an absolute majority in the state legislature and several important municipalities, including Xalapa (OPLE 2019).

Since 2006, and as with the rest of Mexico, there has been an enormous increase in violence in Veracruz, especially related to drug trafficking, forced disappearances, and other forms of organized crime. President Felipe Calderón's war on drugs and the related security crisis led to more than five thousand deaths and seven hundred disappearances in Veracruz alone. All regions of the state were affected (Pozos 2021).

In 2019, Veracruz had over forty daily newspapers (Prensa Escrita 2020), 106 TV channels and 1,149 radio stations (RPC 2020). Although there is significant instability in the industry, Mexico's oldest newspaper still in circulation, *El Dictamen*, has been published continuously in the Port of Veracruz since 1898, while other important local newspapers such as *Diario de Xalapa* and *La Opinión* of Poza Rica date from the 1940s (Del Palacio 2015, 130). Journalists in particular were targeted during the wave of violence: at least thirty-five reporters and news editors have been killed or disappeared since 2010 (Del Palacio 2018). Veracruz thus bears the paradox of simultaneously being one of Mexico's richest and most dangerous media systems.

THE EVOLUTION OF THE PUBLIC SPHERE IN VERACRUZ SINCE 2016

How has the media contributed to the democratization of the public sphere in the state of Veracruz since 2016? My hypothesis is that the deep tradition of political coverage, regional media diversity, and the existence of multiple technological platforms in the media in Veracruz have fostered the (neo)plural media system. However, the shortcomings of this system contribute to creating a neoplural polity (Oxhorn 1998). Certain media contribute to the creation of counter-publics that allow for the dissemination and discussion of specific topics on the public agenda in otherwise restricted thematic or sectoral spaces (Fraser 2001).

THE VERACRUZ MEDIA SYSTEM

Since 2016, the media involved in the public sphere in Veracruz have changed remarkably. Many print media – newspapers and magazines – have disappeared, some definitively, others going digital. Beyond the global crisis of print media, the Veracruz government drastically reduced advertising expenditures – even completely suspending them between May and October 2019 – as a response to perceived excesses from the Duarte government, thus drastically reducing the resources available to the Veracruz media, forcing them to survive from sales, subscriptions, and private advertising.

Consequently, many "front" media – which lived off government advertising agreements, with a limited information apparatus ("*chayoteros*"[2] and "*boletineros*"[3]) and without other sources of income (sales or advertising) – disappeared. Among the best known of these were Xalapa's *El Sentinela* and *Política*.

The big traditional newspapers such as *El Dictamen*, *Diario de Xalapa*, *El Buen Tono* (Córdoba and Orizaba), *El Liberal del Sur* (Coatzacoalcos), and *La Opinión* (Poza Rica), among others, continue to appear in print. However, some have reduced their format from standard to tabloid and all of them have reduced their print run and their number of pages per issue. Others, such as *El Mundo* (Córdoba and Orizaba, founded in 1960), *Crónica* (Xalapa), *El Regional* (Coatepec), and *Vanguardia* (Poza Rica), recently became exclusively web-based.

In an attempt to overhaul the Veracruz media system, the subnational Social Communication Law, adopted by Governor García Jiménez seeks to reduce opaque and discretionary government advertising spending. To do this, the law mandated a media registry that requires the receipients of government advertising revenue to be publicly known, be formally registered as companies, bid on contracts, pay taxes, and be accountable.

During the preparation of the register, the Veracruz government spent nothing on advertising. Currently, available resources are relatively limited. However, resource allocation continues to be discretionary and non-transparent: despite a formal request for access to information, the General Coordination of Social Communication (or Spokesperson's Office), which is responsible for the register, claims to have no advertising contracts with the media, thereby contradicting the law, the fact that government advertising is ubiquitous, and several conversations with journalists (Durazo Herrmann 2025).

The creation of independent subnational accountability bodies, such as the Veracruz Institute for Access to Information (Instituto Veracruzano de Acceso a la Información, or IVAI), created in 2007, or the state legislature's auditing office (Órgano de Fiscalización Superior del Estado de Veracruz, or ORFIS, created in 2012), also contributed to the publicizing of the actions of the subnational government. Using information from these bodies, some journalists have highlighted problems such as malpractice in public works and budgetary underspending in certain asgencies (Valdez 2022). However, most access-to-information requests come from academics while journalist ignore these sources (IVAI 2021).

Since 2016, the number of digital media in Veracruz has skyrocketed. In addition to former print media going digital, many other news sites have appeared. Some of these are large companies, have won state journalism awards, and have a relatively large number of reporters and other employees (such as Al Calor Político and AVC Noticias). Others are maintained by autonomous journalists or small teams, such as Istmo Alternativo (Coatzacoalcos), Sigüenza Comunicación (Xalapa), or Monitor Huasteco (Chicontepec).

These media are called "independent" to distinguish them from the large media groups (although, to ensure sufficient income, many reporters work for both types of outlets). However, their political independence is questionable, because, despite political change and legal reform, these media remain – by their own admission – dependent on government advertising contracts and *chayotes*.

In big cities, many of these media consist of formal websites, with well kept and frequently updated web pages. Most often, reporters at these media have university dgrees in journalism or related subjects and follow the values of professional journalism in both form and content. In contrast, in small cities and rural areas, journalists are often self-taught and frequently present their news – without necessarily verifying its veracity – on simple Facebook pages or poorly organized websites, with little editorial care and irregular frequency.

In some cases, the smaller media allow their owners to cover issues and social groups with which they have political affinities, thus bringing issues related to women's rights, the environment, or human rights to the public agenda (Testigo Púrpura, Defensa Verde). This journalism – called "alternative" to distinguish it from independent media – sometimes does not clearly separate information from political affinity; moreover, these media are frequently short lived.

The Veracruz tradition of opinion journalism, dating from the mid-twentieth century (Del Palacio 2015), continues. Printed newspapers, such as *Notiver* in Veracruz or *Diario de Xalapa*, devote a large portion of each edition (up to 50 per cent) to regular columns that comment on the issues of the day with clear positions for or against the government (municipal or subnational). As discussed earlier, these columns disseminate gossip and political speculation that sometimes confuse rather than clarify public debate (Freije 2020). Outside the public spotlight, some columnists also demand *chayote* in exchange for favourable coverage.

In the case of the public broadcaster, after MORENA came to power in 2018, RTV developed new programming with political content, including reports, open-microphone debates, and public service programs on health, agriculture, education, etc. It has also made efforts to extend its coverage, reaching 100 per cent of the Veracruz territory through radio, although only 60 per cent through television. However, RTV continues to serve the political interests of the subnational government in power, in particular by promoting its graphic identity and frequently broadcasting exclusive interviews with the governor and other high-level officials (RTV 2023).

Some community or sectoral media have also become consolidated. This is the case of the community radio stations of Teocelo and Huayacocotla, in Indigenous areas of the state, and of the news service Insurgencia Magisterial within the subnational section of the national teachers' union. Managed as cooperatives, these media hold strong symbolic meaning for those who identify with them. In addition, in the case of Indigenous radio stations, they are frequently the only local media, since these localities do not hold any economic or journalistic interest for other media (Ramos 2007).

The political diversity of the Veracruz media is impressive, both among print and digital media. In Xalapa and the Port of Veracruz there are newspapers with conflicting political positions that sometimes communicate with each other or refute positions published by their competitors (cf. *Diario de Xalapa* and *La Jornada Veracruz* in the state capital or *Imagen* and *Notiver* in the port). Alternative and independent news sites further enrich this media system.

Despite the large number of existing media and their thematic and regional diversity, the expansion of the Veracruz public sphere has given rise to neopluralism. The relative opacity of the content and financing of the Veracruz media continues to undermine their credibility, especially among social movements (Aguilar Sánchez 2019) and – surprisingly – among the journalists themselves, who in this way exemplify the mistrust and competition that characterizes their industry.

In Veracruz, media dynamics fragment the public space while upholding formal democratic procedures. Pluralism underscores a clear division between large media – traditional or web based – and small – independent or alternative. The former monopolize most of the audience and most of government advertising, creating a vicious circle in which a handful of large media organizations continue to grow, while a large number of smaller media survive precariously.

Paradoxically, the growing presence of exclusively web-based media concentrates media diversity – and the access to the information it produces, however biased it may be – in urban areas, where access to the Internet for both journalists and the public is guaranteed. Rural areas, especially those in the mountainous areas of Veracruz – incidentally the areas with the highest density of Indigenous populations – have far less cell phone and Internet coverage. There are thus fewer media vehicles, and these are concentrated in Facebook pages, or small commercial or community radio stations with little reach. Fragmentation and isolation significantly contribute to the neoplural nature of the Veracruz media system.

The arrival of MORENA to subnational power changed the dynamics between the government and the media. Beyond the implementation of the media register and the opaque management of subnational advertising resources, Governor García Jiménez and his officials publicly and systematically disqualified opposition media, accusing them of hypocrisy and spreading false news, while constantly praising government media (García Jiménez 2023).[4] The angry reactions of the affected media also contributed to polarizing the public debate (Oliva Radio 2023; Quezada Bielma and Sánchez Abreu 2023).

The violence that has plagued Veracruz since the beginning of the twenty-first century has had important consequences on its media system, especially as journalists became frequent victims (del Palacio 2018; Olvera 2018). In response to the violence, in 2012 the government set up the State Commission for the Attention and Protection of Journalists (Comisión Estatal para la Atención y Protección de los Periodistas, or CEAPP). However, the commission's lack of legal capacity, the scarce resources allocated to it, and an ambiguous internal governance model have limited its work (Cervantes Díaz 2024).

In an attempt to consolidate its institutional position and increase its legitimacy, both vis-à-vis the state and among journalists, the CEAPP has expanded its original protection mandate to include professionalization and social recognition programs, including the State Journalism Prize in various categories (special feature, chronicle, photojournalism, etc.). The CEAPP thus seeks to increase its political relevance while strengthening the Veracruz media system and, consequently, the public sphere.

However, these programs have widened the gap between so-called "professional" journalists – those with college degrees and more stable, higher paying jobs than average – from "empirical" journalists, who work in more marginal areas with much fewer resources, both material and human. However, "empirical" journalists are the ones who are most exposed to violence because they work far from the big cities and cover the most violent areas, where the state and its justice procurement systems are largely absent (Bustos González 2016). The resulting elitism creates a hierarchical and exclusive system that further fragments the Veracruz media system (Cervantes Díaz 2024). The resulting neoplural tensions increase the mistrust that afflicts the Veracruz media system both internally and externally, and significantly reduce its contribution to the subnational public sphere.

Despite profound political change, the media continue to reproduce the factors that foster both the political and economic marginalization inherited from the authoritarian regime, and neo-pluralism (Oxhorn 2014). The transition to web-based media exacerbates this marginalization by dividing the state geographically into zones of exclusion and inclusion – and these, further, into thriving and relatively prosperous elite spaces with marginalized and fragmented media.

THE ACTORS OF THE VERACRUZ PUBLIC SPHERE

The Veracruz public sphere has many access points. In a striking parallel with the Habermasian model (1962/1992), cafés are, in Veracruz, important loci of public discussion. Present in the main squares of all large cities – and in many medium-sized ones (Veracruz and Xalapa, but also Coatzacoalcos, Córdoba, and Huatusco, among others) – these cafés serve as platforms for spontaneous declarations and as arenas of deliberation, protected by a relaxed and cordial atmosphere (Zamudio Román 2005).

These political cafés are frequented by federal, subnational, and municipal officials who wish to make public statements and offer collective interviews. Organized social movements – unions, sports, or neighbourhood associations – and individual people seeking to add a topic to the public debate – businessmen, relatives of disappeared persons, religious leaders – also visit these spaces. Journalists – both cause and consequence of this deliberative dynamic – patronize these cafés even when governors, mayors, or party leaders are not holding press conferences in them.

Despite cafés being thought of as open spaces, visiting a café entails significant financial costs for those wishing to set the public agenda. Tradition dictates that the person addressing the media offer breakfast to the journalists present, a proposition that can easily cost 8,000 pesos (about US$400).[5] Although some people do not offer breakfast, their ability to attract journalists – and to enter the public debate – declines significantly as a result, becoming more dependent on their personal relationships with the journalists present than on the content of their statement.

Furthermore, these statements frequently end up being "saved up," postponed for another day, for a slower news day, thus losing their immediacy and relevance. For instance, on 11 October 2022, a poor woman made a statement to defend her plot of land from encroachment by a big hotel corporation, but it was only published on 13 October in the inner pages of just one newspaper (Pérez Melo 2022). A neopluralistic system thus hinders access to the public sphere for small, subordinate actors.

Press conferences are a more formal space to set the media agenda and intervene in public deliberation. In some cases, they are regular and open, such as the weekly press conferences of the PAN and the PT. These parties offer breakfasts to the participating journalists and small gifts on certain occasions, such as St Valentine's Day. They are also the occasion – more or less discrete – to distribute *chayotes*. At these press conferences, discussion between reporters and politicians is heated, questions are sharp, and answers are frank. These dynamics, however, are not reflected in news publications, which often uncritically repeat formal declarations and official press releases; in this instance, hybridization – using democratic procedures to legitimate undemocratic ones – is clearly at play.

Other press conferences are frequent, but irregular, such as those of the governor or parliamentary leaders. Others are intermittent, such as those of the General Prosecutor's Office or the ORFIS. In these cases, journalists only attend by invitation, which allows the political actor to select the participants at their discretion – and thus reward journalists with access (or punish them with lack of access) to important first-hand information. Journalists informally criticize this practice, but do not presume to have the ability to change it. Therefore, institutional political actors have a guaranteed voice in the public sphere, slanting deliberation in their favour.

Among social actors, however, access to the media and the public sphere is unequal, despite the diversity of the Veracruz media system. On the one hand, some civil associations formed by businessmen have privileged access to the media due to the friendship and business ties between their leaders and the owners of certain media outlets. This is the case of the Veracruz Tourism Council, made up of hoteliers, restaurateurs, and transporters. Its director has a permanent and regular column, as well as a live broadcast space (*Al Calor Empresarial*) on Al Calor Político, one of the most important news websites in Veracruz. Combining its members' resources and taking advantage of its government contacts, the Tourism Council constantly organizes festivals and other events that promote its members' businesses and receive wide and favourable coverage in the media.

Other organizations must make greater efforts to receive media attention. This is the case for the groups of relatives of the disappeared

– one of the main manifestations of violence in Veracruz – who are forced to come up with more innovative initiatives to attract some media attention, since their press conferences and weekly demonstrations are no longer enough. To do this, they cover the trees in front of the municipal and state government palaces in Xalapa with decorative balls during the Christmas season, constantly carry photographs of their missing relatives, and begin any public intervention by talking about their relatives, the circumstances of their disappearance, and the state of their case – though usually with no noteworthy progress (Zavaleta 2023).

In still other cases, as befits a neoplural system, mistrust and conflict mark the relationships between social movements and the media, such as when feminist activists expel male journalists from their demonstrations or other public activities, or when student associations accuse reporters (of any gender) of being university or government infiltrators. Because of physical aggressions against journalists on these occasions, coverage is often negative and focuses on the violent dimensions of these movements. These movements' lack of strategies to garner greater presence and better coverage in the media is quite evident – consider the posters from the "Marcha Kon Nosotres" demonstration on 8 March 2023, in the Port of Veracruz, which aggressively excluded any journalistic coverage (Fernández 2023).

Organizers from several social movements, such as from the major LGBTQI+ organization and the search collectives – those searching for disappeared persons – confirmed this lack of a media strategy but said they had other priorities – mostly building direct channels with public officials and legislators. Remarkably, competition for the attention of political authorities outside of public scrutiny is one of the key features of neopluralism (Oxhorn 2003).

The weak presence of the state is another (Oxhorn 1998). In terms of the media system, and despite its efforts to renew itself, RTV's contribution to the expansion of the public sphere has been relatively poor. For instance, the public broadcaster has a single reporter to cover the thirty-four municipalities of the Huasteca, which has a population of over one million but whose roads are in extremely poor condition. Many regional social groups inevitably escape this reporter's attention. Furthermore, local media devote little attention to these groups, since they are more focused on covering the "general" (political) and crime beats. For the case of Indigenous communities, they receive essentially no coverage whatsoever, even in municipalities with a population over 90 per cent Indigenous.

As pointed out above, some social movements have created their own media. In some cases, these have lasted for decades. La Voz Campesina, from Huayacocotla in the Huasteca region in the northern part of the state, was founded in 1961 and is the oldest community radio in Mexico. It shares its programming widely with community radio stations in Veracruz and other parts of the country. The Xalapa-based Insurgencia Magisterial also exchanges content with similar outlets throughout Latin America. Democratization and recent federal communications reforms have reduced political pressure and judicial harassment against alternative media, but, given their limited audience outside their immediate circle, these media still function more as counter-publics than as instruments for accessing the public sphere.

Despite consistent efforts to develop social clout, these media have a limited reach: unable to penetrate the general sphere of deliberation, because of their geographic isolation and their thematic specificity, these media create stable counter-publics rather than become effective vehicles for intervention in the subnational public sphere. The more recent alternative media suffer from a lack of recognition, or even opposition, in their own localities, while the more established ones face challenges in renewing themselves and in keeping their counter-public mobilized. It is worth noting that, despite the size and strength of their social organizations, the search collectives and LGBTQI+ groups in Veracruz have not developed their own media.

The prevailing violence in Veracruz produces paradoxical effects in terms of access to the public sphere. On the one hand, the self-censorship exercised by the media and journalists leads to a silencing of the activities, motivations, and participants of social groups. Violence thus clearly handicaps the subnational public sphere.

On the other hand, coverage of the victims of violence is one of the only ways that the popular classes can receive journalistic coverage in a way in which they can recognize themselves. These features reflect how hybridization affects the public sphere – produced by the combination of caciques (local political bosses), little affected by democratization, and with criminal violence (Ortega Vidal 2022). Along with the contemporary inclination for spectacular coverage, the perverse form of inclusion that the "yellow press," or sensationalist press, produces, explains its popularity and its oversized presence in the Veracruz media.

THE TOPICS OF PUBLIC DEBATE

In Veracruz, the issues that institutional actors – government, the legislature, political parties – bring to the public agenda are considered "general," and deserving of the most important coverage. They are, together with criminal affairs, the main journalistic beat, especially among the so-called empirical journalists. Therefore, journalists organize their work routines around the contingent political situation and the institutional agenda. In other words, institutional political actors set the media agenda – and that of the public sphere.

Press conferences – whether in the café, at government facilities, or at party headquarters – include a formal statement, often accompanied by a printed bulletin, and a question-and-answer period. These exchanges are the occasion for heated debates and severe criticism, but they are rarely published, as opposed to the politicians' statements and bulletins, which often make the front page. Thus, the interaction between politicians and journalists has a highly ritualized formal and public dimension that is controlled by institutional actors, and an informal and open feature that is not published (Zamudio Román 2005). This dynamic reflects the stifling effects of *chayotes* and advertising contracts on public debate.

Journalistic routines reinforce the outsized weight that institutional actors have in the public agenda. In addition to the global trend towards statement-based journalism, in which the lack of time and resources prevents journalists from consulting other sources, the economic precariousness of the Veracruz media and their journalists makes them dependent on advertising contracts (essentially governmental) and handouts (including *chayotes*). Only a few professional journalists, working mostly for opposition media, resort to official statistics or access to information requests to verify official claims (IVAI 2019).

The endemic nature of the violence in Veracruz is reflected in the content of the media. Further away from large urban areas, where political activities are concentrated, the presence of the yellow press is overwhelming. A journalist from Coatzacoalcos said that, in their city, "the crime beat is the only source of news." In Tierra Blanca, another reporter commented: "half of our news is motorcycle accidents."

The yellow press concentrates the best photojournalists in the state, producing photojournalism that is macabre in both graphic and narrative terms. Coverage is so explicit that the specialized newspaper *Órale!* – available in local editions in Coatzacoalcos, Veracruz, and Xalapa – bears the warning, "not for sale to minors." Currently, all print newspapers have a crime section; *La Jornada Veracruz*, which lacked one until the end of 2019, included a crime section at the behest of street vendors, who favour these themes when announcing the newspapers they sell, as they attract more customers. A good number of commercial radio newscasts and websites are also entirely dedicated to crime coverage.

In a significant paradox, and despite its omnipresence and its graphic and explicit nature, the Veracruz yellow press has a marked tendency toward self-censorship. Both media and journalists consciously limit the topics they cover and publish to avoid putting themselves at risk, simultaneously limiting the public discussion of one of the state's most important problems: violence and its causes.

The Veracruz media rarely identify those responsible for the crimes committed, or their motives, especially when dealing with organized crime, and instead focus mainly on the victims and the injuries they sustained. The media only identifies criminal actors when official sources make their names and affiliations public – frequently after they have been killed by the police (García et al. 2022). Publicity thus suffers and, with it, the democratic nature of the Veracruz public sphere.

The yellow press is ubiquitous and extremely detailed, but its coverage is superficial and lacks follow-up. Self-censorship also limits the search for exclusive news, as well as competition between journalists and investigative journalism, giving a superficial and repetitive character to the general content of the media. Some in-depth reporting has appeared, though mostly in the form of books published by publishers located in Mexico City (Mateos 2021; Zavaleta 2023). The contribution of the yellow press to the expansion of public debate is therefore quite limited.

Given the relevance that violence has in Veracruz, the coverage of public security policies is also frequent. However, informal political restrictions and self-censorship by the press mean that follow-up coverage is limited, let alone sufficient context in the initial reporting ("No hay guerra," 2019). Moreover, the media frequently enable the government's attempts to revictimize victims of murders, disappearances, or other attacks by accusing them of being involved in criminal activities or other wrongdoings (@CEAPP_V 2022). The media thus transmit into the public sphere the fragmentation dynamics characteristic of neopluralism.

Another form of opaque coverage is that which, under the pretext of covering a certain event, actually seeks to strike a political adversary. An example is the intense coverage of the mobilization against sexual harassment at the Universidad Veracruzana in the fall of 2022. The media covered the movement from afar, since their relations with the student associations were antagonistic and students excluded journalists from their demonstrations.

This did not stop the media from severely criticizing the university authorities (Castilla 2022). However, in private conversations, several journalists from Xalapa and the Port of Veracruz confirmed that the actual goal, encouraged through *chayotes*, from within the university itself and by sectors of the subnational government, was to destabilize the new rector and undermine his reform initiatives.

The effects of bad faith between the media and social groups have also been evident in the coverage of feminist movements, and especially of the march on 8 March, International Women's Day. The march was "separatist," exclusively for women, and thus excluded male journalists. When male journalists tried to cover the march from Xalapa's main park, some demonstrators forcefully asked them to leave. Media coverage the next day placed as much emphasis on the destruction caused by the march and the aggression suffered by a television reporter and his cameraman as on the protesters' demands ("¡Marea Morada!" 2023).

For their part, the demands of Indigenous peoples go almost entirely unnoticed in the Veracruz media system. In Xalapa, the press conferences and other activities of Indigenous movements receive marginal coverage, and is dependent on the friendly relations between activists and certain reporters, established during their student years (Hernández 2023). In the rural regions with the highest Indigenous population density, journalists claim that the difficulty of accessing the communities and their closure to foreigners prevents journalistic coverage. They also recount cases of retaliation following unfavourable coverage.

Some journalists espouse a notion of public service journalism in which social activities and demands are covered on a benevolent and voluntary basis. In some cases, this coverage is patronizing and condescending, as well as irregular and instrumental.

Oftentimes, reporters "save" news that is related to social groups to fill their production quota on lean days. Social coverage is thus often belated, losing its relevance. Moreover, these stories rarely make front page news.

Faced with this exclusionary system, some alternative media have been created in Veracruz seeking to build counter-publics where marginalized actors can discuss issues that have been excluded from public debate. They are thus examples of extant mechanisms for the political participation of poor people, but also of the challenges facing the social construction of citizenship (see Montambeault and Hilgers, this volume).

These counter-publics can be thematic in nature, like Testigo Púrpura, or union-based, like Insurgencia Magisterial, or they can be community media, like Radio Teocelo or La Voz Campesina. Although they do not cover all social mobilization fronts in Veracruz, these media seek to advance their political demands and to affirm a collective identity.

In some cases, coverage of social movements is the result of personal ideological commitments. For example, Testigo Púrpura conceived of itself as a news agency with a gender focus, regardless of the news covered. In addition to its own platform, Testigo Púrpura sought to make its own journalistic content available to other media. It was also one of the few Veracruz media engaged in fact-checking (Martínez García 2023). However, because of financial problems, Testigo Púrpura closed its doors in April 2023, underscoring the fragility of issue-based alternative journalism in Veracruz (Testigo Púrpura 2023).

La Voz Campesina in Huayacocotla is dedicated to defending natural resources and comunal access to them, and to broadcasting programs in Indigenous languages. Radio Teocelo promotes land rights and agrarian issues. Insurgencia Magisterial broadcasts the efforts of a group of local teachers to counteract the federal educational reform, promote union democracy, and disseminate the best education practices based on the teachings of Paulo Freire.

In conclusion, in the public debate, social demands are markedly subordinated to the official discourse and to the yellow press. There are spaces for open discussion among mainstream journalists, but these are hidden from the general public. Alternative media have divergent logics, do not meet in the public sphere, and do not develop effective coalitions with each other. The distrust among social movements and their lack of media strategies reproduce and exacerbate this marginalization. In this way, despite the existence of numerous media, covering the entire state of Veracruz and available on various platforms, the Veracruz media system contributes to the formation and reproduction of a neoplural political system.

VERACRUZ: A NEOPLURAL PUBLIC SPHERE

This study of Veracruz media uncovers the workings of a neoplural public sphere. The replacement of a hegemonic party – the PRI – by a democratically elected majoritarian party – MORENA – with little willingness to engage social organizations in open public debate is solid proof of this. The criminal violence that continues to plague Veracruz is another element of closure of the public sphere (Bustos González 2019). I found no formal evidence of elite agreements restraining democracy in Veracruz, but there is a clear accommodation of undemocratic actors, such as local caciques, giving rise to a hybrid regime (Aguilar Sánchez et al. 2021; Ortega Vidal 2022).

The imperfect penetration of the state also contributes to neopluralism, both in geographical terms, with significant blackout areas in rural and Indigenous regions, and in terms of the effective application of the spirit and letter of the law. The operation of the CEAPP and of the new Social Communication Law illustrate the reproduction of corruption and coercion dynamics that curb the development of a democratic public sphere, supporting legislation notwithstanding. As Oxhorn argues in this volume, through state weakness, neopluralism compromises the consolidation of the rule of law.

The recognition of political diversity and competition for the state's increasingly scarce resources have also fragmented the public sphere. The condescending tone with which the mainstream and so-called independent media treat social demands and the secondary importance given to these demands in their coverage, as well as the deep mistrust that social groups have of these media, leads to a hierarchical, or vertically controlled, and fragmented representation of social actors and their demands in the Veracruz public sphere (see also Bonner, this volume).

While some community radio and alternative digital media have managed to create durable counter-publics, others have failed due to insurmountable political and financial obstacles. Nonetheless, these counter-publics remain isolated and have not been able to harmonize divergent social demands. Their direct contribution to the Veracruz public sphere has thus been limited. Not surprisingly, in some cases, social movements prefer to deal directly with the government, even though this maintains their relative invisibility in the public sphere and makes them vulnerable to cooptation.

In conclusion, this chapter validates the original proposition that Veracruz's tradition of political coverage, regional media diversity, and the existence of multiple technological platforms have fostered a (neo)plural media system, which includes numerous actors and themes. However, geographic and sectoral fragmentation, political marginalization, and controlled inclusion all contribute to a neoplural political system, in which democratic procedures are formally in force, but which also reproduces and normalizes significant authoritarian practices.

By reducing the politico-territorial extent of the study, my subnational approach contributes to fleshing out pluralism as a political mechanism. This is because the effects of neopluralism are mostly informal and informed by local-level institutions and understandings. By clearly identifying the actors involved and better explaining the dynamics in which they engage, the insights of my study of Veracruz can easily be applied to other cases.

What remains less clear is the direction of causation. The exploratory work that I present here suggests that the media system is both a cause and a consequence of Veracruz neopluralism, in a complex relationship in which the media both serve as an arena for currently existing public deliberation and are participating actors in this arena. How this Janus-type paradox is resolved on the ground is a question for future research.

NOTES

I gratefully acknowledge the comments and suggestions received from the organizers and participants at the conference Still the Era of Neopluralism? Celebrating Philip Oxhorn's Legacy, at McGill University, and the Taller de investigación en comunicación y política, at the Facultad de Ciencias de la Comunicación of the Universidad Veracruzana. Funding for this research came from SSHRC grant no. 435-2017-1466, "Médias régionales et démocratisation subnationale en Amérique latine."

1 The first subnational state to undergo alternation in Mexico was Baja California, in 1989. The first federal alternation took place in 2000 (Carrasco Brihuega 2013).
2 *Chayotes* are money handouts that a politician or a public official gives to a journalist in exchange for favourable coverage for themselves or for attacking political adversaries in the media. *Chayoteros* are thus media and journalists that accept *chayotes* (Serna 2015).
3 A *boletinero* media or journalist publishes statements uncritically, without verifying their content or seeking other sources (Serna 2015).
4 In so doing, they followed the example of President López Obrador (López Obrador 2023).
5 For comparative purposes, the average monthly salary in Veracruz in the last quarter of 2022 was 4,590 pesos (Data México 2023).

REFERENCES

@CEAPP_V. 2022. "Exhorta #CEAPP a Poder Ejecutivo de #Veracruz evitar criminalizar a #periodista agraviado." Twitter, 24 November. Accessed 25 November 2022.

Aguilar Sánchez, Martín. 2019. "Mouvements sociaux et politique de gauche dans l'État de Veracruz, Mexique, 2010–2016." In *Les espaces publics, la démocratie et les gauches en Amérique latine*, edited by Julián Durazo Herrmann, 213–35. Quebec: Presses de l'Université Laval.

Aguilar Sánchez, Martín, Saúl Horacio Moreno Andrade, and Yolanda Francisca González Molohua. 2021. *Protestas y movilizaciones sociales en el Golfo de México*. Xalapa, Mexico: Universidad Veracruzana.

Azevedo, Fernando Antônio. 2004. "Agendamento da política." In *Comunicação e política*, edited by Antônio Canelas Rubim, 41–71. Salvador, Brazil: Compós/EDUFBA/UNESP.

Bustos González, Felipe. 2016. "Violencia y periodismo en Veracruz, 2004–2012." In *Resistencia y protesta social en el Sureste de México*, coordinated by Martín Aguilar Sánchez, 301–30. Mexico City: Universidad Autónoma Metropolitana.

Bustos González, Felipe. 2019. *Violencia contra periodistas en Veracruz: una pugna por la notoriedad pública, 2004–2016*. Thesis, Universidad Veracruzana, Xalapa, Mexico.

Carrasco Brihuega, Daniel. 2013. "Concurrence politique et démocratisation au Mexique." In *Réflexions sur le centenaire de la Révolution mexicaine: Un siècle bigarré*, edited by Julián Durazo Herrmann, 131–54. Quebec: Presses de l'Université du Québec.

Castilla, Juan David. 2022. "Caos en Facultad de Psicología UV," *El Heraldo de Xalapa*, 25 October, 1.

Cervantes Díaz, Antonio. 2024. *"Hemos crecido con esas instituciones": Análisis de la política pública para la atención y protección de los periodistas en Veracruz (2012–2022)*. Thesis, CIESAS-Golfo, Xalapa, Mexico.

Dahl, Robert. 1971. *Polyarchy*. New Haven, CT: Yale University Press.

Data México. 2023. "Veracruz de Ignacio de la Llave." Accessed 27 April 2023.

Defensa Verde. 2011. Accessed 28 April 2023.

Del Palacio, Celia. 2015. *Pasado y presente: 220 años de prensa veracruzana*. Xalapa, Mexico: Universidad Veracruzana.

Del Palacio, Celia. 2018. *Callar o morir en Veracruz: Violencia y medios de comunicación en el sexenio de Javier Duarte (2010–2016)*. Mexico City: Juan Pablos.

Durazo Herrmann, Julián. 2010. "Neo-Patrimonialism and Subnational Authoritarianism in Mexico: The Case of Oaxaca." *Journal of Politics in Latin America* 2, no. 2: 85–112.

Durazo Herrmann, Julián. 2025. "Las vicisitudes de la comunicación social." In *El Veracruz que vemos, el Veracruz que queremos*, edited by José Luis Ortega Vidal and Guadalupe Mar Vázquez, 23–32. Mexico City: Tirant lo Blanc.

Fernández, Sina. 2023. "5 claves que debes saber de las marchas del 8M en Veracruz" [5 keys you should know about the March 8th marches in Veracruz], *La Silla Rota Veracruz*, Xalapa, Mexico, 6 March. Accessed 7 March 2023.

Fraser, Nancy. 2001. "Repenser la sphère publique: Une contribution à la critique de la démocratie telle qu'elle existe réellement." *Hermès, La Revue* 31, no. 3: 125–56.

Freije, Vanesa. 2020. *Citizens of Scandal. Journalism, Secrecy, and the Politics of Reckoning in Mexico*. Durham, NC: Duke University Press.

García, Daflin, Abel Valdez, and Omar Celiseo. 2022. "Orizaba, 'Wounded' by Shootout." *El Mundo*, Orizaba, 13 September, 1.

García Jiménez, Cuitláhuac. 2023. Facebook post. Accessed 28 April 2023.

González Casanova, Pablo. 2013. *La democracia en México*. Mexico City: Era. Originally published 1965.

Habermas, Jürgen. 1992. *L'espace public*. París: Payot. Originally published 1962.

Hernández, Ángel. 2023. "International Mother Language Day and its Passage through Veracruz." TV *Azteca Veracruz*, Xalapa, Mexico, 21 February. Accessed 21 February 2023.

INEGI (Instituto Nacional de Estadística, Geografía e Informática). 2024. Accessed 8 March 2024.

Isunza, Ernesto, coord. 2013. *Controles democráticos no electorales y régimen de rendición de cuentas*. Mexico City: CIESAS.

IVAI (Instituto Veracruzano de Acceso a la Información [Veracruz Institute for Access to Information]). 2019. "The Exercise of the Right to Know Grew by 54% in Veracruz." *Accesa: Revista del IVAI*, no. 22 (January–June): 45–6.

IVAI (Instituto Veracruzano de Acceso a la Información [Veracruz Institute for Access to Information]). 2021. *Informe de actividades*. Xalapa, Mexico.

Levy, Charmain, and Andrea Martínez, eds. 2019. *Genre, féminismes et développement: Une trilogie en construction*. Ottawa: Presses de l'Université d'Ottawa.

López Obrador, Andrés Manuel. 2023. "Stenographic Version of the Morning Press Conference of President Andrés Manuel López Obrador." *AMLO: Official Site of Andrés Manuel López Obrador*, 21 April. Accessed 28 April 2023.

"¡Marea Morada!" 2023. *Notiver*, Veracruz, Mexico, 8 March, 1.

Mariscal, Judith. 2011. *Condiciones del mercado de televisión abierta en México*. Mexico City: Comisión Federal de Telecomunicaciones – Centro de Investigación y Docencia Económica.

Marques-Pereira, Bérengère, and David Garibay. 2011. *La politique en Amérique latine: Histoires, institutions et citoyennetés*. Paris: Armand Colin.

Martínez García, Luisa. 2023. "Experiencias de investigación sobre violencia machista." Conference at the Universidad Veracruzana, Boca del Río, Mexico, 10 March.

Mateos, Juan Eduardo. 2021. *Reguero de cadáveres*. Mexico City: Los libros del perro.

Matos, Carolina. 2012. *Media and Politics in Latin America*. London: I.B. Tauris.

Mazzuca, Sebastián. 2010. "Access to Power Versus Exercise of Power: Reconceptualizing the Quality of Democracy in Latin America." *Studies in Comparative International Development* 45: 334–57.

Muñiz, Carlos. 2015. "La política como debate temático o estratégico: Framing de la campaña electoral mexicana de 2012 en la prensa digital." *Comunicación y Sociedad* 23: 67–95.

"No hay guerra en contra de la Fiscalía General: CGJ." 2019. *El Dictamen*, Veracruz, Mexico, 13 August. Accessed 3 May 2023.

O'Donnell, Guillermo, and Philippe Schmitter. 1986. *Transitions from Authoritarian Rule: Tentative Conclusions about Uncertain Democracies*. Baltimore, MD: Johns Hopkins University Press.

Oliva Radio. 2023. Press release, 14 March.

Olvera Alberto, coord. 2018. *Veracruz en su laberinto*. Xalapa, Mexico: Universidad Veracruzana.

OPLE (Organismo Público Local Electoral). 2019. https://ine.mx/voto-y-elecciones/opl. Accessed 14 September 2020.

Ortega Vidal, José Luis. 2022. *Democracia violenta*. Coatzacoalcos, Mexico: Publitex.

Oxhorn, Philip. 1998. "Is the Century of Corporatism Over?" In *What Kind of Democracy? What Kind of Market*, edited by Philip Oxhorn and Graciela Ducatenzeiler, 195–217. University Park, PA: Penn State University Press.

Oxhorn, Philip. 2003. "Cuando la democracia no es tan democrática: La exclusión social y los límites de la esfera pública en América Latina." *Revista Mexicana de Ciencias Políticas y Sociales* 46: 131–76.

Oxhorn, Philip. 2014. "La sociedad civil de adentro hacia afuera: Comunidad, organización y desafío de la influencia política." *Revista Mexicana de Ciencias Políticas y Sociales* 59: 257–78.

Pérez Melo, Irineo. 2022. "Hoteliers in Martínez de la Torre Seek to Dispossess a Housewife of Her Land." *Jornada Veracruz*, Xalapa, Mexico, 13 October, 4.

Pozos, A. 2021. *Derecho y desaparición de personas: El cuerpo ausente como sujeto político*. Mexico City: Tirant lo Blanch.

Prensa Escrita. 2020. https://www.prensaescrita.com. Accessed 25 August.

Prudêncio, Kelly, Carla Rizzotto, and Rafael Cardoso Sampaio. 2022. *Atores coletivos em tensão: Uma década de pesquisa em comunicação e participação política*. Curitiba, Brazil: Editora CRV.

Quezada Bielma, Omar, and Juan Sánchez Abreu. 2023. Press release. Mexican Association of Communicators and Journalists, 14 March.

Ramos, Víctor. 2007. "La radio comunitaria frente a los grupos de poder." *Razón y Palabra* 59. Accessed on 3 May 2023.

RPC (Registro Público de Concesiones). 2020. Instituto Federal de Telecomunicaciones. https://rpc.ift.org.mx/vrpc. Accessed on 25 August 2020.

RTV (Radio y Televisión de Veracruz). 2023. https://www.rtv.org.mx. Accessed 28 April 2023.

Serna, Ana María. 2015. "Se solicitan reporteros." *Historia oral del periodismo mexicano en la segunda mitad del siglo XX*. Mexico City: Instituto Mora.

Snyder, Richard. 2001. "Scaling Down: The Subnational Comparative Method." *Studies in Comparative International Development* 36: 93–110.

Testigo Púrpura. 2023. https://testigopurpura.wordpress.com. Accessed 4 May 2023.

Valdez, Noemí. 2022. "¡'Año de Hidalgo'!" *Notiver*, Veracruz, Mexico, 1 October, 1.

Weber, Max. 1999. "Sociología de la prensa." *Revista Colombiana de Educación* 38–9. Originally published in German in 1910.

Zamudio Román, Isabel. 2005. *El café de La Parroquia de Veracruz: ¿Fuente de información o hábito reporteril?* Thesis, Universidad Veracruzana, Boca del Río, Mexico.

Zavaleta, Noé. 2023. *Las buscadoras: Madres que buscan a personas desaparecidas en México*. Mexico City: Harper Collins.

SECTION TWO

Comparative Perspectives

7

The Making of Immigrant Inequality in the US: The Privileging of Cubans

Susan Eckstein

Historically, governments have extended social, economic, and political rights, often sequentially. So, too, have they extended rights differentially, privileging certain groups over others. Phil Oxhorn has addressed these concerns in many of his writings over the years (see the introduction to this volume). Yet, he has not addressed how the lives of immigrants have shaped and been shaped by governments' differential awarding of rights. Although immigration is at a record high, we know little about how and why governments have granted different immigrant groups different rights, and the consequences of these decisions.

The US has been highly inegalitarian in its awarding of rights to immigrants, including rights to citizenship. Its political, geopolitical, and economic interests, as well as racial biases, have shaped the entitlements awarded to different immigrant groups, and its framing of immigrants' rights to certain rights. Yet, the differential awarding of entitlements has also been contingent on group influences. Below, I illustrate the interplay between societal and state dynamics in shaping Cuban and Haitian immigrant entitlements and how, as recipients of extensive entitlements, Cubans have become a force unto themselves, able to press for additional entitlements, furthering immigrant group inequities. Our understanding of citizenship and citizenship rights needs to be extended to immigrants.

US immigration policy was notoriously racist and exclusionary in the early to mid-twentieth century. While the US was not explicitly admitting foreigners based on skin colour, in the 1920s Congress passed legislation to limit country admissions to 3 per cent of the number of immigrants from that country who were living in the US in 1890, over thirty years in the past, when most immigrants were White, from northern Europe.

The landmark 1965 immigration reform, which remains in effect, introduced a so-called preference system that ostensibly put to rest racist country-based admissions. Instead, it prioritized the admission of relatives of US residents and persons with skills useful for the economy. Quite remarkably, however, at the November 1965 ceremony where President Lyndon Johnson signed the new legislation into law, after announcing that "from this day forth those wishing to emigrate to America shall be admitted on the basis of their skills and their close relationship to those already here," and no longer on the basis of where they were born, he extended an open-ended invitation to Cubans, and only Cubans, on the basis of their country of origin (see Eckstein 2022, 17). Cubans stood to gain not only from the shift in US immigration policy but also from declining European interest in immigration as opportunities in Europe improved after the Second World War. Cubans became one of the main immigrant groups, despite coming from a small country of around seven million people in 1960 and barely more than eleven million people sixty years later.

In formalizing the privileging of Cubans over other nationals, Johnson built on entitlements that both Presidents Dwight Eisenhower and John F. Kennedy previously had granted to Cubans. Since Castro came to power in January 1959, successive administrations extended a broad range of unique entitlements to Cubans that highlight inequities in Washington's treatment of immigrants. Below, I consider, theoretically, the role governments assume in the construction of citizenship. Then, I briefly summarize the entitlements the US offered to Cubans for over half a century, after which I detail how and why first President Barack Obama and then President Donald Trump retracted entitlements, though only partially. Comparisons with the US treatment of Haitians during the same years highlight how Washington has leveraged immigration to favour certain foreign-born immigrants over others in a manner that has infused new life into racist biases of old.

GOVERNMENT ROLE IN THE CONSTRUCTION OF CITIZENSHIP

Oxhorn has argued for a political economy perspective on civil society and citizenship. His body of work analyzes how reigning economic paradigms interact with politics to shape citizenship rights, and how economic context impacts civil society mobilization and inclusion (1998a, 1998b, 2011). Emphasizing not only historical problems of inequality and exclusion, but also opportunities for change, Oxhorn has written about the social construction of citizenship. Ideally, he argues, state and society act in synergy, with the state providing opportunities for civil society organization and civil society cooperating with the state to create policy, while holding the state accountable. Where civil society is representative of the panoply of interests – including the subaltern – that make up society, organizing autonomously and capable of both competing and cooperating with each other, its demands for inclusion can create a citizenship based on equal social rights (Oxhorn 2011).

While Oxhorn's empirical focus has largely been Latin America, his theoretical contributions are constructed on comparisons with North American and European political economies. He argues that Latin American civil society is comparatively fragmented and weak due to the timing and effect of industrialization and urbanization. Late, rapid industrialization in Latin America was capital intensive, limiting the expansion of industrial jobs and forcing an influx of rural migrants into the informal sector. The popular classes lacked the cohesion necessary to play a primary role in constructing citizenship. Conversely, early and comparatively slower industrialization and urbanization in Western Europe and North America created labour-intensive industrial sectors, with organized workers capable of taking agency and demanding social rights (Oxhorn 1998a).

Rather than focusing on the economic context as a driving factor behind state–society relations, I point to the role that state political interests may play. I show that international and domestic politics may drive governments to extend entitlements to certain subaltern groups, who then go on to promote greater entitlements for "their own." Cold War strategic concerns led US administrations to extend unique opportunities to Cuban immigrants, which enabled them to become politically influential to the point that they have been able to shape immigration policy to their own advantage, including after the Cold War's end. In contrast, with Haiti not serving Washington's geopolitical interests, Washington implemented exclusionary policies towards Haitian immigrants and aspiring Haitian immigrants. I show the political interests of governments to shape the social construction of social, economic, and political citizenship, in ways that may divide immigrant groups.

UNIQUE CUBAN IMMIGRATION ENTITLEMENTS

Unique entitlements granted to Cubans include special entry privileges, special rights to become lawful permanent residents and citizens if they entered the US without authorization, and special rights to benefits once settled in the US.[1] Successive presidents used their discretionary power to pile new entitlements onto entitlements granted by earlier administrations, and, on several occasions, Congress legislated unique prerogatives for Cuban immigrants.

For one, Cubans were granted multiple entry privileges. Presidents arranged, in total, for nearly one third of a million Cubans to be flown to America at the expense of US taxpayers, first with temporary and later with permanent entry rights that included a path to citizenship. They also admitted Cubans as tourists and as refugees when known to be neither, and permitted unauthorized Cubans to be paroled into the US, namely, given temporary entry and work rights, regardless of where they entered the country, whereas other immigrants could only be admitted at official ports of entry with immigration visas. In addition, Cubans have been admitted under a family reunification program while waiting for their visa priority dates to become current. While waiting, they, too, enjoyed work rights. Presidents even created unique immigration statuses to admit Cubans who circumvented Congressional entry restrictions;[2] they also allowed Cubans living in the US to operate a unique private program to admit new Cuban immigrants, and agreed to admit a minimum of twenty thousand Cubans yearly, a guarantee offered to nationals of no other country. Congress, in turn, passed the Cuban Adjustment Act (CAA), which grants unauthorized Cuban entrants unique rights to lawful permanent residency after one year in the US, with a path to citizenship (including a unique fast-track path to citizenship, and, accordingly, quicker qualification for Medicare, available only to citizens, and quicker attainment of voting rights) (Eckstein 2022, 57).

Moreover, once settled in the US, Cuban entrants received unique benefits to help them adapt. They were beneficiaries of the most generous refugee program in US history, even when they did not meet the near-universally agreed-upon criteria for refugee status – that of fleeing persecution. If they arrived after January 1959, they were automatically considered refugees, and on that basis offered unique entitlements, whether or not they fled persecution. Cubans also qualify for federally funded welfare benefits upon entry, irrespective of whether they immigrated lawfully. Authorized immigrants from other countries are ineligible for welfare benefits during their first five years in the US, and unauthorized immigrants from other countries never qualify.

For over half a century, Democrat and Republican administrations alike granted Cubans new entitlements and honoured entitlements initiated by earlier administrations. Obama was the first president to break the precedent. He granted Cubans no new entitlements, and in his last full week in office, in January 2017, he ended Cuban exceptionalism "as we knew it," to paraphrase President Bill Clinton when he enacted the 1996 welfare reform.[3] Obama revoked Cuban rights to parole entry, the basis on which most Cubans had been admitted to the US. Nonetheless, legislated entitlements that only Congress can retract remained in effect, most notably the CAA, which grants unauthorized Cuban entrants a path to lawful permanent residence and then citizenship.

In January 2023, President Joe Biden proceeded to (re)introduce yet new entitlements for Cubans. He agreed to admit, monthly, thirty thousand Cubans, together with Haitians, Venezuelans, and Nicaraguans, but no other aspiring immigrants, two-year parole entry, and the right of the Cubans, along with the Haitians, to refugee benefits. However, because the CAA continued to be the law of the land, Biden's 2023 initiative enabled Cubans – and only Cubans – to leverage their parole entry to become lawful permanent residents after one year in the US, and subsequently US citizens.

WHY CUBANS WERE PRIVILEGED

The Cuban experience reveals that neither presidents, with their discretionary power, nor Congress, with its legislative power, treat all immigrants and all aspiring immigrants equally and equitably. Fortunate for Cubans, both presidents and Congress singled them out for special entitlements.

In the throes of the Cold War, presidents and Congress initially leveraged Cuban immigration for foreign policy gain. Eisenhower and his immediate successors privileged Cuban immigrants with hopes of thereby causing the Castro-led government to collapse – by draining Cuba of its "best and brightest," by demonstrating Cubans' preference for a capitalist democracy as they fled to US shores, and by drawing on Cubans for covert activity to destabilize the revolutionary regime. Paradoxically, however, in admitting Castro's opponents, Washington may have unwittingly strengthened his hold on power. If these Cubans had been forced to stay in Cuba they might have instigated regime change.

In turn, Cuban immigrants became agents of the privileging of "their people." They pressed for the continued honouring of previously granted entitlements, for new entitlements, and for expanding the number of Cuban beneficiaries of entitlements. They lobbied (with guidance and funding initially from the Reagan administration); they made campaign contributions; they bloc-voted, thereby strengthening their influence through electoral channels; and they mobilized in the streets of Miami and Washington to defend and promote their interests (see Eckstein 2009, chap. 3). Because the CAA offered a path to citizenship, Cubans enjoyed voting rights that were denied to unauthorized entrants from other countries, which they parlayed for special entitlements. Also, the Cuban Refugee Program helped Cubans get a college education and professional training, which enabled them to become economically successful, and thereby able to finance campaigns of politicians committed to advancing Cuban immigrant interests.

Settling mainly in Florida contributed to their political clout. Florida's electoral college votes rose from ten to thirty between 1960 and 2024, as ever more people settled in the state. As Florida came to have the third largest number of electoral college votes and became the largest "swing state," politicians responded to the requests and demands of Cuban Americans in order to win their votes.

Cuban immigrants accordingly attained outsized political influence despite comprising less than 1 per cent of the US population. In the process, domestic politics became the driving force behind the continued privileging of Cuban immigrants. This was true already during the Cold War, but especially afterwards, when Washington's foreign policy priorities no longer justified singling out Cubans for unique entitlements. Cuban immigrants themselves, along with the federal government, became agents of immigrant inequality.

RETRACTION OF CUBAN ENTITLEMENTS

After more than fifty years, Obama, followed by Trump, reined in Cuban entitlements. In so doing, both presidents contributed to greater immigrant equality – but they did so by retracting entitlements for Cubans, not by extending the rights granted to Cubans to other immigrant groups. While Obama hoped to rein in unauthorized Cuban immigration in revoking Cuban prerogatives, Trump sought to contain authorized as well as unauthorized Cuban immigration, in conjunction with his "war on immigrants."

OBAMA ADMINISTRATION TERMINATION OF UNAUTHORIZED ENTRANTS' PATH TO LAWFUL RESIDENCE AND CITIZENSHIP

In his last full week in office, Obama retracted the so-called dry foot policy that allowed unauthorized Cubans, alone among immigrants who entered without US-granted visas, to be paroled into the country. Absent parole rights, unauthorized Cuban entrants were to be subject to detention and deportation, like other unauthorized entrants, and be denied work and welfare, along with other legal rights.

Why did Obama break with precedent and retract Cubans' special entry rights that had served as a springboard for other entitlements? When announcing the policy change, he claimed that "[t]oday the United States is taking important steps forward to normalize relations with Cuba to bring greater consistency to our immigration policy." The US would treat "Cuban migrants the same way we treat migrants from other countries." He added that "Cuban nationals who attempt to enter the United States illegally and do not qualify for humanitarian relief will be subject to removal."[4] Political asylum remained an option, but only, in principle, for Cubans who demonstrated well-founded evidence that they had fled actual or likely persecution.

Obama had reasons other than improving immigrant equality for revoking Cuban parole rights. He sought thereby to halt soaring unauthorized Cuban immigration. He changed US policy in the process of lengthy negotiations with the Cuban government to normalize bilateral relations. Nearly fifty-seven thousand unauthorized Cubans had presented themselves at the US border in 2016. Human smugglers had guided them thousands of miles under dangerous conditions over difficult terrain through Central American countries and Mexico to the US border. Since the mid-1990s, Coast Guard policing of the Florida Straits had made the most direct, ninety-mile route to the US near impossible. In revoking Cuban parole rights, Obama hoped the US would regain control over its borders.

Obama revoked the parole rights when unconstrained by Cuban American political pressure, including from Cuban American members of Congress, who normally influenced US–Cuba policy. He made the policy change in his parting days in office, when unconcerned about courting Cuban American voters, and against the backdrop of changes in the Cuban American community that spared him political pushback. During Obama's presidency, Cuban American politicians, who came from families who immigrated in the early years of the Cuban Revolution, began to criticize Cuban immigrant entitlements that they until then had defended and promoted. Viewing themselves as exiles,[5] they were committed to building a "wall" across the Florida Straits to economically isolate and strangulate "Castro's Cuba" (under the leadership, sequentially, of Fidel, his brother Raúl, and, beginning in 2019, Miguel Díaz-Canel). They were hostile to the post–Soviet-era arrivals, whom I call the "New Cubans," who defied the cross-border, people-to-people embargo to which the exiles were politically committed.[6] Wanting to bond with, and help, family they had left behind, New Cubans had, in increasing numbers, been taking advantage of the lifting of restrictions on travel and remittances under Obama. Their sense of transnational family morality conflicted with the political morality of the exiles.[7]

Beginning in 2015, Cuban American politicians who were hostile to the New Cubans' cross-border ties – among them Representatives Mario Díaz-Balart and Carlos Curbelo, and Senators Marco Rubio and Bob Menendez – argued for restricting Cuban immigration and for reserving entitlements for those Cuban entrants who made no homeland trips. In making their arguments they cited a series of articles published in October 2015 in the South Florida newspaper *Sun Sentinel* that described Cuban Americans breaking the law, including in ways embedded in cross-border ties. The articles reported crimes that were committed to pay debts to smugglers who brought Cubans to the US. They also reported on highly organized Miami-based criminal networks that were reputedly rooted in the ease with which Cubans could gain entry into the US without a visa, with ringleaders frequently travelling back and forth to Cuba, smuggling millions of dollars and bringing Cubans to the US to work as foot soldiers in their criminal organizations. In essence, the Cuban American politicians argued that the transnational ties of Cuban immigrants were not merely morally reprehensible, in defying the personal embargo to which they were politically committed, but also embedded in illicit activity.

In their efforts to retract entitlements for Cuban immigrants who defied the people-to-people embargo (which was not enshrined in US law), Curbelo and Rubio proposed legislation in 2015 to terminate Cuban immigrants' unique rights to welfare, which Congressman Lincoln Díaz-Balart (Mario's older brother) had managed to get inserted into the welfare reform passed by Congress under Clinton. Curbelo and Rubio's proposed legislation called for restricting welfare rights to Cuban immigrants who made no homeland trips (Kestin and O'Matz 2016). With Curbelo and Rubio unsuccessful at securing sufficient support from other legislators, Congress continued to fund near-automatic welfare rights for Cuban immigrants – and only Cuban immigrants – on the basis of nationality.

Meanwhile, the Cuban American legislators who were critical of continued Cuban immigrant entitlements did not support legislation proposed to sunset the CAA. In 2015, Republican Paul Gosar, along with nine other members of Congress, introduced a bill to terminate the CAA (Kestin and O'Matz 2016). In not supporting Gosar's proposed legislation, the Cuban American legislators revealed that they were not really interested in repealing one of the most exceptional of entitlements for Cubans. Rather, they wished to threaten to repeal the CAA to pressure the New Cubans to comply with a people-to-people embargo.

The divergent views toward cross-border ties among the earlier and more recent Cuban immigrants stemmed from their different experiences in Cuba before being uprooted. Exiles typically wanted nothing to do with the country as it had been transformed under Castro's rule and sought to bring the regime to heel. In contrast, the New Cubans, who had "lived the revolution" but became disillusioned with it when experiencing the crisis caused by the Soviet Union's collapse and the consequent abrupt ending of Soviet aid and trade, perceived themselves as immigrants. Like immigrants from other countries, after moving to America they wanted to visit and financially help family they had left behind. They also wanted family in Cuba to enjoy the same immigration prerogatives they had enjoyed (see Eckstein 2009, especially chap. 4). However, with no political organizations or political leadership of their own, and without the financial resources to make political contributions to convince politicians to promote their interests, they did not publicly challenge the critique of Cuban immigrant entitlements being made by exiles – and, increasingly, by their children, who upon coming of age had also become politically influential. Under these circumstances, Obama faced little opposition to ending Cuban parole rights.

TRUMP 1.0 ADMINISTRATION INTERVENTIONS TO BLOCK CUBANS FROM ENTRY

Although unintended, Obama's parting reforms appealed to Trump's anti-immigrant base. Trump fervently attacked immigrants, and made no exception for Cubans. He accordingly further retracted Cuban immigrant entitlements, although his actions were more de facto than de jure. Cubans who tried to circumvent the new barriers he imposed became victims of his general "war on immigrants." Trump also had little interest in reinstating immigration entitlements that would provide an "escape valve" for disgruntled Cubans; if unable to immigrate they might press for regime change in Cuba. In addition, Rubio, to whom Trump turned for Cuba policy advice (first as Senator and, in his second presidential term, as Secretary of State), favoured restricting the immigration of Cubans who were likely to make homeland trips.

While remaining officially committed to a 1994 bilateral agreement that guaranteed a minimum of twenty thousand Cuban immigration visas yearly, between 2016 and 2018 the Trump administration issued no more than half that number of visas to Cubans, and as few as four thousand in 2018 (see DHS 2016, 2017, 2018, table 10; CRS 2020). To limit immigration, in 2018 it suspended visa processing at the US embassy in Havana, which meant that Cubans needed to absorb the costs of applying for visas in third countries, with no guarantee that they would be awarded visas in those countries.

To further contain lawful immigration, the Trump administration imposed new hurdles to the family reunification parole program that President George W. Bush had initiated, and then suspended the program altogether. New Cubans had been the main beneficiaries of the family reunification program in that, as more recent arrivals, they had more family in Cuba wanting to immigrate (FIU 2020).

With the Trump administration making lawful immigration difficult, and with parole entry officially no longer an option, determined Cubans turned to a new entry strategy. They reimagined themselves as asylum seekers, and in such large numbers that they became the third largest group of asylum claimants (Bier 2019). If they won their asylum cases they gained lawful entry. While the Trump administration also sought to block asylum seekers, by suspending immigration court proceedings (in the context of the COVID-19 pandemic) that put asylum prospects on hold, Cubans who successfully managed to enter the US could draw on the CAA to attain legal rights to stay after one year, before being called upon for asylum hearings. Although the number of Cubans granted lawful permanent residency did drop during Trump's presidency, from 66,510 in 2016, before Obama terminated Cuban parole rights, to 16,367 in 2020, three-fourths of the Cubans who attained lawful permanent residency did so based on the CAA (DHS 2016, 2020). In essence, appeals for asylum provided Cubans with a new means of privileged entry. The CAA became the basis for lawful permanent residency and citizenship, often before their asylum hearings.

Unsuccessful at blocking asylum seekers, the Trump administration turned to the Mexican and Central American governments for assistance. It required asylum seekers (from all countries, not just from Cuba) to wait in Mexico, often for months, until they were admitted for their asylum hearings. While waiting in Mexican border cities, Cubans were at the mercy of criminal gangs, armed robbers, and kidnappers (Attanasio 2019), and were subjected to worse conditions than those they had fled. In addition, the Trump administration pressured the Mexican government to itself detain and deport Cubans to prevent them from reaching the US border, where they could plead for asylum.

With the outsourcing of immigration control to Mexico also failing to block asylum seekers, the Trump administration sought to offshore US immigration control to the governments of Guatemala, El Salvador, and Honduras. It convinced the Central American governments to sign Asylum Cooperation Agreements that required migrants to seek asylum in the first country through which they passed. If migrants passed through a country before reaching the US, the Trump administration deemed them ineligible for asylum in the US – a ruling that went on to be challenged in the courts (Liptak 2019). The countries through which asylum seekers trekked in their quest to reach the US border had some of the highest homicide rates in the world (Rappaport 2019). Hardly were they safe havens.

The Cubans who did manage to defy the Trump administration's entry barriers faced exclusionary barriers once in the US from which they previously had been shielded. The detention of Cubans soared – 700 per cent between Obama's last year in office and the end of 2018 (Rivero 2019) – and in 2019 the US Immigration and Customs Enforcement (ICE) detained more Cubans than any other nationals (TRAC 2020), and under such deplorable conditions that those who were being detained rebelled (Lanard 2020). If detained, a detainee's asylum hinged on them winning claims in immigration court. If their claims were denied, they risked deportation. Cuban deportations increased more than eighteenfold during Trump's first presidential term. Meanwhile, his administration responded to pressure from exiles to tighten the people-to-people embargo, in order to limit ties between Cubans in the US and those in their homeland. It stopped issuing the multiple entry visas that Obama had introduced, and which had made cross-border family visits easier and less costly. Instead, it reinstituted George W. Bush's single-entry visa policy, and made visas more difficult to attain. It also required Cubans on the island to go to US embassies outside the country to apply for visas for US visits as well as for immigration. The Trump administration was indifferent to the needs of the New Cubans who wished to see family that they left behind (FIU 2020).

The Trump administration also imposed new limits on remittances. It set a $1,000 quarterly cap, and restricted remittance-sending companies from processing payments, which led Western Union, the largest US provider of remittance services, to suspend money transfers to Cuba. In addition, the clampdown on remittances troubled many of the New Cubans, who remained committed to family on the island.

Accordingly, the Trump administration made both authorized and unauthorized Cuban immigration more difficult and it subjected unauthorized entrants to exclusionary measures that had never been applied to Cubans on any scale in the past. It also introduced new barriers to cross-border ties among Cubans. Yet, with Congress maintaining the CAA, Cubans who managed to defy the Trump administration's entry barriers continued to enjoy a unique path to lawful permanent residence.

THE BIDEN ADMINISTRATION: BETWEEN A ROCK AND A HARD PLACE

When campaigning for the presidency, Biden presented himself as more immigrant friendly than Trump. However, during his first two years in office he left Trump's Cuban immigration policies unchanged. He did not task the US Embassy in Havana to increase visa processing, he continued to enforce the Trump administration's pandemic ruling known as Title 42 to block migrants who reached the US–Mexican border from Remain in Mexico program that required Cubans to wait months in Mexico for their US immigration court hearings.

Even after escalating inflation, chronic food and drug shortages, and power outages fuelled the largest protests in Cuba, in 2021, the Biden administration tried to block Cubans from immigrating. Fearing that discouraged Cubans would seek refuge in the US, it commissioned the Coast Guard to step up sea and air watches in the Florida Straits, and the Department of Homeland Security (DHS) to warn Floridians who sought to bring loved ones on the island to the US via boat, as they had in 1980 from the Cuban port of Mariel, that they would be fined $250,000 and face five years in prison. The DHS also warned Cubans who took to the sea that they would be apprehended and returned to Cuba, and not admitted to the US. Should they demonstrate that they would likely face persecution if they were returned, they would be referred to third countries for resettlement. While a growing number of Cubans, under these circumstances, sought (and were awarded) asylum in Mexico, most of the aspiring immigrants continued to focus on US entry.

Notwithstanding the efforts to block Cubans from entry, unauthorized immigration soared. Cubans were helped when Nicaragua lifted its Cuban visa requirements in late 2021, which shortened their land trek to the US. They no longer needed to first fly to Guyana, which until then had been the closest country to the US with no visa requirement. By 2022, Cuban immigration exceeded the two preceding years combined, as well as the 1980 Mariel exodus of over 125,000 Cubans, the largest previous influx of unauthorized entrants in one year.

Meanwhile, once again Cubans were privileged compared to other unauthorized immigrants. Most of them could apply for asylum, and if their cases were not processed within a year they could become lawful permanent residents under the CAA. Hardly any of them were being turned away under Title 42, which the Trump administration introduced to block entry of unauthorized immigrants on alleged health grounds, in the context of the pandemic (Spagat 2022) (an aspect that was helped by the Cuban government refusing to accept deportees).

In May 2022 the Biden administration finally modified some Trump policies – against the backdrop of Cuba's ongoing economic crisis, plus the arrival of soaring numbers of visa-less Cubans. It lifted remittance restrictions so that Cubans in the US could, in principle, assist island family in need, thereby reducing immigration pressures; it increased staff at the US Embassy in Havana to process immigration visa requests; and it reactivated the family reunification parole program to enable Cubans to immigrate while they waited for their visas to be processed (see Nodarse Venancio and Oliver 2022). In (re)opening possibilities to immigrate lawfully, Washington could better control who immigrated, but not before one-half to one million Cubans managed to enter the US unlawfully by the time Trump returned to office in 2025, his second term (beyond the scope of this chapter).

EXCLUSION OF DARK-SKINNED HAITIANS

While honouring entitlements that had been granted to Cubans over the years until his last full week in office, Obama continued to enforce racist Haitian exclusionary policies initiated in the past. Every administration since the 1970s had treated Haitians differently than other migrant groups – blocking their entry, rejecting their asylum claims, and holding them in detention for longer periods. While adopting a more conciliatory approach toward Haitians than previous administrations, Obama mainly only granted Haitians temporary rights, which the Trump administration proceeded to revoke or threaten to revoke.

Haitians have long been subjected to immigrant inequities that have laid bare the racist biases in US immigration policy. They gained the most rights when coming ashore at the same time as the Cubans who exited from the port of Mariel, when the inequitable treatment of Cubans and Haitians became exceptionally transparent and thus unjustifiable. Even then, Haitians were denied citizenship rights that Cubans who arrived via the port of Mariel obtained.

Haitian exclusion was multipronged. For one, the US has limited the lawful immigration of Haitians over the years. Under these circumstances, Haitians, desperate to escape poverty, persecution, and violence in the poorest and most tumultuous country in the hemisphere, tried (like Cubans) to immigrate without authorization. However, they faced successive presidential administrations that interdicted them at sea, that detained them under deplorable conditions, that denied them fair hearings for asylum claims, and that expedited their deportation. The unauthorized Haitians who managed to make it to the US were, in turn, denied rights to work and welfare (except the Haitians who the Carter administration admitted along with the Cubans who arrived from the port of Mariel). On two occasions Congress did offer unauthorized Haitians a way to adjust their status: in 1986, in conjunction with the Immigration Reform and Control Act, which gave all unauthorized immigrants the opportunity to become lawful permanent residents (under specific conditions), and twelve years later when, pressured by Haitian rights groups, it passed the Haitian Refugee Immigration Fairness Act, which provided a brief window for previously excluded Haitians to have their status adjusted.[8]

The Obama administration's Haitian policies need be assessed in particular against the backdrop of the policies of the preceding administration, that of George W. Bush, which offered Haitians no relief when conditions in Haiti went from bad to worse. The Bush administration lent no support to a bill introduced in Congress in 2002 to amend the CAA to apply also to Haitians. Nor did it offer relief to Haitians after Haiti descended into violent chaos in 2004 following a coup that ousted Jean-Bertrand Aristide, a former priest who espoused liberation theology and who was elected president with the greatest popular backing of any Haitian president, or later the same year after a hurricane destroyed most of the domestic crop production and left a quarter million Haitians homeless (Wasem 2005).

Instead, the Bush administration, like previous administrations, focused on interdicting Haitians who were desperately trying to escape the dire conditions in their homeland, and on detaining and deporting unauthorized Haitians who managed to reach US shores. It denied Haitians entry while paroling Cubans into the country who the CAA entitled to lawful permanent residency, and then citizenship.

In the context of 9/11, the Bush administration further discriminated against Haitians but not Cubans. It claimed that Haitians were a national security threat because terrorists could pose as Haitian asylum seekers and because Haitian asylum seekers were diverting the Coast Guard from homeland security duties (Lindskoog 2018, 146). Using this rationale, the Immigration and Naturalization Service (INS) issued new guidelines to fast-track Haitian asylum adjudications without due process and to detain Haitians even if they were not charged with a crime (Lindskoog 2018, 145). It also granted few Haitian asylum seekers "credible fear" hearings and adequate legal representation. As a result, fewer than 5 per cent of Haitians won asylum requests, despite the horrific conditions they fled (Lindskoog 2018, 146). High-ranking INS officials acknowledged that Bush's Haitian detention policy was designed to deter Haitians from seeking asylum in the US, not to address a national security threat (Lindskoog 2018, 146).

Indicative of Obama's more inclusionary stance toward Haitians, following a devasting earthquake in 2010 he granted temporary protected status (TPS) to unauthorized Haitians who were in the US at the time. TPS comes with rights to work and protection from deportation but no rights to public assistance or path to permanent residency and citizenship: in essence, it allows for economic and certain legal rights but no social and political rights. However, Obama denied TPS rights to unauthorized Haitians who arrived after the hurricane, despite conditions in Haiti remaining dire (although his administration extended eligibility for TPS by one year). Unauthorized Haitians who arrived subsequently were subject to the exclusionary practices of the past: to detention and deportation, with the conditions in detention facilities so abysmal that Haitians rioted and staged hunger strikes.

Independently of the TPS, in 2015 the Obama administration initiated a parole-based program to fast-track Haitian family reunification in the US (modelled after the program for Cubans), and in 2016 it granted three-year humanitarian parole to five thousand Haitians without a visa who arrived at the southern California border. These Haitians came mainly via Brazil, where they had fled after the 2010 Haiti earthquake.[9] Following an economic downturn in Brazil in 2016 they sought refuge in the US. Worried that if Trump won the election that year he would implement his campaign promise to build a wall across the US–Mexican border to block immigration, they rushed to reach the US before the November vote.

As in the case of Cubans, parole status did not grant Haitians any longterm rights, and the Obama administration proceeded to announce plans to terminate Haitian TPS rights. However, when Haiti was hit in 2016 by its worst hurricane in over a century, Obama, under pressure from the Haitian American community and influential non-Haitian politicians, both suspended deportations of Haitians and extended Haitians' entitlement to TPS.[10] Yet, unlike Cubans, Haitians had no formal basis for adjusting their status to become lawful permanent residents.

In contrast, the Haitians who the Obama administration admitted as lawful permanent residents in accordance with the immigration preference system enjoyed, like Cubans, work rights, plus a path to citizenship, but unlike Cubans, they could receive no immediate rights to welfare. Moreover, in allowing the admittance of around two and a half times as many Cubans as Haitians (see Eckstein 2022, chap. 8, fig. 8.1), the preference system, which prioritizes relatives of US residents, will privilege the admission of more Cubans than Haitians in the years to come.

Whatever the gains Haitians made under Obama, Trump took Haitian exclusion to a new level. Haitian apprehensions at the border soared, from less than five hundred in 2008 and about one thousand in 2014 to over four thousand in 2020. Also, the Trump administration granted asylum to fewer Haitians than other nationals, despite the high number of Haitian asylum seekers (Morrison et al. 2021). Haitians were granted asylum at the lowest rate of any nationality. In addition, Trump threatened to withdraw Haitian TPS rights, such that some fifty-five thousand Haitians worried that they would be deported and Haitians on the island worried that they would, as a result, be left without family in the US to send them the remittances on which they depended (Haiti being the most remittance-dependent country in the Western Hemisphere). However, his threats notwithstanding, Trump entitled Haitians to TPS for his entire presidency.

Although Biden promised a more immigrant-friendly approach when campaigning, in office he continued the discriminatory immigration policies of the past that targeted Haitians. Most troubling, in 2021, mounted Border Patrol agents in Del Rio, Texas, corralled for rapid deportation more than fifteen thousand Haitian asylum seekers who were trying to cross into the US from Mexico. Drawing on Title 42, border services planned to deny the Haitians asylum hearings. Outraged that Haitians were to be returned to a country racked by deadly natural disasters and political turmoil, the senior US envoy for Haitian policy resigned (Sullivan 2022). Confronted as well with public outrage, Biden criticized the Border Patrol agents' handling of the Haitians, but this did not stop his administration from deporting more than twenty-five thousand Haitians between September 2021 and June 2022.

Biden did grant Haitians some immigration rights, although, as with Obama, only on a temporary basis with no path to citizenship. He officially reinstituted the Haitian family reunification parole program that Trump had ended, but its implementation was delayed because Haiti was believed to be too unsafe for US officials to travel to the country to process applications. Haiti had become overrun by gangs. Biden also extended TPS status to the Haitians who had initially been granted the status by Obama, as well as to Haitians who had moved to the US since 2010. With TPS status, Haitians were entitled to work permits, but not to welfare or citizenship rights. In addition, the Biden administration entitled Haitians to the same humanitarian parole program (CHNV – "Cuba, Haiti, Nicaragua, and Venezuela") as Cubans (along with Nicaraguans and Venezuelans), which Trump discontinued when assuming his second term as president.

In sum, Haitian immigrant rights barely improved over the years. In the main, Haitian entitlements have been of a temporary nature. Haitians have been excluded from entitlements extended to Cubans, even though they are no less worthy.

CONCLUSION

Comparison of the treatment of Cuban and Haitian immigrants, and of aspiring Cuban and Haitian immigrants, highlights how Washington policymakers prioritize their political concerns over immigrant equity. Although the 1965 immigration reform was intended to eliminate national origins–based racial inequities in terms of who was admitted into the US, racial biases continue, to Cubans' advantage and Haitians' disadvantage.

Both presidents and their administrations, drawing on their discretionary power, and Congress, drawing on its legislative power, have privileged mainly White Cubans (as self-defined in the US census) over dark-skinned Haitians and other nationals. They have granted Cubans special entry privileges and entitled them upon entry to social, economic, and political rights that are denied to other immigrants. The US government initially privileged Cuban immigrants as part of a Cold War foreign policy strategy to undermine a nationalist, Soviet-allied, anti-American revolution in America's "backyard," but continued to privilege Cubans after the end of the Cold War. Cubans benefited from new entitlements piled onto old – all while Haitians were mainly excluded. Even an African American president, together with an African American attorney general and an African American secretary of Homeland Security, subjected Haitians to a system of detention and deportation from which Cubans were spared.

Nonetheless, the Cuban experience demonstrates that the privileging of certain immigrant groups is not merely an outcome of official design. Early entitlements transformed Cuban immigrants, and, with time, their US-born children, into a force unto themselves. They became, in Oxhorn's frame of analysis, a neopluralist, society-based force. They defended and promoted the continued privileging of Cuban immigration when Washington no longer had reason, after the Cold War, to prioritize Cuban immigration for foreign policy gain. Even when presidents, beginning with Obama, whittled away at Cuban entitlements, and influential Cuban exiles stopped defending and promoting Cuban entitlements, ordinary Cubans defied efforts to make immigration rights more egalitarian. For how long they will be able to do so remains to be seen. Through the years of the Biden administration, they did manage to continue to receive unique entitlements and suceed in evading regulations that were not advantagious to them. Initial entitlements, the bedrock for subsequent entitlements, have worked to the long-term advantage of Cuban immigrants.

NOTES

1 I discuss the gambit of entitlements in greater detail in *Cuban Privilege: The Making of Immigrant Inequality in America* (2022).

2 President Carter, for example, created the category of "Entrant: Status Pending" to grant temporary entry rights to some 125,000 unauthorized arrivals from the Cuban port of Mariel, claiming that they did not qualify

for admission as refugees. President Reagan proceeded to grant the "entrants" refugee status in the absence of evidence that they had fled persecution, the internationally agreed-upon criteria for refugee status, so that they could become lawful permanent residents.

3 President Clinton had initiated the "wet foot/dry foot" policy. The "wet foot" component required the Coast Guard, for the first time, to repatriate Cubans who they interdicted at sea. However, the "dry foot" component affirmed the rights of unauthorized entrants to be paroled into the country. President Clinton also extended other entitlements to Cubans. See Eckstein, *Cuban Privilege*, chapter 5.

4 "Statement by the President on Cuban Immigration Policy," 12 January 2017. https://obamawhitehouse.archives.gov/the-press-office/2017/01/12

5 Marco Rubio, a former Florida senator and current secretary of state under Donald Trump, and Bob Menendez, a former New Jersey senator, came from families who immigrated shortly before the revolution. However, they identified with the exiles, from whom they received substantial political contributions over the years. Indeed, Rubio claimed to be an exile when first running for the Senate. He considered it in his political interests to do so. The media revealed his false claims.

6 The term "people-to-people embargo" refers to limits on cross-border personal relations, particularly visits and remittance-sending to Cuba.

7 See my book *The Immigrant Divide* for more detail on the differences between the immigrant waves.

8 Haitians had deliberately been excluded from legislated immigration entitlements that were previously granted to Nicaraguans, as well as Cubans, Guatemalans, and Salvadorans, in the 1997 Nicaraguan Adjustment and Central American Relief Act.

9 See Semple 2016 for an excellent description of Haitian immigration to the US via Brazil.

10 For a report of human rights conditions in Haiti, see US Department of State, "Haiti 2013 Human Rights Report," in Country Reports on Human Rights Practices for 2013 (Washington, DC: Bureau of Democracy, Human Rights, and Labor), https://2009-2017.state.gov/documents/organization/220661.pdf.

REFERENCES

Attanasio, Cedar. 2019. "Migrants Face Violence as US Makes Them Wait in Mexico." AP News, 27 June.

Bier, David. 2019. "Cuban Credible Fear Asylum Claims Surge after Ending Wet Foot, Dry Foot." *Cato at Liberty*. Washington DC: Cato Institute, 20 March.

CRS (Congressional Research Service). 2020. *Cuba: US Policy in the 116th Congress*, 14 May.

DHS (Department of Homeland Security). *Yearbooks of Immigration Statistics FY 2016–2018*.

Eckstein, Susan. 2009. *The Immigrant Divide: How Cuban Americans Changed the US and Their Homeland*. New York: Routledge.

Eckstein, Susan. 2022. *Cuban Privilege: The Making of Immigrant Inequality in America*. Cambridge UK: Cambridge University Press.

FIU (Florida International University). 2020. *2020 FIU Cuba Poll: How Cuban Americans in Miami View U.S. Policies toward Cuba*. Miami: FIU, Steven J. Green School of International and Public Affairs.

Kestin, Sally, and Megan O'Matz. 2016. "Rubio Bill would Curb Welfare abuses by Cuban Immigrants." *Sun Sentinel*, 12 January.

Lanard, Noah. 2020. "Trump Panders to Cubans, Nicaraguans, and Venezuelans While He Deports and Detains Them." *Mother Jones*, 5 February.

Lindskoog, Carl. 2018. *Detain and Punish: Haitian Refugees and the Rise of the World's Largest Detention System*. Gainesville, FL: University Press of Florida Press.

Liptak, Adam. 2019. "Justices Permit U.S. to Exclude More Asylum Seekers." *New York Times*, 12 September.

Morrison, Aaron, Astrid Galvan, and Jasen Los. 2021. "Haitians See History of Racist Policies in Migrant Treatment." AP News, 24 September.

Nodarse Venancio, Mariakarla, and Isabella Oliver. 2022. "Cuban Migration Is Changing, the U.S. Must Take Note." Washington, DC: WOLA (Washington Office on Latin America).

O'Matz, Megan, and Sally Kestin. 2016. "Rubio to Propose Bill to Cut Aid to Cuban Migrants." *Sun Sentinel*, 7 January.

Oxhorn, Philip. 1998a. "The Social Foundations of Latin America's Recurrent Populism: Problems of Popular Sectors Class Formation and Collective Action." *Journal of Historical Sociology* 11, no. 2: 212–46.

Oxhorn, Philip. 1998b. "Is the Century of Corporatism Over? Neoliberalism and the Rise of Neopluralism." In *What Kind of Democracy? What Kind of Market?: Latin America in the Age of*

Neoliberalism, edited by Philip Oxhorn and Graciela Ducatenzeiler, 195–217. University Park, PA: Penn State University Press.

Oxhorn, Philip. 2011. *Sustaining Civil Society: Economic Change, Democracy and the Social Construction of Citizenship in Latin America*. University Park, PA: Penn State University Press.

Rappaport, Nolan. 2019. "Trump's Latest Gambit: Send Asylum Seekers to 'Safe Third Countries' That Are Less than Safe." *The Hill*, 24 November.

Rivero, Daniel. 2019. "Number of Cuban Nationals Detained by ICE Has Skyrocketed, New Data Shows." *WLRN-Miami*, 18 June.

Semple, Kirk. 2016. "Haitians, after Perilous Journey, Find Door to U.S. Abruptly Shut." *New York Times*, 24 September.

Sneed, Tierney, and Priscilla Alvarez. 2022. "Biden Reverses Some Trump Policies Related to Cuba, Making It Easier for Families to Visit Relatives in Country." *CNN*, 30 June.

Spagat, Elliot. 2022. "Court Ruling to Maintain Title 42 Extends Uneven Treatment for Asylum-Seekers." 23 May.

Sullivan, Eileen. 2022. "U.S. Accelerated Expulsions of Haitian Migrants in May." *New York Times*, 9 June.

TRAC (Transactional Records Access Clearinghouse). 2020. "*Immigration Asylum and Detention Data*." Accessed 30 October 2020.

"U.S.–Cuba News Brief." Washington, DC: Center for Democracy in the Americas, 17 January 2020.

Wasem, Ruth. 2005. "U.S. Immigration Policy on Haitian Migrants." *Congressional Resource Service Report for Congress*. Washington, DC: Congressional Research Service, 21 January.

8

Civil Society Construction, Hybrid Regimes, and Political Change in the Middle East: Egypt and Syria, Before, During, and After the Arab Spring

Aviad Rubin

Philip Oxhorn's theoretical contribution to comparative politics is built mainly on his extensive research in Latin American cases. The relevance of his theoretical insights, however, stretches far beyond his regional expertise. In this chapter I demonstrate how Oxhorn's lessons about the construction of an autonomous civil society help us understand social mobilization and regime typology in the contemporary Middle East.

The political turmoil that started in the Middle East in 2010 and continues in some of the region's countries until today, provides a rare opportunity to examine the relevance of concepts and theories of comparative politics to the region. In particular, while monarchies of the region have proved rather resilient to political change, given their legitimate inheritance mechanisms, the Arab Spring produced diverse processes and outcomes among Middle Eastern republics, which have proved extremely vulnerable to popular protest and regime change (Brownlee et al. 2015; Frisch 2011; Gause 2013). Among the republics, Tunisia underwent a short, effective, and relatively nonviolent period of political mobilization, which was followed by a decade-long period of democratic stability, which cracked recently. Egypt followed in Tunisia's initial footsteps, but after two years of democratic opening, suffered a backslide to authoritarian rule. Libya, Syria, and Yemen fell into decade-long bloody civil wars. In Algeria and Lebanon, mass protest was marginal and did not lead to political change.

Without dismissing the situational complexity and the weight of elitist, structural, and cultural factors to explain the different outcomes observed in the region (Hinnebusch 2016; Stepan and Linz 2013; Mako and Moghadam 2021), this chapter builds on Oxhorn's work on civil society in the Latin American context, and argues that mass mobilization and proceeding regime transitions in Arab societies are deeply connected to the relative vibrancy and autonomy of civil society that emerged in each country before the eruption of protest. The sociopolitical realities in the Middle East make the dominant, overly liberal school of civil society ill-equipped to explain Middle East political dynamics. Conversely, Oxhorn's theory on the social construction of civil society provides a suitable framework for explaining recent political dynamics and outcomes in the region.

Building on Oxhorn's approach to the social construction of civil society (Oxhorn 2006, 2011), in this chapter I view civil society as the agency of a myriad of heterogenous groups and organizations (rather than an aggregation of interest-maximizing individuals) that come from various cultural backgrounds and socioeconomic strata and interact among themselves and vis-à-vis the state. These groups share only a thin consensus and relatively low levels of trust (rather than a shared liberal worldview). Oxhorn's novel perspective, which broadens the conceptual boundaries of civil society beyond the overly liberal worldview, is particularly insightful for examining the role of religious groups in civil society and their influence on democratic transitions and democratic performance in Middle Eastern societies. Following Oxhorn ideas, which I have developed further elsewhere (Rubin 2013, 2020), religious groups and organizations should not be excluded a priori from the conceptual boundaries of civil society. As long as religious groups and organizations are willing to accept the principles of the thin consensus, they should be conceived as potential members of civil society.

Like Oxhorn, I do not view the state and civil society as two isolated spheres that maintain a permanent conflictual zero-sum game relationship. Rather, the state and civil society engage in a continuous open-ended, reciprocally constitutive process, one that can be mutually constructive, mutually destructive, and everything in between (Migdal 2001). It means that the state has a fundamental role in nurturing (or impeding) the construction of civil society and in shaping its boundaries. It also means that the relative strength and organizational capacity of civil society may impact the state and the political sphere in a considerable way.

In employing this perspective on civil society in the Middle East, my main argument is that the scope and outcome of popular protest on regime change in Middle Eastern republics can be explained by the relative vibrancy, autonomy, and inclusive nature of civil society prior to the protest. Comparing the cases of Egypt and Syria, I show how the existence (or absence) of relatively autonomous spheres of civil activity impacted mass mobilization and political change, something that is at least partly attributable to the nature of the undemocratic regimes in place. In fact, these cases offer a particularly interesting standpoint to address this question comparatively, as while both republics combine features of hybrid regimes (electoral procedures and an absence of liberal constitutionalism) (see Zakaria 1997; Diamond 2002), one can be characterized as fully authoritarian and the other as hybrid, as they do not have the same level of tolerance for civil society activity outside state control. Fully authoritarian regimes exercise (or at least seek) a complete grip on all realms of societal life and repress any societal challenge to their rule. Conversely, hybrid regimes consciously tolerate a certain degree of societal challenge, which is seen by the government as a solution to perceptions of illegitimacy, but that nonetheless provides a platform for the diffusion of ideas and coordination of mass protest. As I show below, Egypt is a hybrid republic that tolerated a relatively autonomous and vibrant civil society, and that underwent rapid and relatively nonviolent regime change following the Arab Spring protests. In contrast, Syria is an authoritarian republic that traditionally repressed civil society activity, provoked an uncoordinated and violent opposition to its rule, and has been torn apart, for thirteen years, in a devastating civil war. In December 2024, the long dictatorial rule of the Assad family in Syria collapsed, but the future of the country remains largely uncertain.

DEMOCRATIC THEORY, HYBRID REGIMES, AND MIDDLE EASTERN POLITICS

The second half of the twentieth century saw a steady rise in the number of democratic regimes in many of the world's regions, which peaked during the last two decades of that century. Several theories, ranging from the structural (Lipset 1981; Almond 1987; Moore Jr

1966), institutionalist (Skocpol 1979; Skocpol 1998; Tilly 2004), and agential (Anderson et al. 2001; Fish 1996; O'Donnell and Schmitter 1986), have been used to try to explain the reasons behind the extension of democratic politics in various countries, and the mechanisms leading to such transitions. Most of this vast research was based on the histories of regions that underwent substantial regime change: primarily southern Europe and Latin America during the 1970s and 1980s, and the former Soviet Bloc during the late 1980s and 1990s.

The Middle East, which until recently had been resistant to political transition, has been largely absent from the early literature on democratic transitions. With the exception of a few case studies (Schwedler 2006; Rutherford 2008) and some regional analyses (Bellin 2004; Brownlee 2011; Hinnebusch 2006; Schwedler 2011; Sadiki 2009), it is the events associated with the Arab Spring that really prompted a wealth of scholarship on the region's political transitions and variety of outcomes. For example, Brownlee et al. (2015) emphasized two structural factors that together account for a transition outcome: oil richness and hereditary mechanisms. For Della Porta (2014, 2016), it is rather the nature of the interactions between elites and social movements – either "pacted" (among elites) or "eventful" (with the active participation of social movements) – that explains the different outcomes of the revolutions throughout the region. These contributions aside, the overall harvest of comparative political research in the Middle East remained modest, and largely detached from the mainstream literature on comparative politics.

Part of the literature on the region has been informed on a theoretical level by the concept of hybrid regimes (Diamond 2002) or its variants – liberal democracy (Zakaria 1997), defective democracy (Merkel 2004), competitive authoritarianism (Levitsky and Way 2010), or electoral authoritarianism (Schedler 2013) – which are conceptualized as regimes that maintain *procedural* (i.e., electoral) democratic systems while retaining many authoritarian practices, and that show little respect for such basic democratic principles as civil rights, universal access to the public sphere, and equal application of the rule of law. Most scholars regard the hybrid regime as a ruling technique that allows the incumbent elite to sustain its grip on political power by maintaining minimum levels of legitimacy through the toleration of institutionalized challenges in the form of multiparty politics and elections. These practices pay lip service to democracy, but lack the constitutional, substantive, and participatory components of democracy.

Notwithstanding the theoretical value of the common understanding of hybrid regimes, this concept has two serious limitations. First, as Oxhorn emphasizes in the conclusion of this book, most applications of the term overemphasize procedural and institutional arrangements and assume electoral practices as a necessary feature of the regime, while paying insufficient attention to the interplay of non-electoral dimensions (Morse 2012; Schedler 2013). Second, most scholars using the term investigate governing practices and competition among the elite, and take a top-down approach to the study of politics and democracy. As Richard Snyder accurately observed:

> [T]he burgeoning literature on contemporary non-democratic regimes ... places an overwhelming emphasis on the electoral process and thus overlooks other fundamental dimensions that are critical for analyzing regimes. ... Understanding the *full spectrum* of non-democratic regimes requires a broader conceptual framework, one that gets beyond the limited focus on electoral politics and competition seen in much recent work. (2006, 292–3)

These pitfalls make the traditional conceptualization of the hybrid regime less applicable to the study of the Arab Middle East, where election practices were, until recently, relatively rare, and definitely not routine, free, fair, and competitive (Brownlee 2011; Gilbert and Mohseni 2011). Given the enduring resistance of the Middle East to political change before 2010, scholars who employed the traditional understanding of the hybrid regime concept to the region were likely to conclude that its utility was either irrelevant or very partial in this context, leaving the Middle East poorly represented in the literature on hybrid regimes (e.g., Levitsky and Way 2010). As we shall see next, instead of disregarding this concept altogether, I argue that a complementary, more nuanced understanding of the term "hybrid regime," one that builds on Oxhorn's scholarship, and concentrates on the construction of an autonomous civil society and its engagement with the state, rather than on elite-initiated top-down policy, might prove theoretically and analytically valuable to the study of political dynamics in Arab societies.

AUTONOMOUS CIVIL SOCIETIES AS AN INDICATOR OF REGIME HYBRIDITY IN THE MIDDLE EAST

While embracing the basic logic of hybrid regimes – namely, the quest to achieve a stable composition of legitimacy and grip on political power through the toleration of a certain degree of challenges to the regime – incorporating insights from Oxhorn's work on the social construction of civil society may offer a more comprehensive understanding of the phenomenon. Specifically, the definition of hybrid regimes should be extended to incorporate the formation and exercise of relatively autonomous civil society activities at the societal level. Rather than limiting the examination of hybrid regimes to the behaviour of political elites and electoral practices at the individual level (i.e., voting), it should include an investigation of societal practices in different realms of society, with an emphasis on a bottom-up construction of civil society at the group level (Oxhorn 2011). As Oxhorn suggests, in places where civil society is more organized, autonomous, and engaged in political activity vis-à-vis the state, it is able to challenge the existing distribution of resources and political power in the state, and promote a more meaningful citizenship and, correspondingly, more substantive democratic practices. Despite the lack of regular elections, non-electoral hybrid regimes differ substantially from fully authoritarian regimes and should not be seen as a mere sub-category of authoritarianism. In other words, my conceptualization of hybrid regimes holds that the distinguishing element between authoritarian and hybrid regimes is the quest of fully authoritarian regimes to maintain comprehensive control over the society and avoid any challenges from below, whereas hybrid regimes are characterized by a conscious toleration of institutionalized challenges (elections and parties) at the political level, *or* uninstitutionalized challenges by an autonomous and engaged civil society at the societal level.

What can explain the willingness of a given regime to allow relatively autonomous civil society activity within its domain? I propose that the incentive of incumbent rulers to tolerate the formation and autonomous activity of civil society organizations is similar to that of post-authoritarian regimes that open the political sphere to procedural competition, namely, to secure a minimum level of legitimacy in order to sustain their grip on political power. There is abundant evidence of this practice in various parts of the world, ranging from Latin America to post-Soviet regimes, to African republics. In the Middle East, however, unlike in other regions, authoritarian regimes that faced legitimacy challenges have chosen a different path to achieve this combined goal. This is precisely where the Middle East experience carries particular theoretical contribution to general theories of regime typology, political transitions, and the construction of civil society. Instead of allowing institutionalized contestation over power – the refusal of which originates from anti-Western bias against democracy and elections as Western practices that are foreign to the region's culture and to Islam (Hinnebusch 2006; Lewis 1994; Price 1999) – a minimum level of popular legitimacy is secured in the short run by allowing relatively autonomous spaces in society that will channel some societal grievances into the public sphere and facilitate the impression of relative freedom of association and an arena for ideational exchange. Such a practice is more likely when the regime's bases of power and support are less solid, which, in turn, relates to the regime's level of public estimation and its ability to provide basic material goods. This cannot be properly understood if we concentrate on electoral procedures or top-down elitist policies. Only an approach that focuses on civil society, one that investigates the intricate dynamics taking place at the societal level, can account for the hybrid nature of such regimes. This is exactly where Oxhorn's works are most insightful.

A societal, non-electoral understanding of hybrid regimes suits the context of the Arab Spring in that it allows for the identification of nonconforming and challenging activities even in the absence of regular elections and in realms outside the state apparatus. The autonomous activity of civil society serves as a platform for mass mobilization in two ways. First, it constitutes spaces of contestation within which democratic practices and advocacy can evolve. Second, it acts as a platform for the coordination of political protest and dissemination of a wide variety of ideas (including dissenting ones). Since it is practically impossible to explore every realm of civil society, I limit my investigation here to one facilitating factor in the public sphere – that of the media and communications – and to two primary spheres of civil society activity: civic organizations and religious associations. In the Middle East, these particular realms constitute the most important platforms for the dissemination of ideas and coordination of popular mobilization.

CIVIC ORGANIZATIONS

Much has been written about the relationship between democratization and the vibrancy of civil society (Almond and Verba 1963; Carothers 1999; Oxhorn 1995; Putnam 1993). Civil society is a realm of associational and voluntary activity conducted by non-governmental organizations (NGOs). As conceptualized here, civil society also includes opposition parties that are not part of the power matrix of the state, as long as they exercise civic (i.e., legal, nonviolent) forms of opposition to the regime.

There are two main scholarly outlooks on civil society. Until recently the main outlook viewed civil society as a voluntary realm, isolated from state influence, in which individual people who share a similar set of values, or a "thick" consensus, and trust each other, gather through self-interest in coordinated activity that facilitates political stability and democracy. In this view, civil society works to curtail state power, and thus its relationship with the state is viewed as a zero-sum game – the stronger civil society is, the weaker the state becomes (Almond and Verba 1963; Putnam 1993; Fukuyama 1996).

The 1990s saw the emergence of an alternative outlook on civil society, one that sees it as an arena of conflict and disagreement. According to this perspective, members of society share a "thin" consensus that relates only to acceptable forms of expression and peaceful conflict resolution in the political arena (Oxhorn 2006). Civil society serves as "the setting of settings" that provides a domain for deliberation without advocating particular ideological content (Walzer 1992). In the new conceptualization, the unit of analysis is not individuals but collectivities from various worldviews and socio-economic backgrounds. As Oxhorn rightly notes, this perspective has a considerable advantage when compared with the overly liberal perspective, because "[m]any societies simply do not recognize the centrality of the individual in the public or political realm, and instead emphasize the communities and larger social networks to which the individual belongs" (Oxhorn 2006, 62).

Indeed, for Oxhorn, democratic performance is contingent on the ability of self-conscious groups from diverse backgrounds to conduct successful struggles to advance their collective interests vis-à-vis other groups and the state. In that respect, Oxhorn emphasized that civil society groups represent a wider variation than do economic classes. In Oxhorn's words:

> [O]ther civil society organizations may include economic sectors and professions, independent territorial communities, ethnic and linguistic groups, religions and sects, voluntary associations, and gender and generational groupings, among others. Shared identities, the ability for self-organization and a history of collective struggle, are sources of power that can enable disadvantaged groups to challenge the status quo. (Oxhorn 2003, 40)

No less important, in this perspective the state is not isolated from civil society, nor does it maintain a zero-sum balance of power with it, but rather it is instrumental in shaping the boundaries of civil society. This is because "basic rights necessary for civil society to flourish can be guaranteed only by the state" (Oxhorn 2006, 66). Oxhorn's conceptualization allows for the incorporation of religious groups in analyses of civil society while recognizing the crucial role of the state in shaping religious behaviour within its borders (more on this below). It is more realistic than the traditional view in that it does not wish to flatten ideological disagreements and it sets a framework for peaceful coexistence of different ideological sectors in society.

A vibrant and autonomous civil society offers groups and organizations a forum within which they can express opinions about – and seek to bring about change in – aspects of the larger society. Therefore, the existence, autonomy, and vibrancy of the organs of civil society should correlate positively with effective mass mobilization and eventual regime change.

RELIGIOUS ACTORS AND ASSOCIATIONS

An ongoing debate exists within the literature as to whether faith-based actors should be included in the realm of civil society. As mentioned earlier, the liberal school of civil society excludes religious actors from this realm. The alternative school of civil society, however, takes a more communitarian approach, and accepts groups with illiberal worldviews, including religious ones, within the bounds of civil society (Putnam and Campbell 2012; Rubin 2020). In my previous work, I reasoned why religious actors should be understood as part of civil society:

> Religious groups and movements are part of the social fabric. They represent a coherent perspective on life and a code of moral

> and practical behaviour. They have an impact on the dynamics within societies as well as between societies and states. In their various activities, they engage with a wide spectrum of social issues, such as education, welfare, and youth organizations, as well as worship services. The legitimacy of the regime and the quality of its democratic governance are dependent to some extent on whether religious groups are accommodated into civil society or are marginalized from it. Hence religious populations should be treated as social actors and potential partners in civil society. (Rubin 2020, 33)

Nevertheless, given the disagreement, and considering the exceptional power of Islamic actors in Middle Eastern societies, I distinguish between religious actors and "mainstream" civic associations.

Islamist movements constituted the most significant political opposition to authoritarian regimes in the Arab world before the Arab Spring. Despite the inherent tension between the absolutism of political religion and the features of democracy, in places where religious groups and organizations abandon a vision of non-democratic revolutionary takeover and accept the rules of the democratic game, they might serve as an important organ of civil society. This trend may be manifested in strategic decisions such as rejecting violence as a means of political transformation (Ashour 2009), and in behaviours such as forming coalitions with secular political parties, collaborating with other organs of civil society, conducting primary elections, and running effective electoral campaigns (Clark 2004; Langhor 2004).

Obviously, not all religious actors fall into the category of civil society. Only some religious actors adopt moderate ideologies and practices, while others uphold a more radical worldview. Islamic movements that adopt moderate ideas and procedures as a strategic choice, and accept democratic principles of government, should be conceived as part of civil society, and their presence and vibrancy should correlate positively with prospects for effective mass mobilization against the regime and for eventual regime change.

Given the huge variation among religious groups and the theological differences among religions, including in relation to their view of state affairs, it is hard to draw a decisive line in the sand above which religious groups and associations would be conceived as part of civil society. Nevertheless, it is possible to specify three necessary prerequiesties for a religious group to qualify as part of civil society. The first and most important condition is the outright denial of any type of violent behaviour for the achievement of political goals. Any permissble approach towards the use of violence therefore disqualifies the group from civil society (Yildirim 2016). The second condition is the support of and adeherence to democaratic procedures as the only way to determine who rules the state. This commitment should hold true at all times and especially under circumstances in which sufficient political power may allow a transition from a democratic to a theocratic regime (Nasr 2005). The third condition should be respect for a pluralistic public sphere, in which different groups with different worldviews can participate without being deligitimized. This is espcially true in the context of Islamic societies with regard to religious minorities, women, and LGBT groups that have been traditionally harrassed and prosecuted (Inglehart and Norris 2003).

MEDIA AND COMMUNICATIONS

Media outlets provide access to information, help shape public opinion, and facilitate coordination among popular groups (Ryan 1991). Authoritarian governments can more easily control traditional outlets such as printed materials, radio, and television by manipulating their content to tailor the information that is available to the public and inculcate particular doctrines or ideas. In recent years, new forms of communication, such as Internet forums, global and regional satellite channels, cellular phones, and web-based social networks, have developed that are much more difficult to regulate.

There is a lively debate in the Arab Spring literature on the relative influence of the media on the eruption and efficacy of mass protests. Some scholars doubt the impact of media traffic during a protest (Aday et al. 2012) and the capacity of that protest to bring about transition in its aftermath (Lynch 2014). But these studies concentrated on a specific type of media (Twitter, through Bitly) that does not account for the entire media domain, and only during the protest, while not evaluating the impact of social media as a platform for the dissemination of ideas long before the eruption of protest. Most scholars, however, acknowledge the enormous impact of media outlets (old and new) as a platform for mobilization and dissemination of ideas and as an enabler of coordination (Bellin 2011; Brynen, Moore et al. 2012; Howard and Hussain 2013). The combined operation of autonomous or unregulated traditional media and new forms of mass media constitutes an important platform for the circulation of diverse (at times dissenting) ideas, as well as a relatively effective platform for social mobilization. As such, these media constitute a key element in the public sphere that serves as the arena within which civil society groups and organizations interact among themselves and with the state (see Bonner, and Durazo Herrmann, this volume). High levels of autonomy and freedom of the press, together with extensive access to Internet-based media and social networks, should correlate positively with effective mass mobilization.

THE IMPACT OF CIVIL SOCIETY CONSTRUCTION ON MASS MOBILIZATION AND POLITICAL CHANGE

The cases of Egypt and Syria represent two archetypal regimes where the connection between civil society and hybrid regimes can be investigated. Prior to the Arab Spring, Egypt had been a non-electoral hybrid regime. Conversely, Syria had been a full-fledged authoritarian regime. While neither of the regimes conducted free and fair elections, the Egyptian state tolerated a relatively vibrant and autonomous civil society, while the Syrian regime denied any autonomous activity at the societal level. The same difference applies to the regimes' treatment of communication and media as an important element of the public sphere. In Egypt, there existed vibrant and relatively free activity in the media domain, while in Syria the regime made serious efforts to repress all media that did not serve as the regime's mouthpiece. As I show below, the striking difference in both cases between the vibrancy and relative autonomy of civil society and the role of the media explains the very different dynamics and results of popular protests and ensuing regime transitions in both states. In Egypt, a vibrant and engaging civil society circulated its ideas via relatively free and diverse media platforms and was thus able to effectively mobilize the masses and confront the regime without violence, leading to regime change and a democratic opening within a few weeks. In Syria, the absence of organized civil society and a free platform for mobilization and the circulation of ideas meant that the resulting popular challenge to the regime was uncoordinated and mostly violent, failing to topple the regime or produce a democratic opening, and instead led to a horrific, decade-long bloody civil war.

CASE STUDY: EGYPT (HYBRID REPUBLIC)

Media and Communications

During the two decades leading up to the Arab Spring, Egypt had undergone a communications revolution. In 2009 Egypt had nineteen daily newspapers with a total circulation of four million; in addition, it had a TV penetration of 93 per cent, including satellite and cable TV penetration of 43 per cent; mobile phone penetration of 72 per cent; and Internet broadband penetration of 7.4 per cent (Ghannam 2011, 26). At the start of the Egyptian revolution, Internet users in Egypt numbered about 21.2 million; 4.2 million people were using Facebook, and 270,000 used Twitter.[1] A report by an Egyptian research centre suggested that, in 2008, around 160 blogs – 30 per cent of all the blogs in the Arab world – were Egyptian; most blog consumers were twenty to thirty years old; and 79 per cent of Egyptian blogs operated from within Egypt.[2] Public and transnational satellite television stations, particularly news channels like Al Jazeera and Al Arabia, were viewed by a substantial segment of the population (Auter et al. 2005). These developments had a profound impact on the ability of individuals and groups to transmit information, values, and norms between the various political levels in local communities, and facilitated the construction of new economic, political, and cultural power structures in areas previously dominated by the political elite and the state.

The far-reaching changes engendered by the Arab digital revolution during this period were manifested in the Egyptian revolution in January 2011. The spread of Internet usage in Egypt derailed the control mechanisms of the political elite, and facilitated coordinated waves of protest against the political, social, and economic reality in ways that would not have been allowed on traditional state- and regime-controlled channels. In 2010, Wael Ghonim, an Egyptian Internet activist and one of the leaders of the Egyptian revolution, founded a Facebook page titled "We are all Khaled Said," in response to the death of a young Egyptian who was tortured to death by police in Alexandria. Ghonim's page garnered three hundred thousand active members and several million hits, and prompted ten thousand people to assemble for demonstrations in Alexandria and other places throughout Egypt. Because the page was instrumental in bringing demonstrators together for 25 January

2011, the "Day of Rage," analysts have credited it with sparking the Egyptian revolution, referred to by Ghonim as the first "Facebook revolution" in the world.

Civic Organizations

Under President Hosni Mubarak, state policies towards civil society became much more tolerant, with increased openness towards opposition factions, support for local and parliamentary elections, and a relative freedom of expression (Al-Awadi 2004). Mubarak promoted reconciliation with opposition factions by allowing them to publish their own newspapers, holding several personal meetings with their leaders (Lust-Okar 2005, 141), and permitting the establishment of new organizations and institutions, which came to play an important role in Egyptian society and politics. The number of Egyptian NGOs grew from 7,593 in 1976 to 13,239 in 1993 and to 16,000 at the beginning of the twenty-first century (Qandel 2003, 76). Since then, the continued expansion of NGOs in Egypt has been quite extraordinary, with estimates of more than twenty-five thousand associations, including five thousand cooperative organizations, four thousand youth and sports clubs, and thirty professional associations, which together make Egypt's NGO community the largest in the developing world. While a quarter of these organizations focus on traditional roles like providing charity, many have begun to focus on issues like poverty alleviation, unemployment, women's empowerment, caring for homeless children, microeconomic projects, and training and development (Brown and Shahin 2010, 208–10).

Religious Actors

Political Islam is not a monolithic movement. Around sixteen different Islamist movements, with distinct political and social views, were active in Egypt on the eve of the popular uprising against Mubarak. These include relatively pragmatic factions like the Muslim Brotherhood (MB), institutional actors like the Al-Azhar University faculty, and militant Ja'maat Salafi and jihadist factions like Takfir Wa-al Higra, and Islamic Jihad (Munib 2012).

Since its founding in the 1920s by Hassan al-Banna, the MB has arguably been the dominant and most institutionalized religious stream in Egypt. The relative tolerance of the movement during the Mubarak era enabled the MB's participation in public and political life (El-Ghobashy 2005), and turned it into a nationwide movement with a religious agenda on social, economic, and political issues. Indeed, the Brotherhood's strategy of continuous participation in political life highlighted the discrepancy between the limited political space allowed to it by the regime and the high level of political support it enjoyed at the mass level. Thanks to its growing legitimacy in the 1980s, the organization gradually expanded its activities and began competing in elections for trade unions and professional associations, including those representing doctors, engineers, lawyers, and journalists. Between 1986 and 1992, the MB won a solid majority in the four most important associations: medicine, engineering, pharmacy, and law (Yohannes 2001).

In March 2004, the movement announced a political platform, the first initiative of this type since its establishment. The platform served as a manifesto on the state of the country, calling for social, economic, and cultural reforms, as well as political reform, in line with Islamic principles.[3] Areas covered by the platform included strengthening civil society; instituting reforms in education and research; battling poverty; introducing social and cultural reforms, including those linked with the status of women and the Coptic minority; and modifying Egypt's foreign policy (Ghanem and Mustafa 2011).

Notably, a lively discussion about democracy existed among Islamic factions in Egypt beyond the MB. For instance, while some militant thinkers from the Ja'maat movements like Al-Mawdudi rejected any attempt to introduce democracy in Islamic society, moderate thinkers like Fahmi Huyadi justified democratic principles and went as far as to distinguish between the source of law, which is God, and the source of sovereignty, which are the people and the state (Yadlin 1998). In sum, the space opened by the regime enabled the MB and other Islamic factions to transform from an illegal and marginalized opposition movement to an effective organ of civil society.

Character and Outcome of Protest

The eighteen-day popular protest against Mubarak's regime – from the "Day of Rage" (25 January 2011) to Mubarak's resignation (11 February 2011) – was short and effective, with an active participation by more than fifteen million demonstrators, many of them staying for days in the place where the protest took place, and with demonstrators occupying different regions, cities, and localities simultaneously.[4] According to the "Report of the Commission to Investigate the Facts of the 25 of January Revolution," between 25 January and 16 February 2011, 846 Egyptian civilians were killed and 6,467 participants were wounded in the revolution.[5] These numbers are relatively low for a revolution against an Arab authoritarian regime of the kind that tended not to hesitate to use brutal repression against their people (Bellin 2011), especially when compared with death tolls in neighbouring countries such as Syria and Libya. Importantly, the state apparatus was the source of almost all of the violence, with only marginal acts of violence conducted by protesters. Another unique feature was the demographic aspect. In a country of eighty-three million people, more than fifteen million participated actively in the revolution, with floods of demonstrators from different social and ideological backgrounds. In Miedan Al-Tahrir (Tahrir Square), the level of coordination between different channels of communication, including social media activists, civil society activists, political activists, and Islamic activists – especially from the MB, which joined the revolution in its second week – was a primary factor behind the capacity of the protest to remove Mubarak from power. This effort was complemented and facilitated by virtual social networks, as Howard and Hussain put it plainly (2013, 32): "The countries with the most tech-savvy civil society groups, such as Tunisia and Egypt, removed their dictators with few casualties."

In June 2011, elections for the presidency brought an Islamic president to office and significantly altered the distribution of power between the elected government and the security forces. In the 2011 parliamentary election, the moderate Freedom and Justice Party, the political arm of the MB, won approximately 47 per cent of the vote, while the militant Salafi faction Al-Nour (the Light) won roughly 25 per cent. The Islamist Mohamed Morsi was elected president in June 2012, defeating Ahmed Shafiq, a former high-ranking figure in the old regime. On 25 December 2012, a new constitution was approved through a referendum, despite arguments, made especially by the liberal factions, against its illiberal and pro-Islamic content.[6]

An elaborate analysis of the counter-revolution in 2013 and the rise of General Mahmood el-Sisi to power is beyond the scope of this chapter. It is important to note, however, that a major aspect of the new president's policy was shrinking the autonomy of civil society in Egyptian society. This policy included the mass arresting of bloggers, increased regulation on the registration and funding of civil society organizations, and the harsh legal and physical repression of the MB, including arresting its leaders and confiscating its property. All these actions arguably drove el-Sisi's regime away from the Egyptian government's status as a hybrid regime.

CASE STUDY: SYRIA (AUTHORITARIAN REPUBLIC)

Media and Communications

The Syrian Ba'ath Party maintained full control over all forms of media throughout its rule. In the 1990s and during the beginning of Bashar al-Assad's presidential incumbency, the regime allowed a limited degree of free speech and criticism against the state, although the latter was limited to reports about bureaucratic corruption, and all published information was strictly controlled by the government (Perthes 2004). Up until the beginning of mass protests in the Syrian periphery, in March 2011, the regime had enforced a sweeping ban on the free use of social networks. Consequently, the rate of Facebook usage in Syria was among the lowest in the Arab world, at less than 2 per cent of the population, and Twitter only 0.2 per cent. In 2011, only 20 per cent were connected to the Internet in Syria, one of the lowest penetration rates in the region.[7] Given this abysmally low penetration rate, the Syrian media did not have the capacity to raise public awareness of political reforms (Biswas and Sipes 2014). Instead, the supervised media served mainly as a control mechanism by the regime.

Civic Organizations

Available sources about the state of Syrian civic organizations during the years before the Arab Spring are rare, given the state's total control over such information and the general weakness of civil society itself. References to Syrian civil society during the second half of the twentieth century focus on traditional communal activities, such as the institutions of the Muslim Waqf and professional associations. These elements of civil society, however, were overseen by the Ba'ath regime and lacked substantial autonomy (Pierret 2013; Ziadeh 2013).

Between 1960 and 1990, the urbanization policies of the regime raised the number of city dwellers from 37 per cent of the population to 50 per cent. Meanwhile, the number of university graduates grew from 5 per cent in 1960 to 28 per cent in 1989, and the middle class also expanded significantly (Hinnebusch 1993). Against this backdrop, signs of liberalization during the 1990s raised the prospect of the empowerment of civic activities. This trend appeared to be strengthening following Assad's rise to power in 2000. A short period, known as the Damascus Spring, saw demands by political activists for expanded political freedoms and civil rights, for the release of political prisoners, and for the right to organize in forums outside the Ba'ath Party's wingspan. However, a year later the positive political trend turned on its head. Criticism of the regime led to the arrest of social and political activists, restrictions on the establishment of civic organizations were kept intact, and restrictions on civic and political activities remained extremely harsh (René 2014). The most significant attempt by civil society groups at coordinated political action took place in October 2005 under the umbrella of the Damascus Declaration,[8] an elitist attempt to promote a civil and democratic agenda. In response, the regime arrested and tortured many of the signatories – liberals, Islamists, minority leaders, and intellectuals – and forcibly dismantled the group (Ziadeh 2013). Indeed, civil society in Syria was an embryonic domain totally controlled and overseen by the Ba'athist regime (Khatib 2013; Khalaf et al. 2014).

Religious Actors

The relationship between the Ba'ath regime and the Islamic factions in Syria reflects a very restrictive dictatorial regime on the one hand, and a violent and uncompromising political Islam on the other hand (Hinnebusch 2002; Wieland 2006). The Syrian branch of the MB was formed in 1945 and soon thereafter became a major actor in parliamentarian politics as an alternative to the communists and the dominant Ba'ath Party (Moussalli 2005, 143). In the mid-1970s, the Syrian MB united with other Islamist factions in the Syrian Islamic Front (SIF). Assad's rise to power in 1970 signified the establishment of an authoritarian regime, and the repression of any form of Islamic activity in Syrian society. In 1976, the SIF began challenging Assad's authoritarian rule. This challenge peaked in 1982 with an Islamic uprising against the regime in the town of Hama, which resulted in harsh government repression, estimates of thirty thousand casualties, and the elimination of the Syrian Islamic opposition movement.

In 1980, the Assad regime enacted Law No. 49, which stipulated the death penalty for membership in the MB, but also provided that members who surrendered would be spared (Porat 2010). Centres of social and organizational action had collapsed, and the SIF was forced to operate only underground or outside the country. The regime denied any attempt at reconciliation with the Islamist sector. The hope that Assad's rise to power would bring tolerance towards religious actors was shattered, as the regime continued to exercise strict secularism (Porat 2010). During the prohibition of the MB, new Islamic forces arose in Syria. These included both local networks, such as reorganized Sufi communities, and Gulf-sponsored missionary movements, which promoted a version of Salafism, particularly after the Second Gulf War in 2003, though both concentrated minimal effort on the public and political realms (Lund 2013). Despite the secular character of the regime, it succeeded in reaching a tacit understanding with the local Islamist elite, fragmented it, and ensured that at least part of it remained permissive of the regime's repressive actions during the eruption of the Syrian civil war (Pierret 2013).

Character and Outcome of Protest

In the absence of vibrant, nonconforming enclaves, the isolated pockets of opposition were unable to coordinate their actions towards effective mass protest in major urban centres and challenge the Assad authoritarian regime. Scattered protests and violent guerrilla operations against the regime began in March 2011, in places like Daraa, A-Zur, and Homs (as opposed to the capital, Damascus), with the participation of at most several hundred or a few thousand protesters. These protests persisted despite harsh repression by the armed forces, but soon gave way to armed resistance, which sparked a vicious cycle of violence and resulted in a steep rise in the death toll. As of 2022, an estimated six hundred thousand citizens have been killed. Out of twenty-three million citizens, more than eleven million are estimated to be refugees, either in Syria or outside its borders. The regime crossed a threshold of violence in the summer of

2013, using chemical weapons as part of its ongoing effort to repress the rebels.[9] As of this writing, the Assad regime has collapsed and different rebel groups have taken control over the war-torn country. It is still too early to say what type of civil society and what type of political regime will emerge in Syria in the coming years.

CONCLUSION

The events that erupted throughout the Middle East in December 2010 produced different political outcomes in different Middle Eastern states. This variation cannot be sufficiently explained by referring to the regime categories that exist in the literature. In remedying this lacuna, the analysis presented here has suggested a complementary understanding of the hybrid regimes, one that is not based on the electoral and constitutional axes but rather on the toleration, or lack thereof, of institutionalized and non-institutionalized challengers of the regime, with the latter being a function of the relative autonomy and vibrancy of civil society, broadly understood.

In particular, by using this novel categorization and exploring the relative vibrancy and autonomy of civil society, as defined by Oxhorn, this work reveals that in hybrid Egypt, where a relatively vibrant and autonomous civil society existed prior to the eruption of the Arab Spring, mass mobilization proved more effective and brought significant political change. The relatively short, peaceful, and successful character of the mobilization was a result of the effective operation of groups in civil society, which served as an arena for the coordination and distribution of ideas. In contrast, the authoritarian Syrian state, which prevented the existence and activity of civil society, was able to thwart mass mobilization and its corresponding potential for bringing about political transition. The result was a violent and politically ineffective protest. The correlation between the character of civil society and political outcomes holds true in other regimes like hybrid Tunisia and authoritarian Libya.

Importantly, this framework does not apply to Algeria and Lebanon. While these outlier cases require in-depth analysis, which is beyond the scope of this chapter, I speculate that a recent history of large-scale violence served as an impediment against mass protest. In Algeria, a civil war that claimed the lives of more than 150,000 people ended only in 1998. This recent bloody experience may have deterred Algerians from mobilizing against the regime and risking the eruption of a new wave of violence. Likewise, Lebanon suffered a relatively recent and very violent civil war, which ended only in 1990, along with recurrent waves of violence with Israel, the most recent of which was in 2006. Of course, this is only a preliminary assumption. These outlier cases require further investigation.

From a theoretical point of view, this chapter applies an alternative conceptualization of civil society, one that treats civil society as a diverse arena of peaceful ideational exchange, constructed from the bottom up, in which groups from different backgrounds and beliefs share a thin consensus and struggle against subordination. This perspective on civil society is more relevant to the study of the Middle East, an illiberal, non-democratic region, in which Islamic religion is an important source of affiliation. This perspective also emphasizes the mutual influence of the state and civil society on each other, rather than viewing them as operating in isolation.

This work also contributes to the literature on hybrid regimes by extending the dominant conceptualization of hybrid regimes, with its emphasis on electoral procedures, through the notion of tolerated challenges to the regime, either in the form of elections and parties, or in the form of a relatively vibrant and autonomous civil society. This more complex understanding of hybridity more substantively captures the conditions that may enable effective mass mobilization, and eventual regime change. Hopefully, doing so will shift more scholarly attention from procedures to the influence of non-electoral practices and orientations on regime transition in the Middle East and elsewhere.

NOTES

1 *Al-Shorouk*. 2011. "The Revolution Changes Egyptian Internet Behavior," 20 March, 16.

2 *Asharq Al-Awsat*. 2008. 6 July.

3 See the interview with Mohammad Mahdi 'Aqef on the Muslim Brotherhood's official site (in Arabic): http://www.ikhwanonline.com/Article.asp?ArtID=5207&SecID=210.

4 Al Jazeera. 2011. "Timeline: Egypt's Revolution." 14 July. Retrieved 18 March 2013, http://www.aljazeera.com/news/middleeast/2011/01/201112515334871490.html.

5 Report of the Commission to Investigate the Facts of the 25th of January Revolution (19 April 2011): 6.

6 See Carnegie Endowment for International Peace (2013).
7 *Arab Social Media Report* (published by the Dubai School of Government). See http://www.arabsocialmediareport.com/UserManagement/PDF/ASMR%202%20Arabic%20Final.pdf (in Arabic).
8 For details about this declaration, see http://carnegie-mec.org/diwan/48514?lang=en, retrieved 9 February 2018.
9 Schmitt, Eric, and David Sanger. 2013. "Hints of Syrian Chemical Push Set Off Global Effort to Stop It," *New York Times*, 7 January; Lynch, Colum. 2013. "U.N. to Investigate Chemical-Weapons Allegations in Syria." *Washington Post*, 21 March; Gearan, Anne, and Scott Wilson. 2013. "U.S., Russia Reach Agreement on Seizure of Syrian Chemical Weapons Arsenal." *Washington Post*, 14 September.

REFERENCES

Aday, Sean, Henry Farrell, Marc Lynch, John Sides, and Deen Freelon. 2012. *New Media and Conflict After the Arab Spring*. Washington, DC: United States Institute of Peace.

Al-Awadi, Hesham. 2004. *In Pursuit of Legitimacy: The Muslim Brothers and Mubarak 1982–2000*. London: I.B. Tauris.

Almond, Gabriel. 1987. "The Development of Political Development." In *Understanding Political Development*, edited by Myron Weiner and Samuel Huntington, 437–90. Boston: Little, Brown and Company.

Almond, Gabriel, and Sidney Verba. 1963. *The Civic Culture: Political Attitudes and Democracy in Five Nations*. Princeton, NJ: Princeton University Press.

Anderson, R. David, Steven M. Fish, Stephen E. Hanson, and Philip G. Roeder. 2001. *Postcommunism and the Theory of Democracy*. Princeton, NJ: Princeton University Press.

Andrain, Charles F., and David Apter. 1995. *Political Protest and Social Change*. New York: New York University Press.

Ashour, Omar. 2009. *The De-Radicalization of Jihadists: Transforming Armed Islamist Movements*. New York: Routledge.

Auter, Philip J., Mohamed Arafa, and Khalid Al-Jaber. 2005. "Identifying with Arabic Journalists: How Al-Jazeera Tapped Parasocial Interaction Gratifications in the Arab World." *International Journal for Communications Studies* 67, no. 2: 189–204.

Bellin, Eva. 2004. "The Robustness of Authoritarianism in the Middle East: Exceptionalism in Comparative Perspective." *Comparative Politics* 36, no. 2: 139–57.

Bellin, Eva. 2011. "Reconsidering the Robustness of Authoritarianism in the Middle East: Lessons from the Arab Spring." *Comparative Politics* 44, no. 2: 127–49.

Biswas, Manish, and Christopher Sipes. 2014. "Social Media in Syria's Uprising and Post-Revolution Libya: An Analysis of Activists' and Blogger's Online Engagement." *Arab Media and Society*, 1–21.

Brown, Nathan J., and Emad Shahin, eds. 2010. *The Struggle over Democracy in the Middle East: Regional Politics and External Policies.* London: Routledge.

Brownlee, Jason. 2011. "Executive Elections in the Arab World: When and How Do They Matter?" *Comparative Political Studies* 44, no. 7: 807–28.

Brownlee, Jason, Tarek Masoud, and Andrew Reynolds. 2015. *The Arab Spring: Pathways of Repression and Reform.* New York: Oxford University Press.

Brynen, Rex, Bahgat Korany, and Paul Noble, eds. 1995. *Political Liberalization and Democratization in the Arab World.* Vol. 1, *Theoretical Perspectives.* Boulder, CO: Lynne Rienner.

Brynen, Rex, Peter W. Moore, Bassel F. Salloukh, and Marie-Joelle Zahar. 2012. *Beyond the Arab Spring: Authoritarianism and Democratization in the Arab Spring.* Boulder, CO: Lynne Rienner.

Carothers, Thomas. 1999. "Civil Society." *Foreign Policy* 117: 18–29.

Clark, Janine A. 2004. *Islam, Charity, and Activism: Middle-Class Networks and Social Welfare in Egypt, Jordan, and Yemen.* Bloomington, IN: Indiana University Press.

Della Porta, Donatella. 2014. *Mobilizing For Democracy: Comparing 1989 and 2011.* Oxford, UK: Oxford University Press.

Della Porta, Donatella. 2016. *Where Did the Revolution Go?* Cambridge, UK: Cambridge University Press.

Diamond, Larry. 2002. "Thinking About Hybrid Regimes." *Journal of Democracy* 13, no. 2: 21–35.

El-Ghobashy, Mona. 2005. "The Metamorphosis of the Egyptian Muslim Brothers." *International Journal of Middle Eastern Studies* 37, no. 3: 373–95.

Fish, Steven M. 1996. *Democracy from Scratch: Opposition and Regime in the New Russian Revolution.* Princeton, NJ: Princeton University Press.

Frisch, Hillel. 2011. "Why Monarchies Persist: Balancing Between Internal and External Vulnerability." *Review of International Studies* 37, no. 1: 167–84.

Fukuyama, Francis. 1996. *Trust: The Social Virtues and the Creation of Prosperity*. New York: Free Press Paperbacks.

Gause, Gregory F. 2013. "Kings for All Seasons: How the Middle East's Monarchies Survived the Arab Spring." Brookings Doha Center Analysis Papers, no. 8.

Ghanem, As'ad, and Mohanad Mustafa. 2011. "Strategies of Electoral Participation by Islamic Movements: The Muslim Brotherhood and Parliamentary Elections in Egypt and Jordan, November 2010." *Contemporary Politics* 17, no. 4: 393–409.

Ghannam, Jessica. 2011. *Social Media in the Arab World: Leading Up to the Uprisings of 2011*. Washington, DC: Center for International Media Assistance.

Gilbert, Leah, and Payam Mohseni. 2011. "Beyond Authoritarianism: The Conceptualization of Hybrid Regimes." *Studies in Comparative International Development* 46, no. 3: 270–97.

Hinnebusch, Raymond. 1993. "State and Civil Society in Syria." *Middle East Journal* 47, no. 2: 243–57.

Hinnebusch, Raymond. 2002. *Syria: The Revolution from Above*. London: Routledge.

Hinnebusch, Raymond. 2006. "Authoritarian Persistence, Democratization Theory and the Middle East: An Overview and Critique." *Democratization* 13, no. 3: 373–95.

Hinnebusch, Raymond. 2016. *After the Arab Uprisings: Between Democratization, Counter-Revolution and State Failure*. Abingdon, UK: Routledge.

Howard, Philip, and Muzammil M. Hussain. 2013. *Democracy's Fourth Wave? Digital Media and the Arab Spring*. Oxford, UK: Oxford University Press.

Inglehart, Ronald, and Pippa Norris. 2003. *Rising Tide: Gender Equality and Cultural Change around the World*. Cambridge, UK: Cambridge University Press.

Inglehart, Ronald, and Pippa Norris. 2016. "Trump, Brexit and the Rise of Populism: Economic Have-Nots and Cultural Backlash." HKS Faculty Working Papers, no. RWP16-026.

Khalaf, Rania, Omar Ramadan, and Fawwaz Stollies. 2014. *Activism in Difficult Times: Civil Society Groups in Syria (2011–2014)*. Beirut: Badael and Friedrich-Ebert-Stiftung.

Khatib, Lina. 2013. "Syria's Civil Society as a Tool for Regime Legitimacy." In *Civil Society in Syria and Iran: Activism in*

Authoritarian Contexts, edited by Petra Aarts and Francesco Cavatorta, 19–38. Boulder, CO: Lynne Rienner.

Langhor, Vickie. 2004. "Too Much Civil Society, Too Little Politics? Egypt and Other Liberalizing Arab Regimes." *Comparative Politics* 36, no. 2: 181–204.

Levitsky, Steven, and Lucan A. Way. 2010. *Competitive Authoritarianism: Hybrid Regimes After the Cold War*. New York: Cambridge University Press.

Lewis, Bernard. 1994. *Islam and the West*. New York: Oxford University Press.

Lipset, Seymour Martin. 1981. *Political Man, the Social Bases of Politics*. Baltimore, MD: Johns Hopkins University Press.

Lund, Aron. 2013. *Struggling to Adapt: The Muslim Brotherhood in a New Syria*. Washington, DC: Carnegie Endowment.

Lust-Okar, Ellen. 2005. *Structuring Conflict in the Arab World: Incumbents, Opponents, and Institutions*. Cambridge, UK: Cambridge University Press.

Lynch, Marc, ed. 2014. *The Arab Uprisings Explained: New Contentious Politics in the Middle East*. New York: Columbia University Press.

Mako, Shadi, and Valentine M. Moghadam. 2021. *After the Arab Uprisings: Progress and Stagnation in the Middle East and North Africa*. New York: Cambridge University Press.

Merkel, Wolfgang. 2004. "Embedded and Defective Democracies." *Democratization* 11, no. 5: 33–58.

Migdal, Joel. 2001. *State in Society: Studying How States and Societies Transform and Constitute One Another*. New York: Cambridge University Press.

Moore Jr., Barrington. 1966. *Social Origins of Dictatorship and Democracy: Lord and Peasant in the Making of the Modern World*. Boston: Beacon Press.

Morse, Yonatan L. 2012. "The Era of Electoral Authoritarianism." *World Politics* 64, no. 1: 161–98.

Moussalli, Ahmad. 2005. *Historical Dictionary of Islamic Fundamentalist Movements in the Arab World, Iran and Turkey*. Beirut: Center for Arab Unity.

Munib, Ahmed-Abdel Monem. 2012. *The Network of Islamic Movements in Egypt*. Cairo: Arab Network for Human Rights.

Nasr, Vali. 2005. The Rise of Muslim Democracy. *Journal of Democracy* 16, no. 2, 13–27.

O'Donnell, Guillermo, and Philippe C. Schmitter. 1986. *Transitions from Authoritarian Rule*. Baltimore, MD: Johns Hopkins University Press.

Oxhorn, Philip. 1995. *Organizing Civil Society: The Popular Sector and the Struggle for Democracy in Chile*. University Park, PA: Pennsylvania State University Press.

Oxhorn, Philip. 2003. "Social Inequality, Civil Society, and the Limits of Citizenship in Latin America." In *What Justice? Whose Justice?: Fighting for Fairness in Latin America*, edited by Eva Susan-Eva and Tom Wikham-Crowley, 35–62. Berkeley, CA: University of California Press.

Oxhorn, Philip. 2006. "Conceptualizing Civil Society from the Bottom Up: A Political Economy Perspective." In *Civil Society and Democracy in Latin America*, edited by Richard Feinberg, Carlos H. Waisman, and Leon Zamosc, 59–84. New York: Palgrave Macmillan.

Oxhorn, Philip. 2011. *Sustaining Civil Society: Economic Change, Democracy, and the Social Construction of Citizenship in Latin America*. University Park, PA: Pennsylvania State University Press.

Penner-Angrist, Michael, and Marc Pripstein-Posusney, eds. 2005. *Authoritarianism in the Middle East: Regimes and Resistance*. Boulder, CO: Lynne Rienner.

Perthes, Volker. 2004. *Syria Under Bashar al-Asad: Modernisation and the Limits of Change*. New York: Routledge.

Pierret, Thomas. 2013. *Religion and State in Syria*. Cambridge, UK: Cambridge University Press.

Porat, Liora. 2010. *The Syrian Muslim Brotherhood and the Asad Regime*. Boston: Crown Center for Middle East Studies.

Price, David. 1999. *Islamic Political Culture, Democracy, and Human Rights: A Comparative Study*. Westport, CT: Praeger.

Putnam, Robert D. 1993. *Making Democracy Work: Civic Traditions in Modern Italy*. Princeton, NJ: Princeton University Press.

Putnam, Robert D., and David E. Campbell. 2012. *American Grace: How Religion Divides and Unites Us*. New York: Simon and Schuster.

Qandel, Amani. 2003. "Mustaqbal Miṣr: Al-Mujtama' al-Madani" [Egypt's Future: The Civil Society]. *Majallat al-Dimuqratiyya* [*Democracy*] 3, no. 9: 69–82.

René, Stéphane. 2014. "State–Civil Society Relations in Syria: EU Good Governance Assistance in an Authoritarian State." Retrieved from Leiden University, Leiden, Netherlands.

Rubin, Aviad. 2013. "The Status of Religion in Emergent Political Regimes: Lessons from Turkey and Israel." *Nations and Nationalism* 19, no. 3: 493–512.

Rubin, Aviad. 2020. *Bounded Integration: State-Religion Relationship and Democratic Performance in Turkey and Israel.* New York: State University of New York Press.

Rutherford, Bruce K. 2008. *Egypt after Mubarak: Liberalism, Islam, and Democracy in the Arab World.* Princeton, NJ: Princeton University Press.

Ryan, Charlotte. 1991. *Prime Time Activism: Media Strategies for Grassroots Organizing.* Boston: South End Press.

Sadiki, Larbi. 2009. *Rethinking Arab Democratization: Elections without Democracy.* Oxford, UK: Oxford University Press.

Schedler, Andreas. 2013. *The Politics of Uncertainty: Sustaining and Subverting Electoral Authoritarianism.* Oxford, UK: Oxford University Press.

Schwedler, Jillian. 2006. *Faith in Moderation: Islamist Parties in Jordan and Yemen.* New York: Cambridge University Press.

Schwedler, Jillian. 2011. "Can Islamists Become Moderates? Rethinking the Inclusion-Moderation Hypothesis." *World Politics* 63, no. 2: 347–76.

Skocpol, Theda. 1979. *States and Social Revolutions: A Comparative Analysis of France, Russia, and China.* New York: Cambridge University Press.

Skocpol, Theda, ed. 1998. *Democracy, Revolution and History.* Ithaca, NY: Cornell University Press.

Snyder, Richard. 2006. "Beyond Electoral Authoritarianism: The Spectrum of Non-Democratic Regimes." In *Electoral Authoritarianism: The Dynamics of Unfree Competition*, edited by Andreas Schedler, 292–310. Boulder, CO: Lynne Rienner.

Stepan, Alfred, and Juan J. Linz. 2013. "Democratization Theory and the 'Arab Spring,'" *Journal of Democracy* 24, no. 2: 15–30.

Tilly, Charles. 2004. *Contention and Democracy in Europe, 1650–2000.* New York: Cambridge University Press.

Walzer, Michael. 1992. "The Civil Society Argument." In *Dimensions of Radical Democracy*, edited by Chantal Mouffe, 89–107. London: Verso.

Wieland, Carsten. 2006. *Syria: Ballots or Bullets? Democracy, Islamism, and Secularism in the Levant.* Seattle, WA: Cune Press.

Yadlin, Rivka. 1998. "Democracy and Peace: The Limits of Universalistic Theory," paper presented at the Leonard Davis Institute for International Relations conference on Regional Peace Making in Comparative Perspective, June 1998.

Yildirim, Kadir A. 2016. *Muslim Democratic Parties in the Middle East.* Bloomington, IN: Indiana University Press.

Yohannes, Okbazghi. 2001. *Political Economy of an Authoritarian Modern State and Religious Nationalism in Egypt.* New York: Edwin Mellen Press.

Zakaria, Fareed. 1997. "The Rise of Illiberal Democracy." *Foreign Affairs* 76, no. 6: 22–43.

Ziadeh, Radwan. 2013. *Power and Polity in Syria.* Beirut: Riad El-Rayyes Books.

9

Neopluralism, Violent Policing, and South Africa's Low-Intensity Democracy

Daniel L. Douek

On 16 August 2012, South African police opened fire on striking mineworkers at the British-owned Lonmin platinum mine at Marikana, killing thirty-four. In a pattern reminiscent of the 1960 police massacre of sixty-nine unarmed protesters at Sharpeville, it later emerged that most of the miners killed at Marikana had been shot in the back or killed execution-style as they fled the heavily armed police (Marinovich 2012). As one surviving mineworker recounted, "you were shot if you put up your hands" (Alexander 2012, 15–42). The Marikana massacre became an instant symbol of the police violence that has plagued post-apartheid South Africa, representing a watershed moment that laid bare a stunning continuity with apartheid-era police violence. Despite restrictions issued in 2011 on police use of force against protesters, due to an increase in serious injuries, an inquest would reveal that at Marikana, South African Police Service (SAPS) officers fired only a few rubber bullets and tear gas rounds before resorting to live ammunition. Evidence from the official inquest into the Marikana massacre suggested that the SAPS's senior officers in command "were behaving as conscious political actors attuned to the needs of a dominant elite aligned to the ruling African National Congress" (Dixon 2019, 203). In this sense, the Marikana massacre embodies the broader trend of police violence that has plagued South Africa after apartheid. It exposes how this violence has served elites' interests at the expense of the majority, who, as during apartheid, remain overwhelmingly Black and poor. It also calls into question the true extent of post-authoritarian change, and indeed, the quality of South Africa's democracy, in ways that echo across the Global South. Today, the Marikana massacre remains emblematic of the violent policing that has become routine in post-apartheid South Africa. Exploring this police violence through the lens of neopluralism promises to shed light on the inherent limitations of democratic change in many post authoritarian Global South countries, where the state deploys its security forces to protect and enforce a socioeconomic status quo fractured by extreme inequality.

Tshepo Madlingozi has argued that South Africa's postcolonial democracy is better understood as a form of "neo-apartheid constitutionalism," whereby apartheid's legal-rational framework has been dismantled, but "the constitutive line of colonialism and apartheid has survived the so-called transition from apartheid to post-apartheid in that impoverished Black people remain ensnared in a zone of stasis" (Madlingozi 2017, 124). This stasis is reinforced by violent encounters between the impoverished masses and the state's security forces, whose mandate to safeguard elites' wealth and property is ever intact. Here, Madlingozi spotlights the intertwined racial and class dimensions of post-authoritarian inequality and marginalization in South Africa, a dynamic strikingly similar to the violent post-authoritarian continuities in many Latin American democracies, where democratic citizenship has largely remained limited and uneven throughout society. As Philip Oxhorn has noted, although this status quo of "inequality and poverty" clearly contradicts the stated goals and values of democratization, it persists so widely across the Global South because neopluralism "deflects public debate away from the structural causes of poverty and toward a focus on its most notorious consequences" (2004, 30, cited in the introduction to this volume). In this case, focusing on the "notorious consequences" of rampant violent crime and systemic police violence has foreclosed a serious examination of how Global South democracies such as South Africa have reproduced key authoritarian legacies by retreating from the public sphere, leaving an increasingly marketized and securitized political landscape in which the promise of democracy goes unfulfilled.

Many Global South countries that democratized as part of the "third wave" have faced intractable challenges to democratic consolidation, including chronically high levels of violent crime, and violent policing that bears authoritarian legacies. Although security force transformation is a key measure of success of democratic consolidation in post-authoritarian states, a growing body of literature now highlights the impact of police violence and corruption on democratic consolidation processes.[1] From South Africa to El Salvador, from Brazil to the Philippines, the violent policing so prevalent throughout much of the Global South serves as an instrument of repression against autonomous civil society mobilization, including political protest and opposition, while aiming to suppress widespread urban violence against a backdrop of vast inequality. Indeed, violent policing in Global South third-wave democratizing countries represents a continuity with authoritarian Cold War–era counterinsurgency strategies (Douek 2020). Violent policing undermines state–society relations in a variety of critically important ways. Because security sector institutions are, by definition, the bearers of authoritarian legacies, they are the most difficult state institutions to reform. Security forces are also one of the most visible and tangible manifestations of state presence for many citizens, and their performance, especially among poorer and more marginalized sectors of the population, tends to have a great impact on citizens' perception of and relationship with the state. Yet our understanding of why post-authoritarian violent policing is so widespread, and how it is so deleterious to democracy, must be located within a broader analysis of the post-authoritarian state and society. As Oxhorn has noted, democratization across much of the Global South has been accompanied by rampant privatization and marketization of the public sphere, combined with the inexorable retreat of the welfare state, resulting in the extension of political rights combined with the shrinking of social and economic rights and increasing authoritarian tendencies (Oxhorn 2007). This results in important continuities with right-wing authoritarian regimes of a previous era, in which, to paraphrase Uruguayan essayist Eduardo Galeano, people went to prison so that markets could be free (Galeano 1997).

NEOPLURALISM AND VIOLENT DEMOCRACIES IN THE GLOBAL SOUTH

Across colonial Africa and among Latin America's Cold War–era right-wing authoritarian regimes, state repression safeguarded the private property of elites, and repressed labour. In these states' negotiated transitions to democracy, elites granted universal political freedoms in exchange for preserving their economic power (Bates

2005); now, markets *and* people were free. Oxhorn's concept of neopluralism describes key post-authoritarian continuities in state–society relations that arose because of this arrangement: these new democracies featured "a market-centred pattern of political incorporation" in which "unprecedented" political rights are accompanied by narrowed "social rights of citizenship," and the incentives for political participation are privatized (Oxhorn 2007, 124–7). Moreover, democratization in many parts of Africa and Latin America has been an inherently violent process, especially in countries that underwent protracted periods of political violence or civil war under authoritarianism (Arias and Goldstein 2010). These post-authoritarian limits to democratic consolidation must be situated within the broader context of post–Cold War neoliberal hegemony (Wacquant 2008). Paraphrasing the counterinsurgency doctrine of "low-intensity warfare," Gills and Rocamora labelled many third-wave democratizers as "low-intensity democracies," in which new "institutions of formal democracy" in the "Third World have failed to broaden popular political participation in a very meaningful way," and have abandoned "social reform agendas that could have established the basis for broader popular participation" (Gills and Rocamora 1992, 501). Guillermo O'Donnell built on these insights with his concept of "low-intensity citizenship," reflecting the disjuncture between state and society in many Latin American third-wave democratizers (O'Donnell 1993, 1,355). To explain the limitations of these democratic openings and their authoritarian continuities, the concept of neopluralism reflects how markets have dictated the configuration of post-transition state–society relations. It is also critical to consider how states themselves have continued to protect elite interests, configured around protecting private wealth and property, via a series of policy mechanisms backed as ever by the threat of brute force.

As state welfare programs are retrenched from a restive, unequal public sphere in Global South post-authoritarian societies, militarized policing and privatized security services fill the vacuum, creating securitized democracies in which high levels of violent crime and chronic insecurity coexist with democratic rights in the political sphere. The state's outsourcing of its monopoly over the use of force contributes to a set of violent equilibria that interact with widespread marketization upon a sociopolitical landscape of violent inequality. Neopluralism thus represents a potentially irrevocable weakening of the social contract, which is inseparable from the simultaneous dismantling of the Weberian state, in which the state maintains a monopoly over the legitimate use of force. This helps to illuminate why the "democracies with adjectives" of the "third wave" era of democratization, in which democratic openings unfolded amidst authoritarian legacies, have become "grey zone" states, trapped between their authoritarian pasts and an increasingly unattainable democratic ideal (Carothers 2022). Many of these "grey zone" states have hardened into "securitized democracies," in which states do not build their authority on protecting citizens' rights, but instead maintain a violent equilibrium characterized by "armed encounters and insidious collusions with violent actors" in the name of security (Pearce 2010). In this context, the concept "low-intensity democracy" takes on its full significance: in Global South countries where authoritarian regimes had previously held power against insurgents by waging "low intensity" wars, that is, counterinsurgency warfare, new democracies in the post–Cold War era now govern by deploying state violence against the poor.

Indeed, as Arias and Goldstein have argued, such violent democracies should not be considered a "social aberration" but rather a "mechanism for keeping in place the very institutions and policies that neoliberal democracies have fashioned over the past several decades" (Arias and Goldstein 2010, 5). In the African context, Achille Mbembe has characterized the third-wave transitions as "recompositions" featuring "the co-existence, within the same dynamic, of elements belonging to warfare as to the conduct of civil politics" (Mbembe 1990, cited in Joseph 1999, 60). These dynamics can be exacerbated by histories of civil war, a common feature across southern African and Latin American states alike that has contributed to the securitization of state–society relations (Buur et al. 2007).

POLICING AS A KEY INDICATOR OF STATE CAPACITY

When security forces switch their normative role from predators to peace officers, the very enterprise of law enforcement is precarious at best. A body of literature has focused on the difficulties of transitioning from a "punitive," authoritarian style of policing that emphasizes repression, to the "investigative" style of policing that is a hallmark of functional democracy (Shaw 2002; Steinberg 2008). The foremost task of authoritarian police forces is to repress dissidents; they bear little or no accountability. Indeed, even as these police forces have attempted to adopt investigative principles suitable for democracy, they have nevertheless displayed alarming signs of reverting to punitive policing in response to post-transition crime and social protest. This has been one of the most important authoritarian legacies in South Africa, and the most difficult to reverse or transform. Across the Global South, the shift from punitive-style authoritarian policing to investigative policing has been laborious and incomplete, highlighting how authoritarian patterns have remained embedded in the post-transition police force, resisting attempts at democratic reform (Macaulay 2012). Moreover, as Bonner has noted, in highly unequal, post-authoritarian societies such as Chile and Argentina, democratic policing is a contested concept, with understandings that vary according to debates around the meaning of democracy itself (Bonner 2020).

The high levels of violent crime in South Africa are connected to state violence because each perpetuates the other, and both undermine the Weberian state in terms of its monopoly over the legitimate use of force. This highlights an important paradox: during the Cold War, South Africa, like many Global South right-wing dictatorships, was an authoritarian "strong state"; yet since undergoing democratization, there has been a decline in the state's ability to assert power over important segments of the population. South Africa's peri-urban townships and inner cities feature huge concentrations of poor, overwhelmingly darker-skinned citizens whose lives are shaped by extreme levels of violent crime and insecurity; like Brazil's favelas, these areas have become "ungoverned spaces" (Muggah and Mulli 2012, 63). Understood differently, these spaces form part of a "hybrid state" in which "multiple governmental actors," including "criminal organizations, politicians, police, and bureaucrats," remain "entangled in a relationship of collusion and divestment, sharing control over urban spaces and populations" (Jaffe 2013, 734). The state's ability to assert power in these spaces, and to deliver services to them, are prerequisites for establishing representative democracy. Yet the violence emanating from these spaces, and the state's violent attempts to assert control over them, have become integral aspects of post-authoritarian politics across the Global South. Thus, policing serves as a particularly important indicator of state capacity.

State power arises not only from a state's capacity to enforce power, but from its legitimacy within civil society, and the citizenry's consent to submit to state authority (Tilly 2007, 179). This takes on particular importance in the study of transitions from authoritarian rule, in which elite-level transformation may leave certain institutions or levels largely unchanged, limiting the significance of the overall transformation for large sectors of society in a variety of important ways. The post-authoritarian underperformance of security forces only reinforces this dynamic, thereby increasing mistrust of the police, further decreasing its legitimacy. This diminished legitimacy and effectiveness in turn contributes to the state resorting to increased violence and militarized tactics to combat crime, which in turn reinforces popular distrust of the police, and by extension, the state.

In many post-authoritarian contexts, the relationship between the state and civil society has been characterized by what Rose and Shin (2001) have called the "low-level equilibrium trap." In this dynamic, the performance of state institutions and public expectations of such performance are components in a causal feedback loop, and as a result, both remain chronically low. This has led to perpetually low levels of state legitimacy. In the case of South Africa, the state security institutions' ineffectiveness and lack of legitimacy have contributed strongly to a low-level equilibrium trap characterized by two mutually reinforcing mechanisms: first, at the level of state institutions, the police force has proven unable to rise above chronic deficits in reputation (legitimacy) and performance (effectiveness). Second, at the level of society, because of the security forces' enduring reputation for brutality, citizens do not, in the main, expect a reformed and effective post-transition security force. The low-level equilibrium trap between state policing and civil society must be understood in the context of a growing distance between citizens and political processes, and growing levels of economic inequality.

South Africa is a paradigmatic case that embodies a pattern increasingly evident throughout much of the Global South: democratization and economic growth do not necessarily diminish levels of urban violence, and may in fact facilitate an equilibrium whereby high levels of violence coexist alongside ostensibly democratic state institutions. A member of the BRICS coalition, South Africa has long been among the most industrialized countries in the Global South; yet it also has a long history of racialized inequality, characterized by one of the largest and most enduring gaps in the world between rich and poor, and it struggles to overcome deep-seated authoritarian legacies in its state institutions, especially the security forces (Douek

2013). The low capacity and legitimacy of state policing in South Africa bring into stark relief the challenges of post-authoritarian governance and the limits of reform. Authoritarian continuities in post-conflict state security forces compromise the ability of these institutions to provide effective internal security, without which "formal democratic rules and equality before the law can mean little in practice" (Call and Stanley 2001, 152). This further reinforces divisions between the state and civil society, ultimately casting doubt upon the quality and durability of democratic consolidation in the Global South.

A range of literature has focused on the phenomenon of post-transition violence (Darby 2005) and the weakness of post-transition state policing (Tanner 2000), pointing to the post-transition intractability of many types of violence, to legacies of violence within the post-authoritarian security institutions (Douek 2013), and to lasting public mistrust of the police (Chikwanha 2005). The South African case is also noteworthy because the country's laws and state institutions, and the degree of media freedom and other speech freedoms ensure a very strong *de jure* democracy, in contrast to the uneven *de facto* implementation of democracy.

Although South Africa's security institutions have attempted to take important strides away from punitive authoritarian policing and towards democratic, investigative policing, incidents such as the Marikana massacre have demonstrated that these institutions still reproduce authoritarian, violent responses. The low capacity and legitimacy of post-authoritarian police forces are exacerbated by the post-transition widening of class inequalities, and by the security forces' role as the guardians of this societal status quo. Anthony Pereira and Mark Ungar emphasize that it is the "degree to which state violence is subject to the rule of law," not the "deployment of violence itself, that distinguishes an authoritarian regime from a democratic regime" (Pereira and Ungar 2004, 264). Bonner, however, rejects the idea that there can be a single "definition of 'democratic policing,'" one which "corresponds to a single understanding of liberal democracy," and which "can be exported as a technical and politically neutral democratic fix" (Bonner 2020, 1,045). Moreover, the "legality" of police violence becomes a slippery slope when the police kill hundreds of citizens per year, often under nebulous circumstances. Furthermore, the sectors of society most affected by this violence are rarely able to mobilize around the issue of police reform or to make their voices heard in the corridors of power. In that sense, the post-authoritarian state's fragile legitimacy can easily be punctured by police violence.

METHODOLOGY

Using the case of South Africa, I identify police violence as a crucial cause of the disassociation of civil society from the state, a phenomenon widespread among Global South democracies, and which constitutes a critical shortcoming in the democratization process. I examine four key variables to measure authoritarian continuities in post-authoritarian policing: police violence, as measured by the numbers of people killed by police, and tactics such as extra-judicial killings and torture, and police militarization; state attitudes, as measured by state elites' pronouncements on policing; public perceptions of security force legitimacy; and security privatization, which serves as an indicator of the state's inability to adequately perform its obligations toward its citizens. My study relies on scholarly and news sources, and survey data, as well as interviews with civil servants and private security officers that I conducted in Pretoria (Tshwane) and Mthatha, South Africa, in November to December 2009.

POLICE VIOLENCE IN POST-APARTHEID SOUTH AFRICA

Class divisions in South Africa have persisted and have remained highly racialized, even as racial discrimination has been abolished (Seekings and Nattrass 2005). During the apartheid era, racist attitudes and policies were strongest within the organs of state coercion, and these attitudes remained chronic in those institutions well after their democratic transitions. South Africa's post-authoritarian constitution, passed in 1994, enshrined principles of racial equality and abolished discrimination; yet in practice, such discrimination has remained widespread in the realm of public security, as darker-skinned citizens are more likely to be the victims of violent crime and police brutality (Mitchell and Wood 1998). In 2002, a South African government inquiry into police force racism initiated by then police minister Sydney Mufamadi was never released (Shaw 2002).

South African police have also responded with excessive force to the widespread protests against inadequate access for large segments of the population to housing, utilities, and basic services, known in South Africa as "service delivery" protests. In April 2012, police officers were charged with "murder, assault, and other offences" in their response to service delivery protests (Amnesty International 2012). Before and since, the SAPS has killed protesters and bystanders with stunning regularity, including fifteen-year-old Lucas Lebyane, shot and killed in February 2015 during protests against the inadequate provision of water in Mpumalanga province ("Police Kill Boy" 2015), and nine-year-old Leo Williams, shot and killed in 2020 during service delivery protests in Western Cape province (Cruywagen 2020). Service delivery protests, and the heavy-handed police response, have unfolded in a context of extreme and persistent inequality, and an inadequate government response, which are hallmarks of neopluralism. Decades after its democratic transitions, South Africa remains one of the most unequal countries in the world, with a Gini coefficient of 0.63 in 2023 (Statista 2023), up from 0.59 in 1993.[2] In this context, the violent police response to citizens protesting the inadequate delivery of basic services highlights continuities with the apartheid past. One SAPS police officer in training highlighted ongoing parallels with apartheid-era policing: "Generally, the police are trigger-happy ... look at what happens when there are service delivery protests: the police shoot retreating protesters from the back" (Rawoot et al. 2009).

CITIZENS KILLED BY POLICE

In July 2021, 354 people died during widespread public protests in South Africa's two most populous provinces, KwaZulu-Natal and Gauteng – most of these killed as a result of the violent police response to the three days of looting (Davis 2024). The protests were caused by a variety of factors, including poor service delivery by the government and outrage at former president Jacob Zuma's imprisonment for contempt of court. The protests resulted in billions of rand in losses, including damaged or destroyed property and looted goods, and thousands of jobs lost as workplaces were closed or destroyed. The magnitude of the crisis led President Cyril Ramaphosa to term it an "insurrection" that "constituted an attack on South Africa's democracy" (Moosa 2021). Reflecting on the police response to the protests, a Human Rights Watch report summarized the key problems that have plagued South African policing since the onset of democracy in 1994: "Serious concerns remain about the conduct and capacity of the South African Police Services (SAPS), particularly its compliance with the lawful use of force and its ability to deal with riots in a rights-respecting manner. Authorities have yet to end the rampant impunity that encourages abusive behaviour by the police" (Human Rights Watch 2022).

These concerns have been exacerbated by numerous widely publicized instances of police brutality across the years: For instance, in July 2023, officers in Deputy President Paul Mashatile's security detail were filmed pulling a man out of his car by the side of a freeway and stomping on his head until he lay motionless, sparking widespread outrage (Imray 2023). In September 2020, police shot and killed Nathaniel Julies, a teenager with intellectual disabilities; according to the *New York Times*, "the police station central to Julies' case has faced over eighty complaints of brutality from 2012 to 2019, with ten involving fatalities, indicating a pattern of abuse" (Chutel 2020). In February 2013, South African police beat to death a taxi driver, Mido Macia, after a parking dispute. Before dying in a police cell, Macia was dragged through the streets from the back of a police van, an act that was filmed by witnesses and became widely viewed online (Nicolson 2013).

Since the fall of apartheid in 1994, South Africa's police have been plagued by violent post-authoritarian legacies, having undergone laborious and uneven reform, that have persisted for decades after the transition. One of the conditions of the negotiated transition between the apartheid regime and the African National Congress (ANC) was a sunset clause that preserved the jobs of tens of thousands of civil servants, including the police (Shaw 2002), and the apartheid security forces preserved many of the same personnel and attitudes from the authoritarian era (Douek 2013). In this context, the SAPS – successor to the apartheid-era South African Police (SAP) – acquired a reputation for corruption and involvement in crime, as well as indiscriminate use of force. From April 1997 to March 2000, 1,548 people died as a result of police action, while 626 people died in police custody; of these, 70 per cent (95 per cent of the deaths as a result of police action and 12 to 16 per cent of deaths in custody) were the result of the use of force by the police (Amnesty International 2012). From 2004 to 2009, there were a further 1,623 documented police killings in South Africa (Amnesty International 2012). One report from 2020 noted that according to the government's own statistics, South African police kill three times more people per capita than police in the United States, with the SAPS killing 538 people in the 2017 to 2018 reporting year and 440 people in the 2018 to 2019 reporting year (Stuurman 2020).

POLICE TORTURE

South Africa's Independent Complaints Directorate (ICD), founded in 1995 to increase public trust in the police force, reported that in the period from April 2007 to March 2008, it received "20 complaints of torture and 739 complaints of assault with intent to cause grievous bodily harm"; during this same period, there were 302 "new reports of deaths in custody and 490 suspects fatally shot by police, an 87 per cent increase over the previous year." The ICD itself continued to suffer from a shortage of resources, and the SAP failed to implement half of its recommendations. The levels of death in police custody continued to rise: in June 2009, the ICD reported a 15 per cent increase "in deaths in custody as a result of police action over the past two years," while from April 2008 to March 2009 the ICD "investigated 828 incidents of assault with intent to cause grievous bodily harm, some of which amounted to torture" (Amnesty International 2011). From April 2009 to March 2010, the ICD received 920 complaints of assault by police "with intent to cause grievous bodily harm, some of which were being investigated for evidence of torture. ... [I]ncidents of torture and extrajudicial executions by police were reported." Seven of the 294 deaths in custody were linked to torture and ninety others to "injuries sustained in custody."

The SAPS still faces accusations of using torture methods against witnesses and suspects that police commonly used during the apartheid era, including choking, suffocation by placing a plastic bag over the victim's head, and "tubing," or suffocation by forcing a rubber or plastic tube down the victim's throat (Mlambo 2023). The ICD also investigated twenty-four complaints of rape by police officers (Amnesty International 2011). In 2013, police personnel were implicated in a series of rapes of women who had called the police for help (Burger 2013). A 2013 seminar in Pretoria on police brutality in South Africa revealed that at least 720 people had died in SAPS custody under suspicious circumstances between April 2011 and March 2012. The seminar further revealed that from 2011 to 2013, over nine hundred police officers had been arrested and charged for a range of crimes in the Gauteng province alone ("Police Conduct Caused" 2013). The 2015 report from the government's Independent Police Investigative Directorate (IPID) found that out of more than 5,500 instances of police criminal offences reported annually, more than 3,500 involved the assault of suspects or witnesses, including torture (IPID 2015). The IPID's 2020 to 2021 report recorded 6,122 cases of police abuse, including 4,228 "assault cases" and 217 deaths in police custody (IPID 2020).

POLICE MILITARIZATION

Urban violence in post-authoritarian South Africa has remained at an intensely high level, a crisis that the police have been largely unable to handle. The security institutions' militarized response to crime is a key indicator that reveals the limits of post-transition democratic consolidation. There has been an increasingly militarized state response to urban violence in South Africa, as the state deploys special units to target lawbreakers, while key leaders have stridently encouraged violent state responses to crime. Several violent instances have highlighted this trend, including the 2012 Marikana massacre, in which heavily armed police units converged on unarmed miners from helicopters and armoured vehicles, and the deployment of twenty thousand troops to quell widespread unrest in July 2021. In most authoritarian regimes, the police and military have been fused in a manner that does "not allow a neat analytical separation between the two," and this legacy often persists post-transition (Pereira and Ungar 2004, 264). Military and paramilitary units that fulfilled policing functions during the authoritarian era often retain these roles, or aspects of them, in the post-authoritarian era. Governments also often deploy their armies domestically to address intractable security problems, especially when their police forces are outgunned, and often outfit their police with military-style weaponry, training, and tactics. Although a militarized response to crime may give the impression of state strength, such displays of force are, paradoxically, indicators of low state capacity, suggesting the state's inability to establish a more quotidian presence within society, and society's unwillingness to acknowledge state authority.

Continuities with apartheid-era militarized policing were evident in South Africa when, in 1995, the newly elected Mandela administration deployed unreformed military units, including the notoriously brutal 32 Battalion, to pacify the restive townships ringing Johannesburg (Reno 1997). Since then, paramilitary responses to crime have been a recurrent feature in South Africa, endangering key tenets of democratic policing (Shaw 2002). One head of a private security company in South Africa's Eastern Cape province emphasized that the state tries to compensate for weak policing by deploying elite tactical units, failing to address the fundamental problems of police inefficiency and corruption, and terrorizing the populace: "kicking down doors – criminals often masquerade as police, so people are suspicious when police knock on their door – suddenly they barge in with torches and guns, traumatizing small kids, women."[3] The dehumanization of lawbreakers by state elites is encoded through the police's increasing willingness to "shoot to kill" (Rawoot et al. 2009).

STATE ATTITUDES TO VIOLENT POLICING

When President Nelson Mandela signed South Africa's democratic constitution into law in 1996, he chose to do it at Sharpeville, the site of the notorious 1960 police massacre, to make an emphatic statement that in the new democracy, the rule of law would be applied to defend human rights (Viljoen 2021). Yet as the economic and social distance between state elites and society has grown inexorably, and as state elites have increasingly aligned with the interests of the wealthy and powerful, their pronouncements about police violence have often been equivocal about, if not outright supportive of, using excessive force.

After the 2012 Marikana massacre, state elites insisted that police had shot the miners in self-defence and commended them for their professionalism; the day after the massacre, police commissioner Riah Phiyega intoned: "[Your] actions represent the best of responsible policing" (Stuurman 2020). However, as details of the massacre emerged, politicians found themselves on the defensive, and several members of the ruling ANC began insisting, absurdly, that the massacre was a national tragedy whose solemnity would be punctured by the casting of blame (Alexander 2012). During the COVID-19 pandemic, after South African National Defense Force (SANDF) soldiers enforcing a lockdown order beat to death a private citizen, Collins Khosa, outside his home in April 2020, Minister of Defense and Military Veterans Thandi Modise proclaimed that citizens "should not provoke" the soldiers, while Police Minister Bheki Cele called for police to "push South Africans back into their homes" if they violated the lockdown (Global Freedom of Expression 2020). Even when elites have acknowledged unjustified police killings, they have been quick to deny any broader, systematic problem of police brutality. For instance, after police shot and killed Mthokozisi Ntumba, a passerby, during the suppression of a student protest in Johannesburg in March 2021, Cele characterized the killing as an inexplicable exception, despite the frequency of such incidents: "I can't explain it, it is something without an inch and has no grain of explanation in it. Somebody, for me, just went crazy" (Viljoen 2021).

In addressing crime and police violence, state elites in new democracies are often conflicted between observing legal restrictions on their power and pandering to popular anti-crime sentiments by encouraging violent state responses to crime. While the shadow of authoritarian policing causes many citizens to demand procedural fairness, others prioritize police effectiveness above all in a high-crime environment such as South Africa (Bradford et al. 2014).

Post-authoritarian governments that try to implement policing reforms may find themselves in no-win situations in which reforms fail to reduce police violence, while high crime levels persist. Politicians' limited ability to respond to these challenges through appropriate channels may lead them to endorse solutions such as increased use of deadly force by police and vigilantism, a response that also threatens to harm innocent bystanders. Following a November 2009 incident in South Africa's Mabopane township, in which police shot and killed a toddler sitting in a car whom they mistook for a criminal, then Police Commissioner Cele had to publicly urge police: "don't be trigger happy." Shortly afterward, Cele said of criminals: "these half-animals do not have a God." On another occasion, in November 2009, Cele insisted: "criminals should be spoken to in a language they understand" ("We Must Avoid" 2009), prompting an opposition party representative to insist that "the proximity between the recent spate of police attacks on civilians and the police commissioner's wild talk about shooting to kill, is surely no coincidence" ("Are South African Police" 2009).

Furthermore, this militarized approach to policing is symptomatic of a fractious political arena in which politicians seek to build individual credibility by publicly taking an uncompromising approach to fighting crime. With a populist flourish, politicians have appealed to widespread anti-crime sentiments by mandating widely publicized police crackdowns. High-ranking South African politicians, including former president Zuma, have taken to making anti-constitutional pronouncements that encourage violent extrajudicial responses against criminals by both the state police and private citizens. Zuma likewise defended Deputy Justice Minister Susan Shabangu when she advocated deadly force as a first response to criminals (Oomen 2004). This outlook is also reflected in the paper trail of the ANC's progressively harsher anti-crime legislation from 1994 onward. This trend has been characterized by business leaders calling for more severe legal sanctions against armed criminals.[4]

PUBLIC PERCEPTIONS OF POLICE LEGITIMACY

Since South Africa's 1994 democratic transition, political institutions have remained plagued by diminishing public trust and high levels of corruption (Patel and Govindasamy 2021). The "frontier capitalist"–style marketization of the public sphere, as encapsulated by neopluralism, has created tremendous opportunities for elites to engage in corruption, exacerbated by a lack of effective government oversight. High levels of corruption and brutality have contributed to a lack of civic trust in the state security forces. In 2022, Minister Modise acknowledged that "low levels of public trust" between members of the public and law enforcement agencies posed a persistent problem (DefenseWeb 2022).

Despite its greater levels of economic development and political freedom compared to the rest of the continent, based on survey data collected from 2021 to 2023, South Africa ranked twenty-sixth out of thirty-nine African countries in public trust of the police: asked whether police "act professionally and respect citizens' rights," 31 per cent responded "rarely or never," 42 per cent responded "sometimes," and only 24 per cent responded "often or always" (Krönke et al. 2024). South Africa also ranked below average for ease of obtaining assistance from police. This trend is not new: South Africa's police ranked eleventh in a 2005 survey of trust in state institutions in twelve African countries; at 35 per cent, the police were also trusted least out of any institution in the country (Chikwanha 2005). Survey data from 2011 indicates that although 59 per cent of

South Africans reported crimes to the police, 39 per cent of respondents did not; furthermore, of those who did not report crimes to the police, 32 per cent did not report because "police do not listen or care" (Wielders 2013). According to national survey data, public opinion of the police's performance sank even lower after the 2012 Marikana massacre; after recovering slightly by 2015, it dropped anew in 2020/2021, correlating with a "strong downward trend" in "public confidence in democratic institutions overall" since 2007 (Roberts and Gordon 2022).

For the period 2021 to 2023, 63 per cent of South African respondents said that "most or all" police are corrupt, surpassed only by the office of the presidency, at 65 per cent, ranking South Africa thirty-first out of thirty-nine African countries in terms of public perception of corruption in the police and other state institutions (Krönke et al. 2024, 13). South Africans also widely perceive the police to be involved in criminal activities: survey data from 2021 to 2023 ranks South Africa third worst out of thirty-nine African countries, with 47 per cent of respondents saying that police "often or always" engage in criminal activities, and a further 29 per cent saying that police "sometimes" engage in criminal activities (Krönke et al. 2024, 14). This reflects a trend since 1994 of a steadily increasing percentage of South Africans regarding their government as corrupt. The percentage of South Africans who regarded corruption as being one of the most important problems facing the country increased from 13 per cent in 2002 to 25 per cent in 2011, while the percentage of people who thought corruption was high among public officials rose from 30 per cent in 2008 to 40 per cent in 2011; meanwhile, in 2011, a majority of South Africans rated the government's performance in fighting corruption as "fairly bad" (30 per cent) or "very bad" (35 per cent) (Wielders 2013). This lack of trust and confidence in state institutions demonstrates that the illegitimacy and unpopularity of the SAPS are part of a broader public crisis of confidence in post-authoritarian state institutions.

As South Africa transitioned to democracy, police corruption and complicity in crime were staggeringly high: in 1995 to 1996, eight thousand police in Gauteng province alone were reported to have committed crimes of one kind or another (Brogden and Nijhar 1998, 93). In Johannesburg in 1996, according to the divisional police chief, who was interviewed at the time, four police a week were suspended for corruption, and 1,076 policemen nationally were under investigation for corruption that same year, an increase from eighty-nine in 1995, fifty-six in 1994, and thirty-two in 1993 to 1994 (Lodge 1998, 22). In the words of one South African civil servant:

> No matter how many police you train, you've got to shift that culture of corruption. Institutions ultimately need to be robust enough to counteract the role of individual agency in facilitating or committing crime. South Africa must reach a point where it's in an individual policeperson's interest to obey the law. If it's in their interest to engage in crime, the institutional channels for corruption will be there.[5]

Furthermore, South African police face a range of critical problems, including a very low case-solving rate, in large part because of police corruption (Steinberg 2008). There is also a great danger in testifying in court, as illustrated by a case in the Western Cape province in which a gang kingpin, while in prison, ordered the killing of anyone who would testify against him. The SAPS also offers little protection for witnesses, and people often refuse the police witness protection program, fearing police corruption. Crime "is encouraged by officialdom," while in urban areas, "police become crime syndicates," such as the police commander in the Eastern Cape province who was caught "running gangs" in 2007. Meanwhile, the SAPS's Vehicle Theft Unit became the butt of widely told jokes because it "literally stole cars" (Steinberg 2008). In 2012, a unit commander in the SAPS's Crime Intelligence Unit was suspended on allegations of murder and corruption; friction then arose between the national police commissioner and the minister of police when the latter ordered that investigations and disciplinary procedures against the unit commander be halted and that he be reinstated (Roelofse 2015). According to the SAPS's own statistics, from April 2013 to March 2014, members of the SAPS faced "corruption and fraud-related charges," including "corruption (332), fraud (207), aiding an escapee (421), defeating the ends of justice (169), extortion (34), and bribery (9), for a total of 1,172" (Roelofse 2015, 110). In 2022, the Department of Defense and Military Veterans announced an investigation into the State Security Agency, an intelligence-gathering body tasked with supporting law enforcement, after "about four members" were found guilty of fraud and corruption (DefenseWeb 2022).

SECURITY PRIVATIZATION

South Africa's burgeoning private security sector showcases the disjuncture and increasing alienation between state and society that is characteristic of neopluralism, as the state outsources one of its core functions: the provision of security to the citizenry. Security privatization embodies the neoliberal economic policies that prescribe the decentralization and outsourcing of state functions, including policing and social control (Bond 2004). Meanwhile, citizens from across the spectrum of race and class have largely turned away from the South African state as a guarantor of security; this trend is evidenced by the rise of private security companies and "community policing" groups whose performance has often resembled that of vigilante outfits meting out violent justice against suspected criminals, further underscoring the state's lack of capacity in protecting its citizens from violent crime (Oomen 2004), and popular distrust of the police's ability to perform this function (Buur and Jensen 2004). Community policing efforts have all too often served as a weak substitute for state institutions over which governments have been unable or unwilling to enforce their authority.

The South African government has embraced a security privatization agenda that has simultaneously reduced its capacity and its public accountability (Baker 2002). Private security companies, whose numbers were already growing steadily during the final decade of apartheid, mushroomed after the transition, compensating for the limitations of post-apartheid state police. In 1994, President Mandela's government initially launched the welfare-oriented Reconstruction and Development Program (RDP), which included ample funding for the provision of security by the state; however, as foreign investors demanded a privatized development model, the RDP was abandoned in favour of the neoliberal Growth, Economic, and Redistribution (GEAR) program, which promoted the marketization of security (Shaw and Shearing 1998, 9). As in other sectors of South Africa's post-apartheid economy, privatization attracted foreign multinational corporations, as private security titans, including Chubb and Wackenhut, joined this burgeoning market. Between 2005 and 2006, the SAPS spent nearly 100 million rand paying private security companies to protect government establishments, effectively outsourcing the role of the state (Gumedze 2007, 198). In a 2007 policy document, the ANC acknowledged the SAPS's low public legitimacy and called for more community involvement in policing as a way of compensating for the SAPS's ineffectiveness. Indeed, by 2007, private security personnel outnumbered SAPS officers by a ratio of four to one (Steinberg 2008); in 2011, South Africa had the world's fifth-highest per capita ratio of private security officers (Small Arms Survey 2011). As one analyst explained, "The growth of the industry has been a result of the crime situation, but also people not believing that they can rely on police" (Davis 2019).

Similarly, in Brazil, increased security privatization has been symptomatic of broader economic privatization and the devolution of state functions, which has facilitated killings by clandestine death squads affiliated with government police forces (Huggins 1997). Overall, the marketization of public security provisions encourages the rise of private security companies and vigilante groups. It reduces the police to being just one more security actor among many, undermining the state's monopoly on the use of force.

DEMOCRACY AND SOCIAL PROTEST

Oxhorn's concept of neopluralism describes a shrinking public sphere characterized by a civil society weakened through the marketization of politics. Nevertheless, in many Global South contexts, political mobilization and participation have actually increased, as reflected in both social protest movements and formal voter participation. In South Africa, the domestic anti-apartheid movement bequeathed to democratic society an assertive, vibrant, and deeply rooted protest culture (Tournadre 2018). This culture has been ever vigilant in the face of elites' abuse of power, as evidenced by frequent and widespread protests and strikes in the post-apartheid era (Tournadre 2022). Yet the democratic state's main response to this widespread political and civic mobilization has been to sideline and repress it, perpetuating the stark inequality upon which violent policing and low state capacity have been overlaid. Indeed, the 2012 police massacre of miners at Marikana occurred precisely in response to the miners' strike and protests for better conditions and pay (Alexander 2012). Such grievances have remained widespread across South Africa and have sparked numerous other protests that the state has likewise violently repressed (Davis 2024). The ANC government's introduction of economic reforms, including the privatization of state utilities such as water and electricity, generated mass social protest movements against inadequate "service delivery" by the state, with high levels of participation by poor people (Barchiesi 1997; Narsiah 2007). The South African government's responses to protesters' grievances and demands have been inadequate and piecemeal, maintaining workers' precarity (Barchiesi 2011). Overall, South Africa's ruling ANC elites have embraced policies that have widened the gap between rich and poor to unprecedented levels, while still claiming to represent the oppressed majority whom they championed during the anti-apartheid struggle, a dynamic captured eloquently by Patrick Bond's 2004 critique of the ANC, *Talk Left, Walk Right*. While the ANC has faced widespread calls from within its ranks to strengthen and expand a "strong developmental state," its elites have instead embraced a model of accelerated privatization (Turok 2008), while leaders such as ex-president Zuma have engaged in prodigious levels of corruption (Burke 2022). Overall, then, the South African case has illustrated neopluralism's juxtaposition of democratic features, such as relatively free and fair elections and the public's right to protest, against high levels of poverty and inequality and the state's entrenched authoritarian tendencies, of which chronic violence is not a bug, but a feature.

CONCLUSION: WHITHER DEMOCRACY?

Violent policing by post-authoritarian security forces, along with their systemic corruption and militarization, underscores the incomplete nature of South Africa's transition to democracy. This has undermined relations between the South African state and civil society in the post-transition era. Despite attempts to civilianize and democratize the police forces, authoritarian tendencies have persisted for decades after South Africa's transition to democracy. State security forces are key actors whose performance serves as a barometer of state–society relations. Democratizing the state and its institutions is not a linear process destined to improve as authoritarian legacies recede into the past. Rather, the South African case illustrates how persistent economic inequality and the hollowing of democracy through the marketization of public goods has securitized politics, at once weakening the state's monopoly on the use of force and (re)inscribing police violence upon the body politic.

The inexorable marketization and securitization of state–society relations in many Global South democratizing nations threatens to sustain high levels of both social protest and police violence. As described by Oxhorn's neopluralism paradigm, this is likely to further erode the state's authority and legitimacy within civil society, thereby limiting the promise of democratic transformation. This corresponds to the predomination in postcolonial southern Africa of what John S. Saul, citing a speech by Issa Shivji, calls "liberal democracy," which prioritizes a market-capitalist economy rooted in private property and controlled by a narrow political elite class representing capital, over "popular democracy," which prioritizes the redress of colonialist inequalities and exploitation, and defines human rights chiefly in terms of economic rights (Saul 2005). The South African state has doubled down on protecting a status quo of sharp inequality, deploying violence to "defend the distribution of space and property," to create a "secure business environment," and to "discipline labour and protect corporate interests" (McMichael 2014, 15).

The 2012 Marikana massacre and the violent police crackdowns on widespread social protest in 2021 (Davis 2024) illustrate the ominous parallels between the authoritarian and post-authoritarian eras in South Africa. Since the country's first free and fair elections in 1994, South African citizens have remained invested in the democratic process, as attested by the consistently high electoral turnout. Yet the past decade has also seen the rise of challengers to the ruling ANC party that threaten a resort to violence: these include the Economic Freedom Fighters party, and the Umkhonto we Sizwe Party, so named to memorialize the former armed wing of the ANC from its liberation struggle era (Pilling and Mark 2024). The emergence of these populist challengers indicates growing public disillusionment with the ability of South African democracy to deliver true equality. In this context, police violence remains both an important source and toxic byproduct of South Africa's ongoing democratic fragility. As state weakness accelerates and democracy faces unprecedented challenges worldwide, systemic police brutality should be considered an early warning sign of even greater perils that lie ahead for representative and accountable government.

NOTES

1 See, for example, Levitsky and Way, *Competitive Authoritarianism*; Gonzàlez, *Authoritarian Police in Democracy*.

2 *Economist.* "Over the Rainbow" (20 October 2012), 22. The Gini coefficient is an index for measuring the degree of income or wealth inequality.
3 Author's confidential interview with a private security company director, Mthatha, South Africa, 6 December 2009.
4 Author's interview with Cheryl Frank, senior researcher, Institute for Security Studies, Tshwane (Pretoria), South Africa, 8 November 2009.
5 Author's confidential interview with a South African civil servant, Pretoria, South Africa, 6 November 2009.

REFERENCES

Alexander, Peter. 2012. "The Massacre: A Narrative Account Based on Workers' Testimonies." In *Marikana: A View from the Mountain and a Case to Answer*, edited by Peter Alexander, Luke S. Sinwell, Thapelo Lekgowa, Botsang Mmope, and Bongani Xezwi, 15–42. Auckland Park, South Africa: Jacana.

Alves, Màrcia, and Desmond Arias. 2011. "Understanding the Fica Vivo Program: Two-Tiered Community Policing in Belo Horizonte, Brazil." *Policing and Society* 22, no. 1: 101–13.

Amnesty International. 2009. *Annual Report: The State of the World's Human Rights – South Africa.* http://www.amnesty.org/en/region/south-africa/report-2009.

Amnesty International. 2010. *Annual Report: The State of the World's Human Rights – South Africa.* http://www.amnesty.org/en/region/south-africa/report-2010.

Amnesty International. 2011. *Annual Report: The State of the World's Human Rights – South Africa. Case Studies of Extrajudicial Executions, Torture and other Ill-Treatment.* http://www.amnesty.org/en/region/south-africa/report-2011.

Amnesty International. 2012. *Annual Report: The State of the World's Human Rights – South Africa.* http://www.amnesty.org/en/region/south-africa/report-2012.

"Are South African Police Trigger Happy?" 2009. BBC News. 11 December.

Arias, Enrique, and Daniel Goldstein, eds. 2010. *Violent Democracies in Latin America.* Durham, NC: Duke University Press.

Arias, Enrique, and Mark Ungar. 2009. "Community Policing and Latin America's Citizen Security Crisis." *Comparative Politics* 4, no. 4: 409–29.

Baker, Bruce. 2002. "Living With Non-State Policing in South Africa: The Issues and Dilemmas." *Journal of Modern African Studies* 40, no. 1: 29–53.

Barchiesi, Franco. 1997. "Delivery From Below, Resistance From Above: Electricity and the Politics of Struggle Over Basic Needs in Tembisa." *Debate*, 4: 12–27.

Barchiesi, Franco. 2011. *Precarious Liberation: Workers, the State, and Contested Social Citizenship in Postapartheid South Africa*. Albany, NY: State University of New York Press.

Bates, Robert H. 2005. "The Economic Bases of Democratization." In *State, Conflict, and Democracy in Africa*, edited by Richard Joseph. Boulder, CO: Lynne Rienner.

Bond, Patrick. 2004. *Talk Left, Walk Right*. Scottsville, South Africa: University of KwaZulu-Natal Press.

Bonner, Michelle D. 2020. "What Democratic Policing Is…and Is Not." *Policing and Society* 30, no. 9: 1044–60.

Bradford, Ben, Aziz Huq, Jonathan Jackson, and Benjamin Roberts. 2014. "What Price Fairness When Security Is at Stake? Police Legitimacy in South Africa." *Regulation and Governance* 8, no. 2: 246–68.

Brands, Hal. 2011. "Crime, Irregular Warfare, and Institutional Failure in Latin America: Guatemala as a Case Study." *Studies in Conflict and Terrorism* 34, no. 3: 228–47.

Brogden, Mike, and Preet Nijhar. 1998. "Corruption and the South African Police." *Crime Law and Social Change* 30, no. 1: 89–106.

Burger, Johan. 2013. "Understanding Police Brutality in South Africa: Challenges and Solutions." Institute of Security Studies. http://www.issafrica.org/events/understanding-police-brutality-in-south-africa-challenges-and-solutions.

Burke, Jason. 2022. "Jacob Zuma Sought to Hand State Assets to Allies, Finds Corruption Report." *Guardian*, 1 May. https://www.theguardian.com/world/2022/may/01/jacob-zuma-sought-to-hand-state-assets-to-business-allies-finds-corruption-report.

Buur, Lars, and Stephen Jensen. 2004. "Introduction: Vigilantism and the Policing of Everyday Life in South Africa." *African Studies* 63, no. 2: 139–52.

Buur, Lars, Steffen Jensen, and Finn Stepputat, eds. 2007. *The Security-Development Nexus: Expressions of Sovereignty and Securitization in South Africa*. Uppsala, Sweden: Nordiska Afrikainstitutet.

Call, Charles, and William Stanley. 2001. "Protecting the People: Public Security Choices After Civil Wars." *Global Governance* 7, no. 2: 151–72.

Carothers, Thomas. 2002. "The End of the Transition Paradigm." *Journal of Democracy* 13, no. 1: 5–21.

Chikwanha, Annie Barbara. 2005. "Trust in Institutions in Sub-Saharan Africa's Emerging Democracies." In *Trust in Public Institutions in South Africa*, edited by Steinar Askvik. Burlington, VT: Ashgate Publishing.

Chutel, Lynsey. 2020. "'Colored Lives Matter': A South African Police Shooting Like No Other." *New York Times*, 21 September.

Cock, Jacklyn. 2005. "Guards and Guns: Towards Privatized Militarism in Post-Apartheid South Africa." *Journal of Southern African Studies* 31, no. 4: 791–803.

Cruywagen, Vincent. 2020. "Rubber Bullet Killed Nine-Year-Old West Coast Boy Leo Williams." *Daily Maverick* (South Africa), 24 August. https://www.dailymaverick.co.za/article/2020-08-24-rubber-bullet-killed-nine-year-old-west-coast-boy-leo-williams.

Dammert, Lucia, and Mary Fran Malone. 2006. "Does It Take a Village? Policing Strategies and Fear of Crime." *Latin American Politics and Society* 48, no. 4: 27–51.

Darby, John. 2005. "Post-Accord Violence in a Changing World." In *Violence and Reconstruction*, edited by John Darby. Notre Dame, IN: University of Notre Dame Press.

Davis, Rebecca. 2019. "As SA Policing Fails, Private Security Steps In – But at a Cost." *Daily Maverick* (South Africa), 15 January. https://www.dailymaverick.co.za/article/2019-01-15-as-sa-policing-fails-private-security-steps-in-but-at-a-cost.

Davis, Rebecca. 2024. "How the Reports into the July 2021 Unrest Let South Africa Down." *Daily Maverick* (South Africa), 30 January. https://www.dailymaverick.co.za/article/2024-01-30-how-the-reports-into-the-july-2021-unrest-let-south-africa-down.

DefenseWeb (South Africa). 2022. "SA's Safety and Security Machinery Will Be Restored – Security Cluster." 28 February. https://www.defenceweb.co.za/featured/sas-safety-and-security-machinery-will-be-restored-security-cluster.

Dixon, Bill. 2019. "Power, Politics and the Police: Lessons from Marikana." *Journal of Modern African Studies* 57, no. 2: 203–21.

Douek, Daniel. 2013. "Counterinsurgency's Impact on Transitions from Authoritarianism: The Case of South Africa." *Politikon* 40, no. 2: 255–75.

Douek, Daniel. 2020. *Insurgency and Counterinsurgency in South Africa.* London: Hurst Publishers.

Galeano, Eduardo. 1997. *Open Veins of Latin America: Five Centuries of the Pillage of a Continent.* New York: Monthly Review Press.

Gills, Barry, and Joel Rocamora. 1992. "Low Intensity Democracy." *Third World Quarterly* 13, no. 3: 501–23.

Global Freedom of Expression. 2020. "Khosa v. Minister of Defense and Military Veterans" (Case analysis). Columbia University. https://globalfreedomofexpression.columbia.edu/cases/khosa-v-minister-of-defence-and-military-veterans.

Gonzàlez, Yanilda María. 2021. *Authoritarian Police in Democracy: Contested Security in Latin America.* Cambridge, UK: Cambridge University Press.

Gumedze, Sabelo. 2007. "Regulating the Private Security Sector in South Africa." *Social Justice* 34, no. 3: 195–207.

Huggins, Martha. 1997. "From Bureaucratic Consolidation to Structural Devolution: Police Death Squads in Brazil." *Policing and Society* 7: 207–34.

Human Rights Watch. 2013. *World Report 2013.* http://www.hrw.org/world-report/2013/country-chapters/brazil.

Human Rights Watch. 2022. *World Report 2022.* https://www.hrw.org/world-report/2022/country-chapters/south-africa#91c186.

Husain, Saima. 2009. "On the Long Road to Demilitarization and Professionalization of the Police in Brazil." In *Policing Insecurity*, edited by Niels Uildriks, 47–76 Lanham, MD: Lexington Press.

Hyslop, Jonathan. 2005. "Political Corruption Before and After Apartheid." *Journal of Southern African Studies* 31, no. 4: 773–89.

Imray, Gerald. 2023. "Outrage Erupts in South Africa Over Video of Deputy President's Security Officers Stomping on a Man." Associated Press, July 4. https://apnews.com/article/police-brutality-south-africa-1593e661d849ef5315c7368b21a0b3e6.

ICD (Independent Complaints Directorate) (South Africa). 2007. "An Investigation Into Deaths As a Result of Police Action in KwaZulu-Natal, Eastern Cape, and Gauteng." http://www.ipid.gov.za/documents/report_released/research_reports/researchreport2007.pdf.

IPID (Independent Police Investigative Directorate) (South Africa). 2015. *Annual Report.* https://www.ipid.gov.za/sites/default/files/documents/IPID_Annual_Report%20_2014-15.pdf.

IPID (Independent Police Investigative Directorate) (South Africa). 2021. *Annual Report*. https://static.pmg.org.za/IPIDs_Annual_Report_2020_21.pdf.

Jaffe, Rivke. 2013. "The Hybrid State: Crime and Citizenship in Urban Jamaica." *American Ethnologist* 40, no. 4: 734–48.

Joseph, Richard. 1999. "The Reconfiguration of Power in Late-Twentieth Century Africa." In *State, Conflict, and Democracy in Africa*, edited by Richard Joseph. Boulder, CO: Lynne Rienner.

Kooning, Kees, and Dirk Kruijt, eds. 1999. *Societies of Fear: The Legacy of Civil War, Violence, and Terror in Latin America*. London: Zed Books.

Krönke, Matthias, Thomas Isbell, and Makanga Ronald Kakumba. 2024. "Law Enforcers or Law Breakers? Beyond Corruption, Africans Cite Brutality and Lack of Professionalism Among Police Failings." Afrobarometer Policy Paper 90. https://www.afrobarometer.org/wp-content/uploads/2024/01/PP90-PAP6-Africans-cite-corruption-and-lack-of-professionalism-among-police-failings-Afrobarometer-26jan24.pdf.

Levitsky, Steven, and Lucan A. Way. 2010. *Competitive Authoritarianism*. New York: Cambridge University Press.

Lodge, Tom. 1998. "Political Corruption in South Africa." *African Affairs* 97, no. 387: 157–87.

Macaulay, Fiona. 2012. "Deepening the Federative Pact? The Dilma Government's Approach to Crime, Justice, and Policing." *Critical Sociology* 38, no. 6: 823–34.

Mac Ginty, Roger. 2006. *No War, No Peace*. New York: Palgrave Macmillan.

Madlingozi, Tshepo. 2017. "Social Justice in a Time of Neo-Apartheid Constitutionalism: Critiquing the Anti-Black Economy of Recognition, Incorporation, and Distribution." *Stellenbosch Law Review* 1: 123–47.

Marinovich, Greg. 2012. "The Cold Murder Fields of Marikana." *Daily Maverick* (South Africa), 8 September.

McMichael, Christopher. 2014. "Police Wars and State Repression in South Africa." *Journal of Asian and African Studies* 51, no. 1: 3–16.

Mitchell, Michael J., and Charles H. Wood. 1998. "Ironies of Citizenship: Skin Color, Police Brutality, and the Challenge to Democracy in Brazil." *Social Forces* 77, no. 3: 1001–20.

Mlambo, Sihle. 2023. "Senzo Meyiwa Murder Accused was Assaulted, Tortured, and Tubed with a Plastic Bag in Police Cells – Defense." IOL Online, 24 October. https://iol.co.za/news/crime-and-courts/2023-10-24-

senzo-meyiwa-murder-accused-was-assaulted-tortured-and-tubed-with-a-plastic-bag-in-police-cells-defence.

Moosa, Mikhail. 2021. *South Africa Reconciliation Barometer Report.* Cape Town: Institute for Justice and Reconciliation. https://www.ijr.org.za/home/wp-content/uploads/2021/12/IJR_SA-Reconciliation-Barometer-2021.pdf.

Muggah, Robert, and Albert Mulli. 2012. "Rio Tries Counterinsurgency." *Current History* (February): 62–4.

Narsiah, Sagie. 2007. "Alternatives to Neoliberal Governmentality in South Africa." *South African Geographical Journal* 89, no. 1: 34–43.

Nicolson, Greg. 2015. "Vultures, Cowards, Capitalists: How We React to the Horror" *Daily Maverick* (South Africa). 4 March.

O'Donnell, Guillermo. 1993. "On the State, Democratization and Some Conceptual Problems: A Latin American View with Glances at Some Postcommunist Countries." *World Development* 21, no. 8: 1355–69.

Oomen, Barbara. 2004. "Vigilantism or Alternative Citizenship? The Rise of Mapogo a Mathamaga." *African Studies* 63, no. 2: 153–71.

Oxhorn, Philip. 2007. "Neopluralism and Citizenship in Latin America." In *Citizenship in Latin America*, edited by Joseph S. Tulchin and Meg Ruthenberg. Boulder, CO: Lynne Rienner.

Patel, Jaynisha, and Preston Govindasamy. 2021. "South Africans See Corruption as Worsening During President Ramaphosa's Tenure." *Afrobarometer Dispatch* no. 476. https://www.afrobarometer.org/wp-content/uploads/2022/02/ad476-south_africans_see_corruption_as_worsening_under_ramaphosa-afrobarometer_dispatch-15sept21.pdf.

Pearce, Jenny. 2010. "Perverse State Formation and Securitized Democracy in Latin America." *Democratization* 17, no. 2: 286–306.

Pereira, Anthony W., and Mark Ungar. 2004. "The Persistence of the Mano Dura: Authoritarian Legacies and Policing in Brazil and the Southern Cone." In *Authoritarian Legacies and Democracy in Latin America and Southern Europe*, edited by Katherine Hite and Paola Cesarini, 263–304. Notre Dame, IN: University of Notre Dame Press.

Pilling, David, and Monica Mark. 2024. "South African Election Turns Populist as Parties Play Anti-Foreigner Card." *Financial Times*, 1 April.

"Police Conduct Caused More than 700 Deaths in 2011-2012." 2013. South African Broadcasting Corporation, 4 November.

Rawoot, Ilham, Sello S. Alcock, and Monako Dibetle. 2009. "Insecurity In the Forces." *Mail and Guardian* (South Africa), 13–19 November.

Reno, Will. 1997. *Warlord Politics and African States.* Boulder, CO: Lynne Rienner.

Roberts, Benjamin, and Steven Gordon. 2022. "South Africans Have Low Trust in their Police. Here's Why." The Conversation, 28 March. https://theconversation.com/south-africans-have-low-trust-in-their-police-heres-why-178821.

Roelofse, Cornelis. 2015. "South Africa: A Schizophrenic System for Combatting the Scourge Police Corruption." In *Police Corruption and Police Reforms in Developing Societies*, edited by Kempe Ronald Hope, Sr., 109–25. New York: Routledge.

Rose, Richard, and Doh Shin. 2001. "Democratization Backwards: The Problem of Third Wave Democracies." *British Journal of Political Science* 31, no. 2: 331–54.

Saul, John S. 2005. *The Next Liberation Struggle: Capitalism, Socialism, and Democracy in Southern Africa.* Scottsville, South Africa: University of KwaZulu-Natal Press.

Seekings, Jeremy, and Nicoli Nattrass. 2005. *Race and Inequality in South Africa.* New Haven, CT: Yale University Press.

Shaw, Mark, and Clifford Shearing. 1998. "Reshaping Security: An Examination of the Governance of Security in South Africa." *African Security Review* 7, no. 3: 3–12.

Shaw, Mark. 2002. *Crime and Policing in Post-Apartheid South Africa.* Bloomington, IN: Indiana University Press.

Small Arms Survey. 2011. *Small Arms Survey 2011: States of Security*, 106. http://www.smallarmssurvey.org/publications/by-type/yearbook/small-arms-survey-2011.html.

Statista. 2023. "20 Countries with the Biggest Inequality in Income Distribution Worldwide in 2023, Based on the Gini Index." https://www.statista.com/statistics/264627/ranking-of-the-20-countries-with-the-biggest-inequality-in-income-distribution.

Steinberg, Jonny. 2008. *Thin Blue: The Unwritten Rules of Policing South Africa.* Johannesburg: Jonathan Ball.

Stuurman, Ziyanda. 2020. "Police Brutality in South Africa Exposed Once Again." *Mail and Guardian* (South Africa), 28 August. https://mg.co.za/thought-leader/opinion.

Tanner, Murray Scot. 2000. "Will the State Bring *You* Back In? Policing and Democratization" (Review article). *Comparative Politics* 33, no. 3 (2000): 101–24.

Tilly, Charles. 2007. *Democracy.* New York: Cambridge University Press.

Tournadre, Jérôme. 2018. *A Turbulent South Africa: Post-Apartheid Social Protest.* Albany, NY: State University of New York Press.

"Police Kill Boy in Mpumalanga Protest" 2015. *Times Live* (South Africa). 27 February. https://www.timeslive.co.za/news/south-africa/2015-02-27-police-kill-boy-in-mpumalanga-protest.

Tournadre, Jérôme. 2022. *The Politics of the Near: On the Edges of Protest in South Africa.* Translated by Andrew Brown. New York: Fordham University Press.

Turok, Ben, ed. 2008. *Wealth Doesn't Trickle Down: The Case for a Developmental State in South Africa.* Cape Town: New Agenda: South African Journal of Social and Economic Policy.

Viljoen, Frans. 2021. "South Africa Needs to Address the Lingering Legacy of its Police Using Excessive Force" The Conversation. 30 March. https://theconversation.com/south-africa-needs-to-address-the-lingering-legacy-of-its-police-using-excessive-force-157695.

Wacquant, Loïc. "The Militarization of Urban Marginality: Lessons from the Brazilian Metropolis." International Political Sociology 2, no.1 (2008): 56–74.

"We Must Avoid Mabopane Incident, Cele Tells Cops." 2009. *Pretoria News*, 7 November.

Wielders, Iris. 2013. "Perception and Realities of Corruption in South Africa." Afrobarometer Briefing Papers. http://www.afrobarometer.org/publications/afrobarometer-briefing-papers/item/713-perceptions-and-realities-of-corruption-in-south-africa. Accessed 16/6/2014.

SECTION THREE

Concluding Reflections

10

Constructing Citizenship at the Margins: Assessing the Work of Transnational Civil Society Through an Oxhornian Lens

Mónica Treviño González

For the past fifteen years, I have been working as a management consultant for international actors working on social, economic, and political development. These include international organizations within the United Nations (UN) system as well as nongovernmental organizations operating at national, regional, and international levels, particularly those whose goals are to work towards a fairer, more just, more inclusive, more sustainable world. My work involves assessing the effectiveness of these organizations' activities and strategies, and advising them on how to achieve their stated objectives. I have found that an Oxhornian understanding of civil society is especially apt for this purpose, both in terms of the neopluralist competition among organized civil society groups and in terms of socially constructing citizenship for those who are not traditionally considered citizens. I will illustrate this with two broad examples: the struggle for women's and gender rights, and the struggle to secure rights for irregular migrants.

BACKGROUND

The organizations with which I work usually operate transnationally. They are not usually, nor exclusively, focused on one particular state, but rather they aim to support groups in different states and to encourage relevant international bodies (such as the UN – in particular its treaty rights entities – as well as regional or global multilateral organizations) to develop norms in support of their inclusion. The majority of these organizations operate on two main levels: advocating for the realization of rights, and providing technical support for the development of legal and institutional structures to enable that realization of rights. I have deliberately chosen to work with this type of organization, in line with one of the primary preoccupations of my doctoral dissertation: what, if any, role do transnational civil society actors have in supporting counterhegemonic actors at the national level?

My clients are, functionally, transnational advocacy networks, defined as "networks of activists, distinguishable largely by the centrality of principled ideas or values in motivating their formation" (Keck and Sikkink 1998, 1). These networks aim to change the behaviour of states and international organizations, by strategically "framing" issues to make them understandable to their target audiences, but also to attract attention to the issues and to encourage action in institutionally acceptable ways. They support counterhegemonic actors in the sense that they work for the inclusion of subaltern populations and to influence state policy at the national and/or international level from this perspective. That is to say, these organizations support women; people with diverse sexual orientation, gender identity, gender expression, and sex characteristics (SOGIESC); and racialized, ethnic, or religious minorities/marginalized groups, within the arena of civil society in particular states, as well as on the multilateral or global stage.

TRANSNATIONAL ADVOCACY, CAPACITY BUILDING, AND WOMEN'S RIGHTS UNDER NEOPLURALISM

In working with organizations seeking to further women's rights and gender equality, such as the Association for Women's Rights in Development (AWID) and the International Civil Society Action Network (ICAN), it becomes apparent that the main thrust of their actions revolves around advocacy on two fronts. On the one hand, they provide financial, technical, and political support for organizations in different regions and/or states to enable them to be effective advocates for themselves in their respective arenas. On the other hand, they advocate directly with states and multilateral organizations in support of the realization of rights for women and people of diverse SOGIESC through the development of norms and policies that further these objectives.

The first component clearly reflects the reality of Oxhorn's conceptualization of neopluralism (Oxhorn 1998): only those entities within civil society that have the requisite human and financial capital are capable of engaging in effective advocacy. Hence the need to provide financial and technical capacities to enable organizations of subaltern groups to engage meaningfully in the struggle for their own inclusion.

AWID's movement strengthening work has made important contributions to strengthening feminist, women's rights, and gender justice movements by enhancing connectivity and promoting collaboration, which enables organizations within these movements to pool their knowledge and experiences. AWID also directly acknowledges the fact that pro-rights actors are in competition with anti-rights actors, and has developed concrete tools and knowledge products to strengthen the capacity of movement actors to develop strategies to effectively challenge anti-rights actors.

For its part, ICAN supports grassroots women's organizations in implementing their peacebuilding projects by providing seed funding to promising initiatives. It provides a holistic package of financial support and capacity building for the implementation of projects, and connects these organizations to key advocacy spaces at the local, regional, and global levels. Concretely, ICAN's support builds the profile and experience of partner organizations by putting them into key advocacy and practitioner spaces, connecting them to other important actors, and supporting their award and funding applications. This means that they can increase their human capital in order to obtain additional financial capital and develop other projects, as well as advance their agendas more widely, contributing to a magnifier effect that can drive further, broader change.

Both organizations also leverage their own human and financial capital to advocate directly in relevant multilateral spaces to develop and/or strengthen international norms that grassroots organizations can then use at the national level.

These ways of working reflect the perhaps unconscious understanding shared by these and similar organizations of the reality of Oxhorn's assessment of the neopluralist characteristics of civil society. My evaluations for and recommendations to these organizations are likewise founded on this understanding, focusing on ensuring the targeting of advocacy efforts in those spaces where the relevant groups have the ability to challenge competing organizations, and on strengthening their capacities in those spaces where they lack this ability.

TRANSNATIONAL ADVOCACY, IRREGULAR MIGRANTS, AND THE SOCIAL CONSTRUCTION OF CITIZENSHIP

From a different perspective, my work also involves supporting organizations like the International Organization for Migration (IOM), which is part of the UN system, in their work promoting safe migration. This highlights a different dimension of the social construction of citizenship, in that it seeks to support and promote the rights of groups and individuals who are not citizens of the states through which they transit and to which they migrate.

Recognizing that many migrants experience violence, exploitation, and abuse during their migratory journey, the IOM developed the Global Compact for Safe, Orderly and Regular Migration in part in order to address and reduce vulnerabilities in migration. There is no internationally accepted definition of a "vulnerable migrant"; there are no clear procedures for identifying them, nor operational guidelines for their protection and assistance (IOM 2019, ix). The IOM undertook the development of the *IOM Handbook on Protection and Assistance for Migrants Vulnerable to Violence, Exploitation and Abuse* to fill this gap. I contributed to this project through the development of assessment tools and guidelines to operationalize the IOM's model, which considers vulnerability and resilience as the result of the interaction of multiple factors at the individual, household/family, community, and structural levels.

The community- and structural-level assessment tools, particularly when applied in transit and destination scenarios, were designed with the understanding that migrants in those locations will usually lack the requisite financial, human, social, and political capital for reducing their own vulnerability. Indeed, they are generally considered to have few if any rights.[1] The challenge in this situation is that the realization of their rights is dependent on a virtual extension of the concept of citizenship. That is to say, as non-citizens, they have few if any avenues to protect themselves against violence, exploitation, and abuse, especially in those cases in which their presence in the given state is considered to be illegal.

The solution to this situation rests very heavily, in practice, on the intervention of transnational actors, such as the IOM but also other UN agencies and international nongovernmental organizations. They take on the role of advocating for the inclusion, however partial, of these vulnerable populations into the realm of civil society and citizenship rights. In this way, they enter the arena of civil society and compete with national civil society groups in seeking the inclusion of migrant populations and the development of policies that enhance their access to basic rights and protection.

This is an interesting extension of Oxhorn's conception of civil society, in two main ways. Firstly, it embeds transnational actors into what has traditionally been a domestic arena, in so far as the populations seeking inclusion are unable to advocate for themselves and require the direct action of transnational actors to protect their rights by proxy. Without the intervention of these transnational actors, there are no obvious avenues for these vulnerable migrants to engage with the state in pursuit of their own interests. This is because they usually have no legal right to be there, and therefore any interaction with state authorities increases their vulnerability. Furthermore, there is little incentive for the state to support their claims, since they are not able to participate in elections. This is especially the case in locations where the host populations also face vulnerabilities and therefore are likely to see irregular migrants as unfairly competing for scarce resources. It is in this sense that efforts to extend rights to these populations are located at the margins of traditional understandings of what constitutes civil society.

Starting from Oxhorn's conceptualization of citizenship as a relational construct resulting from the peaceful coexistence and competition among organized groups makes it possible to conceive of the broadening of the concept of citizenship in this manner. That is to say, non-citizens within a given state can access rights and protection to the extent that they are able to effectively engage (directly or through intermediaries) with the state and/or with other groups in civil society to further their interests. At the same time, this conceptualization makes it possible to envision a legitimate role for non-domestic actors in civil society, as long as they can be seen to follow the rules, and as long as they have the necessary financial and political resources.

CONCLUSION

Based on my work with organizations acting for women's and gender rights, as well as for the provision of protection in migration, I have found that Oxhorn's conceptualization of civil society and citizenship in democracy is extremely useful for practitioners in international development. It provides a powerful explanation for the ways in which different actors behave in their advocacy efforts. But it also provides a useful lens through which to envision the potential for interventions in support of subaltern groups in both authoritarian and nominally democratic contexts. Understanding the reality of civil society as neopluralist enables us to develop pragmatic strategies for strengthening the financial and human capital of organizations to enable them to effectively advance the inclusion of subaltern groups, as well as to creatively leverage international norms to expand the margins of citizenship.

NOTE

1 This refers primarily to those migrants who are not otherwise protected by international refugee law, and those who migrate outside regular migration flows.

REFERENCES

IOM (International Organization for Migration). 2019. *IOM Handbook on Protection and Assistance for Migrants Vulnerable to Violence, Exploitation and Abuse*. Geneva: International Organization for Migration.

Keck, Margaret E., and Kathryn Sikkink. 1998. *Activists Beyond Borders*. Ithaca, NY: Cornell University Press.

Oxhorn, Philip. 1998. "Is the Century of Corporatism Over? Neoliberalism and the Rise of Pluralism." In *What Kind of Market? What Kind of Democracy? Latin America in the Rise of Neoliberalism*, edited by Philip Oxhorn and Graciela Ducatenzeiler. University Park, PA: Pennsylvania State University Park.

CONCLUSION

Bringing Norms Back In: The Neopluralist Legacy and the Need to Rethink Our Assumptions About Democracy

Philip Oxhorn

The study of democracy and the social, economic, and political inclusion of poor, disadvantaged groups in Latin America is bittersweet. The region's history since independence is filled with seemingly countless examples of social, economic, and political innovation with the goal of creating more just societies. Studying these innovations, which have been championed by a myriad of political, social, and economic actors, takes on a certain poignancy given the fact that structural inequality has proved to be one of the most resilient characteristics of Latin America since the colonial period, despite often significant long-term improvements in basic indicators such as poverty, per capita income, and life expectancy. Even the dramatic, unprecedented increases in socioeconomic and political participation by the poor and disadvantaged groups in recent years have failed to reverse this to any significant degree (see Montambeault and Hilgers, this volume). The consequences of this inequality include unacceptably high poverty rates when compared to other countries at similar levels of development over time and extremes of employment insecurity for those lucky enough to have a job. They are also reflected in the region's notorious democratic instability.

While inequality is anything but new in the region, its sociopolitical and economic impact has been fundamentally transformed by the region's legacy of neopluralism. In the approximately fifty years since Chile implemented the economic policies that laid the foundation for neopluralism,[1] throughout Latin America the state's relationship with the economy and society has been changed profoundly. As the chapters in this volume illustrate, this has significant implications for democracy that researchers are only beginning to understand, in Latin America and beyond.

As a starting point, academics and policymakers need to rethink their common assumptions about the relationship between democracy and the poor and disadvantaged groups. For example, since at least the 1930s, the assumption has been that the poor needed to learn the value of democracy before they could participate in and/or advocate for it. The reality, however, is that disadvantaged people already have a good understanding of what "democracy" is, even when they have never experienced it. Democracy is not that hard to figure out! When poor people first mobilized in Latin America, they often did so to demand effective democracy. Elites understand institutional democracy because it is all about power. Their fear of losing power, or the opportunity to seize it, leads them to support non-democratic alternatives. The poor and disadvantaged also understand this power dimension of democracy, but not in the same way as elites who undemocratically exercise power over them. The poor are the targets of the exercise of elite power.

This contradiction has been at the heart of Latin America's political economy since at least the colonial period. It has periodically generated political instability as first the middle classes, followed by the working class and then the popular sectors, mobilized to demand democratic inclusion. Such demands, especially from the working classes and popular sectors, were met by increasingly violent elite opposition. Stability was eventually restored with the democratic transitions of the 1980s and 1990s, but structural change aimed at the root causes of political instability was minimal at best.

Social confrontation and the threat of violence on this scale did not happen because disadvantaged groups suddenly forgot what effective democracy was, and it certainly was not because the poor had given up on the importance of democracy's core values. The poor and disadvantaged adopted pragmatic responses that reflected the unequal social structures that marginalize them, leaving them vulnerable to state and non-state violence, as well as to economic insecurity and to a lack of adequate social policies. The promise of access to even limited resources in exchange for political support, however contingent and regardless of the threat to democracy that this turn toward authoritarian politics and the right represents, is a last resort in the context of growing marginalization. What do the poor and disadvantaged have to lose?

In recent years, as frustration among citizens grows due to perceived economic and/or political crises, elites have tried to take advantage of the situation by introducing the most authoritarian of ideas and ideologies into their public discourse as new solutions that justify their efforts to seize or retain power. At this point, the political situation becomes very volatile, and all bets are off as countries, if not whole regions like Latin America, find themselves increasingly sucked into what I call a new authoritarian dynamic whose goal is to instill non-democratic governance structures and an ultra-right-wing political culture at all levels of society.

To meet the challenge to democracy posed by the legacy of neopluralism and the emergence of the new authoritarian dynamic, I argue that we need to rethink some key assumptions in the study of democracy. I begin with a discussion of an alternative conceptualization of democracy as an *accountable, responsive government through active citizen participation.* I then examine the nature of the new authoritarian dynamic and its relationship to the legacy of neopluralism. In the concluding section, I look at how we need to rethink the role of norms in the study of democracy.

RECONCEPTUALIZING DEMOCRACY

Accountable, Responsive Government Through Active Citizen Participation

The last thing we need is another definition of democracy, with or without adjectives (Collier and Levitsky 1997). It would be far more useful to develop greater clarity and focus on how we understand democracy conceptually. In other words, why have people been willing to risk so much to achieve democracy? This would provide more useful insights into the primary challenges and potential of democracy. Rather than reinventing the wheel or applying the latest research methodologies to reaffirm the validity (that was never in doubt) of what we already know, we should restructure our research to bring to the fore the principal concepts and norms that undergird democracy's legitimacy and efficacy. Evidence-based policies would then be driven by what we need to learn to reinforce democracy and social inclusion, and less by the "puzzles" created by the methodologies we employ and confusion over ends and means.

A classic example of this problem is the highly influential work of Mancur Olson.[2] People had been voting for thousands of years when, much to everyone's surprise, Olson (1965) allegedly demonstrated through his work on collective action and rational choice that it was irrational for people to do so. This is because of the so-called free-rider problem: if no single vote could determine the electoral outcome, yet everyone would be affected by the outcome regardless of whether they voted, why bother to vote? How could voting be understood as more than a waste of time and other scarce resources? Following this conceptualization, democracy at best would be dysfunctional, requiring people to act "irrationally" against their own best interests to complete their democratic duty. As the chapters in this volume clearly demonstrate, however, the people and organizations under study are anything but "irrational." At worst, democracy would be equated with elections independently of the outcomes they produced and the context in which they were held. In other words, elections would be transformed from being one of the principal means for achieving the normative ends of democracy into the only end of democracy.

Historically, democratic instability in Latin America was viewed as the result of elitist biases in the region, undemocratic political cultures, and/or the ignorance (at best) of poor and disadvantaged groups, that is, the majority of Latin Americans.

This is remarkably consistent with Joseph Schumpeter's (1942) definition of democracy as a system of government in which leaders are selected through competitive elections. This classic definition has been extremely influential among academics and policymakers alike around the world. Yet Schumpeter was not much of a democrat. He was so concerned that most citizens did not have the ability to do more than simply decide who would make decisions that he conceptualized democracy narrowly to minimize their influence. He conflated democracy with elections, paving the way for the fallacy of electoralism. Accountability is complicated by the fact that Schumpeter's conceptualization of democracy as the act of selecting leaders would seem to give leaders carte blanche after they are elected.

People do not desire democracy or risk their lives to establish and safeguard democratic regimes simply because democracy offers them the possibility of voting. People decide to make such sacrifices because of the values or norms that democracy entails. Democracy comes to be understood as an end rather than as a means toward other ends. The ability of specific governments to realize these norms, in turn, determines their perceived democratic legitimacy among citizens. In my reconceptualization of democracy, three principal norms are critical in both theory and practice: *accountability*, *responsiveness*, and *active citizen participation*.[3]

These norms are shared by all democracies to a greater or lesser degree and are institutionalized in a myriad of ways. They also clearly are interrelated, reinforcing one another in a variety of manners. Elements of all three norms can also be found under authoritarian regimes, but only democracies can simultaneously embody all three to a meaningful degree. Authoritarian regimes also do not institutionalize these norms to any significant degree. At best, they arbitrarily provide poor and disadvantaged groups with some recourse. At worst, democratic norms are manipulated by elites to deliberately undermine democratic institutions (e.g., the importance of elections under neopluralism, constrained as they are by other aspects of neopluralism).

It is important to emphasize that these norms that define democracy are relatively clear and understandable. In fact, their meaning is largely self-evident, including for people with limited formal education. Rather than confuse and obfuscate, the conceptualization of democracy developed here contributes to transparency and dialogue, which itself is quite democratic.

In many respects, accountability is the most important norm for poor and disadvantaged groups. It represents a generalized demand that people in positions of authority face consequences for the decisions they make, regardless of their position in society. It is closely related to demands for justice, fairness, and the end of impunity, not to mention the rule of law and due process. The importance of accountability also helps explain the centrality of elections in democracy. Free and fair elections are an unambiguous means for securing vertical forms of accountability by simply voting for other candidates or political parties.

Responsiveness goes to the heart of democratic relations between rulers and citizens. In democracies, leaders are expected to be aware of the concerns and interests of citizens and respond accordingly. It is an important part of the powerbase and legitimacy of democratic leaders. Responsiveness is achieved through a variety of means in addition to elections, ranging from institutions of formal representation connected to the state, to a range of mechanisms within civil society and in the public sphere. Regardless of how it is achieved, the democratic quality of responsiveness reflects the role that citizens play in determining what issues or demands are discussed as part of the public agenda, and their relative priority for being addressed.

Participation fundamentally provides a bottom-up perspective on responsiveness. This is because participation tends to be more intensive at the community level. People generally experience democracy at the community level, and many citizen demands and/or expectations are centred there. The community level is also more accessible, especially for poor and disadvantaged groups for whom travel-related expenses (including time) can be prohibitive. As noted above, there are a myriad of means to participate in a democracy, both institutional and informal (see Montambeault and Hilgers, and Hilgers, both in this volume). Such participation is democratic to the extent that two conditions are met: first, those who are participating have the autonomy vis-à-vis other actors, including the state, to define and defend their interests in competition with other actors; second, the right of all groups to such autonomy is respected. These conditions safeguard the transparency of participatory processes and maximize social inclusion. These conditions are also important for confirming the authenticity of the participants' demands and concerns because they help ensure that participants are legitimate interlocutors on behalf of those for whom they claim to speak.

It is important to note that participation itself can be transformative at both the macro/societal and micro/individual levels. People's consciousness changes as they interact with others and learn that their situations are not so different from their own.[4] This can lead to a cascade of new activities, both by individuals and collectively, as people form a variety of self-help organizations. In other words, this participation reflects the growth of civil society. The more varied the participation is, the better, because this strengthens the capacity of poor and disadvantaged groups to mobilize in support of their own demands and priorities, including demands that the three norms defining democracy be enforced. Ultimately, the macro-level transformative process linked to participation is the social construction of citizenship. The breadth of the process in terms of who participates (or does not) and the issues or policy areas affected (or left off the agenda) determines the breadth and depth of citizenship rights in each country. In other words, who participates in the social construction of citizenship and how they participate is a principal determinant of citizenship rights and of inclusion.

Accountability, responsiveness, and participation can be particularly problematic in poorer, highly unequal, and exclusionary societies. To the extent that they face a wider range of pressing needs to address and have relatively fewer resources at their disposal for doing so, responsiveness in the context of high levels of inequality raises the stakes in Latin American politics. This is because even small gains in the standard of living of the poor through social policies can make a relatively huge difference to the recipients, while the concentration of income means that a relatively small number of taxpayers would need to pay for it. This can lead to a prevailing sense of zero-sum politics, as well as political and economic instability. It is a consequence of the contradictory ways that elites and the poor envision power and of how it is exercised, as referred to above. In other words, democracy comes to be seen as the problem by elites who want to at least preserve, if not expand, their power. At best, democracy loses its attraction to poor and disadvantaged groups because of its inability to provide accountable, responsive governance based on participation. At worst, democracy is seen as the problem, dominated by a corrupt political class at the service of powerful elites with little to offer the average person.

By focusing attention on what really matters, this reconceptualization of democracy puts into relief issues of democratization, including the relationship between democracy as an end and as a means for achieving other ends – ends that are often overlooked. In other words, the relevance of the research and the policies that flow from it would increase. Policies based on research carried out in accordance with this conceptualization of democracy would be more relevant. This is because the research would explicitly be driven by what we need to learn to strengthen democracy, not some other agenda only tangentially related to democracy (Olson 1965) – or even worse, research motivated by the goal of undermining democracy.

The conceptualization of democracy developed here can help focus attention on the tensions among the short- and long-term goals driving democratization, as well as among the specific ends and means in each case. For example, Chile has been among the most successful countries in Latin America in terms of having consistently high levels of economic growth. But economic growth is not an end. It is a means for achieving ends like poverty reduction, employment security, better social policies, and so on. Unfortunately, Chile has lagged in achieving such ends. In fact, at the peak of its growth in the 1990s, inequality increased. Chile's challenge is to synchronize the use of the impressive amount of economic resources generated by high growth – its principal means with its democratic ends (see Roberts, this volume).

It would be naïve to expect any conceptualization of democracy to lead to the rapid emergence of a global consensus in favour of democracy simply because the ends it entails appeal to large numbers of people who risked everything in their struggles for democratic transitions in the 1980s, 1990s, and early 2000s. This is true in countries like South Africa, as Douek's chapter in this volume illustrates, and it is particularly true in Latin America, with its history of extreme inequality. What the conceptualization can do is provide new insights into the nature of the challenge and offer potentially better strategies for dealing with it.

A New Authoritarian Dynamic and the Legacy of Neopluralism[5]

When I, along with a handful of other intrepid researchers, began to study civil society in Latin America in the early 1980s, the region was still in the depths of unprecedented levels of political repression. Many of the organizations we studied emerged as survival mechanisms to cope with the violence and the consequences of the region's switch to a market-based development model that exacerbated Latin America's historical challenge of inequality.

Things were *supposed* to be better for the poor and disadvantaged when the countries of the region had undergone democratic transitions. To a certain extent, they were. State repression decreased significantly, elections were largely respected, and new social policies directed at the poor and disadvantaged were promised. Yet, political violence was largely replaced by criminal violence; elected officials seemed out of touch with the people who elected them, or were corrupt and part of the problem; and social policies not only did not keep pace with the needs of the poor but introduced new sources of inequality, as peoples' ability to access their basic citizenship rights was determined by their personal economic resources (see the introduction to this volume). This is the paradox of neopluralism: unacceptable levels of poverty and social exclusion coexisting with meaningful elections that are frequently won by progressive political parties and movements.

This paradox underscores the surprising lack of resiliency of progressive reforms and the political parties and movements that promote them. Brazil is a good example. Its leftist Workers' Party (Partido dos Trabalhadores, or PT) governed Brazil for over a dozen years starting in 2006. It used the revenues generated by a boom in the country's exports as a means for successfully implementing an array of innovative popular reforms intended to address inequality and social exclusion. Citizen participation was often central to their popularity and success, and many participatory mechanisms introduced in Brazil were adopted by other countries, including developed ones. The world similarly took note when, in 2013, millions of Brazilians took to the streets demanding redress from the PT government for a number of issues, particularly people's growing frustration with the lack of socioeconomic fairness and equality. Although the intrinsic unfairness and high inequality in Brazilian society date back to the colonial period, they were becoming intolerable for many in the first half of the 2000s.

None of this, however, insulated Brazil from the threat of the new authoritarian dynamic. In 2018, Jair Bolsonaro won the presidency on a platform epitomizing the most negative aspects of the new authoritarian dynamic – the first person to do so in Latin America. Throughout the region, there is the real risk that a vicious cycle will emerge as the strength of the institutions needed to contain the new authoritarian dynamic (e.g., the courts, a free press, rule of law, and so on) declines at the same time that the new authoritarian dynamic strives to take advantage of the institutional decline to further penetrate state and civil society organizations.

The new authoritarian dynamic that is emerging in Latin America and elsewhere may prove to be the most important political innovation of the twenty-first century. It has shown itself to be a unique conglomeration of political and social actors, ideologies, histories, and personalities. Although the new authoritarian dynamic is fundamentally antithetical to democracy, electoral processes have been the principal means for its champions to take and hold on to power. And they are increasingly good at winning elections. Examples from Latin America include Bolsonaro (president of Brazil from 2019 to 2022, and the first president in the region following this dynamic; he was convicted in September 2025 by a panel of Supreme Court justices of plotting a coup), and the current sitting presidents of Argentina (Javier Milei), Ecuador (Daniel Noboa), El Salvador (Nayib Bukele), Guatemala (Bernardo Arévalo), and Nicaragua (Daniel Ortega). While the new authoritarian dynamic shares some similarities with populism, it is the culmination (albeit unexpected) of neopluralism.[6] The new authoritarian dynamic is a political phenomenon that penetrates societies at all levels, from the grassroots up. Its goal is to lead a process of social change that reaches its peak with the emergence of a new, illiberal political culture that the leadership of the new authoritarian dynamic and its allies would find more favourable to their interests.

The new authoritarian dynamic is associated with all things right-wing – political parties, ideologies, religion, and so on. Nationalism, particularly racially based nationalism, is especially important because it intrinsically thrives on division – an "us" versus "them" mentality – to isolate its presumed enemies and mobilize its own base. The ideological imprecision of the new authoritarian dynamic provides greater flexibility to construct winning electoral coalitions, while illiberalism provides an overarching source of unity for people identifying with the new authoritarian dynamic.

The new authoritarian dynamic relies on various illiberal sources of political power. In addition to religion, race ideology, culture, and social media, it purposely focuses on the fears of citizens to mobilize support based on ambiguous, often contradictory, ideas and beliefs. This illiberalism further enables the new authoritarian dynamic to feed off violence, fear, and division to further its own interests. The result is confusion and obfuscation rather than clarity and transparency.

From excessive reliance on market principles and an important yet ambiguous role for elections to undermining institutions and civil society, the new authoritarian dynamic is intimately intertwined with the legacy of neopluralism and continued efforts by Latin American elites to preserve it. The structural reforms have increased the stakes in Latin American politics, while the obvious inequity that those reforms institutionalized have added to growing citizen frustration and distrust in existing institutions.[7]

One of the most pronounced (and fundamentally unfair) contradictions in the legacy of neopluralism is the de facto privatization of programs central to social mobility, including education and health care – access to which is often considered in democratic countries to be a citizenship right because of their importance – while intolerable levels of economic insecurity and poverty make it increasingly difficult for the majority to pay for these services. Ingrained structures of inequality deepen and become harder to reduce as people with economic resources purchase the best private services they can, and the poor and disadvantaged groups are forced to rely on underfunded and deficient public services.

A similar situation exists regarding civil rights. People with economic resources not only receive better treatment by the police and judicial system when they are victimized by crime, but their legal transgressions are far more likely to avoid sanction. Conversely, the poor and disadvantaged groups are not only more likely to be victimized by the police because of often endemic levels of violence, but they are often made scapegoats so that more powerful people can avoid accountability and so that citizen frustration with rising crime rates can be somewhat appeased.

Another series of contradictions stems from the impact of economistic norms on participation. Under neopluralism, voters are conceptualized as casting their votes in a free market of votes, just as consumers spend their scarce economic resources on goods and services in markets. Voting becomes a quintessential self-interested activity (hence Olson's challenge to figure out why people bother), ignoring the various public and collective dimensions of voting, which include reinforcing the three norms defining the ends of democracy. The neopluralist conceptualization also supports the competing illiberal norm that merely holding elections is sufficient for democracy to exist, what Schmitter and Karl (1991) call the "fallacy of electoralism." Democratic ends are confused with the means for achieving them to justify the norm that the person who receives the most votes wins. No other criteria are offered for evaluating democracy or determining who wins elections. This would be true regardless of the conditions under which elections are held. At the same time, an almost exclusive focus on elections makes key support institutions (courts, a free press, education, and so on) more vulnerable to external manipulation (see both Bonner and Durazo Herrmann in this volume). This includes having few checks on what the winners of elections can do, as long as they continue to win elections. Restrictions on who can run and on the issues that can be raised directly affect all three democratic norms, yet this is unimportant under neopluralism.

The legacy of neopluralism is equally devastating for other forms of participation. The norm of individual self-interest determining citizen behaviour implies that people will participate in organizations or other collective activities only when they think doing so is in their personal best interest. Decisions to participate therefore are fluid, always subject to reconsideration as the individual person's circumstances change. Collective identities similarly lose any intrinsic value because identifying with them is contingent on factors external to the identity.[8]

Neopluralism reinforces a norm of individual self-interest in several ways. First, social welfare policies such as targeted assistance are designed to help people cope economically until they find employment. Any collective dimension to the aid is kept to a minimum, reinforcing the tendency in civil society toward fragmentation. Assistance is expected to be only short-term until the labour market recovers sufficiently to provide people with needed employment. To ensure that this happens, policies of labour market flexibilization make it easier to hire and fire workers, with the expectation that this will keep wages sufficiently low to clear the labour market.

Policies like these inevitably weaken labour movements. Like a self-fulfilling prophecy, changes in workers' policies and the economy under neopluralism have left workers with few alternatives to competing with one another in the pursuit of their self-interest. Those fortunate enough to have a unionized job, especially their leaders, are now more than ever a narrowly self-interested actor – preserving the interests and privileges of the labour elite, while fragmenting the working class even more.[9]

Neopluralism has fundamentally changed the politics of inequality in Latin America, but not in the ways or for the reasons one might have anticipated. After over five hundred years as the most unequal region in the world, inequality had become a given in Latin America. Marginal increases or decreases have attracted little attention because their impact on the day-to-day life struggles of the poor was not obvious. Neoliberal reforms increased inequality, but more importantly, it became clear that the state no longer had the institutional ability to redistribute resources in favour of the poor. Paradoxically, this was because the percentage of household income going to the poor was so low – that is, too marginal to the overall level of economic activity. In fact, income inequality in Chile increased during the country's peak period of economic growth in the 1990s, despite a significant concomitant decrease in poverty rates. Similarly, Brazil's widely recognized Bolsa Familia targeted assistance program helped 25 per cent of Brazilians and reduced extreme poverty by 12 to 19 per cent, at a cost of just 5 per cent of household income (Veras Soares et al. 2010).

While the relatively low cost of programs like the Bolsa Familia is positive, it also began to shift public discourse to increasingly focus on norms of fairness, which subsumes discussions of norms of equality.

Filling the Normative Void

The new authoritarian dynamic represents a real normative challenge to democracy. Illiberal norms may triumph because the poor and disadvantaged prefer an illiberal normative alternative. After centuries of structural inequality and democratic instability, the frustration of the poor and disadvantaged groups may have reached a tipping point.

At the same time, the growth in participation by the poor and disadvantaged groups has not had the kind of positive impact that research on social construction would have predicted.[10] The weakness of more traditional collective identities (worker, women, peasant, and so on) has undermined attempts to mobilize the poor and disadvantaged groups in numbers large enough to have a realistic chance of actually bringing about structural change.[11] Instead, participation takes place in a variety of forms, both formal and informal. It remains fragmented and tends to reinforce social heterogeneity and exclusion rather than social cohesion and inclusion.

Together, these trends contribute to a democratic normative void that makes it even harder for the poor and disadvantaged to collectively resist the spread of the new authoritarian dynamic, assuming that they even want to. Indeed, in this context, the poor and disadvantaged may even turn to actively supporting candidates representing the new authoritarian dynamic, as a response to inequality.

Ironically, the new authoritarian dynamic seeks to fill the normative void created by the overly economistic worldview of neopluralism. It may be easier than we realize.

The right wing Unión Demócrata Independiente (UDI) political party in Chile was responsible for the design and implementation of the policies that would define neopluralism in Latin America. In

1986, Chile was wracked by massive protests demanding an end to the military regime and a transition to democracy. When the military government responded by increasing political repression to levels not seen in Chile since the first years after the 1973 military coup, it certainly came as no surprise.[12]

What was surprising in 1986 was how the far right attempted to complement repression with social policies and a normative discourse that seem to anticipate those associated with the new authoritarian dynamic when it began to emerge approximately four decades later. As the UDI official responsible for the party's work in the shantytowns explained to me in 1986 during a meeting in a pro-Pinochet shantytown in Santiago, the UDI had two messages for the poor, which had largely been received successfully: first, unlike the left, the UDI appreciated them for who they were, so *everyone can be happy recognizing that no one is equal*; and second, the UDI has access to state resources (personal interview, Santiago, Chile; emphasis mine).

The combination of elitist conceptualizations of democracy and neopluralism would seem to overdetermine the spread of the new authoritarian dynamic. Yet its triumph is by no means guaranteed. This is one reason why governments throughout the region generally seek to avoid the stigma of openly rejecting the democratic label. Democracy still enjoys considerable legitimacy, just as there is substantial opposition to the new authoritarian dynamic. Instead, governments linked to the new authoritarian dynamic continue to take advantage of the various constraints that neopluralism places on democratic governance as they look for opportunities to take power.

As countries that until recently epitomized democratic political norms find themselves confronting growing threats from the far right and the new authoritarian dynamic,[13] we cannot afford to be on the defensive. Fortunately, after delving deeper into the problem of the universality of democracy, cultural relativism, and the ability of poor groups to participate in democratic politics, it quickly becomes clear that many of the assumptions behind elitist, minimalist approaches to democratization are mistaken and/or irrelevant. We need to be firm in our resolve. Our mistaken assumptions can become self-fulfilling prophecies if we are not careful. In particular, we can no longer afford a lack of respect towards people with whom we will need to collaborate to address many of today's challenges. Otherwise, we run the risk of further democratic backsliding.

It would be equally mistaken not to recognize that the potentially universal appeal of democracy does not mean that all other forms of governance will disappear or lose their legitimacy to democracy. Numerous non-democratic forms of governance have been considered legitimate for extended periods. These include revolutionary regimes in Iran, Cuba, China, Yugoslavia, and Mexico. Non-democratic ends that could legitimize a regime include realizing the goals of a revolution and/or ideology, and ends associated with a religion or particular lifestyle, physical security, a fairer society, and so on. It is also premature to rule out the possibility that a new regime type might appear based on the still-emerging new authoritarian dynamic, while non-democratic, illegitimate regimes can remain in power for decades.

We are far from exhausting the political alternatives that are available to choose from, including democratic, authoritarian, and hybrid political alternatives (see Rubin, this volume). Just the opposite: the weaker and more defensive democracy appears to be, the more likely it is that alternatives will emerge (for better or worse) to take advantage of the vulnerability of democracy.

It is up to us to imagine what they might be. It is also imperative that when engaging in such "imagining," we not lose sight of what is most important. As I have argued here, in the case of democracy, we cannot ignore the specific norms that legitimate it: accountability, responsiveness, and participation. Otherwise, democracy may appear to be, at best, irrelevant for understanding a particular problem, or, at worst, part of the problem.

Given the range of issues that the region confronts, it is difficult to know where to start. One issue or area in particular stands out: the unprecedented surge in participation in recent years by the poor and disadvantaged groups, the concomitant atomization of civil society, and the potential of *cooperative competition* to find meaningful solutions (see Montambeault and Hilgers, this volume). Although still quite preliminary, the basic ideas at play here overlap well with the core issues addressed in the present volume: civil society, neopluralism, and the social construction of citizenship, to name the most prominent. Important unanswered questions for guiding research include: How and by whom will the basic contours of cooperation be established? Is cooperative competition a general, conceptual framework for understanding social relations based on collaboration and/or a formal institutional mechanism tasked with promoting compromise?

Of course, this is just one potential topic for research. Given the nature of the many challenges Latin America has successfully met since it achieved independence two hundred years ago, as well as those that are still pending – and not to mention those that have yet to appear – we do not need to fear for a lack of interesting and important research topics. What the present volume is more concerned about is developing useful theoretical and empirical research methodologies. The reader will be the judge whether we succeeded.

As a political scientist, I find transparency and the relevance of my work to the people I study to be an important aspect of my work. This will not prevent me from being critical in my work, but it helps me remain objective and responsible. These issues are particularly important when studying democracy. How society governs itself is something that only that society can decide, although I feel free to offer unsolicited advice.

Finally, in reconceptualizing democracy and trying to understand the nature of a regional (if not global) swing to the right so that it can be moderated, if not stalled, I hope to facilitate compromise and remind us all why we believe in democracy. Hopefully, my unsolicited advice will help others in similar efforts.

By way of concluding: projects of this nature necessarily involve several generations of scholars and researchers working in a wide range of disciplines on a myriad of themes all over the globe. There are few experiences quite like it, although there are some important similarities with successful innovation labs. The results, as this volume attests, include all kinds of new, unexpected insights into some of the most important topics of the day. It also brings new us friends and acquaintances, which is another benefit of what we do. We are indeed very fortunate.

As I finish the final sentences of a multiyear project, I want to thank the people who actually wrote the book. I would also like to thank all of the many people who attended the conference and shared their thoughts, as well as the many more people who over the years shared their thoughts and opinions with me personally. Finally, a special thanks to Françoise and Tina, the volume's editors and the people who graciously kept us on our toes.

NOTES

1 These policies were eventually labeled neoliberalism or the Washington Consensus. Poorly defined, neoliberalism is too narrow to be a mode of interest intermediation cable of structuring whole societies. It is blamed for most of the region's economic and political ills, with little recognition of its positive contributions (e.g., the control of hyperinflation). For many, neoliberalism has become the bogeyman of the twenty-first century.
2 I am not criticizing Olson's work, only its blind application to all human endeavours, without recognizing that alternative logics or rationalities may be more relevant depending on the circumstances.
3 The list is not meant to be exhaustive. Philippe Schmitter (1983), for example, adds competition and accessibility. Both also are much more dependent on other norms to be considered democratic ends.
4 This is especially important for women, who traditionally must overcome a variety of obstacles that limit their activities outside the household, as Stéphanie Rousseau's chapter in this volume shows.
5 Although I am focusing on Latin America, very similar patterns can be found in virtually every region of the world, as the chapters by Douek, Rubin, and Eckstein in this collection illustrate. The discussion tends to be more theoretical given the fact that the new authoritarian dynamic is so new.
6 Unlike populism, the new authoritarian dynamic is committed to long-term social change in the form of a new conservative political culture.
7 Not everything associated with neopluralism was bad. Neopluralism was instrumental in bringing the region's hyperinflation – which disproportionately hurts the poor because their meagre resources cannot keep up – under control after decades of failed efforts by civilian and military governments. Neopluralism was also critical in the establishment of elections as the principal means for legitimating executive and legislative authority throughout Latin America.
8 Indigenous peoples are an important partial exception, as discussed by Robert and Brunet-Bélanger in their chapter in this volume, though an examination of this aspect is beyond the scope of this conclusion.
9 It is important to note that, as is often the case in Latin America, economic sectors with large numbers of unions belie a weak workers movement. The leverage that these organizations provide the poor and disadvantaged is lost.
10 The following draws on the chapter by Montambeault and Hilger in this volume.

11 And if organizations mobilizing for such structural change did emerge, it is not at all clear what they would demand.

12 Regime supporters, however, were shocked by the level of violence when a military patrol burned alive two shantytown youth.

13 This is by no means a problem unique to Latin America, as the re-election of Donald Trump to the US presidency attests.

REFERENCES

Collier, David, and Steven Levitsky. 1997. "Democracy with Adjectives: Conceptual Innovation in Comparative Research." *World Politics* 49, no. 3: 430–51.

Lipset, Seymore Martin, 1959. "Some Social Requisites of Democracy: Economic Development and Political Legitimacy." *American Political Science Review* 53, no. 9.

Olson, Mancur. 1965. *The Logic of Collective Action: Public Goods and the Theory of Groups*. Cambridge, MA: Harvard University Press.

Oxhorn, Philip, 1995. *Organizing Civil Society: Popular Organizations and the Struggle for Democracy in Chile*. University Park, PA: Pennsylvania State University Press.

Schmitter, Philippe C. 1983. "Democratic Theory and Neocorporatist Practice." *Social Research* 50, 885–928.

Schmitter, Philippe C., and Terry Lynn Karl. 1991. "What Democracy Is… and Is Not." *Journal of Democracy* 2, no. 3: 75–88.

Schumpeter, Joseph. 1942. *Capitalism, Socialism and Democracy*. New York: Harper and Bros.

Soares, Fábio Veras, Rafael Pérez Ribas, and Rafael Guerreiro Osório. 2010. "Evaluating the Impact of Brazil's Bolsa Família: Cash Transfer Programs in Comparative Perspective." *Latin American Research Review* 45 (2): 173–90.

Williamson, John. 1990. "Latin American Adjustment: How Much Has Happened?" *Choice Reviews* 28(4). https://doi.org/10.1016/0305-750x(93)90046-c.

Contributors

MICHELLE D. BONNER is professor of political science at the University of Victoria. Her research examines authoritarian practices in democracy. In particular, it explores the role of media and civil society organizations in holding police violence to account. She is the author of numerous books, articles, and chapters. Her most recent book is *Tough on Crime: The Rise of Punitive Populism in Latin America* (Pittsburgh, 2019). Her book *Policing Protest in Argentina and Chile* (Lynne Rienner, 2014) won the 2016 Canadian Political Science Association's Comparative Politics Book Prize. Her articles have been published in journals such as the *Journal of Latin American Studies*, the *International Journal of Press/Politics*, and the *International Journal of Transitional Justice*. She is currently working on a SSHRC-funded project on the political communication of enforced disappearances in democratic Latin America.

ANDRÉANNE BRUNET-BÉLANGER is a postdoctoral researcher at Saint Paul University and Nipissing University, with a PhD in political science from the University of Montreal. Her research focuses on social movements and activism, both legal and political, among historically marginalized groups, particularly Indigenous communities and diasporas. She examines judicialization processes, social justice struggles, and the impact of social movements on policy change in Quebec and Paraguay. Her recent scholarship investigates informal philanthropy and motherhood as avenues for social and political engagement among immigrant mothers in Quebec. Her publications have appeared in *Lien social et politiques*, *Migration and Development*, the *Canadian Journal of Law and Society*, the *International Journal on Minority and Group Rights*, and *Diaspora Studies*, among others, and several edited volumes.

DANIEL L. DOUEK is a faculty lecturer in the Department of Political Science at McGill University. His teaching focuses on international relations and comparative politics in Africa and the Middle East, and on civil wars and political violence. He is passionate about researching rebel movements and state security forces in Southern Africa, especially during transitions from colonialism to independence. Douek has written extensively about the African National Congress' armed wing, Umkhonto we Sizwe. He is the author of *Insurgency and Counterinsurgency in South Africa* (Hurst, 2020) and has published several articles in *Third World Quarterly* and *Journal of Southern African Studies*.

JULIÁN DURAZO HERRMANN is a professor of comparative politics at Université du Québec à Montréal (UQAM). His current research deals with the role of local media in democratizing the public sphere, especially at the subnational level. He has done extensive fieldwork in Bahia (Brazil) and Veracruz (Mexico). His most recent publications include "Political Stability and Subnational Media Systems: Comparing Bahia and the Federal District of Brazil," *Communication Research and Practice* 8, no. 3 (2022), co-authored with F.H. Pereira; and "Espaces publics et conglomérats médiatiques: Le cas de Bahia (Brésil)," in *Les espaces publics, la démocratie et les gauches en Amérique latine* (Presses de l'Université Laval, 2019). He has edited numerous books and special issues, most notably "Populism, Media and Journalism," *Brazilian Journalism Research* 17, no. 3 (2021); *Les espaces publics, la démocratie et les gauches en Amérique latine* (Presses de l'Université Laval, 2019); and "Études comparatives sur le journalisme, les médias et la politique," *Sur le journalisme* 6, no. 2 (2017).

SUSAN ECKSTEIN is a professor in the Pardee School of Global Studies and in the Sociology Department at Boston University. She has written numerous books and articles on Mexican urban poor, political-economic developments in Cuba, Cuban immigrants, immigration policy, and the impacts of Latin American revolutions, and has edited books on Latin American social movements and social rights, and on immigrant impacts in their homelands. Most recently, she published *Cuban Privilege: The Making of Immigrant Inequality in America*. Previously she has published *How Immigrants Impact Their Homelands* (co-editor), *The Immigrant Divide: How Cuban Americans Changed the US and Their Homeland*, *What Justice? Whose Justice?: Fighting for Fairness in Latin America* (co-editor), *Struggles for Social Rights in Latin America* (co-editor), *Back from the Future: Cuba Under Castro*, *Power and Popular Protest: Latin American Social Movements* (editor), *The Poverty of Revolution: The State and Urban Poor in Mexico*, and *The Impact of Revolution: A Comparative Analysis of Mexico and Bolivia*. She is the recipient of fellowships from the John Simon Guggenheim Memorial Foundation, the Radcliffe Institute for Advanced Study, the American Council of Learned Societies, the Ford Foundation, John D. and Catherine T. MacArthur Foundation, the Rockefeller Foundation, the Tinker Foundation, and the Christopher Reynolds Foundation. She has received a number of awards for her publications.

TINA HILGERS is associate professor in the Department of Political Science at Concordia University (Montreal). She is director of the Lab for Latin American and Caribbean Studies and a researcher on the Fonds de recherche du Québec (FRQ)-funded Équipe de recherche sur l'inclusion et la gouvernance en Amérique latine (ÉRIGAL). Her research interests lie in urban and grassroots informal politics and her projects focus on clientelism, violence, and forms of resistance and resilience in low-income communities in Latin America and the Caribbean. She is the editor of *Clientelism in Everyday Latin American Politics* (Palgrave, 2012), *Violence in Latin America and the Caribbean: Subnational Structures, Institutions, and Clientelistic Networks* (with Laura Macdonald, Cambridge, 2017), and *Identidade, território e política no contexto de violência na América latina* (with Jorge Luiz Barbosa, Observatório de Favelas, 2017). Her articles have appeared in *Development and Change*, *Latin American Research Review*, *Latin American Politics and Society*, *Policing and Society*, and *Theory and Society*, among others.

FRANÇOISE MONTAMBEAULT is professor of political science at the Université de Montréal, and Canada Research Chair in Participation and Citizenship. Her research looks at participatory spaces, institutions, and practices, and at their role in the construction of democratic citizenship in Latin America, and beyond. Since 2016, she is director of Équipe de recherche interuniversitaire sur l'inclusion et la gouvernance en Amérique latine (ÉRIGAL). Her publications include: *L'engagement pousse là où on le sème* (Écosociété, 2021), *The Politics of Participatory Democracy in Latin America: Institutions, Actors and Interactions* (Stanford, 2015), the co-edited *Legacies of the Left in Latin America: The Promise of Inclusive Citizenship* (Notre Dame, 2020), and *The Participatory Democracy Turn* (Palgrave, 2019). Her research has been published in the *International Journal of Urban and Regional Research*, the *International Journal of Human Rights*, the *Journal of Latin American Studies*, *Latin American Politics and Society*, the *Journal of Civil Society*, and *Politics and Society*, among others.

PHILIP OXHORN is a retired professor of political science from McGill University, where he also was associate provost (international), the founding director of McGill's Institute for the Study of International Development, and associate dean (graduate studies). In addition, Professor Oxhorn was the editor-in-chief of the international journal *Latin American Research Review*. Most recently, he served as dean of international education at Vancouver Island University. His research focuses on the comparative study of civil society and its role in supporting democratic regimes, particularly in Latin America. His publications include *Sustaining Civil Society: Economic Change, Democracy and the Social Construction of Citizenship in Latin America* (Penn State University Press, 2011) and *Organizing Civil Society: The Popular Sectors and the Struggle for Democracy in Chile* (Penn State University Press, 1995), as well as numerous articles and four co-edited volumes: *What Kind of Democracy? What Kind of Market?: Latin America in the Age of Neoliberalism* (with Graciela Ducatenzeiler, Penn State University Press, 1998), *The Market and Democracy in Latin America: Convergence or Divergence?* (with Pamela Starr, Lynne Rienner Publishers, 1999), *Decentralization, Civil Society, and Democratic Governance: Comparative*

Perspectives from Latin America, Africa, and Asia (with Joseph S. Tulchin and Andrew Selee, Woodrow Wilson Center Press/Johns Hopkins University Press, 2004), and *Beyond Neoliberalism?: Patterns, Responses, and New Directions in Latin America and the Caribbean* (with Kenneth Roberts and John Burdick, Palgrave Macmillan, 2009).

GARANCE ROBERT is a PhD candidate in political science at the Université de Montréal. She holds a master's degree (2013) in social sciences from the École des hautes études en sciences sociales (EHESS), majoring in political studies. Her early research focused on the emergence and appropriation of human rights language by Nicaraguan political actors during the revolutionary period (1979–90). Her doctoral work extends these reflections to the construction of human rights interpretation and practice after peace accords through a comparison of Nicaragua and Guatemala. She was coordinator of the CERI-CÉRIUM Chair in International Affairs (2020–22) and is now coordinator of Équipe de recherche sur l'inclusion et la gouvernance en Amérique latine (ÉRIGAL) (2021–). She is an associate member of the Centre d'études mexicaines et centraméricaines (CEMCA) and member of the Canada Research Chair in Participation and Citizenship(s), the Centre de recherche sur les politiques et le développement social (CPDS), and the Observatoire des droits de la personne du CÉRIUM (ODPC). Her articles have been published in *Cahiers des Amériques latines* and *Problèmes d'Amérique latine*.

KENNETH M. ROBERTS is the Richard J. Schwartz Professor of Government at Cornell University and a faculty fellow of the Democratic Threats and Resilience initiative at Cornell's Mario Einaudi Center for International Studies. He earned his PhD from Stanford University, with teaching and research interests that lie at the intersection of political parties, social movements, populism, and crises of democratic representation in Latin America and beyond. His publications include *Changing Course in Latin America: Party Systems in the Neoliberal Era* (Cambridge University Press, 2014), *Deepening Democracy?: The Modern Left and Social Movements in Chile and Peru* (Stanford University Press, 1999), and the co-edited volume *The Resurgence of the Latin American Left* (Johns Hopkins University Press, 2011). His research has been published in *World Politics*, *American Political Science Review*, *Perspectives on Politics*, *Comparative Political Studies*, *Comparative Politics*, *Latin American Politics and Society*, and other scholarly journals. His current research explores polarization and democracy in contemporary Latin American politics.

STÉPHANIE ROUSSEAU is a full professor of political science at the Department of Social Sciences, Pontificia Universidad Católica del Perú. She has a PhD in political science from McGill University. She worked as an associate professor of sociology at Université Laval (Quebec, Canada) from 2005 to 2013. Her research interests are social movements and citizenship, gender, social policy, and ethnicity in Peru. In 2016, she won the José Maria Arguedas Award for the Best Article published on Peru, from the Peru Section of the Latin American Studies Association. She is the author of *Women's Citizenship in Peru: The Paradoxes of Neopopulism in Latin America* (Palgrave Macmillan, 2009) and co-author of *Indigenous Women's Movements in Latin America: Gender and Ethnicity in Peru, Mexico and Bolivia* (Palgrave Macmillan, 2017). She has published articles in *Latin American Research Review*, the *Journal of Latin American Studies*, *Latin American Politics and Society*, *Social Politics*, and the *Journal of Politics in Latin America*, among others.

AVIAD RUBIN is associate professor in the Division of Government and Political Theory, School of Political Science, at the University of Haifa. He holds a PhD in political science from McGill University. Professor Rubin specializes in the intersection between collective identities and political regimes, with particular emphasis on religion and state, nationalist movements and protracted conflicts in the Middle East, and has published extensively on these topics. His most recent book project, *Bounded Integration: The Religion–State Relationship and Democratic Performance in Turkey and Israel* (SUNY, 2020), explores the impact of the religion–state relationship in Turkey and Israel on democratic performance in both countries.

MÓNICA TREVIÑO GONZÁLEZ is founder and director of Merits Partnership, a client-focused management consulting firm whose core sectors of expertise include international development, humanitarian and peacekeeping interventions, results-based management, and social science research. With over twenty years of experience in research and evaluation of international development projects and programs, she has worked with clients such as the International Organization For Migration (IOM), the Organization of American States (OAS), UNESCO, the United Nations Children's Fund (UNICEF), UN Women, and the World Bank, as well as nongovernmental organizations such as Oxfam, the International Civil Society Action Network (ICAN), and the Association for Women's Rights in Development (AWID). Thematically, her work has focused on projects including human rights–based approaches, advocacy interventions, education and capacity-building, women's rights promotion, institution strengthening, migration, and social protection. She has led research and evaluation teams in multicultural contexts throughout Latin America and the Caribbean, Africa, the Middle East, and Southeast Asia.

Index

acarreo (political practice), 38
al-Assad, Bashar, 223
Allende, Salvador, 59, 65, 136–7
apartheid: and the African National Congress (ANC), 245, 255; neo-apartheid constitutionalism, 236; post-apartheid transitions and legacies, 243–4, 245, 246, 247, 253, 254
authoritarian regimes: appeal of, 38, 91, 92, 130; authoritarian drift, 15, 20, 21; defined, 8, 209; examples of, 8, 14, 28, 33, 99, 218, 223, 224–5; legacies of, 236–7, 239–40, 245, 247, 255; and the media, 167, 217; and neoliberal reforms, 80; new authoritarian dynamic, 14, 275, 280, 281–2, 285–7; in opposition to, 216, 222, 225; post-authoritarian contexts and transitions, 18, 212, 235–8, 240–3, 247, 249, 251; practices and tendencies, 158, 177, 210, 255, 277; and repression, 148, 226; and the resurrection of civil society, 10, 52–3; versus hybrid regimes, 17, 212

Bachelet, Michelle, 59, 64, 66
Berni, Sergio, 144
Biden, Joe, 189, 197, 198, 201–2, 203
Boric, Gabriel, 54–5, 66, 67–71
bottom up, 7, 212, 227, 278
Bush, George W., 194, 196, 199–200

caciques, 171, 176
Calderón, Felipe, 162
Cárdenas, Cuauhtémoc, 43
Cariola, Karol, 66
Carrillo Vidal, Alondra, 71
Castro, Fidel, 186, 190, 192, 193
caudillo (strongman) leaders, 34
Cele, Bheki, 249
Cerezo, Vinicio, 102
"Chicago Boys," 58
Chicago school, 58, 64
citizenship: and agency, ix, 6, 7, 8, 10, 15, 16, 77, 98, 99, 101, 131; anti-rights actors, 269; civil rights, 5, 6, 29, 30, 37, 83, 85, 131, 142, 210, 224, 283; coerced marginalization, 8, 130, 131, 133, 137, 148, 150; as consumption, 8, 10, 20, 29, 32,

33, 44, 77, 99, 138, 139, 148, 151; and controlled inclusion, 7, 8, 28, 30, 33, 130, 131, 135–7, 143, 150, 177; as cooptation, 6, 8, 29, 33, 34, 44, 62, 105, 130, 136, 149; corporatist, 44; exclusionary citizenship regimes, 5, 8, 20, 78, 82, 96, 97, 98, 99, 100, 187; extension of citizenship rights, 2, 31, 100, 127, 131, 270; functionalist and deterministic nature of, 5; low-intensity citizenship, 235; non-linear, 101; political rights, ix, 3, 5, 7, 8, 29, 83, 131, 139, 185, 200, 203, 237, 238; as a relational construct, 5, 15, 16, 271; social construction of, 4, 5, 6, 8, 15, 18–21, 28, 98, 99, 101, 106–11, 120, 129, 131–5, 142; social rights, 3, 4, 5, 6, 7, 8, 10, 30, 37, 57, 70, 131, 187, 238; thick consensus, 214; thin consensus, 208, 214, 227; unequal access to the civil, political, and social rights of citizenship, 4

civil society
- Argentina: Coordinadora contra la Represión Policial e Institucional (CORREPI), 145
- autonomous: and citizenship, 15; and economic structures, 27; functional groups within, 6, 28; and hybrid regimes, 17, 211, 212; and the media, 132, 133, 137, 150; relations with the state, 5, 8, 29, 132, 142, 218, 237
- Chile: Amnesty International Chile, 145; Centro de Estudios Públicos (Centre for Public Studies, or CEP), 141; Central Unitaria de Trabajadores de Chile (United Workers Central, or CUT), 65; Confederación de Estudiantes de Chile (Confederation of Chilean Students, or CONFECH), 65; Paz Ciudadana (Citizen Peace), 140–1, 144–5; the Ethical Commission Against Torture, Chile, 145
- cooperative competition, 6, 7, 15, 18–20, 287
- Guatemala: Academy of Mayan Languages (Academia de Lenguas Mayas de Guatemala), 102; Council of Mayan Organizations of Guatemala (COMG), 102; Instance of Mayan Unity and Consensus (Instancia de Unidad y Consenso Maya, or IUCM), 102; Mutual Support Group (Grupo de Apoyo Mutuo, or GAM), 102; National Coordination of Widows of Guatemala (Coordinadora Nacional de Viudas de Guatemala, or CONAVIGUA), 102; Peasant Unity Committee (Comité de Unidad Campesina, or CUC), 102
- Mexico: Asamblea de Barrios (Neighbourhood Assembly, or AB), Mexico City, 36; Coordinadora *Única* de Damnificados (Single Coordinating Committee of Earthquake Victims, or CUD), Mexico City, 35; Frente Popular

Francisco Villa (Francisco Villa Popular Front, or FPFV), Mexico City, 36; Confederación Nacional de Organizaciones Populares (National Confederation of Popular Organizations, or CNOP), 34, 35
– mobilization 1968, 35; coverage of, 175; cyclical, 56, 63; economic context, 187; Indigenous mobilization, 17, 97, 98, 115, 118, 237, 254; and the international sphere, 107, 110; and the media, 217, 218; and the Movimiento Urbano Popular (Urban Popular Movement, or MUP), 36, 39; and religious associations, 19, 213; and repression, 8, 33, 34, 53, 58, 59; resisting constitutionalization, 54, 61, 65; student mobilization, 60; sustained mobilization, 31, 56; and undemocratice regimes, 209; and urban housing needs, 33; weak collective mobilization, 14; women's mobilization, 78, 79, 85
– weak civil society, 4, 150, 238, 254; civil society organizations: Association for Women's Rights in Development (AWID), 268–9; International Civil Society Action Network (ICAN), 268–9
Claro, Ricardo, 138
class, 15; conflicts, 5, 66, 139, 243; economic classes, 214; formation and positions, 56, 58; inequalities, 30, 60, 91, 159, 236, 242; lower class, 8, 10, 29, 35, 157; working class, 274, 284; popular classes/sectors, 33, 149, 171, 187, 274; labour, 8, 34; middle classes, 34, 36, 224, 274; upper classes, 40, 256
clientelism, 10, 27, 29, 30, 44, 89, 130, 136; under authoritarian-sim, 33–6; under democracy, 36–8; as a form of democratic participation, 33; as an informal mechanism of social inclusion, 28, 29; under neopluralism, 30–3; patrons and clients, 33, 39, 40, 42, 43, 44
Clinton, Bill, 189, 193, 204n3
constituent power, 54–72
constitutional convention, Chile, 68–71
counterhegemonic actors, 268
counter-publics, 156, 159, 163, 171, 175, 176
COVID-19, xii, 18, 31, 61, 78, 79, 80, 90, 91, 195, 248. *See also* pandemic
Cuban immigrant entitlements: Asylum Cooperation Agreements, 195; the Cuban Adjustment Act (CAA), 188, 189, 190, 193, 196, 198, 199; "dry foot" policy, 191, 204n3; homeland trips, 192, 193, 194; "New Cubans," 192–3, 194, 196; parole rights, 191, 192, 194, 195; people-to-people embargo, 192, 193, 196; Remain in Mexico program, 197; single entry visa policy, 196

Damascus Declaration, 224
Damascus Spring, 224
decolonization, 12

de la Madrid, Miguel (President), 35
demobilization, 52, 53, 56, 57, 63, 72, 89, 105
democracy: classic definition, 276; *democracia de los acuerdos* (democracy of agreements), 53; democracies with adjectives, 239, 275; democratic backsliding, 15, 286; democratic erosion, 3, 15, 20, 21, 80, 150; democratic regime transitions, 3; democratization, 157; the fallacy of electoralism, 276, 283; Global South democracies/democratizing, 236, 237, 243, 255; liberal democracy, 3, 157, 158, 210, 242, 256; low-intensity democracies, 18, 235; post-authoritarian inequality, 236; reconceptualization of democracy, 277; securitized democracies, 238, 239; third wave democratizers/democratization, 236, 237, 238, 239; weak democracies, 6
demos, 62
double movement, 60
Duarte, Javier, 162, 163

Echeverría, Luis, 35
Edwards, Agustín, 144
Eisenhower, Dwight D., 186, 190
electoral sanctions, 39
exclusion: and citizenship regimes, 5, 8, 20, 78, 82, 96, 97, 98, 99, 100, 187; economic exclusion, 6, 14, 77, 114; in immigration policies,185, 188, 196, 198, 199, 200, 201; and media systems, 175; social exclusion, 8, 14, 16, 17, 19, 29, 279, 280, 281, 285
extractive development projects: Fenix nickel mine, El Estor, Izabal, Guatemala, 104; hydroelectric project, Santa Cruz Barillas, Huehuetenango, Guatemala, 104; Marlin Mine, San Marcos, Guatemala, 104; mobilizing against, 106; Paraguayan–Brazilian Itaipu hydroelectric dam, 112; San Rafael mine, Santa Rosa, Guatemala, 104

Fernández de Kirchner, Cristina, 143, 144, 145, 149–50
Fontaine Aldunate, Arturo, 141
free-rider problem, 276
Freire, Paulo, 175

García Jiménez, Cuitláhuac, 161, 162, 164, 167
Garré, Nilda, 161, 162, 164, 167
Ghonim, Wael, 219–20
grey zone states, 239

Haitian immigrant entitlements: "credible fear" hearings, 200; Haitian family reunification parole program, 202; Haitian Refugee Immigration Fairness Act, 199; temporary protected status (TPS), 200–1
Humala, Ollanta, 89
hybrid regimes, 17, 287; and citizenship, 20; in the Middle East, 209–13, 218, 219, 223, 226, 227; and South Africa, 240;

and subnational polities, 157–8, 169, 176

immigrant rights: 1965 immigration reform, United States, 186, 202; Immigration Reform and Control Act, United States, 199; Title 42, United States, 197, 198, 202
Indigenous actors and Peoples: Akaṭeka, 109; *alcaldía indigena* [Indigenous mayoralty] of the Ixil of Nebaj, 108; Chuj, 109; Garifuna, 104, 121n3; Maquín, Mama, 108; Maya, 104, 105, 107; Popti', 109; Q'anjob'al, 109; Sawhoyamaxa community, 116; Xákmok Kásek community, 116; Xinca, 104, 121n3; Yakye Axa community, 116
Indigenous citizenship: Article 64 of the Constitution, Paraguay, 112, 113; Article 98 of the Agrarian Statute, Paraguay, 115; Article 142 of the Penal Code, Paraguay, 115; and autonomy, 97, 102, 111, 121; Convention 169 (C169), ILO Indigenous and Tribal Peoples Convention, 96, 103, 106, 112, 115; collective ownership, 112; Indigenous People Rights law office, Guatemala, 109; Ka'a Poty Square, 117; Law 1863 on agrarian status, 113; Law 904/81, "Estatuto de las Comunidades Indígenas," Paraguay, 111, 112; *Maya Kaqchikel Peoples of Sumpango et al. v. Guatemala*, 107; Maya movement, 105, 106; *Maya Q'eqchi' Indigenous Community of Agua Caliente v. Guatemala*, 107; the Peace Accords, Guatemala, 103, 110; the rational use of land, 113; the right to free, previous, and informed consultation (FPIC), 103, 104, 106; self-determination, 96, 99; transitional justice, Guatemala, 102; United Nations Special Rapporteur on the Rights of Indigenous Peoples, 114
industrialization: dependent industrialization, 7, 56; European industrialization (or early and comparatively slower), 6, 7, 56, 187; import substitution industrialization (ISI), 7–8, 9, 34, 36; Latin American industrialization (late and rapid) 7, 187
informal authoritarian practices, 158; channels, 31; effects of neopluralism, 172; housing, shelters, 24, 41; mechanisms of inclusion, 28; work/sector, 7, 9, 11, 13, 41, 80, 81, 187
Inter-American Court of Human Rights (IACtHR), 101, 107, 113, 116–18, 119
International Labour Organization (ILO), 96, 103, 106, 112

Jackson, Giorgio, 66, 67, 70
Johnson, Lyndon, 186

Kast, José Antonio, 55, 67, 69, 70, 71

Kennedy, John F., 186
Keynesian/ism, 9, 58
Khosa, Collins, 248

labour, organized, 9, 11, 52, 59, 64, 65, 135, 237, 284
Lagos, Ricardo, 59, 64
Latinobarómetro survey, 37
Law No. 49, 225
Lebyane, Lucas, 244
LGBTQI+ rights, 70, 83, 170, 171
Loncón, Elisa, 69
López Obrador, Andrés Manuel, 39, 40, 43, 162
lo social, 62
"lost decades," 36
low-intensity warfare, 235
low-level equilibrium trap, 241

market society, 58, 60
Mashatile, Paul, 245
media coverage: *boletinero*, uncritical journalist, 163, 178n3; *chayote*, in exchange for favourable coverage, 163–5, 169, 172, 174, 178n2; crime beat, 146, 170, 172; general coverage (the government, the legislature, political parties), 161, 170, 172, 173; Indigenous movements, 170–1, 174; mobilization against sexual harassment, 174; polls, 140–2; press conferences, 161, 168–70, 172, 174; public relations, 131, 139, 142–5; social coverage, 174–7; street vendors' coverage requests, 173; under military regimes, 143; victims of violence, 171, 173
media framing and effects: agenda setting, priming and framing, 133; enforcing and reproducing existing hierarchies, 139, 160; protest-as-crime frame, 149; self-censorship, 171, 173
media reach: blackout areas, 176; low penetration rate, 223; rural access versus urban access, 157, 166
media types and models: alternative media, 165; democratic corporatist media model, 134; "empirical" journalists, 167, 172; in its ideal form, 132; independent media, 165, 176; liberal model/deregulated private media, 134–5; "professional" journalists, 167; social media, 63, 70, 129, 133, 139, 141, 144, 217, 282; "yellow press," or sensationalist press, 171, 172–3, 175
Menchú, Rigoberta, 103
Menem, Carlos, 137
migrant rights: Global Compact for Safe, Orderly and Regular Migration, 270; International Organization for Migration (IOM), 270; *IOM Handbook on Protection and Assistance for Migrants Vulnerable to Violence, Exploitation and Abuse*, 270; vulnerable migrants, 271
Ministry for Development and Social Inclusion (MIDIS), Peru, 89
Modise, Thandi, 249
Morales, Evo, 12, 97
Morsi, Mohamed, 222

Mubarak, Hosni, 220, 221–2
Mufamadi, Sydney, 243
multiculturalism, cosmetic, 97

neoliberalism: anti-neoliberalist sentiment and protests, 57, 60, 65, 69; and class cleavage, 66; as an economic development model, 4, 9, 11, 12, 17, 18, 20, 21, 29, 33, 36, 53, 57–9, 64, 79, 80, 82, 157, 238, 239, 253, 284; and Indigenous populations, 98; neoliberal multiculturalism, 97; and security privitization, 253; and social atomization and heterogeneity, 56
neopluralism: and authoritarian backlash, 11, 14; defined, 130–1, 157–8; and economic insecurity, 99; as eroding state authority and democratic institutions, 4, 256, 277, 283; as favouring those with economic and political resources, 145; and forced competition, 19, 20, 158, 170; and fragmentation/alienation, 32, 99, 142, 145, 157, 174, 253; and Indigenous citizenship rights, 97, 99; and inequality, 4, 10, 11, 244; and interest intermediation, 16, 21, 29, 269; as legacy, 4, 273–4, 275, 282, 284, 285; and media systems, 20, 131, 135, 137–9, 140, 142, 143, 147, 159–60, 166, 167–8, 177; neopluralist maternalism, 78, 79; and opportunities for corruption, 250; as paradox, 14, 280; plebsicitary nature of, 139–40, 141, 142, 143; and police violence, 236; and post-authoritarian democracies, 236, 238; and poverty, 236; as replacing corporatism, 16, 29; and rule of law, 176; and self-interest, 284; and space for protests, 146, 148; versus pluralism, 10, 29; and weak civil society, 4, 150, 238, 254
Ntumba, Mthokozisi, 249

Obama, Barack, 186, 189, 191–4, 195, 196, 198–202, 203

pandemic, 12; and care work, 18, 78, 79, 90; and effects on protest, 68; and enforced lockdowns, 248; post-pandemic crisis, 80, 91, 92; and the Trump administration, 195, 197, 198; and unemployment, 149
parity dollars, 80
Perón, Juan Domingo, 136
Piñera, José, 64
Piñera, Sebastián, 60–1, 64, 67, 68, 147
"pink boom," 31
"pink tide," 11, 12, 31
Pinochet, Augusto: and the Carabinaros, 143; challenges to Pinochet, 59, 137; Chicago school technocrats, 58, 64; institutional legacies, 53, 55, 58, 59, 61, 65, 66, 68, 138; market-based economic reforms, 138, 141, 146; plebiscite on leadership, 140; post-Pinochet, 9, 60; pro-Pinochet, 71, 138, 141, 286; regime, viii, 52, 143

police/paramilitary/security organizations: 32 Battalion, 248; the Carabineros and public relations, 143, 147, 148; CORREPI, 145; Independent Police Investigative Directoratc (IPID), South Africa, 247; South African National Defense Force (SANDF), 248; South African Police Service (SAPS), 235, 244, 245–6, 251, 252, 253–4
policing: investigative style policing, 239, 240, 242; Marikana massacre, 235–6, 242, 247, 248, 251, 254, 256; police militarization, 18, 243, 247–8, 255; punitive style policing, 239–40, 242; security privatization, 18, 243, 253–4; torture methods, 246–7
political opportunity structure, 36
political parties
– Bolivia: Movimiento al Socialismo (Movement Toward Socialism, or MAS), 62
– Brazil: Partido dos Trabalhadores (Workers' Party, or PT), 62, 281
– Chile: Concertación alliance, 58, 64; *Frente Amplio* (Broad Front), 67, 69; *Lista del Pueblo*, 69; *Nueva Mayoría* (New Majority), 66, 67; Partido Comunista de Chile (Communist Party, or PCCh), 65, 66, 69; Partido Demócrata Cristiano (Christian Democratic Party, or PDC), 55, 66, 67, 71; Partido Socialista de Chile (Chilean Socialist Party, or PSCh), 55, 65, 67, 71; Unión Demócrata Independiente (UDI), 285–6
– Egypt: the Muslim Brotherhood (MB), 220–3
– Mexico: Movimiento Regeneración Nacional (National Regeneration Movement, or MORENA), 27, 28, 37, 38–9, 40–2, 42–4, 45, 156, 161, 162, 165, 166, 176; Partido de la Revolución Democrática (Democratic Revolutionary Party, or PRD), 27, 28, 37, 38–40, 40–2, 42–3, 44, 156; Partido del Trabajo (Labour Party, or PT), 161, 169; Partido Revolucionario Institucional (PRI), 28, 33–6, 37, 38, 40, 42, 44, 156, 161, 162, 176
– South Africa: African National Congress (ANC), 235, 245, 248, 253, 254, 255, 256; Economic Freedom Fighters party, South Africa, 256; Umkhonto we Sizwe Party, 256
– Syria: Muslim Brotherhood (MB), 224, 225; Syrian Islamic Front (SIF), 224–5

Ramaphosa, Cyril, 244

Sánchez, Beatriz, 67
Shabangu, Susan, 250
social movements: Arab Spring, 207, 209, 210, 213, 216, 217, 218, 219, 223, 226; Damascus Spring, Syria, 224; Day of Rage, Egypt, 220, 221; *estallido*, Chile, 53, 54, 57, 60, 61, 67, 68; Ni Una Menos (not one more) campaign, Argentina, 85; No campaign, Chile, 137; *Pingüino*

(penguin) rebellion, Chile, 60, 63; *piqueteros* movement, Argentina, 63; *poder popular*, 61; protest cycles, Chile, 57, 67; Mexican student movement of 1968, 35; Movimiento Urbano Popular (Urban Popular Movement or MUP), Mexico, 27, 28, 33, 36–7, 38, 9, 41, 42; service delivery protests, South Africa, 88, 244; "We are all Khaled Said," Egypt, 219
social programs: Bolsa Familia, Brazil, 285; collective kitchens, or *ollas comúnes*, Peru, 89, 92; Cuna Más, Peru, 87, 88, 89; Fondo de Cooperación para el Desarrollo Social (FONCODES), Peru, 87; Pensión 65, Peru, 87; Programa de Apoyo Directo a los Más Pobres – Juntos, Peru, 87, 88; Programa Nacional de Alimentación Escolar – Qali Warma, Peru, 87, 88; Wawa Wasi program, Peru, 90
State Commission for the Attention and Protection of Journalists (Comisión Estatal para la Atención y Protección de los Periodistas, or CEAPP), Mexico, 167, 176
state corporatism, 7, 8, 10, 33, 130, 136
Stroessner, Alfredo, 112
subaltern groups, support and inclusion of, 16, 130, 187, 268, 269, 272

Trivelli, Carolina, 89–90
Trump, Donald, 186, 191, 194–6, 197, 198, 200, 201–2

United Nations Declaration on the Rights of Indigenous Peoples (UNDRIP), 113

Vallejo, Camila, 66, 70
Veracruz Institute for Access to Information (Instituto Veracruzano de Acceso a la Información, or IVAI), Mexico, 164
Vidal, Alondra Carrillo, 71
"voice and exit," 40

Williams, Leo, 244
women's rights and gender justice movements: benefits, exclusion from, 81; care work, 77, 85, 86, 90, 91–2; conditional cash transfers, 87; gender-based violence, 83, 84, 85, 91; gender gap, 80–1; maternal mortality, 18, 84, 86; morning-after pill, 84; neopluralist maternalism, 77, 78–9, 82, 86, 91; Ni Una Menos (not one more) campaign, 85; reconciling caring and income-generating activities, 81; reproductive rights, 17, 79, 83, 84, 85, 91; sexual minority rights, 83

Yunes Linares, Miguel Ángel, 161

zero-sum, 208, 214, 215, 279
Zuma, Jacob, 244, 250, 255

DEMOCRACY, DIVERSITY, AND CITIZEN ENGAGEMENT SERIES

Series editors: Alain-G. Gagnon and Yasmeen Abu-Laban

1 The Parliaments of Autonomous Nations
Edited by Guy Laforest and André Lecours

2 A Liberal Theory of Collective Rights
Michel Seymour

3 The National Question and Electoral Politics in Quebec and Scotland
Éric Bélanger, Richard Nadeau, Ailsa Henderson, and Eve Hepburn

4 Trust, Distrust, and Mistrust in Multinational Democracies
Comparative Perspectives
Edited by Dimitrios Karmis and François Rocher

5 Constitutional Politics in Multinational Democracies
Edited by André Lecours, Nikola Brassard-Dion, and Guy Laforest

6 Fiscal Federalism in Multinational States
Autonomy, Equality, and Diversity
Edited by François Boucher and Alain Noël

7 The Symbolic State
Minority Recognition, Majority Backlash, and Secession in Multinational Countries
Karlo Basta

8 Taking Pluralism Seriously
Complex Societies under Scrutiny
Félix Mathieu

9 A Written Constitution for Quebec?
Edited by Richard Albert and Léonid Sirota

10 Civic Freedom in an Age of Diversity
The Public Philosophy of James Tully
Edited by Dimitrios Karmis and Jocelyn Maclure

11 Contemporary Federalist Thought in Quebec
Historical Perspectives
Edited by Antoine Brousseau Desaulniers and Stéphane Savard

12 Territories of Inequality
How Federalism and Redistribution Interact
Edited by Olivier Jacques and Alain Noël

13 Civic Parties in Divided Societies
Northern Ireland and Bosnia-Herzegovina
Cera Murtagh

14 Fragile Nations
The Promise and Perils of Multinational Democracies
Félix Mathieu

15 Unequal Democracy
The Social Construction of Citizenship in Latin America
Edited by Françoise Montambeault and Tina Hilgers